D1029573

HEALING THE SPLIT

Integrating Spirit Into Our Understanding of the Mentally Ill

REVISED EDITION

JOHN E. NELSON, M.D.

Foreword by Ken Wilber

Preface by Michael Washburn

HEALING THE SPLIT

◆

SUNY Series in the Philosophy of Psychology
Michael Washburn, Editor

HEALING
THE SPLIT

Integrating Spirit
Into Our Understanding
of the Mentally Ill

Revised Edition

JOHN E. NELSON, M.D.

STATE UNIVERSITY OF NEW YORK PRESS

Illustration of the chakras by Lydia dePole appears on page 270 by kind permission of Georg Feuerstein.

Published by
State University of New York Press, Albany

For information, address State University of New York
Press, State University Plaza, Albany, N.Y., 12246

Production by E. Moore
Marketing by Dana E. Yanulavich

Library of Congress Cataloging-in-Publication Data
Nelson, John E., 1937-
    Healing the split : integrating spirit into our understanding of
the mentally ill / John E. Nelson. — Rev. ed.
        p.   cm. — (SUNY series in the philosophy of psychology)
    Includes bibliographical references and index.
    ISBN 0-7914-1986-X (PB : acid-free paper). — ISBN 0-7914-1985-1
(CH : acid-free paper)
    1. Transpersonal psychotherapy. 2. Mental illness. 3. Chakras.
I: Title.   II. Series.
RC489.T75N45   1994
616.89'1—dc20   93-32115
                                                        CIP

10   9   8   7   6   5   4   3   2

CONTENTS

Author's Note

◈

I AM DELIGHTED that Ken Wilber agreed to write the fore-word to *Healing the Split*. For this, my first book, I could ask for no better introduction than from the leading philosopher of the transpersonal movement whose ideas and inspirations grace the pages to follow.

Transpersonal psychology is a relatively new and rapidly grow-ing discipline that deals with fundamental questions about the deepest aspects of human nature that may never be answered to everyone's satisfaction. A lively debate regarding the nature of con-sciousness—or Spirit—and its relation to human development now enlivens the movement. Many of Wilber's central ideas have been criticized by transpersonal philosopher Michael Washburn, and Wilbur has published an astute reply. Because I find great value in both Wilber's and Washburn's points of view, I have attempted to partially reconcile them in *Healing the Split*, sometimes adding my own unique perspective that diverges from both theories. In the spirit of advancing an ongoing exchange of ideas, the SUNY edition adds a preface by Michael Washburn, whose thinking is also seminal within transpersonal psychology and which I gratefully blended into my effort to find a practical application for rather lofty philosophi-cal principles.

In the second half of his foreword, Wilber clearly states out his position and clarifies ways in which it differs from Washburn's, and sometimes my own. I believe that this is an important addition to a fascinating debate, and am honored to include it here. However, the reader may find him or herself confronted with a rather technical counterpoint before encountering the main point of *Healing the Split*. I would therefore suggest that the reader return to that section of the foreword after completing the main body of this book. The reader is also invited to enrich his or her understanding of transper-sonal psychology by consulting Wilber's and Washburn's original works. Three of Ken Wilber's books have been especially influential: *The Spectrum of Consciousness* (Wheaton, Ill.: A Quest Book, 1977); *The Atman Project* (Wheaton, Ill.: A Quest Book, 1980); and *Up From Eden* (Boston: New Science Library, 1986). Michael Washburn's book is titled *The Ego and the Dynamic Ground* (Albany: State University of New York Press, 1987). The debate between Wilber and Washburn is further clarified in companion articles by the two authors in *Journal of Humanistic Psychology*, Vol. 30, No. 3, Summer, 1990.

Foreword

◆

JOHN NELSON HAS written an enormously impressive, profound, and important book, which takes as its simple starting point the fact that Spirit exists. This might seem an utterly obvious place to begin, except for the fact that Dr. Nelson is a member in good standing of the mainstream psychiatric community. And modern psychiatry, for all the relative good it has managed to accomplish, is still by and large totally ignorant of the spiritual and transpersonal dimensions of human experience. This is all the more curious in that psychiatry, whatever else its mission, has been understood from its inception to be the science of the soul. And yet on the subject of the human soul and spirit modern psychiatry has been strangely silent.

Even worse, most of the genuine human experiences of transcendental spirit have been not merely ignored but rather violently pathologized by modern psychiatry. The easiest way to be labeled schizophrenic in our society is to let it be known that you feel that in the deepest part of your being you (and all sentient beings) are one with infinite Spirit, one with the universe, one with the All—an insight that every wisdom culture the world over has held to be not the depths of mental illness but the pinnacle of human understanding. This intuition of the Supreme Identity, shared by all beings, is for such cultures not the ultimate pathology but the ultimate liberation.

The Supreme Identity of the human soul and the transcendental Divine is the cornerstone of the perennial philosophy and the defining insight of the world's greatest mystics and philosophers. As Aldous Huxley put it, "*Philosophia perennis*—the metaphysic that recognizes a divine Reality substantial to the world of things and lives and minds; the psychology that finds in the soul something similar to, or even identical with, divine Reality; the ethic that places man's final end in the knowledge of the immanent and transcendent Ground of all beings—the thing is immemorial and universal."

Erwin Schrödinger, the founder of modern quantum mechanics and himself a profound mystic, explained that if you carefully look through the world's great spiritual and mystical literature, you will find "many beautiful utterances of a similar kind. You are struck by the miraculous agreement between humans of different race, different religion, knowing nothing about each other's existence, separated by centuries and millennia, and by the greatest distances that there are on our globe." This perennial philosophy, as Arthur Lovejoy pointed out, "has, in one form or another, been the dominant philosophy of the larger part of civilized mankind through most of its history" and has been embraced "by the greater number of speculative minds and religious teachers." And so Alan Watts draws the obvious conclusion:

> Thus we are hardly aware of the extreme peculiarity of our own position, and find it difficult to recognize the plain fact that there has otherwise been a single philosophical consensus of universal extent. It has been held by men who report the same insights and teach the same essential doctrine whether living today or six thousand years ago, whether from New Mexico in the Far West or from Japan in the Far East.

The only major culture to ignore or devalue the perennial philosophy has been, alas, our own modern culture of secular materialism and brutish scientism, which has by and large, from the eighteenth century onward, been dominated by that which can be perceived by the senses and manipulated by measurement. The concept of the Great Chain of Being—according to which men and women have at least five major levels of being: matter, body, mind, soul, and spirit— was reduced to mere matter and body. First spirit, then soul, and then mind were rejected by modern psychology and psychiatry, with the disastrous result that men and women were held to be nothing more than sophisticated bundles of material atoms in vaguely animate bodies. Thus our modern "science of the soul," almost from the start, has been a science merely of the physical and bodily components of the entire human being—a reductionistic cultural catastrophe of the first magnitude.

In recent times, however, the school of humanistic psychology has succeeded in reintroducing mind to psychology, thus supplementing and surpassing the empirical-physicalistic schools of behaviorism and the instinctual-bodily-emotional schools of psychoanalysis. And even more recently, transpersonal psychology has gone further still, and reintroduced the dimensions of soul and spirit. The result is a comprehensive or full-spectrum view of human psychology that includes matter, body, mind, soul, and spirit, in both their normal and pathological manifestations.

The aim of transpersonal psychology, then, is to give a psychological presentation of the perennial philosophy and the Great Chain of Being, fully updated and grounded in modern research and scientific developments. It fully acknowledges and *incorporates* the findings of modern psychiatry, behaviorism, and developmental psychology, and then adds, where necessary, the further insights and experiences of the existential and spiritual dimensions of the human being. We might say it starts with psychiatry and ends with mysticism.

And that is exactly the value of *Healing the Split*. It presents one version of a full-spectrum model of human growth and development that incorporates the vast richness of modern psychiatry and neuroscience and then supplements it with transcendental and spiritual dimensions. And one of its chief attractions, as I have said, is that it is authored by a member in good standing of the mainstream psychiatric community. In this regard Dr. Nelson joins the ranks of such pioneering transpersonal psychiatrists as Stanislav Grof, Stanley Dean, Roger Walsh, Edward Podvoll, and Seymour Boorstein. It is an utterly welcome addition, for John Nelson discusses these topics with enormous insight, clarity and, above all, I think, a truly heartfelt compassion, genuine and tender and compelling.

Not all of his theoretical conclusions, of course, will be accepted by all transpersonal theorists. The field is young, and there is plenty of room for healthy disagreements. Although this is somewhat technical, I think the following points of potential disagreement should be very briefly spelled out, because they are rather important:

1 . Dr. Nelson's use of the term *the Spiritual Ground* is, I believe, slightly misleading. He speaks of the Spiritual Ground—that is, infinite Spirit—as "interacting" with the ego or the individual self; he speaks of "the energies of the Ground" and of "the relentless pressure of the Ground." But infinite Spirit, precisely because it is infinite, doesn't *interact* with anything. That which is infinite is not set apart from anything, including the ego, but rather pervades equally all that is, as the water of the ocean pervades each wave. We don't say that water interacts with waves; rather, each and every wave is a *form* of water, just as each and every manifest thing is a form of Spirit. There is no separation between the finite and the infinite such that any "interaction" could occur (interaction happens only between finite events). Likewise, infinite Spirit does not contain "energies" or exert "pressure," any more than water exerts pressure on waves. To main-

tain that the Ground is set apart from the ego and interacts with it is a very subtle but pernicious form of dualism (a mistake, I believe, that Nelson inherited from Michael Washburn's otherwise perceptive and important writings) .

2. Rather, Nelson is using the term *Spiritual Ground* in a very loose sense to mean all the various higher levels and dimensions generally referred to as spiritual or transpersonal. As he says, the Ground is actually "composed" of various bands or wavelengths. These higher bands or levels are sometimes referred to as the psychic, the subtle, and the causal dimensions of existence, but even they are not to be confused with the ultimate or infinite spirit itself, which is no particular level or dimension at all, but rather the reality or suchness of each and every level. Thus, when Dr. Nelson speaks of the interaction of the Ground with the ego or the individual self, he is really speaking of the interaction of one of the subtler levels of existence (psychic, subtle, or causal, which he calls, respectively, the fifth, sixth, and seventh stages of development) with the ego or individual self. Indeed, most of what Nelson refers to as the Ground is really the psychic or beginning dimension of transpersonal existence, which does interact with the ego, and does contain energies, and does exert pressure on the ego (none of which the infinite does) .

3. In particular, the infantile self is not "more open" to infinite Spirit than is the adult self. In fact, the opposite is true. The infantile self is embedded in the material and bodily levels of development, and because its self-boundaries are very weak and fluid, it is open to a dramatic and enormous influx, not from Spirit, but from the immense material and biological energies of those primitive levels, from the overwhelming energies of élan vital, *prana*, libido. The fact that these energies are overwhelming does not mean they are spiritual.

Nelson (following Washburn) maintains that the infantile self is one with infinite Spirit (albeit unselfconsciously). But infinite Spirit is one with *all* levels—matter, body, mind, soul—and thus if the infantile self were one with Spirit (in a way that the ego-mind is not), it would also *have* to be one with *all* levels. But that is impossible, since in the infantile self the symbolic, mental, logical, and conceptual levels haven't emerged yet. No, the infantile self is one with, or fused with, the biomaterial world in general and the mothering one in particular. I believe this early stage is just as important as Dr. Nelson maintains that it is, but not because it is more in touch with Spirit, but because it is lost in the lower, oceanic spheres of existence, with feeble and easily overwhelmed self-boundaries. And, in fact, the material and bodily levels are *less* in touch with Spirit than are the mental levels, which are less in touch than the soul levels.

4. Dr. Nelson speaks of the fifth level of development as the home of creative genius and the sixth level as the home of paranormal abilities. While these are fine as a first approximation, they are slightly problematic. Most transpersonalists do not see creativity or paranormal abilities as an actual *stage* of growth, because a stage by definition is something that everybody *must* proceed through invariably. And it is simply not the case that all mystics, even if enlightened, *necessarily* go through a period of highly developed paranormal abilities. Most, in fact, do not. Rather, creativity and paranormal abilities may or may not develop at various stages of growth, and are not themselves a *particular* stage of growth.

These are all important points, I think. But in the larger view, they are also just nitpicking. Still, John Nelson has succeeded in writing an enormously important and helpful book, which has gone further than any other, I think, in directly grounding transpersonal psychology in the research of modern medical psychiatry, neuroscience, and psychiatric psychotherapy. If this type of book were required reading in all psychiatric schools in this country, we would soon be rejoining the ranks of a common humanity that has unmistakably found in the human soul "something similar to, or even identical with, divine Reality." And John Nelson will have helped that long-overdue return to basic sanity in a major, profound, and compassionate way.

Ken Wilber
Boulder, Colorado

Preface

◆

IN *HEALING THE SPLIT*, psychiatrist John Nelson presents an important new framework for understanding a wide range of nonordinary states of consciousnesss. Most of these states have been pathologized by the psychiatric establishment. Dr. Nelson, however, proceeding from a transpersonal perspective, is able to show that these states are of widely different sorts. Although many of them are properly diagnosed as belonging to known pathological conditions, others, Dr. Nelson explains, are properly understood as awakenings of higher psychic or spiritual potentials. Dr. Nelson has a keen phenomenological eye and is able to describe nonordinary states of consciousness in terms that are comprehensible to the lay reader. His discussions are both scientifically well informed and open to significant possibilities not yet acknowledged by science. Dr. Nelson draws upon recent findings in medical and neuroscientific research to show that there is much more to human experience than is presently accepted by psychiatry.

In pursuing a transpersonal perspective, Dr. Nelson maintains a clear-headed balance that avoids both the prevailing psychiatric prejudice against nonordinary states of consciousness and the anti-psychiatric (e.g., R.D. Laing) glorification of nonordinary states. Dr. Nelson follows Ken Wilber in stressing the pre/trans distinction, the distinction between preegoic states of an infantile or regressive sort on the one hand and transegoic states of a supranormal, ego-transcending sort on the other. This distinction is crucial, since preegoic and transegoic states can be sufficiently similar in superficial ways to lead either to a reduction of the transegoic to the preegoic, that is, to a pathologization of transcendence as regression (the prevailing psychiatric prejudice), or to a promotion of the preegoic to the transegoic, that is, to a rationalization of pathology as transcendence (the anti-psychiatric counterextreme). Dr. Nelson makes neither of these mistakes. He has a good sense of the diagnostic and developmental status of nonordinary states of consciousness and provides the best account available of the differences between psychosis and transcendence. His observations on these matters should be of great value to psychiatrists, to transpersonally oriented developmental theorists, and to everyone engaged in the practice of psychotherapy. His observations should be of special value to psychotherapists treating people undergoing spiritual emergencies.

Dr. Nelson bases his discussion of nonordinary states of consciousness on a very plausible reinterpretation of the ancient chakra system, the Tantric system of bodily energy centers and corresponding modes of experience. The chakra system has been the subject of many books in recent years, most of them of a superficially popular or bewilderingly esoteric sort. Although much has been said about the chakra system, little has been said that plausibly links this system to the findings of Western psychology and psychiatry. It is a credit of Dr. Nelson's book that it establishes just such a link. Setting aside the metaphysical and theological baggage of the chakra system, Dr. Nelson shows how the chakra system can be used as a heuristic to explain states of consciousness associated with specific psychodevelopmental levels, from the lowest preegoic levels (associated with the first two chakras) to higher transegoic levels (associated with the fourth through seventh chakras). Dr. Nelson describes the phenomenology and the psychic functions corresponding to each of the chakras and explains how specific psychiatric conditions and transpersonal awakenings can be understood in terms of the chakra levels.

In addition to its other accomplishments, *Healing the Split* is to be credited for making an important contribution to an ongoing debate in transpersonal theory. Currently, there are two primary paradigms guiding transpersonal inquiry. One of these is a paradigm rooted in the psychoanalytic tradition and, more specifically, in Jungian depth-psychology. This paradigm sees human development as following a *spiral* course of departure and higher return to origins. According to this paradigm, the ego emerges initially from the deep sources of the psyche; the ego then separates itself from these sources during the first half of life, which is a time not only of ego development but also ego predominance; and the ego finally returns to the deep sources of the psyche in the second half of life in order to become integrated with them on a higher, transegoic level. The other major transpersonal paradigm, formulated by Ken Wilber, is rooted in strucuturally oriented psychology (especially cognitive-developmental psychology) and sees development during this lifetime as following a course of straight ascent from preegoic levels to egoic levels to, finally, transegoic levels of development. Wilber's paradigm can be called a *ladder* paradigm, since it conceives the path of development as following a level-by-level ascent up a hierarchy of psychic structures. For Wilber, human development during this lifetime does not spiral back on itself; there is no return to earlier levels on the way to higher, transpersonal levels.

In his foreword to this book, Ken Wilber takes exception to Nelson's use of some of my ideas, which are based on the spiral paradigm. I could reply in turn and charge that Nelson draws upon many of Wilber's ideas, which are based on the ladder paradigm. But such a response would miss what Nelson is trying to do in *Healing the Split*. Just as Nelson is seeking a middle ground between the psychiatric and anti-psychiatric extremes, so he is also seeking a middle ground between the spiral and ladder paradigms. Nelson, I believe, is recommending that essential aspects of the spiral and ladder paradigms can be reconceived in a way that allows them to be fruitfully combined. This is an important recommendation that should not be prejudged.

I want to thank John Nelson for asking me to write this preface. I very much like his book and enthusiastically recommend it to psychiatrists and psychotherapists and to everyone interested in transpersonal psychology.

Michael Washburn

Acknowledgments

❖

THE FUNDAMENTAL PHILOSOPHY of this work emerged from my study of three major transpersonal authors: Ken Wilber, Stanislav Grof, and Michael Washburn.

The ideas that take shape in the following pages percolated within me for nearly twenty years, enriched by many people who have shared them in lively discussions. I especially wish to thank my first draft readers and critics: Gary Bravo, M.D.; Beverly Conlan, L.C.S.W.; Brian Conlan, L.C.S.W.; Andrea Nelson, Ph.D.; Karen Parker, Ph.D.; Rod Carroll; Judy Farrell; Robert Auric, M.D.; Anna Auric, R.N.; Lauren Zuckerman, LCSW; and Mary Solomon. Members of The Circle fed my head in more subtle ways.

It would be difficult to wish for more sensitive editing than the manuscript lovingly received from Connie Zweig. At one crucial point in the genesis of this book, I was fortunate to encounter Mary Goldenson, an unusually empathic healer who helped me overcome a stubborn impediment to my writing during her workshop at Esalen Institute in Big Sur, California. Esalen has been fertile ground for generating many of the ideas in this book.

Mostly I wish to thank my wife, Andrea, whose love and discerning critique of this work created the warm home and cool discipline for me to write this book.

Introduction

◆

Move every stone, try everything, leave nothing unattempted.

ERASUMUS

IN 1633, a calamitous event split the traditional unity of Western science and religion. After years of careful study, the Renaissance scientist Galileo Galilei informed the churchmen of his time that their doctrine of the earth's position at the center of the universe was false, and that he could prove it with his telescope and mathematical calculations. Disquieted by this challenge to their sacred authority, the church's inquisitors refused to consider Galileo's reasoning or even look through his telescope, which they denounced as an instrument of "devious illusion." Instead, they demonstrated to him a few of their own instruments designed to gather information of a far less celestial nature. Realizing that the momentous truths shining through his crude lenses would not require his martyrdom to make their way in the world, the peaceable Italian scholar prudently recanted and retired to quietly refine his data and live out his days in comfort. The year of his natural death marked the birth of Sir Isaac Newton and the passage of that particular inquisition into infamy.

Shock waves from Galileo's tribulation continue to perpetuate the gulf between Western science and religion, especially within the branch of psychiatry that deals with people who have extreme nonordinary experiences. Largely cut off from spiritual considerations, Western psychology stumbles as it encounters the mysteries of how brain and mind interact to bring about the bizarre alterations of consciousness known as schizophrenia, mania, and multiple personality disorder. Similarly isolated, traditional religion seems impotent to halt its slide into irrelevance as it confronts practical problems of life in the late twentieth century.

Ideally, the role of religion is to *lead* science as it searches for ever higher truths. Disciplined spiritual practice has the power to condition human consciousness to rise above the material realm, freeing the mind to generate insights into subtle aspects of reality that lie beyond the grasp of physical science. Rather than opposing science with dogma, religion should help us transcend its limitations. In turn, sciences like medicine and psychiatry would do well to embrace those spiritual insights that take into account the power of consciousness in determining health or sickness.

Yet to avoid a return to the Dark Ages, we must recognize that science and religion deal with distinct categories of human experience—matter and spirit—that are separate, but complementary. To expect religion to explain physical laws in any but a metaphorical way is like expecting science to interpret scripture by making a chemical analysis of the paper on which it was written.

We are now in the early years of a spiritual renaissance in the West. Spawned by the often reckless explorations of consciousness during the psychedelic sixties, the curious mixture of Eastern mysticism, Western Gnosticism, and quantum physics that is loosely known as New Age thought seeks to fill the gap separating science and spirit with an amalgam of both. This movement has given rise to numerous "alternative healers" who claim access to subtle forces that influence the material world in ways that leave the familiar laws of cause and effect far behind. It is natural that they would turn their attention toward the psychoses, which traditionally have been thought of as primary maladies of the spirit with occult implications.

But by rejecting the discipline of the sciences and the traditions of the great religions, this new movement has been vulnerable to charges that it exalts the worst aspects of both. In blending long-discredited healing practices with quirky metaphysics, and then refusing to subject the results to verification, some of these healers have tended to alienate mainstream medicine, which they should strive to influence. Meanwhile, science and religion continue to point accusing fingers at each other, agreeing only in their abhorrence of New Age excess.

HEALING THE SPLIT

No area of Western thought is more in need of input from the spiritual disciplines than our understanding of the psychoses. These mysterious maladies penetrate through the deepest levels of soma and psyche to the roots of the human soul. The resulting personal suffering and waste of valuable talent are unparalleled in any other category of human disease.

The various forms of madness affect about two percent of the population of all cultures in the world. One out of every four hospital beds in North America is occupied by someone diagnosed as schizophrenic or manic-depressive (bipolar disorder) . Thousands of confused people with these maladies roam the streets among the destitute and homeless. Millions of dollars are spent each year in research and rehabilitation.

But the problem persists. Our legal system awkwardly vacillates as it tries to rationally determine the limits of free will and personal responsibility in madness and sanity. We will never untangle these knotty problems as long as we regard psychotic alterations as exclusive disorders of brain, or mind, or spirit. They are aberrations of *consciousness itself,* whatever their manifestation.

The best efforts of neurological science cannot explain the hallucinated voices and visions or sudden unnamed terrors that are the daily reality of people in the midst of psychosis. Psychoanalytic theories that focus on the ravages of faulty parenting fare no better in uncovering the cause of such profound disruptions of selfhood. Yet it is certain that primary disorders of the brain are involved in some severe forms of madness. And we also know that childhood trauma can provide impetus for the emergence of psychotic symptoms later in life. We are therefore challenged to return to the oldest and most basic philosophical question: what is the nature of consciousness and its association with the physical body? How this question is answered draws the battle lines between orthodox and alternative approaches to madness.

My lifetime fascination with this most impenetrable of human mysteries inspired me to write this book. I am a practicing physician, certified by the American Board of Psychiatry and Neurology. For the past twenty years I have nurtured an interest in consciousness research as exemplified by the relatively young discipline of transpersonal psychology. Although the worldview that I derived from my study of Eastern and Western spiritual techniques might have put me hopelessly at odds with mainstream psychiatry, I chose to work within the system, the better to master the powerful tools of science that I was trained to use for the benefit of my severely disturbed patients. Despite its limitations when overextended, I could not deny that the traditional medical model has led the way in virtually eradicating once-dreaded diseases like smallpox and polio, and has contributed significantly to reducing the suffering of many mentally ill people.

Yet during two decades of working closely with troubled people in private practice and hospital psychiatry, I grew aware of serious short-comings in the modern Western approach to extreme alterations in consciousness. Among the psychotic patients who sought my care, I noticed a significant minority who seemed to be experiencing what is described in esoteric literature as signs of impending spiritual realiza-tion. Nothing in my medical training prepared me to distinguish pro-found breakthroughs of higher consciousness from malignant psy-chotic regressions that permanently submerge the self in primitive areas of the psyche.

As I discussed my concerns with my colleagues, I found that many mainstream psychologists and psychiatrists have tended to overinter-pret the compelling biological research of the past thirty years, con-cluding that *all* deviations from conventional reality are no more than brain disorders in cause and cure. They therefore judge any experi-ence outside of ordinary reality to be a hallmark of disease, and their theories exclude the possibility of emerging higher consciousness. For them, therapy should aim to convince psychotic people that their subjective experience is invalid and that they should submit to treat-ment that corrects disorderly brain function. It follows that we should avoid upsetting our patients or their families with approaches that smack of psychologizing or spirituality. Of course, adherents of this view are quick to support their beliefs with hard scientific data that conscientious alternative therapists overlook only at the peril of ignoring some mightily convincing facts.

Because theories that deal only with the brain are ultimately no more satisfactory than theories that deal only with the mind, I con-cluded that we need to focus on the nature of consciousness in its *rela-tions* with the brain to understand what makes people go mad. Seeking to broaden my understanding of alterations of conscious-ness, I began attending workshops in spiritually based therapeutic techniques. I soon found that many alternative healers regard estab-lishment psychiatrists as mind police interested only in reducing the soul to a flux of chemicals in a test tube, squiggles on an oscilloscope, or related events on the grossest level of existence. Accordingly, they seek guidance from astrologers, nutritionists, crystal healers, or shamanic exorcists in their healing practices, which are sometimes strikingly effective in ways incomprehensible to modern medicine.

But I eventually realized, to my dismay, that many of these "holis-tic" practitioners systematically exclude biological science in their approach to psychosis, which they view variously as a misdirected flow of "energy" or as unrecognized spiritual insight. The implications of

these approaches are equally unbalanced. Some alternative therapists act as if psychotics have no bodies at all, or as if their bodies don't
have much to do with what is going on in their minds. Erroneously
thinking that anything scientific is antispiritual, some recommend
discontinuing medicines that, though imperfect, may be the only
glue bonding a psychotic person to an orderly world and to society.
And like their psychiatric adversaries, many alternative therapists fail
to discriminate between regression and transcendence. They then
apply advanced spiritual techniques to people who are so fundamentally impaired that they cannot respond to interventions above the
basic physical level. When their tactics do not work, some of these
therapists abandon their clients in a condition much worse than that
in which they came to them for help.

Extremists on each side of this paradigmatic clash consider the
others to be useless at best and destructive at worst, and so with fruit-
less antagonism they relentlessly undermine each other's efforts to
understand these dreadful affflictions. The significant minority of
humanity whose daily experience of reality varies greatly from that of
their fellow men and women are caught in the crossfire.

The time seems right for a radical new theory of madness that
takes into account the whole of our being. Therefore, I decided to
write this book with the goal of reintegrating spiritual psychologies
with modern medical science. My aim is to make the complexities of
brain disorders intelligible to healers who have little knowledge of
medicine, as well as to render spiritual philosophies palatable to healers who have invested their education in orthodox science.

TRANSPERSONAL PSYCHOLOGY

Transpersonal psychology affords a sturdy foundation for this
reintegration. This vigorous and rapidly growing discipline regards
consciousness as the central dimension of human existence and is
concerned with optimum psychological health and well-being.

The transpersonal perspective views "normal" consciousness as a
necessary and useful, but defensively contracted, state of reduced
awareness that enables the individual to live in a social world but
blinds him or her to greater spiritual potentials that lie beyond the
ego or world-self. Consciousness itself is structured into levels, and a
large spectrum of altered states of consciousness exists, some states
tapping capabilities greater than are possible in the ordinary state,
others being more limited in potential. From any given level, most
human beings have a capacity to expand into higher realms of awareness that possess all the possibilities of the lower levels together with

some additional ones. Under adverse conditions, consciousness may contract into primitive forms, stripping the individual of capabilities necessary for him to adapt to modern society.

Although many seminal works in the transpersonal field are brilliant in theory as they construct detailed maps of consciousness, they can be faulted for lacking practical applications for reducing human suffering. Because they often ignore important physical aspects of mental disorders, they fail to gain the attention of the powers-that-be within the mental-health establishment. *Healing the Split* strives to remedy that shortfall with an afffirmation of the idea that psychological and spiritual theories should not contradict physical facts, just as physical theories should not exclude the experience of real people.

Seeking a working model for reaffirming the lost complementarity between science and religion, *Healing the Split* also looks to the Eastern world, which has never separated the two realms. Eastern religious systems continue to inform and inspire their cultures' healers, who would no more ignore states of consciousness—their own or their patients'—than Western doctors would exclude a physical examination. Because Eastern religions insist on disciplined introspection, they have become as expert in the technology of consciousness as Western medicine has become in neurology. Hence, the vaunted scientific objectivity so dear to Western rationality seems a form of self-deception to the Eastern mind, which recognizes brain, psyche, and spirit as manifestations of a vast, multilayered sea of consciousness immediately shared by all sentient beings.

In this book, I do not espouse any particular religion, Eastern or Western, but I incorporate certain fundamental insights from the core teachings of several religions. I strongly believe that science and spirituality can be combined into a synthesis of essential truths from both worlds.

A transpersonal approach to psychotic experience invites us to rethink the entrenched fallacy that human beings are purely physical objects, spiritless and mechanical, isolated by their skin from the environment, helpless pawns of genetic endowment, biological drives, and the indecipherable complexity of the brain. According to this fallacious view, "crazy" psychotics should surrender responsibility for their disease to "sane" authorities who feed the drug-oriented expectation of quick, painless solutions to problems. In contrast, I would argue that the medium of consciousness imparts to living beings an identity that transcends their material bodies. It is just as correct to say that mental events affect brain events as to say the reverse. Personal responsibility, rather than mindless dependency, thereby follows.

On the opposite side, reafffirming the best of the medical model invites us to rethink an equally extreme fallacy that the individual is a transiently embodied spirit, impervious to the frailties of the physical body, responding only to ill-defined metaphysical forces that can be manipulated by prayer, ritual, or virtuous living, or by releasing blocked emotional energy. This position ignores the demonstrable fact that what affects brain always affects mind, as well as the reverse. Well intentioned though it may be, such a naive approach simply does not work when it confronts a disorder as pervasive as schizophrenia.

Once orthodox and alternative schools of thought rise above these fallacies and begin to communicate in a common language, they will be free to devise specific ways to treat benign psychotic states that herald spiritual emergence, as well as malignant states that portend retreat to primitive mental levels. It is the primary mission of this book to assist healers from diverse backgrounds in distinguishing these levels as they tailor their responses to the confused people who trust their bodies, minds, and spirits to their care. Because I also intend the ideas in *Healing the Split* to be useful to non-medically trained people, including families of psychotic patients and people involved in spiritual practice who may be undergoing disturbing inner experiences, I have taken pains to avoid psychiatric jargon.

Healing the Split is divided into four parts, each with a specific purpose. Part one introduces the reader to the idea of consciousness as a universal reality, capable of assuming various forms. It describes typical psychotic states of consciousness as they are subjectively experienced, including schizophrenia, mania, and multiple personality disorder, and then examines ways in which modern civilization responds to these afflictions.

Part two focuses on the way in which genes, anatomy, and chemistry within the brain contribute to certain kinds of psychotic experience. It reviews the pros and cons of antipsychotic medicines, as well as the intriguing connections that link both madness and mysticism to psychedelic drugs. Finally, it examines the suggestion from quantum physics that the brain may function like a hologram as it interacts with consciousness to produce madness or sanity.

Part three deals with the psychological and spiritual aspects of madness. It employs the ancient Tantric yoga system of the seven chakras to explore the psychotic mind as it takes form in childhood, then assembles its own unique reality in early adulthood. This section includes speculation from parapsychology, occult literature, and Eastern philosophy, and explores the overlapping boundaries between madness, creative inspiration, and mystical enlightenment.

Part four offers a practical application of transpersonal psychology to the *artful* healing of a major source of human suffering, to revamping our obsolete mental-health system, and to aiding the spiritual progress of a long-misunderstood and neglected segment of humanity—the mentally ill. *Artfulness* in healing requires a special kind of awareness that takes into account the state of consciousness of the healer as well as that of the patient.

In sum, this book seeks to heal the split between antagonistic and rarely communicating schools of thought as it offers practical techniques to heal the split within severely disturbed human beings. It is my fervent hope that it will take up the challenge left by that greatest of modern spiritual psychiatrists, Carl Jung:

> It will assuredly be a long time before the physiology and pathology of the brain and the psychology of the unconscious are able to join hands. Till then they must go their separate ways. But psychiatry, whose concern is the total man, is forced by its task of understanding and treating the sick to consider both sides, regardless of the gulf that yawns between the two aspects of the psychic phenomenon. Even if it is not yet granted to our present insight to discover the bridges that connect the visible and tangible nature of the brain with the apparent insubstantiality of psychic forms, the unerring certainty of their presence nevertheless remains. May this certainty safeguard investigators from the impatient error of neglecting one side in favor of the other and, still worse, of wishing to replace one by the other. For indeed, nature would not exist without substance, but neither would she exist for us if she were not reflected in the psyche.

PART 1

MADNESS IN HUMAN CONSCIOUSNESS

CHAPTER 1

Madness, Consciousness, & The Spiritual Ground

◆

The stuff of the world is mind stuff.
SIR ARTHUR EDDINGTON

Looked at, it cannot be seen,
Listened to, it cannot be heard,
Applied, its supply never fails.
LAO-TZU

LONG AGO, the youthful Plato and his mentor, Socrates, paced the streets of Athens pondering the nature of the soul and the enigma of "divine madness." Twenty-four centuries later, the questions they confronted still challenge the best of minds. What is human consciousness? Does it originate from a higher source? How is it connected to the physical body and to reality? What causes it to take a sane or insane form within a given individual?

Perhaps it will remain forever beyond the grasp of humanity to understand its own fundamental nature. But we are now edging closer to a unitive understanding of those realms of solitary experience, alternately revered or reviled, known in modern times as the psychoses.

This book defines psychosis as *any one of several altered states of consciousness, transient or persistent, that prevent integration of sensory or extrasensory data into reality models accepted by the broad consensus of society, and that lead to maladaptive behavior and social sanctions.*

This definition spans several modern diagnostic categories, includ-

3

ing manic-depressive (bipolar) disorder, schizophrenia, multiple personality disorder, brief reactive psychosis, "borderline" states, various kinds of chemical intoxication, and several less common deviations from socially defined reality. To the confusion of many, this definition also describes several potentially *adaptive* altered states of consciousness (ASCs), including premature spiritual realization, prolonged mystical rapture, and the effects of certain consciousness-altering drugs. The experience of some artists during moments of intense inspiration falls in the borderlands of the definition.

Western societies are increasingly divided about the value of these basic shifts in consciousness. Our failure to distinguish between malignant and benign psychotic ASCs in terms of cause, degree of regression, adaptive value, potential for spiritual growth, and treatment strategies bedevils both mainstream psychiatry and alternative schools of thought. Each errs in its own characteristic way by failing to recognize that various psychotic states of consciousness—although apparently similar—differ from each other in important ways that can be readily recognized.

The following two case histories illustrate these errors.

Tom is a nineteen-year-old grocery clerk whose mother brought him to see a marriage, family, and child counselor who advertised herself as a "holistic therapist." Tom was raised alone by his mother after his father committed suicide during one of several psychiatric hospitalizations. She said that Tom recently shaved his head and superficially cut his wrists in response to "orders from the mob," which he later revealed to be hallucinated voices. His mother said that Tom was an introverted child and had been a fair student until his last year of high school, when he began spending long hours alone in his room. His grades declined, and he quit school six months before graduation. He had no close friends. Because his mother often heard him murmuring and laughing to himself when he was alone, she was sure that he was using drugs, but none were ever found, and Tom denied drug use except for occasional experimentation with marijuana.

Tom's therapist found him to be a pale, thin, rather unkempt young man dressed in oddly mismatched clothes. Because she suspected poor nutritional habits, she requested that his family obtain a battery of blood tests and hair analysis to determine any metabolic deficiencies. She then recommended that he take large doses of several vitamin and mineral supplements. The therapist also noted that Tom lacked spontaneity and spoke in an expression-less voice, although he was polite. He had great difficulty in making minor decisions and seemed to be too distracted to discuss his life issues with her. When asked about career plans, he said he wanted to be a psychologist, but had no idea how to achieve that goal. He often smiled during serious moments of their conversation, but when she asked what was funny, he rambled off the point.

Tom's therapist concluded that he was "tense and emotionally constricted," and needed to "loosen up and get in touch with his repressed feelings." She felt that his symptoms represented "blocked emotional energy" from early in life, or possibly from a past lifetime, and that this energy needed to be released if Tom was to be free from his symptoms. After teaching Tom a relaxation technique, she engaged him in a series of "rebirthing" experiences that included deep and rapid breathing and suggestions for visual imagery that simulated his passing through the birth canal. She also prompted Tom to strike a mat with a soft bat while shouting how angry he was at his father for abandoning the family when Tom was five years old. Tom was instructed to practice the relaxation technique and concentrate on his breathing at least once a day.

Tom cooperated with the therapy, but seemed dazed and restless following the first of these sessions. When he returned for his next appointment, he was initially distant, but then coolly told his therapist that he planned to kill her because she was "in cahoots with the mob to steal my brain." When she picked up the phone to call for help, he bolted from her office. Later that day he was apprehended by police when he threatened to jump from a freeway over-pass into oncoming traffic.

The next case illustrates how a similar therapeutic error can occur on the opposite end of the spectrum.

Tina is a successful thirty-six-year-old trial lawyer who sought help from a psychiatrist when she began having panic-like feelings that ordinary events in her life were un-real, as if her surroundings had somehow changed or she were dreaming when she was awake. At other times, she felt that her way of perceiving her own thoughts and feel-ings was different from usual. As she put it, "It's like I'm losing my identity." On two recent occasions, she felt herself to be outside her body, during which she could see her physical body resting immobile at a nearby location. She also described several recent dreams that later came true, including one especially vivid and detailed dream in which a close friend was seriously injured in a skiing accident. This information was unwanted and frightening to her, and she feared that she was going insane.

Tina was in the midst of an acrimonious divorce from a marriage that she entered "to please my parents." She was also uncertain about the future of her career in law and was considering renewing a lifelong ambition to write children's books. Having been raised a strict Catholic, she had undergone a spiritual crisis several months earlier when she began a program of yoga and meditation that led her to question her lifelong beliefs in the religion of her birth. However, she recently stopped attending her meditation classes and simultaneously increased her daily meditation time from forty minutes to two or three hours. Shortly after this change, she noticed that she was unusually sensitive to bright lights and loud noises.

Tina's psychiatrist made no comment about her meditation practices, but advised her to begin psychoanalytic psychotherapy with him. He prescribed a small dose of Valium to take when she felt an anxiety spell coming on. Initially, Tina began to feel less anxious, but during her fourth session with the doctor, she suddenly informed him that she had died and gone to hell. She meant this literally, adding that the world was collapsing upon her from all directions and that she had been abandoned by God. She spoke of vague surges of "heat" flowing upward from her pelvis, through her body, and into her head, where they would leave colorful "trails of light." She also felt that there were demonic "presences" trying to possess her, although she was able to say that she knew these were not real. When she threatened suicide to end her turmoil, the psychiatrist felt he had little choice but to commit her to an acute psychiatric hospital.

In the hospital, Tina was given Haldol, an antipsychotic medicine. Within a few days, she no longer spoke of being threatened by demons, the bursts of inner heat and light had subsided, and the frightening feelings of unreality had ceased. But she also complained of feeling dull-witted and constricted in feeling, "like I'm dead inside." She also complained that she could no longer recall her dreams, and that she could not concentrate on meditation, which she abruptly ceased altogether. Although her psychiatrist gradually tapered the dose of Haldol, the most disturbing of her symptoms did not return. Yet for months afterward, Tina complained of periodic anxiety attacks, "as if something evil is threatening me from within," and unaccustomed episodes of depression, "as if I've lost something very important."

After six months of psychotherapy that focused on her childhood relations with her parents, Tina felt that she was not getting to the root of her problem and quit therapy. Her anxiety and depression progressively worsened, and she was admitted to the hospital on two more occasions after attempting suicide.

Both Tom and Tina showed clear manifestations of a psychotic ASC. Both found their way to healers whose assessment and treatment fit the accepted paradigms of their particular disciplines, but whose responses were unsuited to the symptoms with which they were confronted. Although it could be argued that each patient would have been better served if he or she had consulted the other's therapist, I propose that a healer who could combine *both* ways of thinking and apply them precisely would have come closer to the ideal. This chapter begins the process of uniting these diverse approaches.

CONSCIOUSNESS: TWO VIEWS

Consciousness is difficult to define but impossible to overlook. It is the *within* of us, our essence, the basic felt vibration underlying each experience, the receptive self onto which the senses project their worldly data, the I who observes the I who observes the I . . . We feel it directly in ourselves, recognize it in our fellow men and women, infer it in animals, suspect it in plants, and wonder as to its presence in all creation.

Paradoxically, consciousness seems private, our own. Yet when we behold its vital spark flicker in the eyes of another, we acknowledge it to be the common bond of humanity, a link that affirms an intuitive sense of oneness shared by all who explore it with an open heart. In a sense it seems earthly, bonded to our bodies and brains. Yet many people have compelling experiences that suggest it is much subtler and deeper than the laws of physics or neurology, no matter how refined those may become.

7

In order to better understand madness as a manifestation of consciousness, we need to first review two historically conflicting views of how our minds and bodies interact: the *material*, and the *transpersonal*. These views split science from religion and also divide Western and Eastern worldviews. The material view elevates the physical brain to a primary position, with consciousness its accidental by-product. The transpersonal view regards consciousness as primary, with the brain its humble servant in the physical world.

Materialists regard consciousness as an intangible effect of neurological activity, an impotent fellow traveler passively following the play-by-play action in the synapses of the brain. Some even think of the brain as *secreting* the mind, similar to the way kidneys secrete urine. Accordingly, materialists classify humanity's spiritual intuitions as superstition, thereby denying them status as "reality." Other casualties are free will, survival of personal identity after death, and paranormal events such as telepathy, all of which are explained away as grandiose illusions spawned by a wish to deny the impermanence of life and its mechanistic character.

Superficially, the evidence for the materialist's stance seems sound. After all, when a blow to the head temporarily disrupts brain function, consciousness—at least self-consciousness—seems to disappear, not go somewhere else to wait. And when parts of the brain are altered by surgery or drugs, consciousness is likewise altered in ways that are fairly consistent from person to person. Therefore, the materialistic argument concludes, mental events slavishly follow brain events. No brain, no consciousness—period.

Despite its surface appeal, this materialist view is seriously flawed, for it cannot explain how a physical brain alone could generate events of greater vitality and superior action to itself. Although it is beyond the scope of this book to delve into the complexities of the mind/brain problem, it can briefly be said that the amazing sophistication of modern physics has not explained how even the simplest form of self-awareness, creativity, or intuition could be generated from molecular activity in any biological organ, let alone the richness of human spirit as embodied within such personalities as Beethoven or Einstein.

Transpersonal theorist Stanislav Grof offered an analogy that exposes the weakness in the materialistic view of the mind/brain relationship. Grof likens the brain to a television set, with the quality of the picture and sound critically dependent on the proper functioning of every component. A malfunction in any part causes specific distortions in output, which can be remedied by replacing that particular hardware. A well-functioning mechanism is essential for a coherent program to be viewed. Despite these undisputed facts, not even the most reductionistic scientist would offer this as proof that TV programs are generated by the television set. Yet this is exactly the argument mechanistic science presents in regard to the brain and consciousness.

Materialism also fails to account for "impossible" human abilities, such as telepathy, near-death experiences, out-of-body states, and dream precognition. To explain these common experiences in material terms would require science to revise most of the known laws of physics, but we have included arguments for their existence in chapter 14. Once materialists exclude consciousness from the cause-and-effect system that governs their universe, they create an embarrassing fissure that no amount of reductionistic science can fill.

CONSCIOUSNESS & THE SPIRITUAL GROUND

As an alternative, the transpersonal perspective affords us an opportunity to build a modern scientific theory of madness around a radically expanded view of consciousness. This view acknowledges consciousness as resident within all beings, rather than as a by-product of specialized types of matter called brains. This insight allows a healer to differentiate extraordinary states of consciousness that are more adaptive than the ordinary state from alterations that restrict one's ability to function in the world.

There is one important caveat, however. Although we can reasonably assert that consciousness per se originates from beyond the structure of the physical brain, we must not overlook the certain links between mind and brain simply because they are overinterpreted by materialistic science.

At the root of the transpersonal perspective is the idea that there is a deep level subjectivity, or pure spirit, that infuses all matter and every event. Be it called Brahman, Buddha-mind, Tao, or The Word, this living spirit was breathed into all being at the moment of creation as a manifestation of the divine nature. It is necessary for sentient life, because experience and awareness are possible only through the activating power that flows from this Source. In this book I will refer to it as the *Spiritual Ground.* This vital element fills the universe with Its presence, and It exists on a higher plane of being than material reality.

To speak of It at all, we must resort to paradox. It is eternal and beyond form, yet within It are transient forms and hierarchal levels. When we know It, we realize that It is beyond our knowing, an everpresent Mystery. It is the primary impetus behind all perception, thought, and feeling, so It must manifest itself in the world as *energy.* Yet It is not identical to the four kinds of physical energy that can be measured with instruments, or even the more subtle energies known in oriental medicine as *ch'i* or *prana*. Intense inner contemplation exposes Its presence at the Ground of our being, but those rare adepts who glimpse It directly describe It as no-thing at all, a void, yet ultimately *real*.

Although the Ground is not material, if we are to speak of It, we must *pretend* that It is. In so doing, we reduce It to "it." But we may take this step only with full awareness that the ensuing analogy will be partially defective in its application. For our present purposes of practically applying transpersonal thought to worldly problems, I will extend the theory to conceive of the Spiritual Ground as a *field* of consciousness analogous to gravity, or like the electromagnetic sphere of influence surrounding a magnet.

A field is a *conditioning of space*, a pattern of force that affects matter and other forms of energy within its range. For instance, as a star accrues gravity by accumulating matter, the star adds its particular form to the background gravitational field. The gravitational field becomes part of what a star is. When the pattern of activity within a star changes, perhaps becoming more compact, the surrounding gravitational field always reflects that change. It also overlaps and is affected by gravitational fields of other nearby stars or planets. In the cosmos, as in consciousness, there are fields within fields within fields. . . .

Similarly, we may think of the Ground as entering an intricate field relationship with the individual brain, imparting its fundamental vitality, its spark of life. Consciousness is everywhere, but each brain has a unique capacity to give it the shapes and forms that we call *mind*. As a developing fetus gains complexity, like a vortex the consciousness of the Ground flows and condenses into it, ensouling it, shaping it and taking shape from it in dynamic *interaction*. As the brain grows in size and complexity, so does its associated field of consciousness. As the brain differentiates into its various anatomical structures—cortex, midbrain, and so on—the human mind acquires its unique patterns and capabilities, whether they be mad or sane. Each specialized brain structure is linked with specialized mental functions; when either brain or mind changes, the other does, too. All the while, the mind remains an *open system*, constantly exchanging energy with its Source.

To look at this another way, for millions of years the brain has been evolving into a living link between matter and the Spiritual Ground. The brain imparts human meaning and purpose to the power of the Ground, enfolding within itself a very specialized awareness uniquely suited to thinking and feeling its way around this planet. In order to perform this task successfully, the brain must operate within well-regulated limits, or the mind will regress into less highly evolved forms, as occurs during certain kinds of psychotic ASCs.

Here I must reaffirm the defects in the field analogy of consciousness. A star's gravitational field is *physical* energy that enters into a lawful, mathematically predictable relationship with the star and with other fields. Consciousness, however, is a finer, *nonphysical* force that nonetheless interacts with physical matter. Many have tried, but no one has ever clearly shown how that mysterious and complex interaction takes place. Yet, like a material energy field, consciousness sometimes appears to assume a vibrational or wave form, as we will see when we apply the analogy to psychosis later in this book.

But ultimately consciousness remains above the laws of physics. Its workings are not entirely predictable by any physical law or laws, and it is not limited by the same constraints as physical entities. This permits an open-ended view of human potential that allows for the *possibility* of extrasensory perception, survival of death, and even noncorporeal forms of intelligence that can influence human beings.

CONSCIOUSNESS & SELFHOOD

Life begins in blissful communion and simple unity with the Spiritual Ground. As a child's brain develops from conception throughout the early years of life, it gradually collects and condenses its own share of consciousness from the infinitely larger field that surrounds it.

The child's first essential task is to seal off this portion of consciousness from the Ground, to make it his own. In other words, he forms a *self,* the integrity of which is essential for sanity later in life. The child accomplishes this by forming a psychic "membrane," a self-boundary that allows an individualized sense of I-ness to separate from other selves and from the Ground. At first, this membrane is quite porous, allowing free exchange of energy between self and Ground. As a healthy child matures, his self-boundary expands, incorporating more and more consciousness within his own being. It is this condensed and walled-off portion of the Ground that actively engages the physical brain in mutual interplay.

But soon something is lost. As a child fortifies his self-boundary—a task necessary for survival—he further isolates himself from the Ground. He accomplishes this by gradually *forgetting,* by repressing his once open

11

and blissful communion with the Ground, which then becomes alien, not-self. In other words, the child's psychic membrane grows less permeable, hardened by his focusing attention on the physical world and away from his inner world, where he still feels the steady presence of the Ground. This process, called *original repression* by transpersonal theorist Michael Washburn, is never complete. Although the child may have forfeited immediate awareness of the connection, the Ground remains as deeply embedded in him as he is deeply embedded in it. The memory of his primal union with the Ground subconsciously remains, a source of both fascination and fear.

The self's gradual estrangement from the larger field of consciousness is a necessary and complicated process that is influenced by a child's genetic endowment, his relations with his parents and peers, and the physical health of his body. The psychic membrane surrounding his self will always remain semipermeable to the Ground, which is necessary to sustain sentient life. But this self-boundary can become vulnerable to catastrophic fragmentation during psychotic ASCs, allowing the Ground to inundate and rupture the self—a kind of psychic death. For this reason, it is important that we appreciate the relationship between the bounded self, the larger and unbounded realm of the Ground and the subconscious mind, (see Figure 1–1).

Our self-membranes should not be too tightly sealed, because we require constant inflow from the Ground to renew and sustain our vitality. The infinitely abundant Ground is our life force. When inflow from the Ground wanes, our awareness contracts and becomes colorless, passionless, and shallow. Conversely, most people welcome regular, controlled infusions of the Ground, which quicken experience and stimulate expansion of awareness and spiritual growth. We recognize these as energetic moments of well-being, inspiration, and occasionally extrasensory perception.

Altered states of consciousness change the permeability of self-boundaries. Some psychotic ASCs dramatically *increase* the flow across these psychic membranes, allowing uncontrolled infusions from the Ground to intoxicate an unfortified self. When this occurs, the awesome force of the Ground first excites the subconscious sphere, causing a person to feel unfocused anxiety and inner restlessness. If the inflow goes unchecked, the more strongly bounded core self is overwhelmed, and thinking and feeling become distorted, such as in the case of Tom, described earlier in this chapter. Subconscious contents then intrude into awareness as hallucinations or "alien" thoughts. In contrast, excessive outflows *away* from the self lead to devitalized depressive states, such as those that follow mania and other hyperaroused psychotic ASCs.

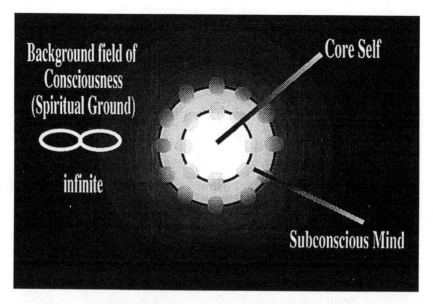

FIGURE 1–1: *The relation of the self and subconscious mind to the universal field of consciousness (Spiritual Ground). Note that both psychic "membranes" bounding these structures are semipermeable, allowing partial entry of energy from the Ground first into the subconscious mind, which acts as a filter, and then into the more firmly bounded area of self-awareness. The inner self-membrane is relatively less permeable to the Ground than the outer membrane. These membranes may be thought of as allowing consciousness to pass in both directions. Therefore, the subconscious mind receives both influx from the Ground and re-pressed contents from the core self. The individual mind also affects the Ground, and potentially other selves. It is helpful to visualize these figures as three-dimensional spheres rather than flat circles.*

Distracted by the lures of the material world, most of us become overly sealed off from this fundamental Source of our being. We can then approach it only though our intellects as an abstract theory. But some people—mystics, creative artists, psychic sensitives—do not have to be convinced of the reality of the Spiritual Ground, because they know its vitalizing presence directly, as they would an old friend. Still others feel the Ground to be a terrifying force threatening to overwhelm their defenses like a rampant floodtide, bearing their vulnerable selves into madness.

Many people who follow a spiritual path practice techniques to gradually reopen their self-membranes to the Ground in a controlled way. This is possible only for those fortunate individuals who have first developed a strong inner self through engaging life's trials and challenges with an open heart. If they follow their path with discipline and honesty, the natural human tendency toward spiritual growth will carry them beyond the need for individuated selfhood and allow them to reunite first with the collective consciousness of humanity and ultimately with the Source of their being.

But the spiritual path can be perilous, and sudden, unplanned openings are not uncommon, such as in the case of Tina, presented above. Psychotic-like states—spiritual emergencies—can fragment self-boundaries, permanently damaging the self if mishandled. Such relatively benign states are well known to experienced spiritual guides, who have at hand time-honored methods to stem the intoxicating influx of the Ground and allow the student to continue on his path. But because these crises superficially resemble pathological states, less experienced guides often confuse the two. This is a cardinal error. Many treatments that are appropriate for malignantly regressive ASCs are contraindicated for spiritual emergencies, and vice versa.

ORDINARY & ALTERED STATES OF CONSCIOUSNESS

An ancient Oriental sage once queried: Last night I was a man dreaming I was a butterfly. How do I know that today I am not a butterfly dreaming I am a man?

As we frame our reply to this unsettling possibility, we might begin by observing the present status of our consciousness. To check this out, we would conduct a quick internal scan of our momentary experience to see if the overall pattern matches those qualities we associate with ordinary waking consciousness. We might further compare our state of mind with one or another altered state with which we are familiar.

If we are law-abiding citizens of a Western culture, this latter exercise will likely be a limited one. Western societies find virtually no use for most ASCs, tend to regard them as pathological, and are quick to rebuke those who make a point of pursuing them. Technological societies warn us to be wary of people who are prone to sudden trances, mystic raptures, and hallucinatory intoxications. Although spontaneous excursions into vivid fantasy worlds were a daily part of our early childhood experience, we learn to repress their memory and our residual craving to explore them as adults.

Safe and socialized, we are allowed but a few deviations from ordinary wakefulness: dreaming sleep, nondreaming sleep, reverie (day-dreaming), alcohol intoxication, sexual orgasm, and, under special circumstances, hypnosis and meditative states. Orthodox Western psychiatry assumes that a person who enters any other ASC is either high on drugs or seriously mentally ill. Such people are labeled psychotic if their ASC is one of several bothersome types defined in psychiatry's diagnostic manual. Even borderline cases are considered a little too abnormal to be trusted or taken seriously. And if such a person were to make a consistent argument against accepted reality? Well, that would simply demonstrate the diabolical cleverness of the psychotic mentality.

This is not the case everywhere. Eastern spiritual systems seem as intent on changing one state of consciousness into another as our system is on maintaining a single state. Sanskrit, an ancient language that evolved along with the practice of yoga, has some twenty nouns that can be translated into the single word "consciousness" in English, and it contains other terms to subdivide these.

Esoteric Eastern philosophies hold that the ordinary state of consciousness is neither innate nor even "normal," but simply one specialized tool for coping with ordinary environments and people. It is useful for some tasks, but inappropriate or even dangerous for others. Yet they do not disparage the ordinary state of consciousness. They recognize that it would be disastrous for a person driving on a highway to slip into a state of ecstasy that overwhelmed his senses. Some Eastern systems teach methods for controlling movement among ASCs, matching them to the individual's circumstances and ability to cope with alternate realities.

THE NATURE OF ALTERED STATES

If therapists or other helpers wish to meet mind to mind with psychotic people in a way that promotes healing, it is important that they be familiar with the attributes of altered inner experience. The following is an introduction to characteristics common to most psychotic ASCs, whether benign or malignant:

- There is a shift in the relationship between self and Ground so that the mind is felt to be somehow different from usual. A person may interpret this as blissful, terrifying, or any point in between.
- An ASC may shift a person either toward primitive modes of thinking and feeling (regression), or toward more advanced modes (transcendence), but either can be confusing to the individual.

15

• Attention turns away from ordinary concerns during ASCs. People may find it difficult to concentrate on matters that seem important to others. Conversely, they may seem deeply absorbed in what is ordinarily considered trivial.

• Space and time are reordered. A person may feel the flow of time speeding up, slowing down, or sometimes stopping altogether. He may perceive empty space as full of "energy" or subtle patterns, like some Van Gogh paintings.

• A person's perception of the material world changes, and objects appear transformed. During extreme shifts, hallucinations may emerge, and new orderings of reality become apparent. One's ability to compare these perceptions with those of the ordinary state—a process known as *reality testing*—may or may not remain intact.

• Perceptual filters may weaken, allowing too much sensory data to bombard a person's awareness, diminishing his ability to focus attention on one thing at a time; instead of being able to listen to one voice in a crowded room, he might perceive all voices with equal intensity. Or these filters may be fortified, resulting in his becoming intensely absorbed in a particular task or process.

• Depending on the ASC, it may be easier or harder for an individual to remember events from the past. Some memories may be changed from what they are in the ordinary state.

• Most ASCs change the way a person expresses himself and uses language. Rules governing the probability of associations change. One's progress along a chain of thought is less predictable— sometimes poetically, at other times incoherently.

• There is a shift in the relationship between what is conscious and subconscious. Self-boundaries may either contract to reduce awareness, or expand into areas that are usually outside of awareness. In the latter case, unfiltered and unprocessed energies from the Ground can exceed an individual's ability to cope. Or he may be overwhelmed by emotionally charged material that he is unprepared to handle. In contrast, adaptive ASCs, such as dreams or states of creative inspiration, can afford access to valuable archetypal or mythical realms.

• A different logical system may replace the one a person ordinarily uses to reach conclusions about reality. He may then form beliefs that contradict what most people consider reasonable, but which sometimes contain extraordinary insights. Ideas that are obviously true in one state of consciousness may be absurd in another, and vice versa.

- Because of these alterations in perception and thinking, a person may discover unusual shades of emotional coloration in ordinary events. He may experience uncharacteristically intense emotions, or conversely, a flattening of feeling-tone. Emotions can range from all-encompassing love to primitive rage or even inner deadness, but they usually are not what society deems appropriate to the immediate worldly situation. This may lead to paranoid terror or insight into the arbitrary character of social conventions.
- Certain ASCs may lead a person to experience his field of consciousness as merging with other fields and exchanging information directly (telepathy). Or his awareness may seem to merge with physical objects (clairvoyance), or even leap ahead of the present moment in time (precognition). These paranormal events may convey useful information or cause confusion and fear.
- A person's sense of self may change to the extent that he disidentifies with his physical body. A new and larger selfhood may then incorporate animals, other people, the planet, or the whole universe. Depending on his preparation for this shift, either spiritual growth or psychotic loss of identity can follow.
- Nearly all ASCs change behavior. This may lead a person to be withdrawn and introverted, as in some forms of schizophrenia, or intrusively extroverted, as in manic states. Mystical ASCs usually increase compassionate feelings. Often the changes persist after ordinary consciousness has returned and may lead a person toward greater or lesser degrees of adaptation to his environment.
- Depending upon his ability to surrender to a particular ASC, a person may experience it as pleasant or threatening. Previous experience with ASCs facilitates the latter outcome.

QUALITY & QUANTITY OF CONSCIOUSNESS

Finally, any ASC can be characterized in terms of quantity and quality. The *quantity* of an ASC refers to the overall level of arousal, the "density" of experience, the units of information processed per unit of time. Small quantitative increases in arousal can be experienced as pleasant and controllable, but larger shifts can exceed the adaptive capacity of the individual and lead to mental disorganization.

For instance, in the early manic phase of the manic-depressive cycle, a person may feel vibrantly alive and creative. Information and ideas flow through him rapidly, inspiring him to bring them together in new ways. Life seems to be rich in meaning and full of possibilities, with too little time to carry them all out. As the ASC intensifies, however, his thoughts start to race tumultuously. He grows irritable and impatient with the slower pace of people in his environment. Finally, what was initially a balanced quantitative increase changes into an unbalanced *qualitative* shift, and his thinking becomes disordered and incoherent.

Shifts in the *quality* of consciousness distort the degree to which the various components within an individual's brain and mind contribute to awareness. Ordinarily, there is a balance between thinking, feeling, instincts, drives, intuitions, and so on that allows us to operate as a coherent self. When this balance is disrupted by an ASC, one or more of these mental functions can overwhelm the checks and balances of the others, which may result in the loss of personal identity we call madness.

For instance, each brain substructure—cerebellum, hypothalamus, limbic system, cortex—makes a specialized contribution to the mind— motor skills, sexuality, emotions, thinking. In the ordinary state of consciousness, these maintain a certain ratio or balance in their contribution to our momentary awareness. Small, controlled shifts in one or another of these functions may enhance our mood or help us focus attention on a desired activity, like shooting a basketball or writing a book. But larger qualitative shifts can overwhelm the brain's delicate balancing mechanisms and lead to paranoid thinking, insatiable cravings, or wildly exaggerated emotional responses.

These two variables—quality and quantity of consciousness—can change independently or in concert during an ASC. When quantity increases independently, and the various components of the field remain in harmonious balance, the individual experiences a state of pure *hyperarousal*. Mild hyperarousal may lead to significant scientific or artistic accomplishment, or even spontaneous states of rapture. But because all mind/brain systems are seldom aroused to the same degree, qualitative shifts inevitably follow. These disrupt the delicate relations among mind/brain substructures—the "jammed computer"—and lead to disorders of thinking and feeling associated with extreme mania and schizophrenia.

The main point is that the common types of madness lie on one end of a spectrum of ASCs that includes creative and mystical states at the opposite end. The range of ordinary states of consciousness is more or less in the middle of the spectrum. There is a good deal of overlap, so that what one person experiences as an ASC may fall into the range of ordinary consciousness for another. For instance, the feeling of merging with the whole of creation may be a blissful daily event for a seasoned meditator, but that same experience could easily overwhelm a naive college freshman. Most societies judge ASCs as desirable or undesirable by the means an individual uses to achieve the state, the amount of control he demonstrates over it, whether it affects him transiently or permanently, and his subsequent inclination to challenge the reality assumptions of his culture or engage in maladaptive social behavior.

For better or worse, most shifts of consciousness result in a reordering of reality. Because a particular culture's definition of psychosis cannot be separated from how it defines reality, we now turn to consider how a given individual's beliefs come to be accepted as reality or to be invalidated as imagination, delusion, or hallucination.

REALITY—WHAT A CONCEPT!

Charlie, a twenty-two-year-old unemployed baker, was hospitalized with a diagnosis of schizophrenia after he entered a school playground and frightened several children by telling them that the end of the world is close at hand. He stated that he did this because he is the center of a plot by satanic extraterrestrial beings to take over the world. They have been waiting for years for just the right moment, but have been thwarted by Charlie's steadfast belief in Christianity. Therefore, he concluded that he was a logical target for their insidious powers, which include turning plastic screws in his joints, whispering sacrilegious obscenities in his ear, zapping his brain with blue lasers, and inserting sexually tinged impulses into his mind. These diabolical beings had taken control of the hospital staff, who conspired to keep Charlie confined to prevent him from spreading the word.

Because Charlie somehow perceived me as uninvolved with this plot, he asked me to arrange his immediate release from the hospital, so he could "save the world before it is too late." When I told him that I did not think that was feasible, he informed me that I, too, had been possessed by Satan and was "one of them." Charlie articulated this belief with the utmost conviction and sincerity, and his behavior was entirely consistent with the urgency of the global threat to humanity as he perceived it. He found evidence of conspiracy in nearly every trivial event—a patient spilling coffee on a newspaper story about space travel, a stray cat that someone had named Luke (Lucifer), the number six appearing three times on a staff member's auto license plate. Whenever anyone tried to demonstrate the irrationality of his belief, Charlie would fix him with the kind of haughty stare one reserves for people who have completely lost touch with reality.

There is little doubt that for Charlie this cosmic conspiracy was *real*. It explained the uncanny sensations that contorted his experience of himself and the world, as well as his caretakers' obstinate disbelief in what to him was obvious. Knowing that his unwanted sexual feelings were implanted from an alien source reduced conflict and helped him define the boundaries of his self, which seemed all too fluid. He felt important and powerful when he realized that he alone had been chosen to thwart this evil plot. And it is not altogether unreasonable for a person who repeatedly hears whispered obscenities coming from nowhere in particular to conclude that there are invisible demonic beings lurking in the vicinity.

For most of us, Charlie's grand delusion seems the quintessence of madness. Yet if we are to examine our own most cherished beliefs—personal, religious, or even scientific—we might find that many of them are also ways with which we explain our unique experience of ourselves in the world. We see that many of our beliefs, like Charlie's, help us view the world as a coherent whole that remains stable and makes "sense." Any belief that reduces uncertainty also relieves tension and helps us feel at ease about ourselves. We tend to summarily reject ideas that do the opposite. But unlike Charlie, we are able to comfort ourselves by finding others who experience the world in a similar way and therefore agree with us about what is real. Without this confirmation, we would be on no firmer ground than most people diagnosed as insane.

It is easy to understand how the idea that there is one true reality came to be accepted. After all, most people—especially influential scientists and politicians—share similar states of consciousness, so they tend to agree on what the world is like. Reality, therefore, is acclaimed by *consensus*. Alternative realities known to psychotics, mystics, and artists are, of course, distortions of that one real world, interesting though they may be. The young genius Sir Isaac Newton shared the consensual reality of his time when he described the universe as consisting of solid particles interacting lawfully and predictably within two force fields, called electromagnetism and gravity. That was how the world looked then, and to most casual observers it still looks that way.

Enter Newton's modern successors, the quantum physicists. Exit the comfortable notion of a solid, material, and predictable universe. First, the original two force fields were found to contain others—the strong and weak forces measurable only at submicroscopic distances.

Then the safe and solid atoms and molecules at the very foundation of reality were found to be made up of even smaller "particles" that, in turn, are not solid, either, but are insubstantial packets of energy, interacting with other fields in the universe in an eternal vibrational dance.

The physicist Sir Arthur Eddington knew this when he wrote that he was simultaneously sitting at "two desks." One was the familiar antique supporting his elbows, made up of hard, brown material. The other desk, equally real, was a shadowy field of energy whirling in mostly empty space. Here and there were local condensations that he had grown accustomed to calling atoms. These spun rapidly through a vastly greater emptiness. The shadow desk had no qualities of hardness or brownness, nor were his elbows more substantial. In fact, there was no "real matter" in either elbows or desk, nothing but a field of energies interacting with other fields of the universe.

Eddington's insight reminds us that our human brains, special though they may be, are composed of basic *physical* particles: molecules, atoms, electrons, mesons, and quarks—fields within fields. These particles interacting in the juices of our neurons and synapses are no more "solid" and behave with no more absolute predictability than they do in the cloud chambers and cyclotrons of the physics labs. So there is a constant interaction among the fields of our mind/brains and the fields of the external world, which isn't so external after all. In this strange new domain where everything blends with everything else, the indistinct self-boundary of the madman, and the mystic's voluntary surrender of personal selfhood, no longer seem so odd.

To confound matters even more, physicists inform us that the mere act of observing a quantum event inescapably alters how that event takes place. If we wish to remain consistent with modern science, we must allow for a potentially infinite number of possible realities to emerge from the various ways we interact with the world. Modern investigations of reality at the quantum level teach us that when we penetrate to the deepest aspects of nature, suddenly, as in a mirror, we meet ourselves. Or as the physicist James Jeans once exclaimed, the closer we look, the more the universe seems to be one great thought!

This is not to say that there is no world "out there," or that sensory perception is, as some Eastern philosophies hold, a thinly disguised illusion. No system that says everything is illusion holds up any more than one that says everything is absolutely real. Reason also fails to confirm the view that reality is *only* a construction of mind, that all you have to do is believe something for it to become true. As transpersonal theorist Ken Wilber points out, the predecessors of the human brain didn't evolve until about 6 million years ago, but the cosmos is about 13 billion years old. There were lots of things around before brains existed.

In a similar vein, the Swiss biochemist and philosopher Albert Hoffman argues that reality requires both a *transmitter*—signals from the external world—and a *receiver*—a subject who experiences by means of antennae formed by the senses.

> The metaphor of reality as the product of a transmitter and a receiver makes evident that the seemingly objective picture of the exterior world that we call reality is in fact a subjective picture in our minds. This fundamental fact means that the picture is not the same for everybody. Everybody bears their own picture of reality produced by their own private receiver . . . The reality we experience is not a fixed state, but is the result of a continuing input of material and energetic signals from the external world and a continuing decoding process in the inner world, transforming these signals into psychic experience . . . It is only in ourselves that the creation becomes reality. Every human being is the creator of a world of his own.

Reality, therefore, resides in neither subject nor object, but arises at the intersection of time and space where subject and object meet. Emerging afresh at the moment the knower encounters the known, reality is neither a thing, nor an illusion, nor a projection of mind. It is an *event*. If we alter either subject or object, the event of reality itself is altered. We neither invent nor discover reality, but we participate in its invention *and* discovery. We can't be uninvolved.

It follows that any given reality is *state bound*—that is to say, dependent upon the state of consciousness, ordinary or altered, of the observer as well as the nature of the observed. If we wish to make judgments about reality events occurring in ASCs, we should keep in mind that our interpretation of any reality event is learned from other minds and from the consensus of society. We are shaped by other people who are as state bound as we are. So for our personal reality to become a meaningful *social* reality, we rely on consensual validation to determine which of many possible descriptions of the world we accept as true.

MADNESS & REALITY

Many behaviors judged insane are efforts by people in ASCs to share nonconsensual versions of reality in ways that profoundly disturb their associates. These communications are so disagreeable because successfully socialized people are usually convinced that the consensus-reality events of their culture define the limits of possible experience. Psychotics frighten us when they remind us that those limits are easily surpassed.

To illustrate the power of the consensus to influence our ideas about what is real, imagine meeting a stranger at a bus stop. You find each other's company interesting enough to make plans to meet again, and you do so several times. But when you introduce your new friend to an older acquaintance, the latter gives you a puzzled stare and exclaims that he sees no one there. You try two or three more introductions, but each time you receive a vigorous denial that a third party is present, along with pointed suggestions that your vacation is definitely overdue.

At this point you may continue to see and converse with your consensually invalidated companion, but your confidence about your ability to discriminate reality from hallucination is likely to be severely shaken, and you may be reluctant to test the matter further. Still, the question of your new friend's reality is far from settled by his selective invisibility. Certainly a real event in consciousness has taken place. Were your older friends too quick in judging your nonconsensual experience as lacking an objective counterpart? How many opinions are necessary before you conclude that you are hallucinating rather than that they are missing something? This is the problem faced by a person in a psychotic ASC who cannot account for a solitary reality he is compelled to deny.

Living in a particular society conditions us to maintain a state of consciousness acceptable to its consensus. At birth human beings make little sense of visual or other sensory inputs. During the first several months of life, an infant reconnoiters the world with few preconceptions, finding magic and mystery everywhere, until he learns to see things in a way that gains the approval of most people in his culture. In so doing, the toddler gradually stabilizes one of many possible states of consciousness that fixes a system of *rules* for perceiving things. Events very early in life have some power to restructure rules while they are still flexible.

As the growing child interacts with his environment, these rules in turn direct the formation of *models* of how to make sense of the world. An example of model-matching is in Figure 1–2. To use a computer analogy, rules are hard-wired—built into the structure of the system—while models are soft-wired—part of the programming. Without rules, there would be no common ground of experience and no basis for communication with each other. Without models we could make no sense of a constantly changing world. The human mind needs its maps and models in order to tame complexity. To illustrate:

FIGURE 1-2: *At first glance, most people do not see that the sentence in the triangle contains two thes. It does not conform to a model from past experience, so the second the is not perceived. But a new model has now been created, so that when we look again, the superfluous the almost jumps off the page in its glaring inappropriateness. What we perceived was not the pattern of words on our retinas, but a model the pattern seemed to match. Research has demonstrated that the process of model matching is so powerful that nerve impulses traveling in reverse from the brain to the eye can actually alter the receptivity of the retina, so that it does not react to a pattern for which there is no model. If our cultural conditioning does not provide models to recognize certain events, we may simply not perceive them. We do not see what we are looking at so much as what we are looking for.*

A person's rules of how he constructs reality are fixed at a very early age, but his models can be modified by new experiences such as psychotherapy. Rules can be altered only by changes in the anatomy or chemistry of the brain, such as occurs in severe psychoses. Transient ASCs, such as a mild marijuana high, merely alter models and cause a person to experience the world as "strange" for a while. However, prolonged ASCs like chronic schizophrenia permanently restructure a person's basic rules and so result in radically shifted models for reality. As the individual adapts to his ASC, what was initially an unfathomable world becomes modeled by these new rules, and he grows comfortable with a nonconsensual reality.

We can imagine the experience of a young adult who develops a psychotic ASC that renders him unable to match his sensory inputs with familiar models. Everyday events seem weirdly distorted and lose their consensual meaning. After a fear-ridden struggle to find new meanings, his ability to make sense of things is overwhelmed, and new models gradually coalesce into a delusional system. He desperately clings to these nonconsensual beliefs, which are his only certainty in a world gone mad.

EXPANDED REALITIES

There is another way that some ASCs can expand the limits of a narrowly construed reality. Not only can shifts in consciousness alter models acquired from social experience, they can also extend the bandwidth of sensory or extrasensory perception into realms for which we have never acquired models.

The world picture that our minds create is painted with only five colors. Each of our senses ordinarily responds to a restricted range of possible stimuli. Human eyes, for instance, process data only from a narrow channel of frequencies in the midrange of the electromagnetic spectrum, the whole of which includes invisible infrared and ultraviolet light, X rays, and cosmic rays. The world would seem radically different if our eyes were sensitive to another band of the spectrum. For example, if we could see the long waves of the radio bandwidth, we could see into distant lands. If our eyes were receptive to X rays, we could see through solid objects, which would seem semitransparent to us. Such a transparent world would then be as real as this nontransparent world is now.

Similarly, human ears are deaf to high-frequency vibrations that dogs hear easily, just as a dog's range of smell also far exceeds our own. The dog lives in another reality, constructed of canine-specific models for sounds and odors that would be incomprehensible to us. Similarly, some psychotic ASCs render people exquisitely sensitive to nearby high-tension electrical power lines or the fields surrounding fluorescent light fixtures. These extra inputs create subtle nonconsensual realities. The feeling of these "expanded bandwidth" ASCs may be easier to grasp if we imagine what reality is like for a dolphin sensing a tidal shift, or a migrating bird navigating by fluctuations in the earth's magnetic field.

During ASCs that render self-membranes relatively open to the Ground, some people experience extrasensory perception. This can be telepathic influence from other localized fields of consciousness, or even information about events far removed in time or space. Very few people reach adulthood with perceptual rules adequate to the task of making coherent models for these kinds of data, which then become disorienting.

The difficulties encountered by people whose psychotic ASC suddenly extends their perception into unmodeled realms parallels the ordeal of people blinded from birth by congenital cataracts who later in life have their sight restored by surgery. Although the operation may be technically successful, and coherent visual patterns fall on functioning eyes, many of these people are unable to make use of their newfound sight. Because they never formed the requisite models for perception, or even rules for acquiring new models, most of these people see only a chaotic jumble of light. For instance, when shown a triangle-shaped block, newly sighted people are usually unable to identify its shape. But if they can touch the block, they recognize it immediately. Some find the whole experience so unpleasant that they ask to be blinded again.

Similarly, people from nontechnological cultures that have different perceptual expectations develop models that vary so much from ours that they may be thought of as living in a different world. For instance, the author Lawrence Blair wrote that when Magellan's expedition landed at the southernmost tip of South America, his massive ships were so far beyond the natives' experience that they were invisible to them, although the natives could perceive smaller landing ships. European explorers learned of this when the natives described how their village shaman, who was accustomed to dealing with unconventional realities, pointed out that the strangers had arrived in something that, although preposterous, could actually be seen if one looked carefully. We might consider such people psychotic if we failed to take their cultural heritage into account. James Fadiman and Donald Kewman offered the following thought exercise to illustrate this point.

Imagine yourself shipwrecked, exhausted, and hungry on an isolated tropical island. You manage to salvage a radio transmitter, only slightly damaged, with tools and spare parts to repair it. But when the local inhabitants, who know nothing of radios, find you working on it, they are glad to provide abundant food and shelter. However, it is difficult to convince them that you need the peculiar equipment. Their chief orders them to confiscate your radio to divert you from the fantasy that you can access unseen and powerful forces in ways that cannot be reasonably explained and that may offend the local gods. When they politely, but pointedly, ignore your demands about your radio, you become extremely upset and "difficult." To soothe you and keep you usefully occupied, the chief assigns helpful natives to instruct you in fishing and basket weaving in the hope that these sensible, constructive activities will supplant your dream world and convert you into a functioning member of their society.

Are radio waves "real" on that island? Not in a personal way. For unless the radio is fixed, they are not part of a reality event, only a "delusional" belief. Not in a socially meaningful way, either, for consensual reality requires two ingredients—personal experience and social validation—neither of which is present in the above situation. You had best attend to basket weaving or risk the fate of those hapless souls everywhere who are judged to have lost touch with reality. Expecting the natives to accept the reality of talking radio waves is as futile as a patient's expecting the staff of a modern mental institution to accept that he is in telepathic communication with demonic extraterrestrials.

In sum, reality depends upon the state of consciousness of the person who perceives it, and upon how his perception fits with models built from his past experience. It is unwarranted to automatically assign a superior status to consensual reality. Some people experience nonconsensual realities in altered states of consciousness that represent events that lie outside the narrow bandwidth of sensory experience, such as telepathy or precognition. And some rare individuals learn to manipulate their inner rules and models of reality at will, affording them extraordinary personal powers.

But when an individual's personal reality is consistently at odds with social reality, he is usually at a great disadvantage and is likely to be judged insane. In the next two chapters we take a closer look at the subjective experience of people who cross the line into a homemade reality that lies outside the human world of useful notions, shared symbols, and socially acceptable conventions.

CHAPTER 2

Madness as an Altered State of Consciousness

◆

Enormous herds of naked souls I saw,
lamenting till their eyes were burned of tears;
they seemed condemned by an unequal law,
for some were stretched supine upon the ground,
some squatted with their arms about themselves,
and others without pause roamed round and round.

DANTE

Insanity is terrific on the Late Show . . . but in the real world it's shit.

DORY PREVIN

WHEN I WAS a medical student, I was once summoned to the emergency room late at night to see an acutely disturbed man who had deliberately plunged a sharp knife into his right eye. As I helped prepare him for surgery, I could not help but ask him what could have motivated such an unthinkable act. Although he was in great pain, he immediately quoted Saint Matthew: *And if thy right eye offend thee, pluck it out and cast it from thee. For it is profitible for thee that one of thy members should perish and not that thy whole body should be cast into hell.*

The gaunt man went on to assert that this appalling act of self-mutilation was in truth an act of salvation, for he was unable to stop himself from lusting after women he saw on the street. Immediately prior to his act, he clearly heard the voice of what he believed was a heavenly messenger commanding him to destroy the offending organ lest it lead to his eternal damnation. Despite his agony, he smiled and assured me that he was at last happy to be cleansed of his sinful cravings.

Stunned by the perversity of this man's reasoning as he interpreted the meaning of scriptures that were presumably intended to illuminate a path away from suffering, I was confronted for the first time with the gravity of what it means to be mad. His grotesque act had actually lessened his intolerable pain and reaffirmed his quest for meaning in his existence.

Such people overwhelmed by psychotic ASCs know them to be cataclysmic events that uproot their basic capacity for reason and set them apart from society. A psychotic ASC can so shatter a person's fundamental sense of selfhood that it leaves him or her devoid of the inner unity and consistency necessary for life to be satisfying or meaningful. Those who eventually return to the ordinary state of consciousness often do so with a crippled trust in their sense of self that lasts a lifetime.

Yet the most sublime forms of art, philosophy, religion, and science also have been profoundly influenced by people whose perception ranged from the uncommon to the mysterious. Hence madness has been alternately glorified and reviled, considered to be a sudden opening into unplumbed depths of meaning and a seditious threat to the social order. In his *Phaedrus*, Plato calls madness "a divine gift, the source of the chiefest blessings granted to men." During medieval times, "divine madness" was thought to be a sign of a heavenly calling. And in recent decades, the idea that psychosis is linked to mystical insight and creative inspiration has resurfaced. Some who have personally experienced psychotic ASCs characterize them as the most ruinous events of their lifetime; others feel they are the richest humanizing experiences they have ever known.

In modern times, madness has become the province of organized medicine, especially psychiatry, which tends to categorize spontaneous, waking ASCs as pathological and treat them accordingly. It is likely that in the last century medical investigators have spent more time, money, and energy on psychosis than on all other mental-health problems combined. Despite this, the controversy over its cause, treatment, and even definition remains mired in an obstinate tangle of conceptual difficulties. Bitterly competitive theories, each promising complete resolution, fall in and out of fashion with each successive "breakthrough."

In recent decades, a radical countercurrent to the prevailing view holds that psychosis, especially schizophrenia, is not a medical disorder, but a fiction invented by authorities determined to suppress antitechnological thinking and nonconformist lifestyles. In this view, the diagnosis *creates* the disease. However, those of us who work intimately with psychotic people recognize the authenticity of their suffering, their incapacity for self-restitution, and their need for compassionate assistance. These unwanted and disabling ASCs lay waste to the lives of people in much the same way as do cancer and diabetes. Denying their existence does not diminish their destructive power.

So if we are to discuss altered-state experience meaningfully, we must categorize it according to observable patterns. I will therefore avoid escalating the conceptual chaos that surrounds the subject. Instead, I accept that many, but not all, psychotic ASCs are maladaptive shifts of consciousness that fall within current psychiatric diagnoses—arbitrary, imperfect, and overapplied though those may be. My goal is not to overthrow a hundred years of halting progress in understanding madness, but to hone our ability to discern subtle variations in order to apply the insights of the transpersonal perspective to healing them.

Schizophrenia and the manic-depressive (bipolar) disorder are the two major forms of psychotic ASCs. They represent one of the major health problems of our age. This chapter will focus on the subjective experience of these psychotic ASCs as they warp an individual's basic sense of selfhood and his connection with society.

In their early stages, mania and schizophrenia look alike. As the acute stage of either ASC runs its course, depression and devitalization usually follow. Although there are different genetic underpinnings for each of these ASCs, only after days or weeks of skillful observation does the distinction become evident, and even then there may still be a confusing similarity of symptoms. But because there are significant differences in the treatment and outcome of the two ASCs, there is a practical reason to separate them in terms of the quality and quantity of their shifts in consciousness.

SCHIZOPHRENIA: A QUALITATIVE SHIFT

Qualitative changes—disharmony among the interacting components of mind and brain—as well as a tendency toward an unremitting and disabling course mark a person's encounter with any of the several ASCs called schizophrenia. One of my patients described her experience of a schizophrenic break.

> At first my whole mind felt jazzed up, but later it was like gears in my head were spinning at different speeds, and when I tried to pull my thoughts together they would grind, like when you miss a shift in your car. My thinking went off in one direction, and my feelings in another, and what was happening in the world still another. I just couldn't fit all these things together in a way that made sense. I didn't

know who I was anymore, or if there were really a person
living in my body at all.

Given the labyrinthine complexity of the human mind and brain, it
is no surprise that the various ASCs we call schizophrenia are only
vaguely alike. Symptoms can range from having an unreasoning fear of
strangers to feeling that one is communicating directly with God. Bizarre thoughts prominent in one statement are absent in the next. Hallucinations come and go, seemingly following their own plan. Some
schizophrenic people are warm and ingratiating, while others are icy
cold. Some occasionally gain power over large groups of people, while
others assume an obsequious manner and a subservient role. Once the
ASC takes hold, it may never let go. Or it may maintain its grip for a
while, only to disappear into the dark of night and never return. The
only constant is inconstancy.

That inconstancy also is reflected in psychiatry's definitions of schizophrenia and other psychotic ASCs. These are rewritten every decade or
so, adding to the air of mystery that surrounds this form of madness.

In the U.S.S.R. it has been commonplace to use *schizophrenia* as a political term to discredit people who vocally dissent from the party line.
In the United States, however, recent custom strictly limits the term to
severe and deteriorating states that last for six months or more. Similar
ASCs of shorter duration are called *brief reactive psychoses* (less than two
weeks) or *schizophreniform disorders* (two weeks to six months). Official
texts also distinguish schizophrenia from multiple personality disorder.
Despite the added complexity, these recent changes are an advance. At
least the stigmatizing term *schizophrenic* is no longer permanently ap-
pended to people experiencing brief psychotic ASCs that mark transitions into higher levels of consciousness.

The following portrait of the schizophrenic ASC is painted with a
broad brush. Not all schizophrenic people manifest every characteristic
described. People who maintain a stable sense of self despite conspicuous social deviance—eccentrics, psychopaths, hysterics, religious
fanatics—are definitely *not* included. Also exempt are people undergoing temporary states of regression that are part of a life crisis. Nevertheless, there are several ways to be schizophrenic, and each has a certain
universality about it. What follows is a sketch of typical features of the
schizophrenic spectrum and some of its subtypes.

Regression: The Key to the Schizophrenic ASC

As we search for a common thread in the warp and woof of the
schizophrenic ASC, we encounter a general principle of the mind: we

cope with life as best we can by using the highest mental skills available to us; but if we lose access to these faculties, or if we consistently fail to achieve our goals, we revert to the next lowest, then the next, and so on. This is called *regression*, and it may encompass all or some mental functions, including perception, feeling, and thinking.

The schizophrenic ASC follows such a regressive path, turning an individual away from his higher potentials and initiating retreat to a more primitive mode of functioning. Regression can occur in terms of personal history—that is, toward an earlier stage of life. Or it can take place in terms of phylogeny—that is, toward a more primitive evolutionary stage.

For example, frogs and other amphibians have hearts whose rhythm is paced by the primitive A-V node, which drives it at forty beats per minute. In contrast, humans and other mammals have evolved the S-A node, which overrides the A-V node with a more efficient cadence of seventy-two beats per minute. However, if the S-A node is damaged by interruption of its blood supply, the dormant A-V node ends its silent vigil and resumes pacing the heart at a slower, but lifesaving, rhythm.

Mental regression can be equally adaptive, allowing a person to retreat and marshal his remaining resources with the aim of holding on to a functioning self. For instance, following the death of a loved one, an adult might regress to a childlike state for a few days, engaging in soothing but unrealistic fantasies and requiring others to care for his basic needs while he integrates the meaning of his loss and prepares to carry on alone. In this case regression is said to be *in the service of the ego*. Regression may also be a necessary preparation for emergence into higher stages of consciousness, including spiritual levels. In this case regression is said to be *in the service of transcendence*. Or regression can become fixed and hardened along with the psychotic ASC that spawned it. In chronic schizophrenia, regression is a key process involving reemergence of primitive thinking and feeling, as well as reactivation of primitive regions of the brain. Such malignant regression can be easily confused with early stages of transcendence.

The Disruption of Self

A reliable ego—the mental organ that searches for meaning, makes decisions, and directs the body to carry them out—depends on a harmonious balance among the components of the mind and brain. But as a schizophrenic ASC takes hold, the ego fragments, and with it goes one's sense of individuality and uniqueness. In contrast, some non-psychotic ASCs actually *fortify* the ego's boundaries, but schizophrenia enfeebles these psychic membranes, rendering them more porous. Then the normal filters that limit sensory and extrasensory inputs in order to make the flow of information manageable permit energies from the Ground to rush inward with a fury.

Despite the consciousness-expanding potentials of such an inpouring of spirit, the shift into a schizophrenic state is far from a mystical experience or an enchanting psychedelic trip. It is an ASC of cataclysmic proportions that ravages a person's ability to differentiate self from not-self along with his status as a discrete being centered in a civilized world. What replaces his fragmented ego is a churning broth of energy from the subconscious sphere, including disowned sexual and wrathful impulses cast in bizarre imagery. Indeed, the deepest levels of the subconscious mind empty themselves into the schizophrenic's awareness, violently distorting his personality and its ingrained habits and dispositions. One patient described this loss of self-boundaries.

> I'd be watching TV, and I'd become the hero or the villain; if they'd get hurt, I'd feel pain in the same place. When my doctor spoke to me, I couldn't tell if it was him talking or myself. One day I'd be Jesus healing the sick, and the next day I'd turn into Satan. Sometimes I'd go outdoors and sit under a tree, and then I'd *be* the tree, feeling my arms spreading out like branches, and my toes growing into the soil.

People unaccustomed to a relatively free flow of psychic energies lack models to give meaning to these kinds of perceptions, so they seem intrusive, strange, unreal. Waking experience takes on the eeriness of a dream, but without a merciful awakening. As in a nightmare, the individual feels himself to be in the presence of an unnamed and unnameable force drawing him downward toward a dreadful unknown. His eyes may reflect this implacable inner force by taking on a fierce stare that unsettles anyone who meets it directly.

The Betrayal of the Senses

As the schizophrenic ASC deepens, psychic energies ordinarily held in check by the self-boundary flow away from the self, eventually depleting the individual's vitality. Perhaps a subliminal awareness of this outflowing energy is responsible for the eerie sensation in the hairs on the back of their neck that an experienced therapist sometimes feels when interviewing a person in a highly charged schizophrenic ASC. Perception is also affected. At first, this may merely cause the material world to appear strangely distorted or affect depth perception.

But as the ASC intensifies, sensory distortions give way to even more threatening mental events. The one percent of humanity who experience schizophrenic ASCs dwell in a world haunted by ghostly apparitions, unearthly voices, and diabolic conspiracies hatched by clandestine forces intent on usurping the integrity of self. With minds bared to their environment, they see, hear, and intuit more than others do, but in so doing they forfeit their ability to separate the important from the trivial. Lacking consensual models of experience, they are unable to make sense of their sensory acuity. Desperately retreating from the unknown, they fortify their self-boundaries by narrowing their attention to the relative comfort of an inner world of hallucinated beings.

The shelter afforded by this defensive retreat is scant indeed. Although a few people find the voices and visions to be friendly, most confront an extremely low order of personality. The voices assume any and every kind of relationship with a person. Before they gain power, they are low and wispy, like the wind, calling his name over and over. As their grip on the psyche intensifies, they threaten, criticize, curse, mock, or command absurd acts, such as taking several baths in succession. They shout, hiss, sneer, whine, or tauntingly describe everything the individual does: "He's opening the door. He's taking off his coat . . ." Sometimes several voices of both sexes heatedly argue among themselves about the merits and deficiencies of the person, who passively listens. They may originate in air ducts or ventilators, and so take on a hollow echo. One woman told of a watery voice coming from her toilet gurgling, "Eat shit!" They are not above offering gratuitous advice, usually foolish, including stern admonitions not to inform others of their existence.

Try as they might, people in schizophrenic ASCs cannot ignore these insistent presences, who are as close as everything they call "I," who are unhindered by walls or distances, whose rancor is neither diminished by muffling the ears nor drowned out by their own screaming. Yet after a while, an individual may learn to converse with his voices and find some to be helpful. In a personal account of his psychotic experience, Mark Vonnegut described his hallucinated voices.

> The voices weren't much fun in the beginning. Part of it was simply my being uncomfortable about hearing voices no matter what they had to say, but the early voices were mostly bearers of bad news. Besides, they didn't seem to like me much, and there was no way I could talk back to them . . . But later the voices could be very pleasant. They'd often be the voice of someone I loved, and even if they weren't, I could talk, too, asking questions about this or that and getting reasonable answers.

Vonnegut concluded ominously:

> Once you hear the voices, you realize they've always been there. It's just a matter of being tuned to them.

These voices that so persistently crowd their way into awareness will not long be ignored, and the individual soon answers them aloud. During an ordinary conversation he may softly whisper asides to his voices every few seconds. The legions of homeless souls with vacant eyes, wandering the streets and teased by children for talking to themselves, are living testament to the noxious power of these mysterious presences.

The Delusional Solution

Hearing disembodied voices several times a day leads a person to question who, or what, is in charge of his inner life. It is no surprise that hallucinating people soon conclude that the world is constructed along lines far different from ordinary conceptions of reality. These beliefs, which conflict with the prevailing reality models of society, are called *delusions.*

As delusions take root within the psyche, they assume several distinct forms, all of which are desperate attempts by the psychotic person to stay centered in the sensible world, to compensate for losing consensual reality by making new rules and models that fit the altered state. He tries to communicate in ordinary language an experience that bears scant correspondence to the consensus world view from which language arises. So great is the human need to impose meaning and order onto the formless or uncanny that a delusion is seldom relinquished until the experience that spawned it is long in the past.

For example, one person who began hearing voices concluded that they were emanating from microscopic speakers implanted in his dental fillings. If speakers were implanted, then so were microphones that enabled his dentist to monitor his conversations. This meant that the dentist was part of a conspiracy involving the Mafia, which was intent on brainwashing him so that he would join their organization as a hit man.

This is an example of the most common delusion, the paranoid type. Paranoid delusions are variations on the theme of dreadful interconnectedness, of grand conspiracies behind the most mundane events, of malign purposefulness in a world where nothing happens by accident. The paranoid plunges into an abyss seething with menace. His environs are populated by omnipresent agents sent to observe and report to even more sinister figures, vaguely identified as "they," or "communists," or "the CIA." Convinced that it is human nature to dissemble, the paranoid is suspicious of all. No sooner does he leave a room full of people than those remaining plot against him. Conspirators include his closest friends and family members, who adulterate his food with insidious poisons and mind-altering drugs. There is no safe shelter, no one to trust, no recourse in love or friendship. His worst fears are confirmed when those to whom he speaks of his terrible insight recoil with a hasty denial that exposes them as participants in the plot.

It is natural for most people confronting a paranoid person to resort to reason. This invariably turns out to be an exercise in futility. The keen edge of logic is quickly blunted against the unyielding granite of necessity, for paranoid "insight" is chiseled from a need more compelling than lofty rationality. The paranoid *knows* his delusions are true with a certainty few people experience. Anyone who cannot connect these self-evident events in his way must be insane. A first-year psychiatric resident once reported to me this humorously illustrative dialogue:

Doctor: I'd like you to tell me what's bothering you.
Patient: I can't, because you're an FBI agent.
Doctor: What makes you think so?
Patient: All FBI agents carry a badge in their billfolds. You have a badge in there, so you must be one too.
Doctor: Look, I'll show you my wallet. See, there's no badge.
Patient: Hmmm. I must have been wrong then.
Doctor: (assuredly) Oh?
Patient: Yes. I guess all FBI agents *don't* carry badges in their wallets!

Delusions of control are akin to paranoid delusions in that they also arise from a weakening of self-boundaries. A person concludes that his innermost thoughts are not his own, but are alien ideas implanted into his mind. These ideas are usually so unspeakably vile that he is sure they could not originate from his own being. He believes the medium of influence to be laser beams, telepathy, electronic waves emanating from household appliances, or surgical implants in various parts of his body. One hospitalized woman believed that when a particular phone rang it was a secret command for her to masturbate. Accounts from pretechnological periods indicate that magnetism and witchcraft played similar delusional roles in the past.

Other kinds of paranoid delusions are *thought blocking,* (a person concludes that his thoughts are being stolen by others) and *thought broadcasting* (a person believes he causes other people to think and feel what he is thinking and feeling, or that his thoughts act in some direct way upon the physical world). Each of these delusions reflects a loss of self-boundaries, which afford the welcome sense of mental privacy most of us take for granted in the ordinary state of consciousness.

As an enfeebled self-membrane grows permeable, it allows an influx of energies from other people or the Ground that are filtered out during the ordinary state of consciousness. Although most of this information is jumbled and useless, occasionally it may be coherent enough so that the person in a schizophrenic ASC has an accurate premonition or authentic telepathic exchange. He then makes a valiant but vain effort to match these nonconsensual perceptions with models from consensual reality, and may, for instance, conclude that he is influenced by laser rays from a satellite.

We will return to the possibility of telepathy in psychotic ASCs in a later chapter, but for now suffice it to say that the exaggerated vigilance and open self-boundaries of paranoid psychoses seem to enhance this latent human potential, although seldom in a coherent way. Delusions of control dramatically demonstrate a person's frantic effort to generate "reasonable" accounts of experiences others view as unreasonable.

Sometimes a delusional system takes a messianic turn. The individual may "logically" conclude that because he is at the hub of so much conspiratorial activity, he must be of great importance. *Grandiose delusions* often take the form of religious images popular in the culture: the person believes that he is Jesus, or the Virgin, or a prophet chosen to save the world. John Hinkley was in such an altered state when he concluded that if he shot the president, a glamorous movie star whom he had never met would move into the White House with him.

Referential delusions are a frequent companion of grandiose thinking. Here the person concludes that lyrics of popular songs, television-show jokes, or innocent comments of fellow passengers on a bus are uttered with an intention of conveying cryptic messages and encoded directions to him. This can lead to outlandish behavior and occasional acts of violence. A dark example of referential thinking is found in the accounts of Charles Manson, who believed that the words of certain Beatles songs personally instructed him to lead his followers on death missions designed to start a worldwide race war.

Although sensational stories of murders and assassinations by people in psychotic ASCs gain notoriety, usually for their bizarre motivation and unpredictability, statistics show that schizophrenics are actually *less* violent than the general population. In fact, their vulnerability and frequent homeless status render them more likely to be victims than assailants. When they do commit crimes, they do so in imagined self-defense. Schizophrenics are more likely to be a danger to themselves, committing suicide at a rate several times that of the general population, and injuring themselves by following hallucinated commands or grandiose delusions that they are impervious to harm.

Splitting Feeling from Thinking

The feeling-tone, or affect, that follows a dissolution of self-boundaries during a schizophrenic break highlights the qualitative shift that is the hallmark of that ASC. As the components of the psyche lose their balance and harmony, the relative contribution of emotions to the totality of awareness is sharply altered. During the early stages of the ASC, emotions may be wildly exaggerated, but as the individual defensively turns his attention inward, they gradually become divorced from thinking.

This split between feeling and thinking reveals itself as glaringly inappropriate emotional responses. The person may giggle while speaking of tragic events, appear sad while doing something that he enjoys, or show indifference to pain. Or, as his fragmenting self contracts behind a wall of introversion, he may show no surface emotional charge at all, a symptom known as *flat affect*. This emotional blunting may lead others to regard him as wooden and lifeless; he alone knows the depth of his nameless dread as he teeters on the edge of imminent annihilation of selfhood.

The flow of time—a comfortably constant progression in ordinary states of consciousness—changes in most ASCs, either speeding up or slowing down. In adaptive states of consciousness, this enlivens the psyche with intimations of eternity, but in schizophrenic states time is distorted into an unreliable means of marking existence. It may seem to stop altogether, stranding the individual in a stagnant present without future or past, like a solitary island in a horizonless sea of remotely passing events. He loses his sense of order, sequence, and the dependable flow of cause and effect. He may feel that whatever he does alters history, or that he is aware of every event a moment before it happens.

Schizophrenic ASCs are no kinder to a person's sense of body integrity. The ordinary feeling of a skin-bounded body of stable dimensions is replaced by a fluidly changing form. The body seems to swell or shrink, sometimes losing various parts, such as hands or feet, sometimes feeling like someone else's body, or like a machine. Most people in the ordinary state of consciousness feel their mind to be centered in their heads, but schizophrenics often say that their minds operate from some other location, such as their livers, or wander from place to place.

Although hysterics and hypochondriacs also misinterpret somatic sensations, only a schizophrenic will proclaim that his brain is melting or that an animal has taken up residence in his genitals. One patient of mine frequently halted her thoughts in midsentence to politely request that I stop sucking the marrow from her bones.

Such fundamental shifts in time and space unsettle the foundations of orderly experience and skew thinking away from consensual lines. This is reflected in the speech of people in schizophrenic ASCs, which seems confused, oddly connected, and off the point. Schizophrenics leap from idea to idea as images stampede through their minds with no watchful shepherd to ward off irrelevancies and herd them along the main point of discourse.

As regression continues, the individual invents new words—called *neologisms*—to describe perceptions that are unmodeled by him and unnamed by the consensus. For instance, *gerigidy-planup* was a neologism I heard recently, referring to an invisible gnomelike entity that dwelled at the periphery of the patient's awareness. When asked to define these original words, the schizophrenic responds with more neologisms, or rhymes the word with several others in rapid succession. Schizophrenic ASCs turn attention away from the abstract meanings of words and toward their *sounds,* to subtle changes in inflection that convey information on another level. This information is usually distorted, but it occasionally bears an element of truth, especially about the speaker's hidden intentions.

The shattered speech of schizophrenic ASCs is a manifestation of a general inability to direct attention, to abstract what is important from what is not, to place events into a context of meaning shared by others. Schizophrenic speech reflects a mind dwelling directly downstream from a broken dam of sensory and extrasensory stimulation flooding all in its path. Such a deluge of unmodeled perceptions renders a person incapable of grasping the significance of issues because he is continually distracted by minor details or internal sensations that people in ordinary states of consciousness easily disregard.

Even after he returns to the consensual state of consciousness, a schizophrenic may recall his experience as so out of the ordinary that he concocts archaic and fanciful images to explain what happened to him. These tales of moonstruckness, demon possession, or accidental ingestion of psychedelic drugs lack the intensity of delusions formed during the ASC, but they reveal the difficulty in describing events that have no counterpart in ordinary experience. Of course these explanations, when repeated to most mental-health professionals, are perceived as yet another example of bizarre thinking.

THE COURSE OF SCHIZOPHRENIA

Just as there is no "typical" schizophrenic ASC (although there are enough common features to allow us to use the term in a meaningful way), there is also no single outcome for schizophrenia that can be predicted with certainty, at least during its early stages. Yet once an extreme qualitative shift in consciousness "locks in," it establishes vicious cycles that tend to acquire a malignant self-sustaining force.

For this reason, a schizophrenic ASC is far more menacing than a "hang-up" to be overcome by blowing off steam. The derangements of a schizophrenic regression reach so deeply into the mind that they will not be relieved by uncovering childhood trauma or poor parenting. Schizophrenia is a frontal assault on what is most human in us all, an exile to a distant land, a condemnation to a life of suffering beyond any human's deserving.

Despite the best efforts of many intelligent and sensitive therapists, the outcome of schizophrenia in civilized societies is grim. Yet this ASC can be readily altered by fortuitous life circumstances and—for better or worse—by therapeutic intervention that is started at an early stage. With the caveat that all schizophrenic ASCs may not follow a typical course, there are nevertheless four recognizable stages of the regression.

The Formative Stages

Although the dramatic shifts of consciousness associated with schizophrenia typically arise in early adulthood, many schizophrenics recall their childhood as haunted by a vague feeling of being somehow *different*. This difference was not celebrated as a tribute to the uniqueness of the individual human spirit, but as a humiliating stigma best concealed from view.

In the childhood of such a predisposed person, there often develops an exaggerated need to dissemble, to assume roles that are socially appropriate but do not reflect what he truly feels. Concealed behind this papier-mâché armor is the soft flesh of a child for whom the consensual world is untrustworthy, of an adolescent whose raw sensitivity confers an exquisitely felt vulnerability to rejection, of a young adult who sees through the superficiality of others, whom he despises and envies for their social grace.

This inward turning, coupled with a fragile shield of defensive arrogance, is called the *schizoid personality*, after the schism between inner experience and outer behavior that characterizes the formative years of many who later become schizophrenic. Such a cleavage between true and false selves establishes a chain of vicious circles. Maintaining a

41

façade of social conformity without a corresponding conformity of personal experience turns the future schizophrenic ever more toward his precariously constructed interior world. The result is an adolescent loner whose discomfort with others kindles in them a feeling that they have invaded his secret realm. Their rejections in turn foster an alienation that prevents him from mastering the social skills gained during the camaraderie and courtship play of adolescence. The more he divests himself of common social symbols, the harder it is to assume roles that others expect of him. Privacy becomes the solace he venerates above all others.

This estrangement from peers who respond to him as awkward or weird spawns a cycle of rejection and isolation that spins the future schizophrenic into an unshared world of his own making. Having forsaken the interpersonal for the intrapsychic, he finds that his defensive armor affords no safe haven. His inner self that once seemed so trustworthy turns out to be as unreliable as the social world. Unable to stave off destabilizing influxes of Ground energy, he feels a constant sense of lurking danger. A little stress at this point is all that is necessary to drag him into the quicksand of madness. Often the stress is the loss of a hoped-for lover who thought him too peculiar, or getting fired from a job because his boss found him too "spaced out" to concentrate. Even a move into an unfamiliar setting, like college or the military, can be enough to initiate the ASC.

As the schizophrenic ASC redirects the delicate balance of energies within mind and brain, the victim finds his concentration fleeting, his sensibilities beset by bewildering crosscurrents of ideas and feelings that crowd into a shrinking circle of attention. His sense of smell and taste goes awry, and his favorite foods seem tainted with suspiciously unfamiliar flavors. Unrecognizable fumes fill his airless room. Terrified that the ASC will never stop, he discovers that he can protect himself by dimming awareness. At this point he withdraws further, sequestering himself from the world as he becomes charged with a mounting energy that has no outlet. But this vain effort to resuscitate his failing selfhood only compounds his problem as the schizophrenic ASC deepens without the steadying influence of feedback from friends or family.

As the ASC tightens its grip, the individual experiences an escalating inner arousal. This is vaguely sexual, gradually spreading in waves upward throughout his body. He feels an irresistible force compelling him to pace about restlessly, stirring his senses to a level of acuity that renders the faintest sound, touch, or shaft of light too painful to bear. His awareness becomes suffused with sensations from subconscious realms, archetypal images that assume terrifying visages as they filter through his fear and confusion, or repressed primal urges that seem alien and foreboding as they return from years of exile.

The schizophrenic-to-be stands poised at the brink of a sudden realization of what he is *not*—namely, an individualized being. As his self disintegrates, he feels precariously differentiated from his environment, more insubstantial than solid, in danger of engulfment by powers that would blot out his personal identity. R. D. Laing called this moment *implosion,* a full-on terror that the world is about to crash in upon the self, crushing ego and identity, as a gas rushes in to obliterate a vacuum.

At this point in the progression of a schizophrenic ASC, some people retreat from the unbridled power of the Ground, contriving ways to remain real, struggling to keep from becoming an *it.* But for most, a lifetime of futile efforts to be what they are not exhausts them and renders retreat impossible. They take the last fateful step across a boundary past which all other boundaries collapse, into a realm where objects, people, and time sequences spin crazily into a churning whirlpool of fragmented consciousness where once there was a self.

This is ego loss, symbolic death of the "I" as knower, chooser, and doer. The newly psychotic self is like that of an infant, incompletely partitioned, its boundaries diffuse and permeable, unable to hold at bay the relentless pressure of the Ground. Conscious energies flow into the mind directly, bypassing the senses, which are too limited to deal with this expanded world. The power of pure spirit is seductive, just as it is for those more fortunate individuals whose lives have prepared them for spiritual realization. Such an irresistible force calls out for *surrender.*

But this new and more primitively defined self is not ready for surrender, for it is rife with fear, and not just the old familiar fear of people and society. A nascent dread arises from the ruins of the inner self, that onetime safe refuge, now the least trustworthy of all. Surrender is impossible; it would only be a submission to randomness, a final annihilation. There follows a death struggle against this insistent chaos, a struggle to impose order and meaning at any cost. Under such conditions, the collective standards of society no longer apply, and only a solitary insight prevails: *all is not what it seems.*

But soon a transformed self arises from the ashes of the old. This is a regressed and contracted self that holds in check the tension between Spiritual Ground and individualized ego, so that survival of a sort is possible. The earlier terrifying sense of inner disorder is replaced by a profound sense of relatedness that fills both inner and outer worlds. The individual feels that no event occurs anywhere that does not immediately affect him. And all that he thinks and feels directly influences not only other people, but even the inanimate world.

At this point the first hallucinated voice makes itself heard, bestowing a semblance of form to the chaotic energies intruding randomly into awareness. This hallucinatory world is a precarious one to be sure, but it is a vast improvement over what preceded, for at least there is company, and with it understanding. An avalanche of discovery of hidden relationships between previously disconnected events exposes what had been concealed. What are to most people everyday happenings, hardly noticed, become conspiratorial threats to survival.

The light of reason and order *seems* to have returned. The individual realizes that all the strange things happening must be clues of some sort. Someone, or worse, some *thing* is his enemy, is after him. Events of vast proportions are unfolding—dangerous events!—and it is clear that he has an important role in what is being played out. Persecution and conspiracy rule the domain of meaning as pacifying antidotes to the inner anarchy that threatened to annihilate the self. An apparently reasonable explanation for what he felt to be inhuman thoughts and feelings takes shape, and with it comes a welcome sense of relief, a closure of his terrible alienation from humanity. This cascade of twisted meaning is aptly called *psychotic insight,* and it marks the transition to the second stage of the schizophrenic regression.

The Middle Stages

From this point on, the person in a schizophrenic ASC reverts to a primitive form of logic to make sense of what is already evident to him. If his food tastes odd, he "reasonably" assumes that someone is adding poison to it. Familiar possessions, like his shaving cream or phonograph records, are tainted by the hand of an unseen enemy. He searches for corroborative evidence, finding it if a noise is heard in the night, if a neighbor uses a special word, if a stranger walks down the street. There is no need to demonstrate the truth of this revelation; he *knows* with an inner certitude that is beyond demonstration. That is enough.

Once he takes this step, the individual reaches a crucial juncture. While he may not be at a point of *no* return, he certainly is at a point of *difficult* return, from which few emerge intact. In Western cultures, the remainder of this story is usually one of tentative attempts to convince others of his delusion, of frightening someone with an angry outburst, of reluctant involvement in a mental-health system, of medicines that blunt both his fear and expanded perception, of relapse and despair.

A person who crosses this line into the middle stages of a schizophrenic regression gradually solidifies his delusions, which thereafter take on a fixed form. He becomes less excitable, with blunted emotions and speech limited in content and spontaneity. Disruptive outbursts are less frequent. Hallucinated voices grow kinder as his resistance to them is worn down and they become accustomed to being obeyed. Whereas earlier he desperately sought some form of social contact or under-standing, now he turns his back on importune attempts to invade his privacy. The arousal and sensory acuity once so prominent become concealed beneath a gray cloak of routine activity designed to avoid unpredictable situations. Life becomes bland and monotonous, but he never complains of boredom.

Whereas the first stage of a schizophrenic ASC is characterized by an intoxicating influx of the Spiritual Ground, the second is marked by a contraction of self-boundaries in a desperate attempt to stave off its power and salvage what is left of the self. This leads to depression, dampening of vital functions, loss of hope and meaning, and a numb-ing feeling of uselessness. A person in the midst of such a depression begins to look exactly as we might expect someone to look who is sealed off from the Source of his being.

Involvement in religious life would seem a plausible detour from the path of regression that follows a premature unveiling of the Spiritual Ground. After all, religions claim to specialize in matters of the spirit and afford models for understanding nonphysical energies. Indeed, many people in schizophrenic ASCs become infatuated with religious symbols as they search for meaning in their otherworldly experience. They dart from creed to creed, searching for an external guide to help them navigate their inner chaos. They may float from fundamental Christianity to occult metaphysics to exploitative cults, but they are usually unable to incorporate any of these into a coherent self-structure. Each failure leads to another search.

As the middle stages of the schizophrenic ASC unfold, variations become apparent, determined by the individual's constitution and environment. The most dramatic is the increasingly rare *catatonic* type, which has been likened to a voodoo trance. This ASC is one of intense inner arousal concealed behind a pervasive paralysis of will. A cataton-ic person can sit frozen and motionless for days, neglecting his needs for food and elimination. If an external force raises his arm or leg, it remains in that position for hours, well beyond the ordinary tolerance for fatigue. Some catatonics lose only their *own* volition; if ordered to perform outrageous acts, such as sticking a pin through their tongue, they unhesitatingly obey like a robot. Others do exactly the opposite of what is asked of them. Yet a person in this ASC is far from cut off from the external world. One need only look into his eyes to see an unfor-gettable acuity, a vigilance that is inclusive of every minor detail of his surroundings, eyes that flick toward the slightest sound or movement unnoticed by others.

Catatonics are more likely than other schizophrenics to spontaneously return to the ordinary state of consciousness. They often later recall delusions and hallucinations of a universal quality, images of vast expanses of time and space or of the end of the world. Yet few describe an accompanying feeling of divine presence, as in a mystical experience. Instead, there is a sense that all is wrong, that they have perpetrated an irredeemable cosmic crime, or are responsible for all the world's ills. These people tell of senses turned up to painful levels, a relentlessly acute awareness, glimpses of realities in which thought and language are meaningless and individual action impossible. No wonder the catatonic ASC often terminates by erupting into volcanic rage.

A rarer schizophrenic subtype with a less favorable course was classically called *hebephrenic* and has recently been renamed *disorganized type*. The older name seems more apt, derived as it is from *Hebe*, daughter of Zeus and cupbearer to the gods, best remembered for her low tolerance for the beverages she served and for her giddy, clownish ways. Hebe's namesake ASC is characterized by antic behavior with shallow feeling-tone and odd grimacing and posturing. Compulsive hypersexuality and feelings that one's body is distorted are common. Hallucinations are fancifully tinted and often pleasant. These people regress to childlike states and establish personal relationships with objects or otherworldly beings. Abstract thinking is forsaken early in the hebephrenic ASC, to be supplanted by an artless literalness that led one patient to drink the cleaning product Vanish because she wanted to disappear. Hebephrenic speech lapses into a series of unrelated rhymes or a nonstop word salad. Only rarely do hebephrenics regain even a measure of social function.

The *paranoid* type of schizophrenia is found in pure form, but paranoia is also a general reaction that can color any ASC. Many nonschizophrenic people habitually make paranoid-tinged interpretations of events and even form delusions. The global suspiciousness and wide eyed vigilance of paranoia are a throwback to a less temperate era of human history, when people struggled to survive in a menacing world populated by cunning nocturnal predators. Although it is usually concealed by a veneer of domestication, paranoia is built into us all and readily mobilized when we feel that unexplained or uncontrollable events are undermining the integrity of our egos.

These types of the schizophrenic ASC are seldom firmly fixed within an individual. Some who appear hebephrenic one day may be catatonic the next. I have observed people changing from one type to another during the course of an interview. Paranoia seems to be the common denominator. When interviewed by a tired, aloof, or disdainful examiner, a hebephrenic can swiftly become paranoid and hostile.

The End Stages

In many instances, the final chapters of a schizophrenic regression chronicle life in a mental institution or on the squalid streets of an inner city. However, a few people grasp the thread of unity that was theirs for a moment and use it to mend the rent fabric of their lives, reweaving a texture stronger than the original. Others need the help of medicines to regain a semblance of the consensus state of consciousness, but never fully recover from the shock of self-loss. They remain fragile and vulnerable to minor stresses that most people easily shake off. Still others inexorably deteriorate into infantile or vegetative states.

Scientists who study the long-term outcome of people who enter the mental-health system in an acute psychotic ASC have a "rule of threes." One-third of these people regain the ordinary state of consciousness, never to relapse; another third also return to the ordinary state but eventually develop more psychotic ASCs; the final third undergo a progressively deteriorating course and require a lifetime of care.

As schizophrenic regression continues over the years, a chronic stage imperceptibly takes hold. Existence turns vegetative as the emotional aspects of the ASC lose their charge. Emotions become like objects, ideas take on physical form, time is disjointed, and feeling and perception inseparably blend. The discrete types of the middle stages gradually merge into what is unflatteringly called "chronic undifferentiated type." Regression descends to the level of a child in the toddler phase, but the exuberant vitality of a healthy child is conspicuously absent.

People in this stage of regression spend a typical day stimulating themselves with rhythmic movements—swaying, pacing back and forth, repetitively masturbating. Self-decoration with feathers, bright pieces of string, or scraps of colorful rubbish becomes a fetish, as does compulsive hoarding (a behavior trait also common to prisoners). Eyes lose their fiercely penetrating stare and take on a glassy hollowness.

The major earthquake that struck Southern California in 1971 demonstrated to me the imperturbability of people with late-stage psychosis. At that early hour I was the sole physician on the grounds of a state hospital where thousands of such patients were housed. When the temblor jolted me from my bed to the floor, I expected that the patients would be in a frenzy, and that I would be overwhelmed with requests for sedatives. But as the day progressed, it was clear that the patients made little of the event; it was the *staff* who were most in need of sedation.

Most people who regress to the vegetative stage of the schizophrenic ASC live out their days in the numb comfort of institutional routine.

Even for the third of all schizophrenics destined to follow a chronic course, only a few deteriorate into the infantile stage, which occurs decades after the original psychotic episode.

This final stage is notable only for a profoundly regressed and rudimentary mental life that is more neurological than psychological in character. Communication is rare and incoherent, and the mouth becomes a primary means of exploring an unfamiliar object. A person in this stage may habitually grab every small object and put it into his mouth, paying no attention to its edibleness. Although he consumes food without savor, his appetite increases markedly, and he may resort to mouthing his own feces when food is not immediately available. His perception of pain diminishes, and he may injure himself by standing passively in a scalding shower. He meets most events, pleasant or noxious, with a wooden indifference as he mindlessly awaits his death.

There is persuasive evidence that such profoundly regressed people are victims of a genetic push toward degeneration of vital brain centers and personality. Their path is one of profound *atavism*, a de-evolution to ever more primitive modes of function, a stagnation of mind unmatched by any other human condition. Yet recent evidence indicates that even this group of severely impaired people, long thought to be hopeless, may eventually recover a surprising degree of social function if met with enlightened treatment approaches designed for their particular level of regression.

As noted earlier, only a minority of people who experience ASCs that resemble the first stages of schizophrenia ever regress to the final stages. An even smaller minority use an acute psychotic ASC as an impetus toward accelerating spiritual growth into higher levels of awareness. It is a recurring theme of this book that a more *artful* response by those who attempt to treat psychoses would redirect a significant number of people away from a regressive path and toward the progressive expansion of consciousness that is our birthright and the central task of our lives.

THE MANIC-DEPRESSIVE ASC

As a manic ASC takes hold, a person initially feels pleasantly alert, vibrantly alive, at the brink of new insights. Although several sleepless nights pass, he feels no sense of fatigue, only a gradual opening of exceptional clarity. Sleep is superfluous, a needless waste of precious time. Sights and sounds are brilliant, vivid; indeed, all the senses come alive, and there may be an excited tingling running up the spinal column. There is a feeling of stepping beyond the limitations of ordinary thought, of being privy to a wealth of insight beyond the reach of others, of unfettered freedom to feel and act as never before. Things that before had been mysterious reveal their secrets. The early manic is empowered with a newfound vision of the essence of things—not merely how the world functions, but the subtle reasons behind it.

It is diflficult to convince someone in such an extraordinary frame of mind that he is in imminent peril of going mad. The sane world has little to match his raptures, and he has never felt more rational in his life. There is no way to keep such important truths to himself. An ebullient extroversion infects the early manic phase, no matter how introverted the core personality. His high-velocity stream of ideas whirls into a torrent of words. He jumps into every situation that catches his fancy, and there are many, for he seldom persists in any undertaking past the point where the next intriguing novelty intrudes. His sexual drive becomes enlivened, insatiably so, by a rush of vitalizing energy.

Time rushes for the manic; there is never enough of it. There are no limits to what he can accomplish by pure will alone if others would just get out of his way. And there are no consequences, no dues to pay tomorrow. Personal responsibility and guilt are impediments reserved for the unilluminated. There is a glorious scattering of money for the sheer fun of spending, and credit cards are his means to meet the unquenchable challenge of finding new and interesting ways to dispense it.

A *quantitative* shift of consciousness marks the early stages of a manic episode. Unlike qualitatively shifted schizophrenic ASCs, which from their onset unbalance the various components of the mind and brain, in early mania there is simply more consciousness condensed into a given time frame, with a corresponding increase in the overall density of experience. Perception, thinking, feeling, and intuition are equally amplified. Qualitative shifts into psychotic states may or may not follow.

As long as the ASC remains only quantitatively shifted, the manic maintains coherent self-boundaries and forfeits little social or vocational competence. Indeed, the inpouring of Ground energies enhances his ability to master new tasks and make creative connections. His infectious confidence and enthusiasm enable him to seduce others into relinquishing their conservative scruples. One manic patient of mine, a rather dowdy, straight-laced mother of five, suddenly left her family and took an apartment in a nearby city so as to indulge a whim to take flying lessons. Her indefatigable capacity for study gained her a pilot's license in near-record time, but she was soon grounded for practicing aerial acrobatics over a populated area. Her manic ASC then faded as abruptly as it arose. She sheepishly returned to her family, never again to find the confidence to enter a cockpit.

Often, arousal stabilizes before qualitative shifts occur, a state known as *hypomania*. Many hypomanics are creative and successful people, becoming leaders in business, science, and the arts. They seem to have the knack of flouting authority and convention while halting one step short of crossing the line into psychosis. Ronald Fieve, a physician who spent his lifetime studying manic people, wrote that such luminaries as Abraham Lincoln, Teddy Roosevelt, Ernest Hemingway, Winston Churchill, and George Patton were beset by episodes of hypomania during the times of their most significant accomplishments.

The 1 percent of the population who develop full-blown manic episodes are less fortunate. Countless careers, marriages, and families have been wrecked by this disruptive ASC when it spirals out of control. As a quantitative increase in arousal escalates beyond a certain threshold, qualitative shifts in the balance of various mind/brain systems inevitably follow. A condition resembling the exaggerated inner acuity of paranoid schizophrenia follows, but with a hypercharged and extroverted ego running the show. As the psychic membranes separating the bounded self from the surrounding field of consciousness stretch thin, they begin to allow uncontrolled influxes from the Ground. By their nature, manic ASCs propel the individual to transcendental planes where subject and object unite, where earthly references become absurd.

Nothing in society prepares one for such a metamorphosis. Because most young adults who enter their first manic ASC are at a stage of life that is naturally focused on the material world, they lack models to integrate finer conscious energies. Nevertheless, people prone to manic ASCs generally possess egos that are less battered from early life than schizophrenics. They are therefore able to withstand sudden inflowings of unfamiliar forms of consciousness without the disabling fear that marks an early schizophrenic ASC. At first a manic may experience quasi-mystical rapture as his naive ego beholds the power of unrepressed spirit. Telepathic or precognitive information may intrude into his awareness. His relatively strong ego is usually able to partially integrate these energies without the psychic intoxication they induce in schizophrenics.

Nevertheless, this state of affairs is too unstable to persist indefinitely. Except in those rare cases in which a person who enters a manic ASC has conditioned himself to tolerate Ground input through spiritual training, his ego will finally begin to crack, along with consensual reality. The fissure may be imperceptible at first. His friends may hardly notice his intense preoccupation with esoteric metaphysics or occultist lore. Accustomed to the harmlessly fascinating quirkiness of individuals prone to hypomanic episodes, they may think little of his irritably rejecting their efforts to ply him with common sense. Impervious to feedback, he simply and sincerely denies that anything is wrong.

An explosively volatile ASC lurks behind this rapidly faltering ego. Hallucinations, as often visual as auditory, begin to blend with objects of the material world. Hallucinated printed matter may even replace or combine with words written in the newspaper or books. Delusions, the ego's last gasp efforts to model the uncanny, soon follow. These tend to be tinged with a cosmic or mythic quality, imparting a messianic sense of mission to save the world, or even the universe. But unlike a catatonic, a manic has no guilt-ridden inhibitions that paralyze his implacable will to action. Paranoia, which is a final common pathway for psychotic ASCs, leads to exaggerated defensive reactions against anyone unwise enough to stand in the manic's way. Many a manic gets roughed up by uncomprehending police after flouting trivial social conventions.

Like Icarus, whose wings of wax lifted him too near the source of ultimate power, manics await a hard fall to earth. A porous self-boundary allows an *outflow* as well as inflow of conscious energies, and a manic consumes his vital inner resources at a rate too swift to be contained. A precipitous descent from sunny heights into the dark caves of depression soon follows.

The devitalized state that follows a manic ASC is much more than the "blues" that follow a setback in normal life. The spent ashes of the manic state blacken each experience, taunting reminders of a momentary flirtation with the Source. There remains only a soft whisper of something left undone, an important truth just barely missed, now seemingly forever beyond reach. Where there was once an abundance of purpose to life, now there is a void, a loss of hope of finding meaning in existence, a sealing off of a newly contracted self from the life-giving energies of the Spiritual Ground.

The average course of a manic episode is about three months, and that of the following depression about nine months—a stagnant eternity that can end in suicide. The depressive ASC is one of daylong fatigue and nightlong insomnia, of unfocused restlessness, of irritable withdrawal from family and friends. The depressed individual is impervious to the pleasure of beautiful music or good food. His will is insufficient to concentrate on the daily newspaper, and he immerses himself in guilt-ridden fantasies that he is contaminating the world with his foul presence.

Yet this, too, eventually passes. One morning he awakens to a pleasing shaft of morning light through a window, or takes joy in the song of a bird. There is a gradual restoration of the ordinary state of consciousness, and with it the premanic personality. He finds no noticeable reason for this happy shift, just as the manic state emerged without apparent cause. Unlike the personalities of schizophrenics in remission, the character of manic-depressives differs little from that of the population at large. When neither manic nor depressed, their self-boundaries remain just as firmly structured as anyone else's. Many are free from everyday neuroses and are sorely distressed by the disruptive interludes in their otherwise goal-directed lives. Even more worrisome is the prospect of another unpredictable manic-depressive cycle in the future.

CHAPTER 3

The Many Faces of Madness

◆

Forgive, O Lord, my little jokes on Thee
And I'll forgive Thy great big one on me.
ROBERT FROST

The self is itself a society.
EMILE DURKHEIM

THERE ARE LOTS of ways to be psychotic. Once the human mind
releases its grip on the consensus view, the orderings and reorderings
of possible realities are countless.

Although schizophrenic and manic-depressive ASCs are the most
common forms of psychosis, several other ASCs also lead to experiences
our society does not accept as valid. This chapter examines some of these
less well known conditions, including "borderline" states and multiple
personality disorder. It also reviews nonpsychotic ASCs that are frequently confused with schizophrenia but are of a more benign nature,
such as sensory-deprivation hallucinations, out-of-body experiences,
and unusual hypnotic trance phenomena. A later chapter describes
transcendent ASCs that are also confused with the major psychoses.

THE BORDERLINE PERSONALITY

Unflattering though it may be, *borderline* is the official psychiatric
term for people who spend their lives precariously perched on the edge
between psychotic and ordinary states of consciousness. Psychiatrists
append this term to "difficult" patients who are neither insane nor neurotic and who are generally immune to standard therapies.

Borderlines are the walking wounded in the universal battle to find a secure place in life for the self. While regression from a relatively mature level characterizes manic and schizophrenic ASCs, borderlines simply have never grown up. Like children still forming self-boundaries, borderlines experience their indistinct selfhood as partially merged with other people and the Ground. This leads them to form "sticky" relationships based on being cared for by powerful others. They desperately cling to these relationships by passively complying to the will of the other, or by manipulation. To lose the relationship is perceived as psychic death, for as one patient told me, "When I'm alone, I cease to exist."

Borderlines are adept at uncovering deep feelings of inadequacy and helplessness in their psychotherapists. These people neither mobilize the compassion in their caregivers that accrues to the severely psychotic, nor the therapeutic zeal that neurotics readily stimulate. Unwilling to share the naked pain that accompanies this form of turmoil, experienced clinicians tend to refer these patients to novice therapists, who are often unprepared to unravel the knot of contradictory feelings that emerge in therapy. What then follows is a cycle of mutual misunderstanding that further fragments the borderline's vulnerable sense of self, quickly catapulting her or him into a frankly psychotic ASC.

At the core of the borderline syndrome is a weakly constructed self, resulting from a failure to form an adequate self/other boundary during early childhood. Such a state of affairs renders a borderline vulnerable to spontaneous psychotic ASCs whenever his easily fragmented selfhood is threatened. This is why borderlines have been aptly described as being like toddlers whose mothers have permanently left the room. Unlike schizophrenic and manic ASCs, in which the self is undermined from within, psychotic states in borderline individuals arise from parts of the self that involve *others*. The psychoanalyst Heinz Kohut aptly named those people whom borderlines include in their selves *selfobjects*.

Because the borderline's selfhood is constructed partly from his own authentic nature and partly from bits and pieces of idealized selfobjects, any failure of these segments roughly tears away a portion of his self. This leaves a gaping hole in the psyche that allows intoxicating energies to rush in from the subconscious mind and from the Ground. Hallucinations and delusions then crystallize around these energies. As the borderline's unsupported self fragments, it regresses to an earlier mode of coping to salvage its integrity. The result is an ASC properly called *brief reactive psychosis* to distinguish it from malignant psychotic ASCs. Similar disruptions of the self-boundary take place during schizophrenic ASCs, but the arm's-length relationships of schizophrenics are less likely to trigger a break than are the need-ridden, emotionally charged relationships of borderlines.

Because of their unreliable interpersonal lives, borderlines bathe themselves in deeply regressive fantasies, constantly balancing their frail self-image against the unbearable facts of their chaotic existence. Their self-presentation is one of partial truth teetering on a shaky foundation of imagination, halfway between delusion and outright lying. Although they can relinquish their fantasies when confronted with contradictory evidence, these people are compelled to revive these imaginings as their need for affirmation from a powerful selfobject dictates. If we find it difficult to tell whether their falsehoods are actually delusional or expressed with an intent to deceive, that is because borderlines themselves are confused as to the difference.

For example, a patient spoke lovingly of her infant daughter repeatedly over her first few therapy sessions with me, only to abruptly blurt out that she was childless. This followed a surge of anger when I refused her request for tranquilizers, telling her that she needed to remain alert to her child's needs. Despite her revelation, she subsequently revived her motherhood pose whenever she felt a need to view herself as an involved and nurturing person. My naive efforts to confront her with this discrepancy of course proved ill advised. Although she again admitted that she had no child, she furiously accused me of not understanding her and entered a psychotic ASC that persisted until I reestablished myself as a reliably supportive person in her life. This meant once I learned to consistently acknowledge the feeling behind her imagination rather than challenging its reality, her motherhood fantasy disappeared.

The following is a review of the cardinal features of the borderline syndrome. Each is a desperate attempt to maintain the integrity of a fragile selfhood by merging with overidealized others.

- A borderline individual maintains an intense, clinging dependency that reflects his need for exclusive and engulfing relationships. He desperately maintains these by manipulation, including threats of suicide.
- He rapidly elevates new friends, lovers, or therapists into hero or savior roles. At their first failure to gratify his dependency, he just as rapidly devalues them into enemies or persecutors.
- Self-destructive acts such as drug overdosing and superficial wrist slashing are his way of exacting rescuing responses from others. The suicide rate among severe borderlines approaches 10 percent.
- He experiences extreme discomfort or panic at being alone. An allied fear is that those on whom he feels dependent will abandon him. His efforts to cling to a relationship often become so exaggerated that the original fear becomes self-fulfilling.
- He tends to reason loosely and organize his ideas in a way that

is difficult to follow when structure is not provided by outside sources.

• A stubborn type of restless depression and feelings of inner emptiness characterize his subjective state. He projects these unpleasant feelings outward as bitterness or sarcasm directed at a "screwed-up world" that has selected him to be its victim.

• He has great difficulty consistently identifying himself as a man or woman. His sexual confusion often engenders a need to affect characteristics of both sexes.

• When confronted with an ambiguous situation, he may lose touch with consensual reality. This usually manifests itself as mild paranoia or grandiose delusions in which he believes that he is chosen for a special mission, tinged with fantasies of rescuing an idealized person from some imagined threat.

• He often shows exquisite sensitivity to the thoughts and feelings of others, sometimes suggesting telepathic rapport, but usually expressed as superstition or magical thinking.

• He is notorious for his impulsivity, including running away, drunken binges, unreasoned use of drugs, sexual excesses, and explosive tantrums.

• He may display exaggerated acts of will designed to establish or fortify his self-boundary. Anorexia, overinvolvement in endurance sports, and occasional acts of self-mutilation are among the ways he may affirm his selfhood.

• Multiple marriages, career changes, and other upheavals mark the life histories of borderline people who act upon their fantasy that a utopian world lies just over the horizon. This causes them to be consistent underachievers, despite intellectual or creative abilities suggestive of a potential for higher functioning.

If we wish to avoid treatments that prompt regression and aggravate the borderline's predicament, we must carefully distinguish this relatively benign malady from malignant psychosis. Although a borderline psychotic ASC may superficially resemble schizophrenia, the consensus state of consciousness can be quickly restored in a supportive, empathic environment. Specific forms of psychotherapy that are useless in schizophrenia and mania are often curative in borderline conditions.

MULTIPLE PERSONALITY DISORDER

No condition known to modern psychiatry is more disruptive to conventional notions of the interactions between body and mind than multiple personality disorder (MPD). Perhaps that is why psychiatry found MPD too preposterous to acknowledge until the book and movie *The Three Faces of Eve* stirred up the interest of the general public.

Despite these dramatized accounts of two or more selves sharing one body, even experienced therapists confuse MPD with schizophrenia. This is because individuals who harbor several *alters*—the term used for intruding personalities other than the core self—tend to be secretive about their many selves. Instead, they may say they are under external influence, that thoughts are inserted or withdrawn from their minds, or that they hear voices arguing in their heads or discussing their personal thoughts and actions—all classic symptoms of schizophrenia.

The crucial difference is that schizophrenics have trouble holding *one* personality together, never mind several. A keen observer is alerted to the presence of MPD when he notes his patient using "we" to describe himself, wondering who keeps filling his gasoline tank, or commenting, "Somebody rearranged my room again." MPD victims speak of strangers greeting them with unfamiliar names as if they knew them, of finding oddly styled clothes in their closets, and of receiving bills for items they did not purchase.

Observing an alter surface during an intimate conversation is an unforgettable experience. The first time this rare event occurred in my presence, I was not merely startled, but jolted into slack-jawed paralysis. As I struggled to regain my composure and make sense of the situation, I was unable to deny a gripping intuition that I was in the presence of *another person*. What struck me most was the change in my patient's eyes, which afforded me a glimpse into the interior of a perfect stranger.

As I resumed the conversation, I noticed less tangible changes that are difficult to fake. Facial expressions, speech inflections, body language, hand gestures, emotional reactions, style of humor, way of laughing—all were those of an impish adolescent male occupying the physical being of my familiar patient, a conservative and rather dour middle-aged woman. Finally, I watched the intruder depart with a sidelong glance and a conspiratorial wink, never to return in my presence. What remained was a sincerely confused and frightened woman, aware only of a "blank space" in her experience of our psychotherapy hour. When I told her what I had just encountered, she became certain that this alter had defaced several of her prized oil paintings over the preceding several months.

As I later reflected upon these events and reviewed the psychological explanations for multiple personalities that I had studied during my years of psychiatric training, I realized how inadequate they were to account for what I had witnessed. At that time less was known about the condition than now. The basic idea is that alters are somehow created by the core personality, sometimes at the prompting of a gullible thera-pist, as a means of ridding the self of unacceptable impulses and drives of a hostile or sexual nature. This view is supported by observations that alternate personalities freely act out angry or sexual urges that are for-bidden expression by the straitlaced scruples of the core personality.

Like many theories accounting for altered-state phenomena in terms of materialistic worldviews, most of these explanations overlook the incredible complexity of the psyche. Alters in MPD are far from one-dimensional entities who express one or two disowned feelings. Each has its own cognitive style, circle of friends, food preferences, personal tastes in art and clothing, addictions, hobbies, sexual preferences, musi-cal talent, religious beliefs, ethical standards, penchant for violence, mathematical ability, craving for drugs, and overall agenda for living. Regional accents and even spoken languages may vary, and most alters maintain separate memories of their life histories. Some alters choose separate therapists from their hosts and receive different diagnoses, confirmed by psychological testing, before the facts of their existence are discovered.

Physiological studies of MPD patients also belie the cherished "one brain equals one self" rule of materialistic science. These studies show that alters can differ from their host personalities in handedness, color blindness, and response to drugs. A few even have different allergies or chronic illnesses, like diabetes. An alter who is fatigued or drunk can yield to another who is alert and sober. An alter who is in pain can sur-render to one who is anesthetic to pain.

Scientists who study brain waves of MPD patients and their alters find telltale differences in electrical patterns when various alters are in control. Sophisticated research has measured visual and auditory evoked potentials—unique "fingerprints" of the brain's responses to light and sound. Several of these carefully executed studies showed sig-nificant differences in response patterns among various alters and their host. Controls feigning alternate personalities could not duplicate these shifts. There were also changes in heart rate, blood pressure, and re-corded voice patterns as the alters switched. Such findings suggest an interaction between the unique consciousness of the alter and the host's body. After studying the tracing from a patient with three alters, one research group concluded that it was "as if four different people had been tested."

Research reveals other facts about MPD that give pause to theorists who maintain materialistic views of psyche and soma. Alters can first appear during childhood and accompany the core personality as it grows up, or they can arrive fully formed at later stages of life. They may be of either sex, younger or older than the core personality, and they usually age along with the host. The number of alters vying for control of one body ranges from one to more than ninety, with about ten being most common. There are known instances of an imaginary playmate—in most cases a normal and harmless childhood experience—forming a nidus around which an alter later crystallizes.

Some alters are gentle and kind, others hostile and violent. The host may be in constant communication with some or all of these entities, or be completely unaware of them. "Civil wars" for control of the body erupt, during which several personalities form alliances. Occasionally alters get sick and die. Or they try to kill one another, oblivious to the idea that death of the body dooms all. The host may be schizophrenic, manic-depressive, borderline, or none of those, and the alters may also show signs of psychosis. Some alters are classically evil, capable of abominable behavior. It is likely that many undiagnosed MPD sufferers have been punished for out-of-character crimes after claiming amnesia, a defense so common among offenders that it is usually discounted in court.

Many people hear the voice of an alter for weeks or months prior to its first "occupation." Once established, an alter may criticize or praise the host's actions while he is not occupying the body. When hosts hear their alters' voices, they say they come from *inside* their heads, in contrast to the hallucinated voices of schizophrenics, which emanate from external locations. Some MPD victims claim that an alter influenced them through their dreams for years prior to its emergence. An established alter occasionally permanently retreats to these more subtle areas of influence.

I have personally inquired of my patients' alters where they go when not in the body, but I have yet to receive a straight answer. When one tried to explain, she heard another alter's voice warning her to keep that a secret. There are reports of alters saying that when they are not in control they travel to surreal nonphysical domains where they secretly communicate with other alters. Some say they sleep, while others surreptitiously observe the activities of whoever is in the body.

A special source of misery to people who suffer from MPD is persecutor personalities, who try to dominate or destroy other alters. Persecutors are often responsible for violent and sociopathic behavior that gets the core personality in trouble. They also embody the sadistic and masochistic traits so common to MPD victims. The fear that persecutors elicit was described by Dr. Robert de Vito of Loyola University.

> If one could imagine the original personality on stage with one or more alters in the wings watching and talking about him, one could begin to approximate the daily torment experienced by the host. When the [host personality]

becomes aware that an alter or group of alters want to torture, humiliate, or even murder him, each waking moment is filled with dread. As a former patient of mine put it, "It is as if I took out a contract on myself."

Alters have occasionally been known to exhibit paranormal powers, including telepathy and precognition, much to the discomfort of psychotherapists who try to understand what is going on. Armand DiMele is one professional who wrote of the uncanny powers of some alters:

> When it comes in, it comes in so clearly, so beautifully, and filled with information one couldn't have any idea about. I have spoken to "spirit voices" who have come through multiples that have told me things about my own childhood. Specifics, like things that hung in the house.

Virtually all people who develop MPD have survived childhoods marred by harsh discipline, cruel torture, or repeated sexual exploitation. This kind of history is found in 97 percent of MPD sufferers, and the remainder give accounts of long, painful illnesses, involvement in war, or near-death experiences. Many of these stories are so gruesome that they are recalled only by alters who were present at the time. Betrayal of childhood trust through incest is especially damaging, particularly when it takes place in an environment from which there is no possibility of escape.

The only recourse of a helpless child under such intolerable circumstances is psychic escape by altering consciousness. People who sustained abuse during childhood describe "making myself numb," "drifting away from the pain," or "going out of my body to a secret place where they can't hurt me." These self-induced ASCs bear a striking resemblance to hypnotic states of *dissociation*—splitting off the self from the body. Experts who treat MPD take advantage of this similarity by inducing hypnotic ASCs to bring forth covert alters. Adults with MPD are known to be highly hypnotizable. This is almost certainly the result of practice in self-induced dissociative ASCs during their formative years.

When the self dissociates from the physical body, it becomes vulnerable to influxes of energies from the Ground. This is especially true during childhood, when self-boundaries are still weakly fortified. We may speculate that when a highly distressed self is forcibly split off from its bodily attachments, this creates a psychic "vacuum" that allows a separate and autonomous self to condense from the inrushing Ground and become embedded in the body. The second self then absorbs those aspects of the original self that are incompatible with survival in an abusive family environment. This process is repeated anew each time a dissociative ASC occurs in response to intolerable abuse.

Such conjecture may at first seem fantastic to people accustomed to the materialistic viewpoint that brains create consciousness, and that matter occupies a higher level in the universal scheme than spirit. But once we allow for *interaction* between a universal Source of consciousness and individual brains, the idea grows more plausible. After all, if one "soul" can become carnate by this means, why should it not be possible for more than one to do so? The major question generated by this interactive view is why multiple personalities occur so *seldom.*

If we give rein to free-wheeling conjecture for a moment, it is conceivable that partially formed personalities exist in nonphysical free form within the Ground. These entities may lie in wait, so to speak, for an opportunity to intrude through vaporous self-boundaries and take up residence within the subconscious sphere of the core personality. If such entities actually exist, what more fertile soil could they find than a terrified child who has entered a dissociative ASC and strayed from its body?

This idea is, of course, similar to ancient accounts of spirit possession, which once was the accepted explanation of many psychotic phenomena, and which, in light of the facts of MPD, now seems less absurd. A difference is that the alters of MPD seldom resemble the devils and demons described in the occult literature of spirit possession and dramatized in the movie *The Exorcist.* Many alters are just as confused and conflicted about their rightful place in the world as their hosts. Some are undeniably demonic, but others are shy and timid, and still others can be exceptionally knowledgeable and helpful. Hence, alters might be seen as falling along a continuum that includes hallucinated voices of schizophrenics, spirit guides perceived by mediums and modern trance channels, demons of possession states, and other nonconsensual entities from which our waking egos usually screen us.

Healing MPD Personalities

Skilled healers who successfully treat MPD operate within a field model of consciousness and are willing to accept each personality as unequivocally *real.* The therapeutic technique involves establishing personal rapport with each alter, engaging them through hypnosis if necessary, and offering sincere assurances that they will not be banished, killed off, or hypnotized away. Healers then foster communication among alters in a way variously described as group therapy or diplomatic relations. One goal is to encourage alters to share personal traits and skills to cope with the particular environment that they share. Another is to gently convince each personality that it is in its best interest to cooperate with the others for the benefit of the whole.

When this method is sensitively applied over time, a gradual merging of the personalities follows, with many steps forward and back. A new and larger self-boundary slowly includes each of the alters as they achieve unity of purpose and share their individual characteristics. This new self-membrane is then fortified by a lengthy process of "reparenting" the newly unified self.

Because MPD and certain other psychotic ASCs are linked to trancelike ASCs and out-of-body phenomena, we now turn to an examination of these generally benign states, often mislabeled as psychotic.

OUT-OF-BODY EXPERIENCES

Convincing tales of out-of-body experiences (OBEs) told by people who have had a brush with death or who have purposefully cultivated the knack of "astral travel" sorely challenge theorists who would reduce consciousness to material events. Although about one-fourth of the general population has experienced an OBE and reports of OBEs are quite consistent, many psychiatrists and psychologists blithely dismiss these ASCs as hysteria, psychosis, or metaphysical flimflammery.

In a way, it seems appropriate for materialists to single out OBEs as prime examples of New Age thinking gone berserk. After all, if a lucidly aware self can gaze upon its entire body from a distant perspective, or violate physical laws of time and space as it drifts about, sometimes passing through walls and witnessing remote events, then even the most hardened skeptics must concede that the mind can get along quite well without immediate contact with a brain. Once this line is crossed, other hallowed materialist notions, such as the inevitable death of the self with death of the body, become suspect.

The confusion about externalization of mind from body may be partly resolved if we recognize that there are three related ASCs associated with the phenomenon. One is almost invariably pleasant and transformative, but two others are associated with psychosis or severe psychopathology. The first is the OBE; the latter two are known as *depersonalization* and *autoscopy*.

OBEs—called *astral projection* by esoterics—are a universal human potential. This does not mean that everyone has them, but that they have occurred to ordinary people throughout recorded history. Descriptions of them are remarkably similar, whether they come from modern housewives in Texas or ancient Egyptian documents. Near-death OBEs have recently received much publicity. They generally follow a particular sequence that strikingly corresponds with the first several stages of the *Tibetan Book of the Dead,* an ancient text that describes the transformative journey of a soul between incarnations.

People who have had a near-death OBE agree that it feels far more real than a dream or a hallucination. Typically, the "dead" person lucidly witnesses his body from a nearby vantage point, usually near the ceiling, and may watch hospital physicians trying to resuscitate him. In one study, several subjects felt themselves drift to another part of the hospital and observe events there, which were later corroborated. As time passes, the person feels himself falling through a dark tunnel, eventually to emerge in the presence of beings who may conduct a review of his life within an atmosphere of love and acceptance.

Although this progression of events is consistent among thousands of collected reports, it may be interrupted at any stage as the person suddenly returns to his body, often feeling himself reenter through the top of the head or through the navel. A few people report ecstatic experiences of approaching a divine white light before reluctantly returning. Most individuals who have had a near-death experience feel that it was a transformative event in their lives that freed them from fear of death and left them committed to serving others. Many are reluctant to speak of their OBE, however, for fear of being thought psychotic. For more information on the near-death experience, the reader is referred to several recent sources.

Only a fraction of OBEs are associated with near-death situations, however. Whatever their context, most occur in states of mental calmness and relaxation, sometimes during meditation or prayer. There are a few reports of OBEs during altered states induced by psychedelic drugs. During an excursion outside the body, the subject may perceive himself to be in a cloudlike second body that is nearly weightless and drifts like a feather. This ghostlike vehicle is said to pass through walls with ease and to be capable of stretching or contracting beyond its usual shape. OBE adepts claim that this "astral body" is affected by electric fields surrounding power lines, causing navigation problems for even the most experienced travelers.

Despite the fantastic nature of OBEs, when large groups of OBE subjects were studied, they were found to be in an excellent state of psychological health, exceeding that of the norm. Researchers found no tendency toward psychotic thinking or hysteria. They typically experienced their excursion in a state of clarity that in no way resembled a dream. Many changed from a traditional religion to a nontraditional spiritual orientation after an OBE. Even those who were not religious felt they had a profound spiritual experience, and from that time on they were more likely to believe in life after death. The occasional individual who returns confused or frightened from a spontaneous OBE rarely requires any treatment other than reassurance about its benign nature.

Skeptics rightly point out that OBEs conform to accepted definitions of hallucinations in that they are private perceptions with no consensual validity. However, there are well-documented accounts of people returning from far-ranging OBEs with accurate information about distant events and places that they could not have gained by normal means. Parapsychologist Charles Tart once tested a naturally gifted subject who regularly experienced herself floating near the ceiling of her bedroom, looking down at her sleeping body lying on the bed. Under laboratory conditions, Tart placed a piece of paper with a five-digit number on a high shelf adjacent to her as she slept, instructing her to read the number should she experience an OBE. After a few OBEs in which she reported that she did not float high enough to see the number, she finally was able to read it correctly. (The odds against guessing a five-digit number on a single attempt are about one hundred thousand to one.) Tart also monitored her brain-wave patterns during the experiment, finding that when she was subjectively out of her body, her EEG tracings were an odd mixture of those associated with dreaming sleep and relaxed wakefulness.

Some esoteric schools teach techniques designed to facilitate OBEs. When I discussed these methods with a person who practiced the skill extensively and taught others how to have OBEs, he left me with a chilling warning that recalls the self-induced dissociative ASCs of abused children who later develop MPD: "Be careful not to go too far away from the body until you learn how to get back quickly. Something else might get in!"

DEPERSONALIZATION & AUTOSCOPY

Although genuine OBEs are almost invariably pleasant, there are allied ASCs that can be quite disagreeable. Some of these are close to the definition of psychosis and cause the person who experiences them to feel that he is going mad.

Depersonalization is a particularly nasty ASC in which one feels one is no longer personally real. Unlike an OBE, it occurs in connection with depression, panic anxiety, or schizophrenia. Or it may accompany extremely stressful conditions, such as surgery or combat. In its mild form, depersonalization induces an sense of numbness or deadness, accompanied by estrangement from the body and ordinary reality. In its extreme forms, depersonalization results in a complete detachment from the body, including self-observation from a distance. This does not give rise to the transcendent freedom of the OBE, but to a dreadful apprehension that one has died and definitely *not* gone to heaven.

Typically only a part of the body is visible during depersonalized ASCs, and the experience is dreamlike and unpleasant, unlike the lucidity of OBEs. Another distinguishing feature is that the depersonalized self watches the body going about its usual activities, while in OBEs the body is immobile. Subjectively, depersonalization is more like the dissociative ASCs described by abused children than like OBEs. But in either case there can be an opening of the self to the subconscious or to the Ground. A full-blown psychotic ASC may follow.

A final and most eerie dissociative ASC is *autoscopy*—seeing one's own image as a "double," as if looking in a mirror. Autoscopy is common to migraine sufferers, epileptics, and some schizophrenics, but is not limited to those conditions and can be brought on by stress or physical exhaustion. Stories of people meeting their doubles go back at least as far as ancient Greece: Aristotle wrote of a man who could not go for a walk on the streets of Athens without his double walking toward him. Similar tales of doubles are found·in the folklore of most cultures, and the idea was romanticized in numerous nineteenth-century European novels, when doubles were known as *doppelgängers*.

In autoscopic ASCs the subject remains in his own physical body, which remains distinct from the double. The double mirrors the subject's gestures, moving his left hand as the subject moves his right. The double's body may be vaguely defined, or only the face may be visible. It wears the same clothes as the percipient, but it does not cast a shadow. If the subject closes his eyes, this does not separate him from the vision; it remains visible with its own eyes closed. Yet holding an object between the viewer and the apparition blocks his view of it, although the semitransparent double only partially obscures objects behind it. One person punched his double, knocking it aside, but he noticed an absence of tactile sensation in his hand as he did so. The subject may also hear the double "with the mind rather than the ears," and hold a conversation of sorts. The subject recognizes that the double will not pass consensual reality testing, but he also remains emotionally involved with the double, feeling it to be an integral part of his self.

Autoscopy evokes a more emotionally neutral mood than either the euphoria of an OBE or the dysphoria of depersonalization, although feelings of sadness, coldness, or ennui are common. The vision may appear suddenly, without any warning, or be preceded by a vague, dreamlike feeling that persists throughout the experience, which typically lasts several minutes. It may occur once in a lifetime or become a continuous presence in a person's life.

Even materialistic theoreticians are forced to admit that no plausible cause for autoscopy has yet been discovered. Some hold that the double must result from an irritation in brain areas associated with vision, but this can be demonstrated in only a small percentage of patients, and medicines effective for epilepsy usually don't help. Psychodynamic theorists posit that autoscopy is an unconscious projection of memories fulfilling a narcissistic purpose. But the evidence for this is equally lacking, and autoscopic subjects manifest a wide variety of personality types. Our present state of knowledge suggests that the most reasonable approach to dissociative ASCs and multiple personalities is to accept them as unexplained mysteries of human consciousness worthy of further inquiry.

MADNESS & HYPNOTIC ASCS

Because the dissociative phenomena described above take place during trancelike ASCs, a deeper investigation of hypnosis is a logical place to begin such an inquiry. In the years since Anton Mesmer tried to integrate hypnosis into nineteenth-century medicine under the rubric *animal magnetism*, mainstream psychiatry has maintained a love-hate relationship with it. Some have rejected hypnosis as "too mystical," while others who recognize its power to restructure reality models have embraced it as having unparalleled potential for healing.

Hypnosis is related to psychotic ASCs through its ability to induce a dissociative ASC in a willing subject, leaving him with transformed reality models, for better or worse. A skilled hypnotist takes advantage of the enhanced suggestibility inherent in the mild ASC that anyone might experience in a relaxed and monotonous environment. The hypnotist then deepens the trance by directing attention to his voice and giving suggestions that reduce contact with the environment. The result is similar to dreaming ASCs, which combine high internal arousal with external immobility. Such states open the self to the influence of the subconscious mind and the Ground.

Almost all healing techniques that employ imagery, emotional release, or "past-life regression" begin with hypnotic induction, although many practitioners call it by another name, such as deep relaxation. People who are good hypnotic subjects are those who have flexible reality models and are already partially open to the subconscious sphere. Conversely, poor subjects are rigid in their worldviews, with a defensive need to fortify their self-boundaries against outside influence.

One imaginative researcher, Bernard Aaronson, took advantage of the malleable reality models of hypnotic ASCs to explore the common ground between madness and mystical experience. Aaronson hypnotized a group of volunteer college students, leaving them with one suggestion: "When you open your eyes, the dimension of depth will be gone. The world will seem two-dimensional."

Aaronson was surprised to find that when he awakened his subjects their thinking and behavior was virtually identical to certain forms of schizophrenia. His subjects were withdrawn, concrete in thinking, hostile and irritable, with blunted emotional response and paranoid fears. One became catatonic. Another felt as if he were trapped inside a movie film, and that the people around him were robots plotting against him. A third subject described an "implosion" experience, feeling that the world was collapsing in on him. As in advanced stages of schizophrenia, the world seemed flat, artificial, two-dimensional. Some subjects were able to reverse these effects by painting or other creative expression, but most had to be rehypnotized and given suggestions that their vision would return to normal.

Aaronson then varied his technique, giving the volunteers suggestions that they would have *expanded* depth perception, as though looking through a stereopticon. When awakened, his subjects were transported into a world of great beauty and wonder. Sounds, colors, and contours were sensually enhanced, and space was extended beyond physical limitations. Sounds were especially crisp and reverberant. Several subjects felt their experience had profound spiritual overtones, one seeing each object and its worldly placement as part of a divine order.

These effects of enhancing depth perception through hypnosis parallel the early stages of the manic ASC, when one perceives vivid detail and color, and new levels of meaning and insight captivate awareness. Just as the disagreeable psychotic states of the first hypnotic experiment demonstrated the distorting effects of uncontrolled influxes of Ground energies, the latter experiment demonstrated the enhanced insight and transformation that occur when one recontacts that ordinarily repressed spiritual source under favorable conditions.

Nevertheless, Aaronson's experiments underscore how hypnotic ASCs can take turns into psychosis. The fact that any charismatic individual who takes a few minutes to learn induction can bring about a hypnotic ASC in himself or others indicates that we live closer to our subconscious minds than most of us are ready to admit. Anyone inducing these ASCs should take pains to reestablish self-boundaries and consensual reality at the conclusion of the session.

MADNESS AND SENSORY DEPRIVATION

Sensory deprivation can easily induce a psychosislike ASC in even the most "normal," socially adjusted individuals—a fact well known to long-distance truck drivers, isolated radar operators, and prisoners in solitary confinement.

The ASC that follows a few hours in a monotonous environment, or even a few minutes in a totally deprived setting, has been studied by researchers at McGill University. The experiments used volunteer college students with no history of psychosis. The subjects reclined on soft beds in pitch-black soundproof rooms while researchers monitored their reactions. Although most of the subjects planned to take advantage of their prolonged isolation to review their studies or outline term papers, they soon found that they were unable to think clearly about anything.

As the experiment progressed, the students began to see strange images in their darkened chambers. One saw a vision of a rock shaded by a tree. Another was disturbed by mental pictures of crying babies. As time passed, the visions grew more complex, with recognizable figures such as rows of little yellow men with black caps and open mouths. Finally, cartoonlike scenes appeared: processions of squirrels with sacks over their shoulders marching across a field, prehistoric animals treading about in a jungle, a parade of tortoiseshell eyeglasses marching down a street. The subjects, who were warned in advance that they would have unusual experiences, were surprised and amused by these hallucinations and eagerly wondered what would happen next. They found that they could scan these scenes, taking in new images as they moved their eyes as if studying a large picture.

The hallucinations were not only visual. Some subjects heard chimerical people speaking, and several felt touch and movement. One described being hit in the arm by pellets fired from a miniature rocket ship. Another, seeing a doorknob in his vision, reached out to touch it and felt an electric shock. Two subjects spoke of feeling another body lying beside them in the cubicle, and in one case the two bodies overlapped, a sensation reminiscent of the autoscopic hallucinations described above.

After emerging from isolation, many of the students experienced distortions in depth perception similar to that induced in Aaronson's hypnotic experiments. They reported that "near things look small and far things look large," or that "things look curved." Many felt that objects seemed to move about and change size and shape. The disorienting effects of sensory deprivation gradually faded as the students acclimated to a normal environment.

Another exotic series of sensory-deprivation experiments was conducted by the neurophysiologist John Lilly. He had just completed experimenting with dolphins and found himself in possession of several aquatic tanks. He converted these into the ultimate sensory-deprivation chambers by filling them with seawater at body temperature and sealing off all sources of light and sound. When he entered this medium, his only connection with the sensory world was an air hose strapped to his face, which he could easily ignore.

Lilly's initial experiences, which resembled the sensory-deprivation hallucinations of the McGill students, left him unsatisfied. He then tried taking LSD to boost the natural effects of spending several hours far removed from the consensual world. Each of these sessions began with an OBE during which he felt himself first floating out of the tank, then out of his laboratory into what he came to call "psychic spaces." He became adept at navigating in and out of his body and, by his own account, to and from the planet itself. Not surprisingly, after several of these excursions into uncharted fields of consciousness, Lilly felt himself drifting dangerously close to insanity, a line that he might have permanently crossed had it not been for two internal "guides" that warned him to end his experiments, as they considered him to be insufficiently prepared.

Skeptics are quick to attribute Lilly's experiences to drug-induced hallucinations, and Lilly himself begs the question of their ultimate reality, except to imply that we create our own truths. But few people have dared to explore such extreme ASCs, and even fewer return to write coherently of their ventures into nonconsensual realities.

The McGill and Lilly experiments confirm what prisoners in extended solitary confinement have known since the first jailer conceived of this slow but sure method of inducing madness. Although there is more sensory stimulation in a small prison cell than in the McGill experiments, nearly all human beings relinquish consensual reality models when removed from all social contact. Many isolated prisoners tell of strange inner realities so overpowering that they must remain silent for several days after emerging so that they can listen to conversations and slowly reassemble consensual models of sanity. One prison research project found that brain-wave alterations in long-term inmates were strikingly similar to those of chronic schizophrenics.

A milder sensory deprivation of a more insidious sort plays a role in the early stages of schizophrenic ASCs. This is a time when a vulnerable person senses that something is changing within. Concluding that outside forces are impinging upon him, he isolates himself from a society that steadfastly refuses to confirm his altered reality. Vicious cycles set in, confirming how dependent human beings are on social contact to reinforce reality models that were constructed during early childhood through repeated contact with parents and society.

PHYSICAL PATHWAYS TO MADNESS

Lapses from consensual reality during deep hypnosis and sensory deprivation illustrate that psychotic ASCs can result from a number of life events, ranging from biological to psychological, or a combination of both. *Physical* factors that can disrupt the delicate harmonies of the mind include brain inflammations and tumors, hormonal imbalances, epilepsy, head trauma, toxins, nutritional deficiencies, allergies, senility, high fever, alcohol withdrawal, and a variety of common medicines. While it is beyond the scope of this book to describe the specific effects of each of these on consciousness, the reader is referred to a helpful book written for nonmedical healers who deal with these conditions (see references).

However, two kinds of brain malfunctions are especially noteworthy: *delirium* and *dementia*. The former is an acute clouding of consciousness with marked confusion, disorientation as to time, place, and self, and hallucinations. Delirium follows any disruption of brain metabolism, and requires immediate medical attention. Dementia, in contrast, is a chronic loss of intellectual functions and memory, usually associated with loss of brain cells, such as in end-stage alcoholism or Alzheimer's disease. A person who experiences a psychotic ASC of any type should always undergo a competent medical workup to rule out physical abnormalities before proceeding with specific treatment.

CHAPTER 4

The Madman in Society: Psychiatry versus Antipsychiatry

◆

"No, no," said the Queen, "Sentence first—verdict afterwards."
"Stuff and nonsense," said Alice loudly. "The idea of having the sentence first!"
"Hold your tongue," said the Queen, turning purple.

LEWIS CARROLL

I don't break the rules, I make *the rules.*

CHARLES MANSON

"**G**O HOME, SHRINKS!" "Stop the genocide!" shouted a group of angry ex-mental patients picketing outside a scientific session at an American Psychiatric Association convention during the early 1970s. "Why do they hate us so much?" I wondered as I skirted the demonstrators, who cursed and spit on the psychiatrists as they exited the convention hall.

The meeting that had concluded had highlighted several exciting new papers on aging and the neurochemistry of memory, the fruits of some first-rate scientific efforts. Neither the presenters nor the audience seemed much like mass murderers. In fact, most of the men and women I met at these meetings during my first two years in the profession were gentle and thoughtful physicians, genuinely concerned for the welfare of their patients.

I was determined to learn more. With some trepidation, I later approached a young man I recognized from the demonstration, who was handing out leaflets on a streetcorner. From the militant appearance of the picketers, I half expected him to be a wildly psychotic.

"What do you have against psychiatry?" I inquired.

"Plenty," he shot back. "Psychiatry kills. Those guys are real head butchers. They take perfectly sane people who someone wants to shut up or get rid of, then they shoot them up with Thorazine, zap them with shocks to the brain, and turn them into zombies. And they get rich doing it. It's the same thing the Nazi doctors did. They wanted everybody to conform, so they put away all the people who thought differently from the establishment fat cats and military bullies. Once those shrinks get their hands on you, they'll work you over until you get really crazy or they'll never turn you loose. They're mind police. Did you read *One Flew over the Cuckoo's Nest?*"

"Uh, yes, but I don't think they perform lobotomies anymore."

"Yes they do, but they just don't talk about it. Anyway, they don't have to. Their pills and brainwashing are worse because they leave you just screwed up enough so you think you're okay. Did you think McMurphy, the dude whose mind they blasted in cuckoo's nest, was crazy?"

"No. Actually I kind of admired him. The Big Nurse seemed more crazy. But I like to think it couldn't happen that way anymore. What do you think would be a better way to treat people who become insane?"

He brightened at the prospect of making a convert. "Get off their backs for one thing, and help them figure out what's wrong with them, how their parents and society screwed them up. People store up stuff inside that drives them nuts. It wouldn't take long to get clear of it if they had a decent place to go, like out in the country where they could rest and eat the right kind of food and get their shit together without a bunch of pills to mess up their minds even more. A lot of people they call crazy are just artists with something stuck inside of them that needs to come out. Some of them are really talking to God."

"Have you read any psychiatric books?" I asked, feeling a vague need to discredit his frontal assault on my recently chosen profession.

"Naw," he said, giving me an opportunity to ignore his reasoning if I so chose. "They're all crap. Go buy a copy of *Dianetics* by L. Ron Hubbard. He's got the right idea."

At a loss to counter what I had to admit were no more the rantings of a madman than my psychiatric colleagues were Nazi torturers, I took this opportunity for strategic retreat. The book he recommended was easy to find and still is. That bible of the Scientology movement easily outsells most other popular works on mental health. However, as I read it I found it easier to fault Hubbard's strange theory of a mischevious "reactive mind" being the source of all human misery than the street-corner philippic of his disciple. The basis of dianetics proved transparently simplistic and shallow, lacking scientific foundation or metaphysical depth, an inflation of a single—and not very original—premise into a panacea for the world's ills. That work, and the cultish movement it spawned, derive their impact from shouting down other theories while claiming theirs to be the only one that works for every mental problem. Unfortunately, that sure sign of fanatic dogmatism is one to which certain of my psychiatric colleagues have not developed immunity.

Yet at the same time I had to admit that my streetcorner adversary had a point, one that stirred up more than a twinge of guilt. Yes, during my psychiatric training at a state mental hospital I did give large doses of major tranquilizers—a now-discredited fashion of that era—to patients who did not wish treatment. But the conditions under which we operated were awesome, with extremely disturbed, regressed, and sometimes explosively violent patients living in overcrowded conditions, with no thought given to sorting them out for treatment appropriate to their specific symptoms, and certainly no time for psychotherapy. At least, I consoled myself, I led several of my colleagues in refusing to use shock treatment as a means of control, a once-abusive practice now under stricter regulation. And while the pay wasn't bad, I definitely did not get rich.

"Could we do better?" I could not shake the question. The equally unshakable answer? "Of course, a lot better!"

Now, more then fifteen years after that encounter, it seems clear that we have *not* done better, as evidenced by the legions of psychotic people living in squalid conditions in the skid rows of our most affluent cities. The libertarian ideals so well articulated by that young man, and so important to any society that values personal freedom, did catch on for a while. But in the hands of politicians whose awareness of the needs of psychotic people was gleaned from "cost-allocation quotas," those ideals degenerated into *deinstitutionalization*. This meant a massive eviction of helpless mental patients from state hospitals, not into rural retreats dispensing nutritious food and healing human contact, but into cold and hostile cities where they simply found no place to go.

That outcome was not the original intent for this visionary scheme, conceived at the peak of the Kennedy administration's enthusiasm for improving the lot of the mentally ill. The idea was to rescue psychotic patients from the deadening effects of custodial hospitals and direct them toward "full and useful lives" with their families or in community board-and-care homes. Medicine, social assistance, and supportive psychotherapy were to be provided by mental-health centers funded by a generous federal government. Only severe psychotics, retarded children, and people with advanced senility were to remain hospitalized.

The result is quite different. Accustomed to treating higher-functioning neurotics with psychotherapy, community mental-health centers displayed little enthusiasm for treating "poor-prognosis patients," whom they saw as uninteresting, overly needy, unresponsive to psychotherapy, and probably brain damaged anyway. Federal funds that were supposed to be channeled into patient care were absorbed by a Kafkaesque bureaucracy that insisted the best way to treat psychotics is to keep the professional staff busy filling out forms. Proponents of the plan greatly overestimated the ability of antipsychotic medicines to maintain a healthy state of consciousness. In the words of one critic, "The chronic mentally ill patient had his locus of living and care transferred from a single lousy institution to multiple wretched ones."

But the pendulum of social ideology naturally alternates direction. At the utopian conclusion of *One Flew over the Cuckoo's Nest,* Indian Chief Broom, a passively mute symbol of the institutionalized mental patient, escapes from oppressive authority, presumably to spend his days happily spearing salmon in the backcountry rivers of Oregon. However, as one critic pointed out, if a sequel were to be made reflecting the realities of the decade just passed, Chief Broom would likely be depicted among the homeless of Portland, shivering in the cold drizzle, hungry and unwashed, hallucinating in an alley behind a chic department store.

The same liberal sensibilities that were outraged by the authoritarian mind screw of the Big Nurse now recoil at the sight of bedraggled and incoherent street people, who give even more offense to the sense of compassion. The pendulum began its counterswing on the streets of New York City in mid-1987, when the movement toward forcing resistant people back into government hospitals—now decrepit after decades of neglect—started gaining momentum. The public seemed convinced that the Big Nurse had retired, and that her successors in the modern mental health establishment have learned from her mistakes.

A widely publicized case arising from New York's efforts to rid the streets of homeless psychotic people illustrates the range of the pendulum's swing between equally absurd extremes. A homeless black woman, known to city social workers for living on a hot-air vent on Second Avenue, was picked up and held for "treatment" against her will. She was said to have a history of psychiatric hospitalization and was seen defecating on herself, destroying paper money, running into traffic, and shouting obscenities at passers-by. Although she was inadequately clothed to sleep outdoors in the winter, she refused treatment of any sort, insisting that she enjoyed living on the streets.

When the woman was questioned by city psychiatrists, whom she perceived as hostile to her interests, she was found to be delusional and suicidal, suffering from paranoid schizophrenia. When she was questioned by American Civil Liberties Union psychiatrists, whom she perceived to be friendly to her interests, she was found to be rational, so much so that the ACLU gave her a job in their local office. The ACLU interpreted her destroying money as an assertion of personal autonomy and her running into traffic as little different from the daily habits of millions of other harried New Yorkers.

A judge agreed with the woman and the ACLU. He praised her humor, pride, and independence of spirit, adding that she displayed an uncommon aptitude for survival. Echoing a revolutionary credo from an earlier decade, he proclaimed that it is society, not she, that is sick. He hoped that by being an offense to the public's esthetic senses, she and her fellow street people would spur the community to action, the exact nature of which he left unspecified. But the judge was not to have the last word. In a response that captures the essence of the dilemma, the woman's sisters, upon learning of the ruling, said that it was racist and sexist for the judge to decree that the streets were good enough for her.

HUMAN COMPASSION VERSUS PERSONAL LIBERTY

The questions raised by the above case seem impossible to answer in a completely satisfactory way. How much deviance ought a free society to tolerate? What is gained by enshrining the liberty of people whose unwanted ASCs prevent them from understanding that liberty or enjoying its rewards? Can a society that values a civilized ambience allow people to live on its sidewalks? What freedom remains to individuals whose mental state has regressed to a childlike level? We do not hesitate to protect children from freedoms that are beyond their capacity; is there a similar ethical imperative to aid childlike adults whom we see suffering, no matter how vocal their resistance? If we suspend the civil liberties of some, how can we ensure the rights of creative icono-clasts to experiment with alternative or harmlessly deviant lifestyles? And the most perilous question: whom do we trust to make these diffi-cult decisions?

As we think through the various compromises and alternatives to the dilemma of forfeiting our liberties versus suppressing our compas-sionate instincts, it is important to understand how we came to be in our present fix, and what life is like inside the aging mental hospitals to which some propose we return the homeless psychotic population.

It has been said that the hospital has replaced the church as the cen-tral cultural institution of the Western world. If so, it is because the church—once the sole caretaker of people with "the demonic affliction of lunacy"—lost much of its credibility as science flowered during the Age of Reason. The church's decline led to a first wave of deinstitu-tionalization and to conditions even worse than today's. In 1843, the re-formist Dorthea Dix decried the common practice of renting insane people to masters who kept them "in cages, closets, cellars, stalls, pens, chained, naked, beaten with rods, and lashed into obedience." Dix's crusade initiated a century of rapid construction of mental hospitals as the relatively more humane era of the insane asylum gained momentum.

For the next century, society was untroubled by the spectacle of hal-lucinating psychotics starving on the streets. The "drunks and bums" were still there, of course, but people in obvious psychotic ASCs were herded out of sight into large hospitals behind strong fences. Madness was held to follow from moral depravity or dissolute personal habits. Stern, authoritarian control was thought to be a fitting therapeutic tac-tic to rehabilitate the debauched. Despite the good intentions of the early reformers, conditions steadily became more gruesome in these hu-man warehouses as their population swelled. Their notoriety infiltrated back into society, where misbehaving children were brought into line by threats to take them to the "loony bin."

Because politicians who slice up the pie charts of society's wealth know that hospitalized mental patients neither vote nor lobby, and that their solitary ASCs prevent them from organizing spectacular riots in the fashion of abused prisoners, the run-down hospitals became "snake pits," as a realistic 1940s movie of that title graphically portrayed. While most patients withdrew from the daily horror into a vegetative exis-tence, wilder patients were controlled with powerful sedatives available at the time: barbiturates and chloral hydrate. Because people grow tol-erant to these drugs after repeated use, electroshock became the pre-ferred way to induce docility and conformity to institutional rules. And if that failed, there was always lobotomy.

This swing of the pendulum reached its zenith in the 1940s, when half the hospital beds in the United States were for psychiatric patients. The seeds of change were sown early in the next decade when the first antipsychotic medicines became available. For the first time, the surface manifestations of psychotic ASCs could be reduced in some patients to the point where these people were judged fit to return to society in a state of "chemical conformity." The population of state hospitals declined, and a new generation of psychiatrists with an updated view of madness took over.

The therapeutic zeal of these young doctors was fueled by changing ideas about schizophrenia and mania. As psychoanalytic thought reached its zenith in the Western world, Sigmund Freud, Adolph Meyers, and Harry Stack Sullivan spread the word that mental disorders are reactions to aberrant childhood experiences. They viewed psychotics as *victims*. At last there was hope for a cure, if sensitive therapists could tap into their patients' unconscious minds and make healing interpretations. Dedicated psychiatrists such as Freida Fromm-Reichmann—the Dr. Freid of Hannah Green's fictionalized *I Never Promised You a Rose Garden*—devoted years to intense psychotherapy that "reparented" patients who were victims of repressed childhood trauma.

The 1960s brought about a further leftward swing, fueled by three radical new theories about the cause of psychosis. The first posited that madness results from corrupt social institutions, including sexism, racism, poverty, and suppression of nonconforming lifestyles. Radicals challenged the idea, so dear to psychoanalysts, that repressed childhood traumas sowed the seeds of psychosis. The radicals viewed psychosis as an inward escape tactic with mystical import. They condemned authoritarian families as unwitting agents of our failed culture, families that thrived on crazy-making double-bind or no-win scenarios to confound and control naturally freethinking children.

A second group claimed that mental illnesses are not diseases at all, merely convenient labels for imposing political control on the powerless. But it was a third interpretation of mental illness that most directly led to the era of deinstitutionalization. Its proponents claimed that mental illness does not occur naturally; rather, its symptoms are caused by telling people they are sick and putting them into mental hospitals.

Proponents of these three views found enough in common to adopt the provocative term *antipsychiatry* for their movement. Their ideas have exerted a powerful influence on current thinking about madness, so much so that as the pendulum poises for another rightward swing, they deserve a closer look so that we can decide which ideas are worth preserving and which should be relegated to the well-used trash bin of misguided idealism.

THE ANTIPSYCHIATRY CHALLENGE

The three schools of antipsychiatry thought are the iatrogenic (physician caused) school of Ernest Goffman and Thomas Scheff, the political-conspiracy school of Thomas Szasz, and the transcendentalist school of R. D. Laing. Although there are many affinities among them, their differences allow us to consider them separately.

The Iatrogenic School

The iatrogenic school, led by Goffman and Scheff, directs its scorn at mental hospitals and their custom of diagnosing patients who enter them. They characterize hospital admission procedures as *degradation rituals* that indelibly brand patients as misfits and outcasts. This quickly reduces responsible people with minor eccentricities or "problems in living" to the level of inmates imprisoned in a paternalistic institution that strips away their autonomy and dictates that they cannot retain their possessions, arrange their time, or choose what space they will occupy.

After admission, hospital life is designed to convert an acute reaction to difficult life circumstances into a chronic disability, argue the iatrogenic theorists. A patient undergoes a series of mortifying assaults to his self-image. He or she trades clothes and personal belongings for hospital issue. He must ask permission for the most trivial activities that elsewhere are purely volitional, such as smoking, shaving, or taking a shower. He then enters the lowest echelon of a privilege system based on behavior modification in which his personal preferences are held up for public display and judgment. Whereas he was once a person with friends and ties to his community, hospital life binds his activities into a social sphere restricted to his keepers and fellow inmates, themselves in various stages of institutionalization. He conducts each phase of his daily routine as part of a group required to do the same thing at the same time.

Day-to-day life in a mental hospital is one of stifling monotony and practiced uselessness that gradually obliterates a patient's sense of future. For example, the California state hospital in which I completed my psychiatric training once contained on its spacious grounds a picturesque farm on which patients voluntarily worked to produce fresh milk, eggs, and vegetables for the hospital cafeteria. Farm chores provided patients with structure, goals, a feeling of usefulness, and a little pocket money. Most also benefited from the fresh air and exercise. But the farm has long since grown over with weeds, a victim of political protests that claimed patients were exploited for "slave labor" and that its products unfairly competed with private industry. Now the patients have little to do but stare at television sets, often indifferent to whether they are turned on.

In such a "total institution," a governing cadre wields almost complete control of thought and behavior. Such a system, say iatrogenic theorists, would be difficult even for well-adjusted people and is devastating to vulnerable psychotics who struggle to maintain the integrity of a weakly bounded self. Although institutional life is rationalized as being in the patient's best interest, antipsychiatrists believe its real purpose is to break the individual spirit in order to render it more manageable. To be discharged, a patient must repeatedly confirm consensual reality at the expense of his own, including acknowledging that hospitalization has been necessary and beneficial. This recantation is an exorbitant price to pay for readmission to the normal world.

Although hospital staffs are usually well meaning, they are ill equipped to deal with the altered experience of their patients. Staff members are selected to reflect conventional bureaucratic standards. Promotions reward conformity to strictly defined norms. Only those who affirm consensual reality and prevailing social customs squeeze through the filter. Some settle into their jobs to assuage doubts about their own sanity, which they affirm by exaggerating psychic distance between themselves and the patients—"You're crazy, I'm not"— rather than bridging the gap on a personal level—"Let's find out why we see things so differently." Replacing the fabled white coats of yore, prominently displayed ward keys have become the concrete symbols of that chasm.

And, of course, the Big Nurse officiously presides over the whole affair, maintaining imperious control over every aspect of hospital life, wielding absolute authority to administer a rigid system of rewards and punishments that determine which behavior will occur and when it will occur. Docility is rewarded; assertiveness is discouraged under the guise of "setting limits" and "providing structure." No activities are permitted that afford a patient the feeling that he has command over his world. Patients who insist on being heard invite injection with drugs or punitive electroshock. Anyone who dares to seek individual attention from the staff earns the time-worn bughouse put-down: "manipulator."

In this way, say antipsychiatrists, does the mental hospital turn a voyage of self-discovery with a potentially liberating outcome into a catastrophe, a soul-squelching pathological process from which the patient requires a "cure." This cure is seldom forthcoming, however, for a more common outcome is *institutionalism,* a condition in which the patient quietly accepts his role as "crazy" and agrees to spend the rest of his days passively surrendering to regulation, his only concern to avoid incurring the displeasure of his keepers lest he be refused permission to smoke or watch TV. As society now confronts some of these people on our streets, it gets, the antipsychiatrists believe, exactly what it deserves.

Central to the antipsychiatrists' case against psychiatric treatment of mental patients is *labeling theory*. This strikes at the heart of the medical model by attacking the venerable process of making a diagnosis. It maintains that a diagnosis is a covert type of *prophesy* that, once made, fulfills itself. As a patient receives a diagnosis (labeled as deviant) with a prognosis of lifelong disability, those around him thereafter look upon him as crazy, so that is what he becomes. That is, he adopts a crazy image of himself, and his behavior expresses that image.

In other words, the naming of a psychotic ASC is responsible for its continuation. A patient then is rewarded for playing a stereotyped crazy role and punished when he tries to shed his labels and return to conventional roles. Once locked into this endless cycle, he finds it ever more difficult to exit because he is taught to manifest more of the behavior for which he was hospitalized in the first place. This launches a lifetime of mental illness and dependency.

Although short on research proving their theory, labeling theorists draw credibility from a 1972 experiment by Stanford University psychology students who tried to demonstrate that hospital psychiatrists have a shaky grip on what they are doing. To get themselves admitted to several public and private psychiatric hospitals on both coasts of the United States, the students simply complained of hearing voices. Once on the wards, they immediately dropped their pose and acted normally except for taking notes, behavior interpreted by the hospital staff as "bizarre." These notes graphically portray the conditions of psychiatric confinement.

> Personal privacy is minimal. Patient quarters and possessions can be entered and examined by any staff member, for whatever reason. His personal history and anguish is available to any staff member . . . who chooses to read his folder . . . His personal hygiene and waste evacuation are often monitored . . . We had the sense that we were invisible, or at least unworthy of account. Upon being admitted, I and other pseudopatients took the initial physical examination in a semipublic room where staff members went about their own business as if we were not there.

In most cases, the real patients had little trouble seeing through the act. Yet every one of the impostors had difficulty getting out of the hospital; the average hospitalization was nineteen days, and one lasted fifty-two days. During this time, the sham patients averaged only 6.8 minutes per day in the company of credentialed psychiatrists, psychologists, or social workers. When they were finally discharged, most were sent away with the diagnosis "schizophrenia in remission," a label presumably destined to stigmatize them for the rest of their lives. The researchers concluded that it is impossible to distinguish sanity from insanity (apparently disregarding the knack of genuine psychiatric patients to do so).

Of course, anyone could similarly swallow a pint of blood, walk into a hospital emergency room, and dramatically regurgitate the red fluid over white tiles. He would find himself whisked off to surgery, but this would neither argue against life-saving surgical treatment for bleeding ulcers, nor demonstrate the hopeless subjectivity of diagnosis. Nevertheless, the bold prank of the Stanford students exposed widespread inadequacies in psychiatric assessment and treatment of psychotic patients during the early days of deinstitutionalization.

Thomas Szasz: Madness as Conspiracy

A second antipsychiatry school is inspired by the political-conspiracy theories of Thomas Szasz. He stands out among generally left-leaning antipsychiatrists in that he represents a right-wing, libertarian perspective, inspired by the laissez-faire ethic of social Darwinism and the elitist *Übermensch* philosophy of Nietzsche.

In common with other antipsychiatrists, Szasz argues that psychiatric diagnoses are political terms based on entrenched social prejudice. But Szasz is unique in his view that mental illness is not a physical disease, or even a socially induced disorder, but a *myth*. He bases this idea on his belief that no physical abnormality for schizophrenia has been found; therefore, it is incorrect to say that a disease is present. In his view, mental symptoms are ultimately metaphoric: "the mind can be sick only in the sense in which a joke can be sick." And because mental disorders are not legitimate diseases, physicians have no business being psychiatrists.

Szasz views mental hospitals as prisons and those who work in them as jailers and torturers. The power structure arbitrarily assigns to psychiatrists the role of defining and enforcing social norms at the service of society rather than their patients. People are held in mental hospitals for the sole reason that they are subversive to the social order. Psychiatrists are "mind police" following nonjudicial rules for incarcerating anyone exhibiting behavior bothersome to the power elite, then forcing them to submit to brainwashing, mind-bending drugs, and worse.

Szasz therefore stands against all involuntary commitment to mental institutions, considering that to be a disgraceful violation of human freedom and responsibility. In one of his more vitriolic moods, he responded to reports that psychiatrists are being more frequently assaulted, or even murdered, by psychotic patients. Szasz commented that psychiatrists are finally getting their just and long-overdue comeuppance: "now some of the slaves seem to be revolting, and apparently with increasing frequency, are murdering the meddling medicos."

Yet Szasz bears scant sympathy for psychotic patients, holding that most are frauds who simulate insanity. At best, they may be said to have "problems in living." All of them—florid psychotics and imminently suicidal people alike—should be left to determine their own fate unless they actively seek help, after which Szasz encourages them "to adopt a critical attitude toward all rules of conduct . . . and to maximize free choice in adopting either socially accepted or unaccepted rules of conduct."

But Szasz is no anarchist. He would shift responsibility for enforcing society's norms and standards away from the medical arena, which should ideally be free from such judgments, and direct it toward politicians and judges, with whom he feels it belongs. Attacking the insanity defense, Szasz argues that if someone breaks laws, he should go to jail no matter what his reasons. If he violates no laws, society should ignore him unless he requests assistance. Without exception, lawbreakers should be held responsible for their actions.

In sum, Szasz holds that people afflicted with what are considered severe mental illnesses, such as suicidal depression or schizophrenia, must demonstrate the ability and will to request treatment or fend for themselves, even if this means self-destruction. He advances no countertheory of psychotic behavior, instead asserting that a minority of human beings simply act strange, but that does not make them ill; only physical bodies can be diseased. If brain disease leads to peculiar behavior, we should call it something other than mental illness.

R. D. Laing: Madness as Mysticism

Unlike Szasz, the Scottish antipsychiatrist R. D. Laing was in essence an apolitical mystic who did not deny the existence of psychosis, but instead blamed the suffering of the mad on the debasements inherent in civilized society as interpreted by the family. Laing's philosophy was inspired not by a Nietzschean indifference to the marginally endowed, but by the revolutionary philosopher Rousseau's romantic exaltation of the "noble savage," the naturally pure and good man corrupted by modern society. Laing's introspectively tinged writings are a prime source of energy for the antipsychiatry movement. More importantly, his seminal works restored respectability to the ancient Platonic idea that at least some psychotic ASCs bear the seeds of spiritual growth and transcendence.

Laing was more an existentialist philosopher than a political revolutionary. He rejected the scientific method of objectively studying psychotic patients without reference to his own personal passions. Instead, he projected his own psyche into the subjective experience of people in psychotic ASCs, trying to understand them from *within*. Some of the insights that emerged from his method were highly unusual and seldom attained by orthodox psychiatric methods.

Laing's most consistent impression was that psychotics pass through transformational stages that, when allowed to progress to natural conclusions, lead to clear, balanced states of mind beyond what was realized prior to the psychotic ASC. Laing felt that the psychotic process repairs damage wreaked by disturbed families and virulent social institutions. This inevitably drew him toward politics.

In his 1967 manifesto, *The Politics of Experience*, Laing characterized schizophrenia as little more than a dehumanizing label devised by oppressive societies threatened by the outward manifestations of a natural healing process. Psychotic symptoms arise when a sensitive person tries to rid himself of "the appalling state of alienation called normality," of the unholy split between the true and false selves that society, via the family, insists that we maintain. The real split, he said, is in dividing inner from outer experience in the first place, then creating social institutions that insist that the consensual world represents the only acceptable reality.

Because we allow ourselves to be so split, Laing held, half of our experience as human beings is lost. Our rigid distinctions between fantasy and reality, and our forced suppression of imagination, breed a society alienated from its creative wellsprings. This "normal madness" is then transmitted through the family to children. Escape through madness is the only sane solution. Inward-turned psychotics appear pathological only to observers so benighted that they lack the will to extricate themselves from their own social prisons. Psychiatrists, Laing believed, are foremost among the unimaginative who miss the message.

Laing's critics accused him of romanticizing psychosis and ignoring its destructive effects on an individual's life. He countered that it is only our misguided efforts to abort the psychotic inner journey that converts an essentially benign healing process into a shallow travesty, a grotesque caricature of what an inwardly directed state of mind should be. Society's response is the destructive force, not the psychotic process itself.

Viewed from Laing's perspective, tranquilizing patients in a rigidly controlled institution perpetuates an artificial inner-outer dichotomy.

Although medicines can induce a semblance of conformity with the consensus view, they accomplish this by invalidating the self's higher aspirations. Once a transformational experience is stripped of its standing in reality, any hope of renewal and reunion with a higher self is cut off. Instead, Laing would have us guide the psychotic in a free-rein exploration of the inner time and space into which his psychosis has plunged him.

Something is dreadfully wrong, Laing wrote, with societies that killed 100 million people in the last century. Who is crazy, he asked, a psychotic who believes he has a bomb in his belly or a pilot who mechanically drops bombs on unseen victims? Crazy or not, this is where our "outer bound" emphasis on technology has led us. We have deified abstract logic to insane proportions. Instead, we need to return to the raw concrete experience of our moment-to-moment humanity. Psychotics can show us what we lack. Following this line of reasoning, Laing viewed psychotic ASCs less as break*downs* than break*throughs*.

But such natural breakthroughs are rare in modern times, Laing believed. Safely socialized people grow accustomed to numb alienation, to being spiritually asleep, *out-of-their-minds*.

Likening society to a formation of planes flying off course, Laing argued that an individual must be out of formation in order to be on course. We drift off course because society teaches us to disregard our inner world. The forgotten process of entering ASCs and coming back out is normal and natural, but few modern people learn to navigate in these realms. So those who enter spontaneously do so without a compass, becoming frightened and adrift, shipwrecked on the rocks of social incomprehension. We then call them crazy and treat them as if they were sick.

Because of our unfamiliarity with ASCs, Laing wrote, a psychotic forced inward by intolerable life circumstances encounters an uncharted void peopled by unfamiliar visions, voices, and apparitions. These were once called spirits, demons, gods, and angels. People never used to argue about their existence because they experienced them directly as daily realities. They were known and named before civilization turned our eyes outward. The only disagreements were about which were the most powerful and how they might be recruited for guidance.

Now it is difficult *not* to doubt the validity of these denizens of the subconscious because we have diverted our attention away from subjectivity and toward controlling the external world, an obsession that estranges us from intuitive ways of knowing. We have become so accustomed to ignoring these otherworldly entities that it requires ever-greater degrees of open-mindedness even to conceive of their existence. People who retain a capacity for inner vision either develop a knack for secrecy and cunning or risk being labeled as lunatic. Laing thus affirmed Carl Jung's lament that our gods have become diseases.

While Laing traced the origin of most psychoses to destructive social and family interactions, he also accepted the genetic links to madness. Yet he interpreted them in a typically turnabout manner. Laing suggested that an inherited predisposition to psychotic ASCs is a *successful* genetic mutation that represents the next step in human evolution. The psychotics among us are an avant-garde leading us toward salvation through reunion with our inner selves, shock troops in the war against that modern archenemy of the liberated soul, *experiential conformity.*

> Until it was decided by dictate that you're not allowed to see things other people don't see, hear things other people don't hear, or smell things other people don't smell, we all didn't have to hear, smell, and see things the same way. This was never the case in the history of humanity. The ordinary human might, when depressed, see the sky become dark or the sun cloud over. The whole world was once part of man's psyche. But no longer. Everything now has got to be experienced all the time in the same way as everyone else. Experience has become homogenized.

Laing's personality was studiously introverted, and he once remarked that he did his best work alone in a darkened room. This trait led him to rejoice in the unfettered subjectivity of the schizophrenic, whom he viewed as having a natural opening to the mythic realm of the subconscious. Consistent with his view of psychosis as a self-induced "headtrip," a handy vehicle of escape from the emotional battlefields of an insane society, he opposed antipsychotic medicines for even the most regressed schizophrenic. These drugs, he stated, "suppress the mental functions necessary to generate the aberrations which are rated as tokens of disorder." Any medicine or psychiatric treatment that encourages "resocialization" interrupts a natural process of healing and perpetuates social and individual disease.

Laing's radical counterpoint to institutions that breed conformity was no less than "experiential anarchy," a free-zone of consciousness in which "anyone, as a first principle, without any argument, is entitled to experience the universe in the manner he or she happens to." No armchair ideologue, Laing put experiential anarchy into practice when he founded Kingsley Hall, an urban London sanctuary where psychotic patients and therapists lived together in first-name equality and with freedom to howl at the moon and smear the walls with feces if they so chose, which they sometimes did.

Kingsley Hall was a sort of commune where officially doctors were not doctors, patients were not patients, and the only regulation was that there were no regulations. Laing intended it to be a Utopia of sorts, an asylum in every sense of the word, where psychotics could experience the full impact of their ASC without restraint and then emerge, healed, after regression and rebirth.

Intuiting the wellsprings of his own mystical experiences to underlie the ASCs of psychotics in his care, Laing passionately exclaimed: "I have seen the Bird of Paradise, she has spread herself before me, and I shall never be the same again . . . If I could turn you on, if I could drive you out of your wretched mind, if I could tell you I would let you know."

The noble Kingsley Hall attempt to liberate the mystic in the madman faded with the waning zeal of its founder. Announcing that he was "worn out and burned out" after years of practice, Laing moved out of the commune, followed by a number of other doctors. Neighborhood residents complained about the strange behavior of patients and staff alike. The (non)patients held meetings to discuss how Kingsley Hall should be run, but the solitary disorganization of the schizophrenic ASC made cooperative efforts difficult. Laing's utopian desire for experiential anarchy degenerated into anarchy of a less subjective sort. There were reports by dismayed visitors that the stairway was littered with trash and the kitchen overflowed with dirty dishes. Critics delighted in reviving the running joke in which madmen and mad doctors swap identities and are impossible to tell apart. In 1970, after five years, the experiment ended not with a bang, but with a lost lease.

Until his death in 1989, Laing remained the leading philosopher behind the antipsychiatry movement, but his detractors are increasingly vocal, especially in today's less psychedelic times. Some question his romanticizing states of consciousness associated with "regressed social misfits" who may suddenly shoot up a shopping mall or murder a rock star. Others argue that the "noble savages" of primitive societies have among them as many schizophrenics as do technological cultures, but they are treated worse.

Other communal sanctuaries modeled on Kingsley Hall have come and gone, usually failing because of a lack of funds or community support. For example, Soteria House in San Jose, California, rejected the disease model of psychosis, seeing schizophrenia as a "developmental crisis" with positive learning potential. Diabasis, a similar San Francisco–area commune for psychotics, emphasized a Jungian perspective and also excluded antipsychotic medicines. Neither overcame the difficulties inherent in maintaining such projects, although there remain at least four in England and others on both coasts of the United States and Canada.

Society's dismal response to psychotic ASCs invites further experiments with alternative approaches. Yet despite their good intentions, it is likely that these experimental communes will meet the same fate as Kingsley Hall if they do not avoid its error of confusing regressive ASCs with transcendent ones, and applying nonspecific therapeutic techniques to a broad spectrum of psychotics.

BALANCING INTEGRATION

As with most controversies involving the mind, there are persuasive arguments on both sides of the psychiatry-antipsychiatry debate. If we look back on the agenda of the antipsychiatry movement from the perspective of two decades of deinstitutionalization, its glaring failure to meet the needs of hundreds of thousands of psychotic people seems obvious. However, this does not invalidate the idealistic positions of the antipsychiatrists, for it is fair to say that their program has hardly been given a fair trial during a political era more oriented to cost containment than reform.

As we confront the specter of a rightward turn back to the decaying state-hospital system, the time seems right to integrate the legitimate criticisms and insights of the antipsychiatrists with the dedication to scientific research of orthodox psychiatry. We must devise a humane, cost-effective system that recognizes the unique requirements of people in a wide variety of ASCs brought about by an equally wide variety of factors—some physical, some psychodynamic, some spiritual.

THOMAS SZASZ: A CRITIQUE

Of the three schools of antipsychiatry, that of Thomas Szasz is the most out of tune with humanistic ideals and biological science. By sweeping proclamation, Szasz "resolves" the ancient unsolved mystery of mind-body interaction by reviving the seventeenth-century Cartesian split between mind and body. His riposte to the common error of ignoring the effect of mind on matter is to substitute the anachronism of ignoring the effect of matter on mind. From his labeling the schizophrenic ASC as a "fake disease," we can infer that Szasz, following Descartes, believes that mind and brain have little to do with each other.

Modern biotechnological research has uncovered substantial evidence that genetic, anatomic, and metabolic abnormalities are associated with several psychotic ASCs, especially those rendering a person least able to seek help. Although there are no known medical or psychological tests to confirm a diagnosis of schizophrenia or mania, and we must infer their presence from behavior, certain objective procedures strongly suggest their presence, and more will surely follow.

In the next decade, we can expect an explosion of discoveries linking specific mental states with brain states. Of course, none of these will prove that all psychotic ASCs are caused by brain abnormalities any more than they will prove that the brain "causes" the mind, rather than viceversa. The brain may well be a target organ for a psychosomatic process, just as biochemical changes leading to stomach ulcers follow certain cognitive styles of handling stress. Yet Szasz would hardly extend his argument to say that people suffering ulcer pain are not ill.

In his view of mental illness as myth, Szasz denies that psychosis is a disease. By placing schizophrenics, manics, and suicidal depressives in the categories of criminals, spongers, dissemblers, and inadequates, and denying them treatment, Szasz draws sharp lines where in fact there is a continuum of fine gradations. More alarmingly, he would dissolve the distinction between hospital and prison, turning our prisons into latter-day Bedlams where hallucinating and delusional psychotics would be perpetually abused by hardened criminals under conditions that would make the Big Nurse's ward seem like a haven of tolerance and liberty.

However, Szasz makes a telling point in his criticism of the insanity defense. He is correct in pointing out that this is blatantly abused and in conflict with the goals of any free society that values individual responsibility as a condition of liberty. Yet he would hardly argue that young children and mentally retarded adults possess adequate free will to assume criminal responsibility for all of their actions.

Free will is a relatively recent development in the evolution of human consciousness on this planet, one requiring our highest reasoning powers honed by life experience. A capacity for abstract reflection, self-awareness, and refined logic is necessary for a volitional act to occur. Not all human beings possess will in equal measure. Most psychotic ASCs involve profound cognitive regression, sometimes to levels at which one's will is as weak as that of a small child or a retarded person.

Szasz's horror of involuntary commitment would seem more reasonable if, rather than living in the West, he had lived in the U.S.S.R. prior to the recent reforms. Although we may sympathize with his desire to prevent Soviet-style practices from taking hold here, anyone who has worked in real-life psychiatric hospitals in the United States is unlikely to recall even one case of involuntary commitment for political purposes or to punish social deviance. Since the era of deinstitutionalization, it is much harder to get into a mental hospital than it is to get out.

Although institutionalized schizophrenics tend to be less violent than the general population, people who are floridly paranoid do represent a preventable danger to society. These easily identifiable ASCs sometimes lead to random, often spectacular homicides. In 1985 a young woman who had undergone several previous mental hospitalizations shot to death two people and wounded eight others in a shopping mall. She said she did it because of a "black box." Congressman Allard Lowenstein of New York was murdered by a man who believed that Lowenstein controlled a radio receiver implanted in his dental fillings. One woman was barely prevented from opening a pressurized door on a crowded airliner because Satan had verbally commanded her to do so. A divorced mother admitted to giving several enemas a day to her child over a period of years, "to clean the evil spirits out of her so they won't yell at me so much."

Experienced therapists who work with psychotics recognize that events such as these are not as rare or isolated as Szasz claims. Szasz would apply restraint to these people only *after* their acts. Although no foolproof way of predicting violence has yet been devised, and judicial restraint is certainly necessary before anyone's civil rights are compromised, it is in the nature of most psychotic ASCs that people committing these deeds would likely have revealed their intentions if someone had simply asked them.

In sum, Szasz's conflict with psychiatry boils down to a clash in *values*. We must all decide if our increasingly paternalistic government should forcibly hospitalize psychotic people who are so unable to care for themselves that they may starve, or jump off a bridge, or shoot a stranger whose appearance seems suspicious. Do the benefits of enforced control outweigh the dangers of removing legal constraints on personal choice and liberty? And should we, as some politically inspired antipsychiatrists seem to advocate, send forth homeless psychotics as shock troops in a revolutionary class struggle?

The solution is not to abandon the time-honored intuition that something is different about people in psychotic ASCs that places them in a separate category of law as it applies to criminal responsibility. Instead, we should fine-tune our ability to distinguish severely regressive ASCs from creative social deviance, harmless eccentricity, and budding spiritual unfolding. A task awaiting a more enlightened legal system is to gradually integrate these refinements.

LABELING THEORY: A CRITIQUE

A central flaw in antipsychiatry thinking that more than any other undermined Kingsley Hall and similar experiments was the scattershot attack on psychiatric diagnoses, which some antipsychiatrists would eliminate altogether or subsume under the euphemism "problems in living." They claim that aberrant behavior associated with ASCs is of minor consequence until a psychiatrist attaches a "sick" label, after which the deviance hardens and becomes self-perpetuating. Like many other antipsychiatry declarations, this is a partial truth, easily overstated.

For instance, labeling theorists correctly point to the social stigma that adheres to people with psychiatric diagnoses, even long after recovery. It is true that once an individual is labeled as deviant or impaired, those around him stop expecting anything better. Although this is certainly not sufficient to *cause* the profound derangements of psychosis, it may aggravate their course. And the indiscriminate application of labels to benign ASCs associated with sudden spiritual awakening is positively destructive.

On the other hand, experienced therapists know that many psychotic people are relieved upon learning that the source of their solitary distress has a name and is therefore understood as part of the human condition. For a person who feels that he is uniquely alone in his ASC, or interprets his symptoms as evidence of moral transgression, a timely diagnosis can reassure him that he is not being punished by a wrathful deity, and that help is on the way. If used with *artfulness* by a healer who takes time to establish trust and rapport, a diagnosis becomes the first step in establishing the therapeutic alliance necessary for recovery to begin.

A second advantage of a well-thought-out diagnosis is that it directs the healer's mind toward the hard-earned experience of others who encountered similar ASCs in the past. The medical archives, a vast body of literature dating back thousands of years, is a major healing resource of humanity. But this information is beyond the reach of those who refuse to categorize their observations. A careful diagnosis can be a tool of communication, guiding a healer toward the experience of others who once grappled with similar problems. Many psychotic ASCs have easily recognizable characteristics in common. The challenge to an enlightened therapist is to apply these commonalties to his patient as a unique individual. This takes time and skill.

If good is to come from the antipsychiatrists' attack on diagnoses, we might hope that it will inhibit such heavy-handed practices as occurred in 1941, when two psychiatric authors retrospectively diagnosed Socrates as schizophrenic because he was guided by inspiring voices and stood immobile in the freezing cold lost in thought for hours, or in 1964, when more than five hundred American psychiatrists signed a petition diagnosing presidential candidate Barry Goldwater as psychotic. More finesse in diagnosis would certainly help. And as is the practice with other medical terms like *pneumonia* or *appendicitis*, any diagnostic label should be dropped when the condition is no longer apparent.

Ernest Goffman's criticisms of the dehumanizing effects of mental hospitalization are more to the point than either labeling theory or Szasz's blanket denial of the existence of mental illness. Once a psychotic ASC takes hold, an authoritarian, self-squelching environment is unlikely to restore coherence to a person's fragmented ego or help him integrate the unfamiliar energies of the Ground into his reality models.

Goffman is correct in pointing out that large institutions managed by entrenched bureaucracies can aggravate psychosis by reinforcing dependency and eroding the self as a center of initiative and will. We gain nothing by negating the nonconsensual world of a person when that is all he knows of reality. But because invalidation of ASCs is a manifest goal of many hospitals, they rely on drugs and behavior modification as their only modes of treatment rather than as two of *several* therapies addressed to specific states of consciousness.

The bureaucratically encumbered institutions left over from the era of the insane asylum are essentially beyond reclamation. Overwhelmed by insurance regulations, fear of malpractice suits, and useless paperwork, the staff vigilantly guards consensual reality by manipulating the thinking of patients who challenge it. Staff members with the most power within the hierarchy end up having the least to do with patients, and those with the least power spend the most time with patients, who are at the low end of a lengthy pecking order. The need for regulation and control within a large institution fosters a sham egalitarianism that treats all inmates with the same shopworn methods and ignores distinctions between severely regressed people requiring level-specific therapies and higher-functioning people who would benefit from consciousness-expanding strategies.

Small wonder, then, that many ex–mental patients hate psychiatrists with the ferocity of an oppressed minority confronting a tyrannical despot. When an authentic spiritual awakening is suppressed or disparaged by inflexible authority, the victim is left feeling so outraged that he becomes a militant enemy of psychiatry, seeing it as the source of all evil in the world. Many such victims exhibit their hatred openly by picketing, shouting slogans, and invading scientific meetings. Others publish antipsychiatry newsletters vilifying psychiatrists as bullying inquisitors intent on stamping out the heresy of spiritual vision.

Although the antipsychiatry movement advocated deinstitutionalization as a remedy for the dehumanizing effects of mental hospitals, its leaders seemed to lack the stamina and social commitment to direct their brainchild away from the shameful debacle it has become. In later chapters we explore the idea that the Kingsley Hall experiment could, with some modification, be a model for enlightened healing centers of the future, specifically designed for the minority of psychotic ASCs that are harbingers of spiritual advancement.

R. D. LAING'S "BREAKTHROUGH" THEORY: A CRITIQUE

Laing's vision of small therapeutic communities where staff and patients interact in spontaneous I-thou relatedness, and where the inner worlds of people in various ASCs are met with respect and confirmation, is a credible one that is due for revision, not abandonment. Yet we might suppose that if Laing's experiment had turned out significant numbers of formerly psychotic people who could at least pretend to social appropriateness as they rejoiced in their visionary insights, there would be Kingsley Hall clones everywhere happily reproducing that sorely needed success. But this has not occurred, which suggests that Laing's revisionist view of psychosis, as inspired as it was in essence, contains serious flaws.

An obvious place to begin a rethinking process is in Laing's blaming psychotic ASCs on sick societies and families. If his bold apostasy retains a certain antiauthoritarian appeal after decades of stagnation in thinking about psychosis, it is not because it fits the facts of sociology or biology. If the "mystifications" of technological civilizations entice reasonable people to seek refuge in madness, we would expect it to be nonexistent in pristine nontechnological cultures. Or if psychotic ASCs did occur spontaneously, those cultures would appreciate their intrinsic value as they devised social roles for these exceptional people.

There is little reason to believe this is the case. Virtually every pretechnological culture has a word, or label, for psychotic behavior. Subsistence economies are even less likely than technological ones to tolerate people who refuse to perform productive social tasks because, say, they believe they are a god. For instance, the Eskimo word for psychotic behavior is *nuthkavihak,* and tribal elders recognize it as

> talking to oneself, screaming at someone who does not exist, believing that a child or husband was murdered by witchcraft when nobody else believes it, believing oneself to be an animal, refusing to eat for fear eating will kill one, refusing to talk, running away, getting lost, hiding in strange places, making strange grimaces, drinking urine,

becoming strong and violent, killing dogs and threatening people.

Similarly, the Yoruba tribesman of rural Nigeria know psychosis as *were,* a condition that encompasses

> hearing voices and trying to get other people to see their source though none can be seen, laughing when there is nothing to laugh at, talking all the time or not talking at all, asking oneself questions and answering them, picking up sticks for no purpose except to put them in a pile, throwing away food because it is thought to contain *juju,* tearing off one's clothes, defecating in public and then mushing around in the feces, taking up a weapon and suddenly hitting someone with it, breaking things in a state of being stronger than normal, believing that an odor is continuously being emitted from one's body.

The author of the above studies concluded:

> It appears that disturbed thought and behavior are found in most cultures; they are sufficiently distinctive and noticeable that almost everywhere a name has been created for them . . . Rather than being simply violations of the social norms of particular groups, symptoms of mental illness are manifestations of a type of affliction shared by virtually all mankind.

From the above "diagnoses," we might suppose that the less-than-noble labels *nuthkavihak* and *were* are even more broadly applied to deviant behavior than are diagnostic labels in our technological culture. The indigenous Alaskan or African might also take umbrage at suggestions that such behavior is a healthy response to an emotionally oppressive culture. Both societies recognize that the ASCs underlying such behavior are intrinsically maladaptive, and they insist on applying indigenous healing practices to people displaying such symptoms.

Many people in psychotic ASCs exhibit behavior that would cause them to be outcasts in any culture with rudimentary rules of territoriality and decorum. Manics invade others' personal space and interrupt conversations with grandiose impunity. Schizophrenics are unable to master the basic repertoires of their cultural heritage. People so afflicted often stand too close while talking, and either focus their eyes a foot beyond the listener or gaze fixedly in a way that imparts discomfort.

In groups they turn away from each other and avoid holding glances. Their timing is off, like a very bad orchestra. A schizophrenic may praise a desired companion by telling her that she has "tarantula eyes," or unemotionally accuse her of stealing his semen by occult means.

When one observes such people desperately trying to master consensual behaviors, it is apparent that they are not cleverly escaping from insincere social interaction. Their ASC simply prevents their perceiving, thinking, and reacting like people in ordinary states of consciousness. Although the dreadful conditions of institutional hospitalization certainly do not improve socially deviant behavior, antipsychiatrists stretch their point by claiming that those conditions, or deranged societies, are responsible for it.

However, Laing's sociological theory of the cause of psychosis does seem to fit one fact about schizophrenia. Several cross-cultural studies have demonstrated a lower incidence of that ASC among native populations having minimal contact with industrialized and urbanized cultures as compared with natives having more contact. Similarly, a World Health Organization study found the course of schizophrenia to be more benign in nonindustrialized countries.

These findings suggest that technological cultures demand more heavily armored self-boundaries than do hunting and agricultural societies, whose members live closer to the Ground in their daily lives. Because civilized people have abandoned the realm of the mysterious in favor of the functional, spontaneous influxes of Ground energies seem more alien to them than to people whose culture celebrates myths and rituals that reconnect them with the Source. Such "primitive" cultures are usually tolerant of spontaneous ASCs in ritual settings, and they provide meaningful models to help integrate sudden openings. Members of those cultures are not forced to employ extreme defenses to maintain the integrity of self during ASCs.

If we are to make practical use of Laing's often brilliant insights, we need *more* diagnoses, refined to discern subtle shadings of consciousness within psychotic experience. This could help us avoid his error of treating any and all psychotic people with the same methods. If large state hospitals are to be faulted for treating all psychotic ASCs as pathologically regressed, Laing's method of treating all psychotic ASCs as portents of imminent mystical enlightenment is hardly less crude. Although antipsychiatrists called for abolishment of psychiatric labeling, it became obvious that they also labeled the conditions that they observed, but they used different labels and did not share them with their patients.

The idea that madness is a way station on the road to heightened consciousness has been oversold, if not by Laing, who finally softened his position, then by his counterculture following. Not every ASC leads to a liberating communion with the Spiritual Ground. Far from it. Repeated eruptions of psychotic ASCs can reduce psychic life to stony deadness, terminal burnout. No matter how enlightened the therapeutic intervention, unchecked regression has a potential for catastrophic outcome, with calcification of the personality a frequent aftermath.

Careful observation of people in psychotic ASCs reveals some degree of regression common to all. But regression can stabilize at any of several levels, from infantile, to childlike, to adolescent. Some "mini-regressions" actually liberate creative or psychic capabilities. Mainstream psychiatry disregards these distinctions and subdivides schizophrenic ASCs only by duration of symptoms, and by type (paranoid, catatonic, etc.). There is but one category of "borderline personality." Hyperaroused ASCs are divided only into "hypomanic" and "manic" forms. Laing's assessments, however, did not even go that far. By over-applying Rousseau's egalitarian vision, Laing doomed his Kingsley Hall experiment from the start.

But perhaps Laing's worst failing was his inflation of 1960's revolutionary ideology into an oversimplified notion that all psychoses are caused by social or familial oppression. This assigned a terrible burden of guilt to parents already devastated by the horror of watching a child slip away from them into an impenetrable world beyond their understanding. The truth is that only a minority of psychotic ASCs are brought about by faulty parenting. Others are largely the result of genetically programmed alterations in brain metabolism. An important subgroup represents, as Laing argued, harbingers of spiritual emergence. Most psychotic symptoms are an amalgam of forces from all of these levels.

The visionary Scottish antipsychiatrist wisely pointed out that people in psychotic ASCs are best treated in small, homelike, communal settings staffed by healers who are sympathetic toward ASCs and their external manifestations. Healing flows from a therapist's willingness to help reconstruct damaged selves through the medium of warm, non-judgmental human contact. What Laing overlooked was that some psychotic people require intervention on a basic physical level (containment, nutrition, medicines), others on psychological levels (social-skills training, supportive psychotherapy, emotional release), and still others on spiritual levels (contemplative practice, interpretive psychotherapy). It is for the next generation of artful healers to build upon the essential truths underlying Laing's fallible intuition.

PART 2
MADNESS AND THE BRAIN

CHAPTER 5

The Anatomy of Madness

◆

*Each person is at each moment capable of remembering all that has happened
to him and of perceiving everything that is happening everywhere in the
universe. The function of the brain and nervous system is to protect us from
being overwhelmed and confused by this mass of largely useless and irrelevant
knowledge, by shutting out most (of it). According to such a theory,
each of us is potentially Mind at Large.*

ALDOUS HUXLEY

I never believe a madman 'til I have seen his brains.

SHAKESPEARE

HIPPOCRATES, the father of medicine, taught his students that
"from the brain, and from the brain only, arise our pleasures, joys,
laughter, and jests, as well as our sorrows, pains, griefs, and fears." Ever
since, physicians have been seeking the "ghost in the machine," the
origin of the soul in the three pounds of spongy tissue known as the human brain.

They have not found it there. Nor will they.

That is not because the brain doesn't enfold the human *mind* deep
within its labyrinthine caverns. To argue otherwise would reveal a naive
ignorance of modern neuroscience, which has generated a convincing
body of knowledge linking brain states and subjective experience. Yet
science has never demonstrated how consciousness itself—the raw experience of feeling, knowing, and manipulating the physical world—
"arises" from the ebbs and flows of electrochemical activity in the
brain.

Of course physical events in the brain affect our experience by interacting with the universal consciousness of the Spiritual Ground. But to assert that they *create* our mental lives is an overstatement that no careful analyst may reasonably make. When we relate specific experiences to conditions within the brain, we can describe only *correlations*, not cause-and-effect relations. We may say, for instance, that when a person experiences anxiety, certain chemicals activate lower-brain centers. But it does not follow that these chemicals cause the subjective experience of anxiety, any more than anxiety causes the chemicals to accumulate. Both are aspects of a unitary process in which changes in one are reflected in changes in the other.

To put it another way, the brain's role is to mold the consciousness of the Ground into human form, into a cohesive self-in-the-world. Ultimately, the brain provides a vehicle for that self's long and perilous journey back to pure spirit through a lifetime of experience and personal evolution. To do so, the brain must operate competently or its embedded mind will regress into a chaotic jumble of primitive thoughtforms. This regression is exactly what occurs in malignant psychotic ASCs.

As we explore the tortuous pathways through which consciousness flows, we discover levels of complexity from the explicit and gross to the inferred and subtle. In this and the following three chapters, we examine how psychotic ASCs reverberate within the intricate chambers of the brain. We begin with a brief look at the brain's origins: the genetic seeds that set the initial conditions for psychotic ASCs to emerge later in life. We then examine abnormalities in the brain's larger anatomical structures, progress to finer biochemical fluctuations at the level of the synapse, and finally turn to new theories of how the brain resonates as a vibrating field at the subatomic level. Although the complexity of the subject renders these chapters challenging to the nonmedical reader, I have tried to present the material in a way that is accessible to the layperson.

As scientists in the early decades of this century grew familiar with the brain's anatomy, they realized that it wasn't a single organ at all, but a congregation of smaller organs, each of which makes a unique contribution to human awareness. Because they discovered tiny nerve tracts connecting these individual centers, the brain seemed to be like a telephone switchboard, with long-distance lines linking terminals. In this chapter, we will use the switchboard analogy to examine how jammed trunk lines and short-circuiting control centers contribute to psychotic ASCs. But as we shall see in following chapters, this switchboard analogy has been replaced by two new models consistent with the advancing technology of our times.

GENES & MADNESS

Scientists pondering the enigma of madness have long observed that schizophrenic and manic-depressive ASCs run in families. Some families, like the notorious Jukes clan of the 1930s, seem to be made up entirely of psychotics. Of course, speaking French also runs in families, but that trait certainly is not transmitted through the genes. Only recently have we been able to distinguish genetic nature from psychological nurture for the two major psychoses. The situation is less clear for borderline states, multiple personality disorder, and other less common forms of psychosis.

The six million genes arrayed in gracefully spiraling columns within a full set of forty-six human chromosomes act as a kind of species-specific memory. Their task is to store information about four billion years of slow biological improvement. Plying their trade within every cell of a developing fetus, they oversee complex chemical reactions, which in turn determine if the child is to be born with blue eyes, a petite nose, and a brain that can support a state of consciousness more or less like that of other members of our species.

It is not always easy to hook up a hundred billion neurons in a precise and orderly way. In addition to controlling the brain's wiring diagram, genes also influence how these neurons react to the hundreds of chemicals that keep the whole system humming along smoothly. Some three billion genetic brushstrokes are necessary to draw a human being. If only one in a million of these goes wrong, the results would be monstrous. Given its complexity, our genetic system has proven to be quite reliable. But occasionally things go amiss. Damage a single gene, or cluster of genes, and the alterations escalate into profound changes in the final product.

Genetic mutations that misdirect brain growth result from ionizing radiation, environmental toxins, poor nutrition, and intrusive viruses. Repetitive inbreeding exaggerates undesirable genetic traits, such as hemophilia and mental retardation. The effects of genetic damage were tragically demonstrated by the armless thalidomide babies in Europe, and are personally known by sufferers of muscular dystrophy and other inherited maladies. Compelling evidence indicates that malignant forms of schizophrenia, as well as manic-depressive ASCs, can be added to that list.

This determination was not easily gained. Only when researchers recognized the unique potential of the *folkeregister,* a Danish registry containing detailed information about the birth, family history, health records, and circumstances of death of virtually every person in that country, could they separate the effects of genetic endowment from the tribulations of childhood.

The Genetics of Schizophrenia

Using the *folkeregister*, researchers studied entire generations of people with mental problems, cross-referencing their results for dozens of traits. To isolate inherited traits from environmentally induced ones, they focused on children adopted at birth and raised by families unrelated to the natural parents. From their research, they readily determined that children adopted from families of schizophrenic parents are far more likely to become schizophrenic than children adopted from nonschizophrenic parents, no matter what the circumstances of their upbringing.

But when researchers compared identical and fraternal twins who were separated at birth and raised in foster homes, they found the unexpected. The concordance for schizophrenia between identical twins is less than 50 percent. Because identical twins have exactly the same genetic structure from conception, we would expect 100 percent concordance if genes are the *only* cause of schizophrenia. Clearly, genetic influence is powerful, but other forces are involved, too.

We might wonder, then, about close relatives of schizophrenics who never develop a psychotic ASC. Are they "a little psychotic"? This intriguing possibility is far from resolved. While some studies indicate that relatives of schizophrenics are prone to a plethora of emotional problems, including anxiety attacks and antisocial behavior, other studies reveal a tendency toward uncommon creativity and other desirable openings to the Ground. One report noted colorful and precociously talented personalities in a group of genetically predisposed children who did not become psychotic. This suggests that the depth of a schizophrenic ASC may be influenced by several genes interacting with each other. These "schizophrenic genes" are present in varying numbers throughout the schizophrenic's family, with most members carrying none, others carrying a small number, and a few carrying a significant number.

To understand the interaction of genes and madness better, we can make an analogy with a more clear-cut genetic syndrome. Sickle-cell anemia, a blood disease endemic to people of African descent, has two genetic forms. When it is associated with a single gene, the characteristic "sickling" of red blood cells occurs only under conditions of oxygen deprivation. But the sickle cell trait also confers immunity to malaria, which grants considerable *advantage* in mosquito-infested central Africa. However, the double-gene variety causes a much more severe and often fatal blood disease. Although the genetic transmission of schizophrenia and mania is far more complicated, we might speculate that the less genetically "pure" forms confer a potential advantage that fosters visionary or creative thinking by allowing smaller, more manageable, openings to the Spiritual Ground.

Another puzzling question is why the prevalence of both schizophrenia and mania has been increasing in recent decades. Reason would suggest a trend in the opposite direction. For instance, if schizophrenia is inherited, and the disease is so disruptive of normal human interactions as to make marriage and procreation less likely than for non-schizophrenics, why is it still with us? Why hasn't it faded from the human gene pool by the simple laws of natural selection? One possibility is that schizophrenic genes are being newly created through a process of mutation that is higher than any known mutation rate. If this is true, the production of schizophrenic genes must be an *ongoing process* that is currently influencing the evolution of our species. Whether this is an ominous portent for humanity or, as R. D. Laing postulated, an evolutionary breakthrough remains an open question.

Despite decades of research, the exact mode of transmission of schizophrenia remains unclear, and the location of the involved genes unknown, although science is edging toward that anticipated breakthrough. Roughly 90 percent of the people who present themselves to psychiatrists with spontaneous psychotic ASCs do *not* have a parent or close relative so afflicted. Only the more malignant forms of schizophrenia are known to be inherited, and these are associated with conspicuous brain abnormalities described later in this chapter.

In sum, not all psychotic ASCs reflect genetic abnormalities or primary brain disorders. What is inherited is a *predisposition* for idiosyncratic thinking and for developing psychotic ASCs when under stress. And if genes predispose some people to schizophrenia, we might wonder what finishes the job. Besides genes, we know that family and social environments profoundly affect a growing brain, which changes throughout life. The outcome of a genetic predisposition to certain ASCs might be entirely different in different families or cultures.

The Genetics of Mania

Although a different cluster of genes is involved, families prone to manic ASCs confer on their children risks similar to those associated with schizophrenia. The genetic pattern of mania may be easier to trace, however. Geneticists now suspect that one or two genes are involved in most cases, and they have narrowed their search to specific chromosomal sites, one close to a location found to control the production of dopamine, a brain chemical known for its association with psychotic ASCs, and another near a site associated with color blindness. This is probably why almost half of manic-depressives are color blind.

Some genetic patterns that produce hyperaroused ASCs of less than manic proportions are potentially desirable. Moderate increases in brain activity without qualitative distortions are called "hypomanic" to indicate that they fall short of true psychosis. There is reason to believe that people prone to hypomania may have a different genetic pattern than those who regularly cross the line into psychotic manic ASCs. These high-energy states may promote unusual creativity and a "workaholic" temperament that can lead to uncommon achievement.

In sum, the bulk of genetic evidence suggests that the terms *schizophrenia* and *mania* describe a spectrum of related ASCs with different causes—some genetic, others from a variety of environmental factors. A genetic liability to psychosis may foster eccentricities that are adaptive or not, depending on one's social milieu. Smaller deviations from the norm can confer extraordinary talents and creative skills, given a proper environment for their development.

There are two ways in which a genetic predisposition to madness can influence a developing brain. The first is by disfiguring the brain's anatomical structures and the ways they are "wired" together in the fashion of a switchboard. The second is by sabotaging the cellular "factories" that produce and destroy the chemical messengers that keep the whole system running. What follows is a brief sketch of the anatomical differences that underlie psychotic ASCs.

THREE BRAINS IN ONE

Like the mind embedded within it, the brain is arranged in layers, each representing a higher level of functioning. This stratification did not happen by chance, but followed billions of years of slow evolution. For the sake of simplicity, we will divide the anatomical brain into three physical levels, following the triune model proposed by the neurophysiologist Paul McLean.

McLean's idea is that the human brain reflects the stages of evolution, beginning with the primordial oceans of a young planet. From there, the brain adapted to amphibian terrestrial life, and then to the struggles of primitive mammals to find a niche in a world populated by larger and fiercer creatures. Following the last ice age, it expanded to guide our primate ancestors as they abandoned the shelter of the jungle canopy for the harsh challenges of a hunting economy on the savannas.

In the early days of this process, the wormlike sea creatures that dominated biological life needed only a hollow tube of nerve tissue, with branches exiting at intervals to coordinate muscular movement. Their awareness of the world was equally rudimentary. As life became more complicated, a light-sensitive eyespot developed at one end of the tube, and a swelling simultaneously appeared underneath it, indicating that nerve cells—neurons—were gathering to make use of this new source of information. As increasingly intricate life forms followed their evolutionary tangents, they needed more and more sensory information for survival. Ever efficient, nature clustered each new sense organ at the same end as the original eyespot, and the enlarging brain at the head end of the tube developed specialized centers to help it deal with the increasing variety of data available to it.

In this way, the primitive brain expanded to gather energies from a widening contact with the physical world. As new sense organs evolved at the head of the tube, each gave the animal an added dimension of response, a higher level of awareness that made the previous level relatively obsolete. Each higher structure also took over the role of switchboard command post, the center of activity that regulated lower structures and embodied the primordial "self" of the animal.

True to nature's evolutionary scheme, no structure or its associated mental function along the unbroken chain leading to the human brain was lost in the process. Although each early structure underwent modification as higher ones evolved and usurped its command, each brain part—originally designed to serve an eel, fish, frog, dinosaur, tiger, or monkey—remains in the human brain, connecting us in spirit and substance with our ancestors. But every advance of awareness also created a possibility that the control center could regress to an older part of the brain no longer capable of operating the whole switchboard.

Nature faced a major problem at an early stage of evolution. How could a progressively elongating brain fit inside a reasonably shaped head that, at least in its original design, had to move efficiently through water? That dense medium is hardly a suitable forum for pointy-headed intellectuals. The solution, simply enough, was to fold the tube so that each new structure layered on top of the old, forming an "aviator's cap" that surrounded older areas. This general format still exists in the triune human brain in which the second layer, or limbic system, caps the spinal cord and brain stem, and the third layer, or cortex, neatly caps the second, (see Figure 5–1).

McLean named each of these three brain layers and their associated mental functions according to their evolutionary roots. He calls the spinal cord and brain stem the reptile brain. Although the structures within this lower brain were once at the top echelon of some primitive lizard that undoubtedly found it a distinct advantage in competing with its less-endowed rivals, the reptile brain in a human now mediates only

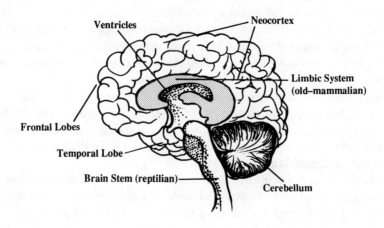

Ventricles

Neocortex

Limbic System
(old–mammalian)

Frontal Lobes

Temporal Lobe

Brain Stem (reptilian)

Cerebellum

F IGURE 5 – 1 : *The human brain made transparent to show the limbic system and related structures encased in the evolutionarily newer neocortex.*

reflexive bodily functions that lack self-awareness. In humans, it expresses itself in imitative and repetitive gestures related to self-preservation, especially in infancy. It probably also contains archetypal instincts that enter our awareness through subliminal memories and dreams. But it isn't much help in learning new approaches to the problems of modern life.

The second layer, or limbic system—called the old-mammalian brain by McLean—is the dwelling place of our emotions, drives, and primitive fantasies. The limbic system was once the crowning evolutionary achievement of our early mammalian ancestors, conferring upon those shy and diminutive creatures the defensive cunning they needed to survive in a world overrun by rapacious dinosaurs. But by today's standards, the old-mammalian brain operates on a crude, unreflectively emotional level. Although a coarse form of "thinking" is associated with limbic-system activity, its role in the human mind revolves around species survival by activating the "four *F*s," as an old medical-school joke has it: feeding, fighting, fleeing, and "procreation." As we shall see, aberrant limbic activity is also associated with psychotic ASCs.

The third and topmost layer, which is highly developed only in humans, whales, and dolphins, and somewhat less so in apes and monkeys, is the *neocortex*. McLean called this newest layer "the mother of invention and father of abstract thought." The reasoning neocortex adds foresight, hindsight, and insight to human awareness. Without it there would be no language, mathematics, symphonies, or nuclear weapons. And as it gradually took over the task of integrating vision and hearing from the lower two strata, the neocortex bestowed the unique faculty of self-reflection and introspection—awareness of awareness—a rare endowment that, for all we know, exists nowhere else in the universe.

This power of consciousness to contemplate itself is essential if a mature and coherent sense of self is to grow and remain stable within the human mind. If the neocortex in which that self is embedded falters, the self's boundary will fragment, and a psychotic ASC follows.

The neocortex has an evolutionary history of its own in that its newest part, the *frontal lobes*, embodies our capacity to manipulate facts, plan strategies, and imagine what is not immediately present. The frontal lobes gather information from all parts of the brain, then coordinate these data to set purposeful goals. Without this advance, we would live in a philosophical vacuum devoid of abstract meaning. Not surprisingly, the frontal lobes are known to function abnormally during regressive ASCs.

THE SELF IN THE BRAIN

As each new layer of the triune brain evolved, its greater ability to think and feel enabled it to rule over the lower levels. In other words, the governing center of neural activity—a rudimentary self-center—advanced to ever higher levels. And with it the subjective feeling of "I" as a center of awareness and will grew more complex and capable of a wider range of activities. Although this "I" did not attain self-reflection until relatively recently in evolutionary terms, a primitive sense of self, separate from the Ground, its awareness confined to bodily sensations and the immediate environment, probably exists even in reptiles.

This same ascent of the governing self-center takes place during a human being's development from conception to maturity. A newborn's neurological center, along with a subjective sense of I-ness that crystallizes around it, is embedded in the reptilian brain, from where it gradually ascends throughout its early years. During this stage, the "I" is preoccupied with feeding, elimination, and security. Next, the toddler's self-center begins its ascent through the limbic system, a perilous climb through a shadowy world of fantasy, raw emotion, and unstable self/other boundaries. This stage normally continues until late adolescence, when the self-center transits to the neocortex and then forward to the frontal lobes, if it can.

This final advance to adulthood is a crucial stage of life, when a person is most vulnerable to a schizophrenic or manic break. A person's ability to establish an identity and compete for a secure place in the world requires a fully operational cortex, especially in the frontal lobes, where strategic planning takes place. The progressive upward thrust of the self-center through levels of mind/brain may be detoured by an abnormal stop command from a gene that inhibits frontal-lobe activity, or by an oppressive environment that arrests its progress.

This is not to say that higher brain levels do not operate until a person reaches maturity. They clearly do. It is only the center of the neural regulator, the seat of governance, reflected in one's predominant mode of thinking and feeling, that steadily advances upward from the reflexive survival mode of the brain stem to the self-aware frontal lobes.

Even when a higher level is gained, if the neurological center fails to maintain its position of control, survival mandates a regression to the next lower level. That is not to say that the higher level ceases to function; it is just not in the "operator's chair" because it is being regulated from a lower level. Thus, when a person's self-center abdicates its position in the cortex and descends to a limbic center, he forfeits his power to use reason to override emotions. Regression takes place in both brain and mind, and it may be total or partial, permanent or temporary. Paradoxically, it may signal an adaptive step back before a major leap forward, or it may portend a plodding retreat away from a higher self.

Once a person's self advances to a higher level, a regressive step back to a lower one feels very peculiar indeed. During the normal ASC of dreaming, for instance, the center of control transiently shifts to the reptilian brain. This weakens self-boundaries and exposes the individual's awareness to the unmodulated energies of the Ground. Higher brain areas are still active during this ASC, but they are under the dominion of an ancient and nonlogical arena of consciousness, and the ensuing experience is impetuous and weird, with archaic emotions running the show. We might take a moment to empathize with the experience of a person in a psychotic ASC whose uncontrolled regression suddenly transports him to this realm of dreams while fully awake.

Even greater regression prevails during profound psychotic ASCs. For instance, in the deepest, most disorganized stages of madness a person may rock his body or repetitiously oscillate an arm or leg, indicating a transfer of control to the reptilian brain stem or cerebellum. During less severe degrees of regression, various survival-based areas may reign, such as the hypervigilant "paranoid" areas in the old-mammalian brain.

At the opposite extreme, certain people learn to willfully raise or lower their center of neural activity and so choose a state of consciousness most adaptive to particular circumstances. These are spiritual adepts, shamans who manipulate their psyches with "power plants" for the benefit of their tribes, creative artists who master the discipline of their crafts while remaining open to the Ground—all students of an inner technology that asserts the power of mind over the physical realm.

MADNESS IN THE NEOCORTEX

While we may marvel over the wondrous outcome of brain evolution, McLean is less than starry-eyed about the human neurological apparatus, even when it is functioning perfectly. He views the triune brain as a grotesque evolutionary error, an impossible mismatch of discordant elements whose inner relations he termed "schizophysiology."

Although there are plentiful nerve tracts to transmit information between the reptilian and old-mammalian brains, McLean believes the rapid evolutionary spurt that produced the neocortex outpaced nature's ability to create adequate links between it and older layers. More ominously, he found that there are many more neurons leading *upward* from limbic system to cortex than in the reverse direction. So the domain of reason can exert only limited power over its emotional forebears. This anatomical shortcoming corresponds to the troublesome human experience of having greater awareness of our fiery emotions than ability to control them through higher reason.

What if this built-in "defect" were to be further exaggerated, and our tenuous capacity to override emotion with reason were compromised even more? During certain psychotic ASCs this seems to be the case. To understand how such a breakdown can occur, we turn to the role of the neocortex in psychosis.

In the past decade, a technological breakthrough called Positron Emission Tomography or PET revolutionized brain science by enabling researchers to observe a living brain in action. Using this technique, researchers found that many people in psychotic ASCs are unable to switch on their frontal lobes in response to tasks designed to activate that area. Scientists refer to this failure of the highest brain center as hypo-frontality.

Further refinements suggest that hypo-frontality is more pronounced on the left side of the frontal lobes in schizophrenics, and on the right side in manics. (However, the total decrease of frontal-lobe activity is considerably less in mania than in schizophrenia.) This may explain why manics usually retain their capacity for logic (left side), but are unable to place events in an appropriate context or accept feedback from others (right side). Schizophrenics, on the other hand, forfeit linear logic early in the ASC, but compensate with exaggerated right-side activity as they overinterpret context to reach paranoid conclusions.

Of course, when higher reasoning capacities of the frontal lobes falter, the individual adapts by falling back to the next-highest cortical level. But in people predisposed to schizophrenia, such a stepwise regression leads only to another unstable equilibrium, for there are still other malfunctions in older cortical areas. The corpus callosum, a flat cable of 250 million nerve fibers connecting the right and left hemispheres of the neocortex, coordinates activities between these two semi-independent information-processing systems. It, too, fails in many psychotic ASCs.

Most people with a passing interest in brain science have during the past two decades been exposed to the (simplified) idea that the dominant left half of the human cortex specializes in logical, linear, verbal thinking with orientation to time, while the right hemisphere processes information in nonverbal wholes, is oriented to space, and gathers meaning through symbols and inference. Also, the right hemisphere shares with the limbic system the task of weaving emotions into awareness, although the old-mammalian emotions of the limbic system are more primitive than those of the right hemisphere—for example, lust rather than love.

Each hemisphere would be lost without the other. The left is so logical as to be literal to a fault, so it relies on its more holistic companion to supply context and nuance. Conversely, the right brain specializes as a fast processor for data that do not require verbal analysis, and as a mismatch decoder that adds intuitive depth to the computerlike left side. But it doesn't do well at figuring out logical sequences.

Rapid-fire communication between the hemispheres is essential to maintain a balanced state of consciousness. This is why the thickened, partially obstructed corpora callosa found in many schizophrenics are so significant. One study found a fourfold delay in information transfer across the corpus callosum in chronic schizophrenics. The static-producing interference is especially prominent in frontal areas, where right and left hemispheres share information about symbols, abstract meanings, and sequences of cause and effect—exactly those capacities most impaired in schizophrenic ASCs.

Paranoia, for instance, follows a failure to interpret nuance, a misreading of cause and effect. This suggests a schism between the brain's hemispheres. Similarly, people whose corpora callosa were severed during surgery for epilepsy simultaneously maintain opposite attitudes toward the same object or event. For instance, they might find their left hand willfully reaching out to prevent the right from performing a task. This suggests that the halting ambivalence so prominent in the schizophrenic ASC could reflect scrambled information transfer across a jammed corpus callosum.

The childlike thinking that Freud called "primary process"—a kind of sublogic that creates chains of associations by taking symbols literally—is a classic mode of regressed schizophrenic thought. Primary-process thinking is nonlogical, emotionally tinged, and overinclusive, and therefore has most of the characteristics of right-brain mentation untempered by the left. It is as though the left brain cannot defend its executive power against an intrusively rebellious right hemisphere empowered with the will to bend logic to its own purposes.

In a worst-case scenario, the above two neocortical failings could join together to shape an especially maladaptive ASC. If the reasoning frontal lobes were to disengage from an overactive limbic system, and the left and right hemispheres also uncoupled their alliance, the ensuing ASC would render an unfortunate individual unable to place his feelings in the context of his life history, as well as unable to mobilize a timely "cognitive override" when confronted by intense emotions. The result would be a disabled person who is circumstantial, distractible, panicky, and incapable of modulating his emotions in order to carry out simple life assignments.

Under these circumstances, the neurological control center would then be divided, with each isolated brain hemisphere acquiring a share of the disjoined self. This final split would lead a person to feel that alien influences were invading his mind, or that unfriendly forces were implanting thoughts and ideas into his stream of consciousness.

MADNESS IN THE OLD-MAMMALIAN BRAIN

Despite this intriguing evidence of malfunction in the topmost areas of the brain, most researchers suspect that the old-mammalian brain, or limbic system, harbors the primary physical correlates of severely psychotic ASCs. And they do so with good reason.

The fist-sized limbic system is in some ways a brain within a brain, but also a mind within a mind, one that "thinks" in raw impressions rather than words. Because we share this consciousness-shaping organ with the ferocious beasts of the jungle, it is easy to imagine how, as higher brain levels falter and regression gathers momentum, the psyche peels layer by layer down to the psychology of lower mammals. The evolutionary struggle of humanity has been to organize our sense of self around higher cortical centers. No wonder we instinctively fear this unreflective remnant of our brutish past. Fictional characters such as Jekyll/Hyde symbolize the danger of the limbic brain's power to emerge from deep within to wrest control from the rational neocortex.

Far from being a simple organ bursting with rude emotions, the limbic system is complex, encompassing within its borders centers that color our awareness with pleasure and pain, rage and fear, aggressiveness and retreat, and recognition of what is strange, familiar, friendly, threatening, and edible. Limbic way stations regulate drive and motivation, remembering and forgetting, our ability to select where to focus attention and what to ignore, and the feeling of continuity of experience so vital to a coherent sense of self.

The location of the limbic system between the reptilian brain and the neocortex places it in a strategic position to transmit information between old and new levels and to modulate traffic between them. Therefore, limbic activity has a profound effect on both lower and higher brain areas—that is, drive and reason—and is profoundly affected by them. To oversimplify a psychoanalytic metaphor, the limbic system is the pathway by which the temperate ego communicates with the unruly instincts of the id.

Scientists have traced activity in several limbic centers to psychotic ASCs. Psychedelic drugs also affect limbic areas, including the prominent temporal lobes. When surgeons stimulate certain temporal areas with microcurrents of electricity, their patients usually experience visual and auditory hallucinations, sometimes of beautiful music. Other temporal areas produce vivid memories from childhood, relived side–by–side with the sense of being in an operating room. Some people with temporal-lobe abnormalities have pseudomemories of events that never occurred, but are recalled with the same certainty as actual memories. All of these phenomena are well known to people in psychotic ASCs.

People suffering from temporal-lobe epilepsy, a condition in which a limbic site becomes explosively overactive, experience ASCs that closely resemble some forms of schizophrenia. Limbic seizures are unique in that the energy liberated is confined to the limbic system and does not spread throughout the brain, allowing a degree of recall impossible in grand mal seizures. The experience varies from person to person, but many people with limbic epilepsy are consumed by dreamlike hallucinations, feelings of persecution, and intuitions that their survival is imminently threatened, even though they rationally conclude that it isn't. Some even develop multiple personalities, although there is only one alter, not the community of selves in a classical MPD.

People with limbic seizures commonly experience déjà vu, an eerie impression that a current event has somehow happened before in precisely the same way, or that they know what is about to be said before the words are spoken. Schizophrenics often have this same sense of portentous familiarity, as do people involved in advanced spiritual practice. Limbic seizures on the right side of the brain usually induce abrupt maniclike mood swings, while left-temporal-lobe seizures provoke schizophreniclike alterations of thinking and paranoia. Between attacks, patients with limbic seizures tend to become fascinated with philosophical and metaphysical matters.

Because schizophrenics are usually unable to express joy or gratification, it is not surprising that the brain circuit that mediates pleasure misfires in schizophrenics. Rats trained to electrically stimulate this circuit by pressing a bar will perform this task obsessively for hours, passing up more mundane allures of food or sex for this quick limbic thrill. But unlike the electrical ecstasies of these rats, the schizophrenic ASC is far from blissful. Instead, a stubborn blockade in the pleasure circuit shows up on an electroencephalogram as abnormal electrical "spikes." (Although research on living animals can yield valuable information, a transpersonal perspective recognizes that consciousness is embedded in all living brains, emanating from the same unitive source as our own. We may hope that future researchers respect the capacity for pain as well as pleasure inherent in all animal biology.)

Many people live with a constant sense of fear or rage, unable to soothe themselves through rewarding activities. These people say that they do not know what happiness is, that they cannot even imagine it. Therapists who work with schizophrenics notice that their patients virtually never speak of falling in love, that they don't fully grasp the feeling. As we reflect for a moment on the role of pleasure and reward in our lives, we recognize that they are essential to feeling that life is worth living and has meaning. Banish these satisfactions that we take for granted and we would feel at loose ends, unable to see a purpose in existence. We would likely withdraw from others into a solitary world where fantasy gradually fills the void.

Still another limbic area, the *hippocampus*, functions abnormally in schizophrenia. Autopsies of schizophrenic brains reveal that neurons in this limbic center, normally arrayed in parallel columns, appear chaotic and tangled. The task of the hippocampus is to store new memories and compare incoming sensations with old memory traces. Any shortfall in the hippocampus impairs a person's ability to recognize consensual behaviors in himself or others, or correct inappropriate behavior through social feedback. People with injuries to the hippocampus show a maniclike inability to stick to a goal, as well as a reckless fascination with danger.

CAVITIES IN THE BRAIN

No brain abnormality underlying psychotic ASCs is more ominous than enlarged cerebral *ventricles*. Only the most severely impaired schizophrenics manifest this malformation, which distinguishes malignant disorders those with potential for restoration.

In a normal brain, the ventricles are fluid-filled cavities that surround and cushion the limbic system. If a person suffers a disease or injury that causes his cortex to lose cells, such as Alzheimer's disease or encephalitis, his cortex steadily shrinks away from the underlying limbic system. The ventricles compensate by enlarging to take up the missing space. Caught in the middle, the old-mammalian brain is pushed upward and gradually crushed. That individual's emotional life is an unfortunate casualty.

Using crude X rays, scientists first noted enlarged ventricles in severe schizophrenics during the 1930s. As of this writing, almost two dozen studies using sophisticated technology perfected in the last decade have confirmed this finding. Enlarged ventricles imply a strong genetic predisposition to the most regressive forms of schizophrenia, and a poor prospect for the individual's ever regaining a consensual state of consciousness. As the ventricles expand, they do so at the expense of brain areas that enable a person to experience a full range of human emotions.

About a third of the people who meet the diagnostic criteria for schizophrenia have enlarged ventricles, whether or not they have ever taken antipsychotic medicines. Intelligence as measured by IQ tests, which is usually normal in psychotics with normal-sized ventricles, is almost always impaired in people with this lamentable clinical sign. Ventricular enlargement strikes such a devastating and irreversible blow to a human mind that it portends a lifetime of dependency.

MADNESS IN THE REPTILIAN BRAIN

The ancient reptilian brain also holds keys to both manic and schizophrenic ASCs. Deep within this ancient stratum is a diffuse network of cells called the *reticular activating system* (RAS). The RAS is strategically placed at the junction of spinal column and brain to monitor messages between body and mind. It sends branches far and wide, keeping track of the overall pattern of brain activity, switching on or off various sectors as it decides which incoming messages enter awareness, and where to send them to be processed.

In other words, the RAS is a guardian of the gates, the first in a chain of "filters" that screen signals from the sense organs. It preferentially grants access to inputs that are the most exotic or compelling, turning aside the rest for the sake of attending to what is important for survival. In this way, it contributes to self-boundaries and helps seal off the Ground from ordinary awareness. Without the RAS filter, we would find ourselves in a state of informational overload, both from the sensory world and from the extrasensory one. In highly distractible schizo-phrenic and manic ASCs, one's ability to focus and hold attention is eroded by a flood of confusing stimuli, indicating that the RAS has fallen asleep at its guardpost. With no way to reduce bombardment by invading sensory inputs, there is little recourse but a desperate fight or panicky flight.

If we surgically remove the RAS, a person plunges into an irrevers-ible coma. If we electrically stimulate it, a sleeper instantly awakens. If we increase the stimulation, the entire brain becomes hyperaroused, vaulting into an electrically induced manic ASC that ceases when the current is switched off. Not surprisingly, stimulants like caffeine and co-caine act directly upon the RAS. The psychedelic effects of mescaline also arise from this switching station, which conditions a variety of al-tered states, psychotic and otherwise.

Another crucial structure in the reptilian brain is involved in the schizophrenic ASC—the *cerebellar vermis,* a worm-shaped trunk line of neurons that transmits information to and from the cerebellum. It is often underdeveloped in both schizophrenics and autistic children. The peach-sized cerebellum, a wrinkled protuberance tucked under the back end of the neocortex, was long thought to make no contribution to awareness as it quietly goes about its role of coordinating the body to move about gracefully. But recent research showed that stimulating this ancient brain structure excites pleasure centers and inhibits rage cen-ters in the higher limbic system. In turn, these limbic centers connect with complex sheets of neurons in the thinking neocortex, so that a mal-function in the cerebellum triggers a chain reaction that moves to higher centers.

Sensory-deprivation experiments demonstrate that in order to main-tain a stable sense of self, we must constantly integrate sensory experi-ence into our stream of feeling and thinking. To do so, we must have a healthy cerebellar-limbic-neocortical relay loop. Without it, we would perceive the world as a chaotic jumble of sensations and disconnected feelings. Because a newborn's cerebellum doesn't fully develop until af-ter birth, it is possible that during infancy rocking movements help the cerebellum connect with pleasure centers in the limbic system. Without this stimulation, a deprived infant may not learn to derive satisfaction from being near others, which will impair his social functioning later in life.

Both schizophrenics and late-stage manics suffer from body images and self-boundaries that won't stay put. During times of stress, their bodies may feel grotesquely deformed and their selfhood may merge with other people, or even animals. Typically, these disturbances can be detected in the early stages of a psychotic ASC, well before hallucinations and delusions emerge. An impaired cerebellar-limbic connection is the likely culprit, since any force that distorts information flowing along this vital pathway warps a person's subjective body image and self-boundary.

Each of the above anatomical deviations linked to psychotic ASCs can be observed with the naked eye, sometimes aided by modern imaging technology. We now turn from gross anatomy to a level of *function*. This molecular level is relatively more inaccessible, but is also profoundly involved in mediating states of consciousness linked to madness.

CHAPTER 6

The Chemistry of Madness

❖

*As we acquire more knowledge, things do not become more comprehensible,
but more mysterious.*

ALBERT SCHWEITZER

EARLY IN THE evening of September 21, 1988, a New York "street
person" quietly walked into St. Patrick's Cathedral in downtown
Manhattan. When the attending priest greeted him, he ranted incoherently. Fearing the disheveled stranger would become violent if provoked,
the priest ignored him, and the man wandered back to the crowded street
mumbling to himself.

His return visit was different. The man maintained an eerie silence
as he purposefully cast off his clothing and strode naked up the aisle.
When he encountered an elderly church usher, he grabbed an iron
stanchion and savagely bludgeoned the helpless man to death. He also
seriously injured a priest and a policeman who tried to restrain him before a police bullet brought his rampage to a fatal conclusion.

What human motive could spark such an inhumanly violent act? Was
his frenzy "commanded" by demonic voices known only to himself? In
his deranged state, could he have felt threatened by powerful religious
symbols within the cathedral? Or did his maniacal fury spring from a
subterranean source beyond our comprehension, one so primitive as to
be devoid of thought or reason? All we know is that he was a loner with
no friends. His dark secret remained nested deep in his soul to the end.

Modern science claims to be edging closer to solving the mystery of
such berserk acts by examining the chemistry of the brain. This view
holds that the madman was in thrall to outlaw brain hormones, probably

brought about by overactivity of *dopamine,* a chemical that is widely distributed throughout the human brain.

Are we to believe that human beings are so vulnerable that a slight shift in the concentration of a half-dozen hormones in the limbic system could transform the most self-controlled of us into raging killers? Is the only difference between heaven and hell a few molecules at the synapse? This chapter will look at the disquieting evidence that this may be partially true.

THE BRAIN AS COMPUTER

The technology of his time prompted Sigmund Freud to view the mind much as he viewed the brain, as a structure with discrete interconnected compartments: id, ego, and superego. But as scientists searched for the physical counterparts of the mind during the last three decades, they could no longer view the brain as a 1930s telephone switchboard with trunk lines connecting neatly divided compartments, like rooms in an office building.

Underlying the switchboard, scientists uncovered a deeper level of brain function—complex molecules engaged in chemical reactions that affect mood, thought, and emotion. This led them to a new model of the brain: as a computer. In this cybernetic analogy, tiny filaments of living tissue carry byte-sized packets of information digitally, using an on-off binary code that stores data in reverberating electrical circuits. At various points along the way, microscopic "resistors" speed up, slow down, or redirect the flow of encoded intelligence along billions of tortuous "circuits," some of which arch back upon themselves to provide feedback.

When we take a close look at the way the brain's neurons operate, a computer analogy becomes nearly irresistible. Each neuron is a specialized cell with an extension, called an *axon,* that may be several millimeters long. The neuron's job is to "fire" an electrical signal down the length of its axon. As the signal reaches the axon's end, it spreads through a multiplicity of tiny branches, each coming into close proximity with another neuron. Where the two approach there is a tiny cleft, a fluid-filled gap called a *synapse.* The importance of the 90 trillion synapses in a human brain cannot be overstated, for they are pivotal elements in the incredibly complex interplay between our physical being and the diffuse consciousness of the Spiritual Ground, both in madness and in health.

The synapse holds such a central role in brain function that many materialist scientists maintain that it is the birthplace of consciousness itself, that each synapse generates a single unit of consciousness that somehow emerges from the molecular rhythms within these tiny clefts. True to their computer model, many of these theoreticians believe the final "printout" to be our subjective experience. Although this materialist perspective is at a loss to explain how that magical conversion from the physical to the subjective might take place, it can help us understand how the brain interacts with the Ground to shape various psychotic ASCs.

There are about 100 billion neurons in an average human brain, and each of them is busy most of the time. When a neuron fires—and most do so continuously at a "resting" base rate of five or six times per second—the burst of energy arrives at the end of the axon where it triggers the release of one of several brain chemicals, called *neurotransmitters*, into the synapse. Like sparks jumping a gap, these neurotransmitters cross the synapse to signal the next neuron in sequence. Some neurotransmitters speed up the rate of firing of the receiving neuron to as high as fifty times per second; others slow it down to one or two times a second. The more receptor sites a neuron has, the more likely it is to change its rate when its favorite transmitter is close by.

The receptive end of each neuron has room for hundreds of synapses, each of which exerts a small influence upon its firing rate. In turn, each neuron governs the firing rates of hundreds of other neurons downstream by dispensing its own neurotransmitters. Once liberated, a molecule of neurotransmitter remains in the synapse for only a fraction of a second while it does its work. It is then either reabsorbed by its source neuron to be recycled, or broken down into waste products by scavenger enzymes that lie in wait in the synapse.

When an event, like taking certain herbs or medicines, upsets this delicate balance, vast chains of interconnected neurons down the line are affected. An altered state of consciousness results. This is why human beings have been fascinated since prehistoric times by neurotransmitter lookalikes from plants that alter consciousness by mimicking natural chemicals at the synapse. *Every* chemical agent that causes an ASC, from caffeine to Thorazine to heroin, does so by either mimicking or blocking the synaptic effects of one or another neurotransmitter, and therefore rerouting the energies of the Ground. Not surprisingly, the ASCs of mania, depression, and schizophrenia also follow the ebbs and flows of neurotransmitters in these tiny clefts.

So far, about thirty-five neurotransmitters have been discovered, their molecular structures analyzed, the enzymes that create and destroy them identified, their vulnerability to various drugs and medicines tested. Because the science of neurobiology is still in its adolescence, it seems certain that many more of these chemical messengers await detection. Although each of the known neurotransmitters probably plays some role in the shifts of thinking and feeling in psychosis, there are three that deserve special attention.

These are *norepinephrine,* known to be involved in mania and depression; *dopamine,* long a suspect in schizophrenia; and *serotonin,* which sets the feeling-tone underlying any state of consciousness and is involved in the psychedelic experience. To complicate matters, each of these influences the effects of the others, and each is itself modified by other brain messengers, such as the morphinelike endorphins. Although the complexity of the subject allows no more than a cursory examination of neurotransmitter function in a single chapter, it is worth taking a brief look at the role of these three chemicals in psychotic ASCs.

MANIA & NOREPINEPHRINE

Norepinephrine, the brain's form of adrenalin, is an agent of *arousal.* It performs its labor throughout all three brain levels, but it originates in the ancient reptilian brain. Here it is manufactured in quantity by a tiny cluster of cells embedded in the brain stem that send branches upward to engage a wide array of higher brain centers. These branching neurons are well positioned to regulate the degree of arousal in the whole brain. Our fluctuating daily levels of alertness, and even seasonal shifts of arousal, are under the dominion of this reptilian center.

Anything that stimulates norepinephrine activity in this ancient brain center boosts the firing rates of large numbers of neurons upstream in the limbic system and cortex. Subjectively, what follows is a quantitative increase in consciousness. Small increases usually result in a pleasant surge of energy and enhanced awareness; larger ones in a state of anxious restlessness; still larger ones in an intolerable internal pressure and an uncontrolled opening to the Ground that approaches psychotic intensity. Stimulants like cocaine and amphetamine, which at high doses induce maniclike ASCs, act by mimicking norepinephrine and tricking chains of neurons into boosting their firing rates.

Neuroscientists cannot directly measure the amount of norepinephrine active in the brain during an ASC. They must infer its activity by measuring its metabolic breakdown product, MHPG, in the fluid obtained from a spinal tap. A sense of well-being, creative energy, and enthusiasm accompany relatively small increases in MHPG. This desirable state holds as long as brain centers for thinking and feeling remain equally amplified.

But when a person enters a manic high, his level of MHPG rises far above normal, indicating increased norepinephrine production and breakdown. As a certain threshold of arousal is reached, *qualitative* shifts take over as other neurotransmitter systems are thrown off balance by excess norepinephrine. Some brain centers are then activated out of proportion to others. Thinking and feeling slip away from consensual modes, and the pleasant early manic buzz escalates into the distortions of a full-blown manic psychosis, tinged with a troublesome degree of paranoid irritability. Once this process gains momentum, there is little anyone can do to halt it, short of prescribing medicines. When the manic episode runs its course, MHPG cascades back toward the baseline as arousal diminishes. It then dips to subnormal levels during the ensuing depressive phase. When the cycle is complete, MHPG—and presumably its parent, norepinephrine—returns to a normal level along with the person's mood.

SCHIZOPHRENIA & DOPAMINE

Just as manic and depressive ASCs are tied to tidal shifts in norepinephrine, schizophrenic ASCs are linked to alterations in its sister neurotransmitter, dopamine. The development of the "dopamine hypothesis" by a team of researchers led by Solomon Snyder is a medical detective story of the first order that sheds light on the way brain chemicals affect states of consciousness, both psychotic and adaptive.

The first clue linking dopamine with schizophrenic ASCs came from heavy users of amphetamine, or "speed," a stimulant long favored by long-distance truck drivers and college students who seek a quick fix for fatigue or sleep deprivation. Although amphetamine initially induces a jolt of maniclike arousal by increasing norepinephrine activity, it does not cause one to develop the characteristic hallucinations and delusions of schizophrenia—immediately. However, as "speed tripping" gained popularity during the late 1960s, admissions officers of mental hospitals in the San Francisco area noticed a mysterious new syndrome.

They encountered an unmistakable epidemic of paranoid psychosis in the Haight-Ashbury area of that city. Even more striking was their observation that the symptoms of that usually tenacious ASC disappeared after a few days of hospitalization, even without antipsychotic-drug treatment. Except for its abbreviated course, this new syndrome—complete with auditory hallucinations, delusions of persecution, and fragmented speech—was indistinguishable from more ominous forms of paranoid schizophrenia. The common factor was that the "three-day psychotics" had been on "speed runs," street parlance for daily use of amphetamine for a week or more, often injected intravenously in escalating doses to postpone "crashing" as users grew tolerant of its energizing effects.

At first, scientists were skeptical that this commonly used "upper" was directly responsible for these temporary incursions into madness. A major objection was that amphetamine is known to reduce the time spent in the dream phase of sleep. Because prolonged sleep deprivation by itself gives rise to an ASC resembling paranoid schizophrenia, investigators surmised that what they were seeing was no more than a reaction that could be induced by anything that kept a person from dreaming.

This objection was soon put to rest by a daring experiment that would be impossible to repeat in today's more cautious climate. Researchers recruited a group of previous amphetamine users who had never been psychotic. They gave them ten milligrams of amphetamine every hour, day and night (a very large dose, even for experienced users). Every one of the subjects became floridly psychotic within two to five days, a length of time far short of that necessary to induce psychosis by sleep deprivation alone. Other researchers then fortified the link by showing that, even in small doses, amphetamine immediately increases schizophrenic symptoms in people who have already developed that ASC. The search for a specific mechanism was on.

A molecule of amphetamine bears a strikingly close resemblance to both norepinephrine and dopamine, which relays emotionally based information within the limbic system. Dopamine also governs the crucial circuit between the limbic system and the frontal lobes that allows feeling and thinking areas of the brain to communicate with each other. Dopamine and norepinephrine are metabolic "siblings," in that they are constantly transformed back and forth into each other by certain brain enzymes. These links led researchers to conclude that "speed" mimics norepinephrine, creating a short-lived maniclike ASC. Excess norepinephrine then gradually converts to dopamine. So taking large doses of amphetamine over several days not only stimulates norepinephrine activity, but also increases dopamine and eventually provokes a schizophreniclike ASC.

Intrigued by these early clues, investigators shifted their attention to a class of medicines, the *antipsychotics,* that diminish some of the more disturbing symptoms of schizophrenia. Because these drugs are quite biologically active and perturb almost every metabolic system in the body, the exact mechanism by which they affect schizophrenia had eluded researchers. If a direct link between antipsychotic drugs and dopamine could be demonstrated, the case linking dopamine with schizophrenia would be greatly strengthened.

Some antipsychotic drugs are much more potent than others in diminishing psychotic symptoms. Research on animals soon demonstrated that there is a direct relationship between the antipsychotic potency of these drugs and their ability to block the effects of dopamine. Moreover, the few antipsychotic drugs that are *ineffective* in reducing psychotic symptoms also have no effect on dopamine.

The next clue came from an unexpected direction. Psychotic patients who take antipsychotic drugs are often plagued by side effects that resemble the disfiguring tremors of Parkinson's disease. The more potent the drug in reducing psychotic symptoms, the more tremors it induces. They also knew that *real* Parkinson's patients have damage in a brain-stem center that uses dopamine to coordinate delicate movements. It was reasonable to conclude that antipsychotic drugs mimic Parkinson's disease by blocking dopamine in these same areas. The next step was to show that schizophrenic symptoms are brought about by an excess of dopamine.

To do this, researchers considered giving dopamine to healthy subjects to see if it would make them psychotic. But the dopamine molecule is too large to cross from the blood directly into the brain. When doctors who treat Parkinson's disease want to increase brain dopamine, they administer *L-dopa*, a medicine that the brain readily absorbs and then converts to dopamine. After a few weeks of L-dopa therapy, a series of side-effects emerged that neatly fit into one of the last gaps of the puzzle. Medicated patients complained of vivid nightmares, increased sexual urges, "forced thoughts," paranoia, and hallucinations.

At this point, all the investigators needed was proof that the brains of schizophrenics contained more dopamine than normal. But experiment after experiment failed to confirm that this was so. The idea still looked good on paper, but its proponents were stymied.

One last set of experiments seemed to close the case, at least for a while. New techniques that involve tagging chemicals with radioactive isotopes, then tracing their progress through the brain with a computerized array of scanners, showed that schizophrenics have an abnormally high number of dopamine *receptors* on some neurons. These extra receptors exaggerate dopamine's effect in limbic areas, even without an excess of dopamine itself. At that point it appeared that schizophrenia was caused by excess dopamine activity, and new and better medicines to block dopamine would be the ideal treatment.

THE DOPAMINE HYPOTHESIS FOR THE 1990s

Unfortunately, in its early form presented above, the dopamine hypothesis failed to account for several important facts about schizophrenia, such as why amphetamines—contrary to the theory—actually *reduce* symptoms in a minority of schizophrenics. Other unanswered questions were why the ASC does not become apparent until early adulthood, and why stress makes symptoms worse.

But recently, Daniel Weinberger of the National Institute of Mental

Health updated the dopamine hypothesis to confirm the view of schizo-phrenia as an imbalance in relations between old- and new-brain levels. Weinberger knew that there are important dopamine centers in the frontal lobes, where rational thought is processed, and in the limbic system, where wish-fulfilling fantasies, paranoia, and hallucinations take root. Both of these areas are switched on by a dopamine production center in the rep-tilian brain. Furthermore, healthy frontal lobes have the power to sup-press dopamine activity in the limbic system, which allows us to over-ride fantasy and strong emotion with reason and common sense. Even at its best, though, this faculty of "self-control" is limited.

Weinberger agreed with the early hypothesis that the so-called posi-tive symptoms of schizophrenia—hallucinations, delusions, perceptual distortions, and irrational fears—are associated with excess dopamine activity in the limbic system. However, he took this one step further to theorize that the "negative symptoms" of schizophrenia—blunted feeling-tone, withdrawal, lack of initiative, impaired intellectual capacity—resulted from *decreased* dopamine activity in the frontal cor-tex. This explained why dopamine-blocking antipsychotic medicines, which are so effective in reducing positive symptoms, often make nega-tive symptoms worse.

In this new theory, schizophrenic ASCs are accompanied by a fail-ure of the dopamine pathway from the brain stem to the frontal lobes, depriving them of this essential neurotransmitter. This sets up a chain reaction in which the frontal lobes are chronically *under*stimulated, dis-rupting their ability to process abstract information accurately. And be-cause healthy frontal lobes can partially dampen the fiery emotions of an overheated limbic system, when they are underactive the old-mammalian brain is liberated from their control and "runs amok." Al-though it is not ethically possible to demonstrate this effect in human beings, it has been shown to be true in rats. When researchers selec-tively destroy dopamine neurons in rats' frontal lobes, their limbic sys-tems quickly become hyperactive.

If a similar situation exists in humans, we can account for both posi-tive and negative symptoms of schizophrenic ASCs. It also explains why amphetamine—by increasing dopamine activity in the frontal lobes—weakens negative symptoms while making positive symptoms stronger.

Figure 6–1 helps make these connections clear.

This update of the dopamine hypothesis also helps to explain why the schizophrenic ASC usually does not emerge until early adulthood. Recent studies show that the frontal lobes are the last brain area to mature during childhood, and may be the only area that continues to mature throughout life. It is not surprising that the most highly evolved—the most human—areas should mature the latest. Mental tasks that

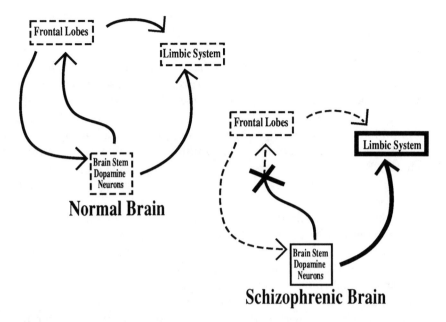

Normal Brain

Schizophrenic Brain

F I G U R E 6 – I : *On the left is a schematic representation of a normal brain in which a feedback system balances dopamine activity among the brain's three levels (see text). The diagram on the right portrays a schizophrenic brain in which dopamine-activated signals from the brain stem to the frontal lobes are disrupted. This inhibits frontal-lobe activity and breaks up the feedback loop. Without essential feedback from the frontal lobes, the brainstem mistakenly increases its dopamine stimulation to the limbic system, overactivating it, and creating conditions for hallucinations and paranoid delusions to emerge into awareness.*

activate the frontal cortex, such as developing long-term strategies for the future based on past experiences, are not characteristic of pre-adolescent thinking.

It follows that an individual could compensate for underactive frontal lobes only before early adulthood, a critical time of life when many new challenges come to the fore. The stress of independent existence in a competitive society could overwhelm fragile defenses that once held an adolescent's emotions in check and his selfhood intact. Yet such a deficiency would not be completely "silent" even during childhood. It would probably be associated with subtle abnormalities such as social awkwardness, extreme shyness, unmodulated fantasies, and odd patterns of thought. These are traits known to characterize the childhoods of many people who later develop severe forms of the schizophrenic ASC.

A schizophrenic's vulnerability to stress also pivots on the dopamine-sensitive frontal lobes. It has long been known that dopamine activity surges when an animal endures stress, such as pain or electric shock. Conceivably, the pathway from reptilian brain to frontal lobes evolved as a means of activating the frontal lobes during times of crisis, when it is important to survey the present in terms of the past so as to make rational choices for the future. Any breakdown in this pathway could render an individual unable to respond to danger. Moreover, when the frontal lobes are cut off from the reptilian brain, they are incapable of providing feedback, leading to rampant limbic overactivity and a psychotic ASC. In this way, the symptoms of schizophrenia may be viewed as a *diminished response to stress on a higher level, accompanied by excessive responses on a lower level.*

Like all theories in the neurosciences, the dopamine hypothesis is inadequate to fully account for the impenetrable complexities of the brain's role in shaping psychotic experience. For instance, we know that there are at least three kinds of dopamine receptors, and that dopamine and norepinephrine interact as they regulate thinking and feeling, so that whatever unbalances one also skews the other. To confuse the situation even more, another mood-regulating neurotransmitter, serotonin, also interacts with dopamine neurons and is involved in certain ASCs, such as those curious states associated with LSD. Serotonin is an *inhibitory* neurotransmitter that prevents other brain systems from running wild and overloading their circuits. Anything that interferes with this check-and-balance system, especially in the limbic system, produces an opening to the Ground that combines the "highs" of mania, the strange ecstasies of temporal-lobe epilepsy, and even the transcendent bliss of mystics.

A SELF-INDUCED PSYCHOTIC ASC

So far, we have seen that dopamine activity is increased in the limbic systems of people experiencing schizophrenic ASCs, while norepinephrine activity runs wild during manic ASCs. But exactly how these neurotransmitters interact to change one's state of consciousness is more difficult to determine.

One bold neuroscientist tested his imaginative theory of the roles of dopamine and norepinephrine in madness by an extraordinary self-experiment. Ernest Hartmann proposed that for a schizophrenic ASC to take hold, both high dopamine activity *and* low norepinephrine activity must be present simultaneously. In other words, a change in the *ratio* of these neurotransmitters underlies what he called the "basic deficit" of schizophrenia. He argued that norepinephrine *alone* mediates higher mental functions, such as focusing attention, abstract thought, and placing memories in their proper context. To maintain stable selfhood, adequate levels of that neurotransmitter must be present.

Hartmann knew that in a normal brain, dopamine is slowly converted to norepinephrine by an enzyme, DBH. But if levels of DBH are inadequate to catalyze this conversion, dopamine could accumulate to excess. It would then release a relentless aggressive pressure, a "push" toward action, an insistent but unfocused restlessness, a feeling that danger is lurking nearby. And because norepinephrine is relatively deficient, there is little consensual-reality processing to help in recognizing the threat. Hartmann reasoned that if such an imbalance were continued over years, it would lead to an unstable sense of self. Stress, or perhaps the hormonal high tide of puberty, then triggers even more dopamine release, further unbalances the ratio, and leads to delusional attempts to rationalize this unnamed dread. But how could he show that disturbing the ratio results in a psychotic ASC?

Hartmann devised a risky experiment that he believed would cause a schizophreniclike ASC by raising dopamine levels while at the same time lowering norepinephrine by inhibiting DBH. But because both L-dopa (which increases brain dopamine) and fusaric acid (which inhibits DBH) have uncomfortable side effects, and in combination pose dangers that make human experimentation perilous, he chose to test the effects of the two chemicals on his own brain.

First taking each agent by itself, Hartmann suffered no more than a stuffy nose and headache. Then on two separate occasions he tried the combination. He described his first experience with low doses.

> I experienced alertness and difficulty getting to sleep, then a nap with a vivid image of someone trying to get into the house. I could not be sure whether this was a dream or a waking fantasy. And I had a half-hour period characterized by a feeling that my mind was racing, and by a generalized, unspecified fear at times coming close to terror.

Finding that he had no lasting ill effects, a month later he tried larger doses of L-dopa and fusaric acid in combination:

> Time passed slowly. I felt good, euphoric for a time. Noises around me seemed especially loud; folding up a paper bag made a noise like thunder. I had a period of one hour or so during which I was constantly pushed, pulled, and distracted—feeling I had to do one thing, but then noticing something else I should get to first, and then a third thing

on the way to that. This was a "pushed" or "driven" state very unusual for me. I felt distinctly weak, pushed around, not in control. I experienced a brief odd fantasy that a good friend (who was to check up on me during the drug experience) would come over and steal things from my house . . . Then my body appeared to be shrinking; I felt afraid to be in a small room alone. All this passed spontaneously after a few minutes . . . I experienced states compatible with a push toward psychosis, or an early phase of psychosis, which I have not experienced at any other time.

Hartmann's daring experiment inspires a thought exercise in which we might imagine ourselves from early adolescence consistently reacting to minor stress by entering an agitated ASC like the one described above. At first we might try to compensate in ways that would seem rather strange to others. Later, evidence of the original ASC would become hard to separate from our defenses against it. Our attempts to cope might eventually mean regression to a dependent existence. However, if we were blessed with unusual intelligence or talents, along with a supportive environment and self-soothing skills, the enhanced energy, along with loose self-boundaries and regular infusions of the Ground, might lead us onto a path well trodden by creative artists, religious prophets, and an occasional mental-health professional.

Hartmann's experiment is unlikely to be repeated on a large scale with human subjects. Nevertheless, it provides us with a tantalizing variation on the dopamine hypothesis that helps to account for many of the core symptoms of the schizophrenic ASC. It also suggests why a genetically transmitted increase in dopamine activity does not always lead to psychosis. Rather, a person with an inherited tendency toward psychotic ASCs, though having higher-than-normal dopamine activity that fosters peculiar ways of thinking and feeling, must also develop a deficiency of norepinephrine before crossing the line into madness.

In sum, each of these complex theories points directly toward limbic overactivity as the primary physical correlate of schizophrenic ASCs. Recall for a moment what we know of the limbic system's role within the human psyche: the seat of our emotions, the theater of our dreams, a filter of sensory experience, a likely receptor site for extrasensory perception, the bidirectional link between mind and body, the guardian of our memories, the regulator of pain and pleasure, a bridge to our evolutionary past. We can see that there is little about the psychotic experience that cannot be understood in terms of an old-mammalian brain run wild.

IS MADNESS PSYCHOSOMATIC?

This is not to say that a genetically programmed abundance of limbic dopamine is the *cause* of schizophrenia in all cases. At this point we reach the same chicken-and-egg conundrum that fuels the ancient debate between materialist and spiritual worldviews. Despite the compelling evidence that aberrant neurotransmitter activity accompanies psychotic ASCs, the mysterious link between mind and brain continues to defy reduction to simple cause and effect in either direction.

The view put forth in this book—that complex events within the brain *interact* with a universal field of consciousness to produce the unique attributes of the human mind—encompasses a greater range of facts about madness than does either the spiritual or material view alone. Mind and brain operate as a *unitary system* in which changes in one go hand in hand with changes in the other. Within such a unity, cause-and-effect relationships blur beyond distinction, and the best we can say is that any force that changes either brain or mind also changes the other. This means that psychotic ASCs are *psychosomatic*, a word that honors the wedding of the mental and physical aspects of our being.

Modern brain research demonstrates the fate of the human mind when genetic endowment leads to a prolonged ASC that turns the mind away from the only reality it has learned to live with. Yet the same outcome could follow when a biochemically normal brain is repeatedly exposed during childhood to erroneous information about people, sex, how to gain worldly power, and how to structure social relationships.

Although it is easier to demonstrate that physically altering the brain changes subjective experience, there is mounting evidence that mental events also leave their imprints within the brain. The old view that a computerlike brain's hardwiring is fixed at birth, or even at maturity, is now passé. Neuroscience has demonstrated again and again that life experience is at least as powerful as genetic programming in shaping both the cellular architecture and chemical activity of the brain. In other words, *plasticity* is a fact of brain functioning, even at the relatively coarse level of the cell and synapse. As science discovers more about the brain's subtle workings at the subatomic level, we will dramatically increase our understanding of the mind's eternal dance with matter.

The pre- and postbirth growth of an infant's nervous system does not proceed apart from experience. Human interaction is the primary element of that experience, arguably even before birth. An infant deprived of personal contact will not sit up, speak, or walk, and it usually dies or grows up to be retarded. A loving tone of voice, a gentle touch, and an admiring gaze are critical in organizing the microstructure of the brain. This lends at least some credence to the psychoanalytic idea that childhood traumas lead to neurosis or psychosis later in life.

This process of rewiring the computer does not end with infancy. A watchmaker refines his delicate touch under a magnifying glass. A jet pilot sharpens his reflexes in countless combat simulations. A Trappist monk spends his life in silent regard of his own being. Their repetitive experiences modify their brains to reflect their skills. If we were to examine a mechanic's brain under a microscope, we would find more nerve branches in areas that control finger and hand agility. Musicians grow more branches in centers that process sound. More branches mean more synapses, which mean a greater potential for directing the energies of the Ground along one's chosen life path.

From the raw material of neurons and synapses, our accumulated thoughts, feelings, and actions sculpt a unique and ever-changing frieze that subtly captures our personal life history. So we might speculate about the effect on a growing brain of an environment in which a child is alternately praised and punished for the same act, or in which double meanings and duplicity are the norm. Considering this, it may not be so surprising that a hereditary basis cannot be found in *most* people prone to psychotic ASCs.

A psychosomatic interaction between mind and brain can work for good or ill. For instance, a person may be born with unusual activity in brain centers that influence his thinking and feeling. Because of this inheritance, he may develop a psychotic ASC at some stressful time of his life. Or he may be fortunate enough to have parents who consistently soothe him during early life, which could permanently reset his limbic dopamine receptors below the threshold for psychosis.

Another person may be born with genetically programmed normal levels of brain messengers. Yet a lack of affirming responses or harsh negativity by his parents may stimulate overgrowth of receptors in brain centers associated with aversive emotions. His failure to learn coping skills may render him just as vulnerable to psychotic ASCs as a genetically predisposed individual. These slowly ticking "time bombs" set the conditions for later regression in response to stresses unique to early adulthood. The end result may look similar, but the causes and treatments would be significantly different.

Furthermore, certain intense spiritual practices, such as prolonged meditation, might increase sensitivity to dopamine in brain areas where attention is focused, or a decrease in norepinephrine in other areas that are repeatedly suppressed. This could predispose a person to temporary psychotic ASCs—so-called spiritual emergencies—that either presage openings to higher realms of mind or, if misunderstood and pathologized, precipitate a downward spiral into madness.

To look at it another way, under certain circumstances the brain becomes a target organ for a psychosomatic process, in much the same way that constant worry alters the chemistry of the stomach to cause an ulcer. A preschizophrenic child protecting himself from a crazy-making environment may shun abstract thinking and interpersonal intimacy— mental activities based in neocortical areas highest in the evolutionary scale. From disuse, these areas weaken, synapses disappear, and the self-center retreats to lower physical and mental planes. Vicious cycles then augment a dizzying regressive spin that further alters brain structure and function.

As regression proceeds, the limbic system gains dominion over the psyche, its level of arousal mediated by shifting tides of dopamine, norepinephrine, and serotonin. As conscious energies detour from neocortical to limbic planes, the lower centers are inadequate to sustain the firm self-boundaries that are necessary for participation in modern societies. As self-boundaries keeping the Ground at bay gradually become more porous, there is a further inpouring, and the unprepared person is overwhelmed by unfamiliar elements of consciousness. Depending on the individual's preparation for the ASC, these shifts may be temporary or permanent, wholesome or morbid, uplifting or destructive.

CHAPTER 7

Madness & Drugs: The Highs & Lows

❖

If your only tool is a hammer, you tend to treat everything like a nail.
ABRAHAM MASLOW

PASSIONATE ADVOCATES OF one class of mind-altering chemicals declare that theirs cast open the portals of heaven. Staunch apologists for a second group of equally powerful chemicals insist that theirs slam shut the gates of hell.

These groups refer to what are arguably the two most controversial consciousness-altering substances known to humanity: psychedelics and antipsychotic medicines (neuroleptics). Each catapults the psyche to a polar extreme of awareness. And as is true for all agents containing such power, the opportunities for misuse nearly surpass the benefits.

Psychedelics stretch the boundaries of the self to the point where the power of the Ground can no longer be held at bay. In so doing, they create an unparalleled opening that can forever expand one's worldview or plunge an unprepared adventurer deep into the abyss of ego loss. Neuroleptics, by contrast, retract and fortify self-boundaries, sealing off the self from the subconscious mind and from its Source. If the former medicines can act as agents of transcendence, the latter can act as agents of mercy. Both kinds of medicines have a place in the armamentarium of a healer of the mind. And despite the fierce antipathy that each elicits from those who have been harmed by their misuse, both are here to stay.

The efflorescence of psychedelic use during the 1960s hardened the battle lines between orthodox psychiatry and its detractors in the antipsychiatry movement. Theorists like R.D. Laing who had positive psychedelic experiences tend to value psychotic ASCs as kinds of protracted acid trips with mystical import. In contrast, people who never felt benefit from an ASC tend to view alterations in consciousness as intrinsically undesirable. Although the former group sees little danger in expanding consciousness with psychedelics, it often takes great exception to those who would use medicines to diminish a troublesome ASC. In contrast, people who find it desirable to abolish disagreeable ASCs with antipsychotic medicines feel that it is criminal to expand consciousness with chemical agents.

The task of this chapter is to penetrate the haze of misinformation, overstatement, and outright hysteria that has condensed around these psychoactive substances, in the hope that healers of future decades can choose from among several precise technologies to match the specific state of consciousness, stage of personal development, and degree of regression of those in their care.

ANTIPSYCHOTIC DRUGS: PRO & CON

It is an oddity of human nature that any craftsperson tends to overvalue tools to which he or she has access, and to undervalue others. Because psychiatrists possess an exclusive franchise for prescribing antipsychotic medicines, they tend toward their hasty use, resolutely extinguishing any unplanned opening to Ground consciousness by manipulating the brain with neuroleptics or lithium.

This is far from saying that antipsychotic medicines are inappropriate responses to all psychotic ASCs. For people caught up in malignantly regressive or impossibly expansive ASCs, medicines can mercifully restore contact with consensual reality and allow a fragmented self to reorganize. Even in less extreme instances, it is hardly a trivial matter to remain in a psychotic ASC for several months of one's life. To do so scars the personality by retarding personal and spiritual development.

Even antipsychiatrists begrudgingly acknowledge the pitiful lack of alternative treatments for the hundreds of thousands of people who spontaneously develop psychotic ASCs each year. Despite their shortcomings, neuroleptics and lithium are preferable to the addictive and less effective barbiturates routinely used in past decades to subdue psychotic people. Historically, the introduction of antipsychotic medicines has humanized the grotesque atmosphere of psychiatric hospitals and saved countless lives. It is certainly progress that the back wards of mental hospitals are no longer filled with terrified patients thrashing about in straitjackets as they scream and rage into the night.

Fill a conference hall, however, with nonmedical psychotherapists, especially humanistic or transpersonally oriented ones, mention the word *Thorazine,* and the room will resound with groans of repugnance as eyes roll heavenward: "There they go again, those heavy-handed shrinks, tranquilizing their helpless patients into zombie land! Are they too blind to see what psychotic people *really* need?"

This clash of opinion revolves around each side's difficulty in distinguishing malignant psychotic ASCs that respond only to physical intervention from benign ASCs that yield to psychological or spiritual tactics. It is inhumane to withhold medicines from a tormented person locked into a self-perpetuating regressive slide that is immune to higher-level interventions. Yet it can be equally destructive to force a temporarily fragmented self that is learning to cope with unfamiliar areas of the Ground back to unquestioning conformity with the constricted reality of the consensus.

Part of the problem is that it is not always easy to distinguish among the various ways of being psychotic. But another difficulty, resting squarely on the shoulders of mainstream psychiatry, is simply that antipsychotic medicines are often given in excessive doses for too long a time. And worse, they are occasionally forced upon people who don't need them at all. Let's take a look at the effects of these imperfect medicines on the mind and body so that we may consider how to use them well.

MAGIC BULLETS OR ZOMBIE POTIONS?

From ancient times, physicians have been fascinated by nostrums that restructure the psyche. So it is not surprising that they would be eager to try these charms on people in unremitting psychotic ASCs. The priests of Æsculapius soothed their disturbed patients with opium, and medieval witches plied their trade with a vast pharmacopoeia of powders and tonics derived from belladonna, mandrake, and other herbs.

Modern antipsychotic medicines trace their origin to a red-flowered plant called snakeroot, which has long been used by southern Asians as a palliative for the psychotic ASC known locally as moonsickness. Snakeroot contains a sedative that became the forerunner of today's neuroleptics—orthodox psychiatry's "treatment of choice" for hospitalized psychotics since the early 1950s.

Although neuroleptics are best known for reducing schizophrenic symptoms, they also restore a consensus orientation to many other psychotic ASCs, whether those arise from extreme mania, brain trauma, bad drug trips, senile confusion, or toxic delirium. Many maladaptive ASCs are accompanied by excess activity of the neurotransmitter dopamine, which kindles an inner agitation that gradually erodes consensual thinking and feeling. In the brain, disturbances of dopamine are prominent in the very areas where neuroleptics are most active. Psychotic people who take neuroleptics lose the volume of feeling that crystallizes around their delusional ideas, which then dissolve back into that murky reservoir of benign quirkiness borne by us all.

Today there are about twenty neuroleptics marketed, each varying in potency and side effects. A few of their trade names are Thorazine, Stelazine, Mellaril, Prolixin, Navane, and Haldol. Although they are all tranquilizers in a sense, they differ from minor tranquilizers like Valium, Ativan, and Xanax, which have little effect on dopamine and merely reduce anxiety, leaving the underlying psychotic symptoms intact. Neuroleptics are therefore unique in their ability to seal off the self from the Ground, and thereby reduce the more dramatic manifestations of psychosis. But by isolating the psyche from its vitalizing Source, they also massively interfere with the feeling system.

In other words, neuroleptics counteract a psychotic ASC by inducing its *reciprocal* ASC. Rather than being intoxicated by the Ground, the self becomes alienated from the Ground's enlivening energies. Although neuroleptics decrease anxiety, aggression, and hallucinations, they aggravate the *negative* symptoms of psychosis—apathy, numbed emotions, withdrawal, impoverished thought, avoidance of change, lack of pleasure responses, deadening of creativity, and depression. These defensive late-stage effects of madness signal a contraction of the self-boundary and a compensatory withdrawal from the Ground.

One of my patients—whom I probably overmedicated—described her experience with neuroleptics.

> The pills only subtract, never add anything. They close in my life from both sides and make me less aware. When I'm having those weird feelings or falling apart, that's okay, but they keep me from tuning in to the good things, too. They cloud up my thinking and my senses like a smoke screen between me and the world. When I take them I feel less of a person, less than all I am.

Another patient had a different reaction.

> Man, I was really out of it before you gave me this medicine. You know, I couldn't get rid of the nutty idea that I

should kill my child because I thought he was possessed by the devil. Now the voices leave me alone so that I can sleep and think my own thoughts. My wife is giving me another chance, and my boss let me come back to work. I feel like a regular person again instead of another screwball on a mission to save the world. I can live with the side effects a lot easier than I could live with those crazy thoughts and feelings.

Clearly, the question of whether to give neuroleptics to a person in a psychotic ASC is complex. Nonmedical healers often work closely with psychiatrists and are in an ideal position to advise them about their patients' responses to medicines and make recommendations about raising or lowering doses. Any healer—physician or not—who chooses to work with a psychotic population should become expert on the appropriate use of these medicines and the dangers of their misuse.

MALIGN CONSEQUENCES

Although neuroleptics are unparalleled in controlling the florid symptoms of psychosis, it is no accident that they are despised by militant groups of ex–mental patients who campaign for their banishment. All medicines have side effects, but neuroleptics are especially biologically active, perturbing nearly every system in the body. Some side effects are relatively mild, such as a dry mouth, constipation, and accelerated heart rhythm. Others, however, can be permanently disfiguring and even life threatening.

About two decades ago, the psychiatric profession was shocked to learn of the alarming number—as many as 20 percent—of chronic mental patients who developed *tardive dyskinesia,* an often irreversible disorder caused by taking high doses of neuroleptics over many years. These people lose the ability to control their facial movements, especially the tongue, which takes on a grotesque life of its own as it protrudes and twists about uncontrollably. There is yet no cure for this incapacitating side effect, which results from chronically blocking dopamine in brain areas that have nothing to do with the schizophrenic ASC.

Even worse is the *neuroleptic malignant syndrome,* a rare but often fatal combination of high fever, muscular rigidity, and rampant hypertension. Neuroleptics also adversely impact the liver, heart, bone marrow, immune system, sexual capacity, vision, and the parasympathetic nervous system. In keeping with their dopamine-blocking effects, neuroleptics cause side effects resembling Parkinson's disease—tremors, restless legs, immobile facial expression, and rigid muscles. This side effect is so disagreeable that psychiatrists feel obliged to prescribe a second group of drugs to counteract it.

About half of all people given a single dose of any neuroleptic refuse to take a second, apparently preferring a psychotic existence to the effects of the medicine. (This is a decision that courts are increasingly granting psychiatric patients.) But it is not hard to spot people with impending difficulty shortly after they begin taking a neuroleptic if one simply takes the trouble to ask them how they are feeling. Most are experiencing an extremely unpleasant side effect known as *akathisia*, which is superimposed on their original ASC.

Akathisia is a restless feeling of impending doom brought on by a keyed-up tension that demands release through movement. But there is no relief to be found in any position. A person so afflicted anxiously rocks from foot to foot while standing in one spot. He will say that he feels wound up like a tightly coiled spring. Overworked psychiatrists often dismiss this side effect as just another aberration of a sick mind—an inexcusable empathic failure on their part that infuriates and alienates the sufferer, often permanently. It is likely that people who have been treated this way are behind the legal battles over the right to refuse medication.

Despite these well-publicized dangers, some psychiatric emergency wards practice *rapid neuroleptization,* a technique based on the premise that an acute psychosis is always a medical emergency. The goal is to abbreviate an expensive hospital stay by injecting large doses of neuroleptics every hour until evidence of "normalcy" is observed. The dazed patient is then quickly shunted back to the environment in which he developed the ASC in the first place, and given more neuroleptics to prevent the ASC from sneaking back. The idea is that when obvious symptoms are absent, the disease is no longer troublesome. Any attempts to make sense of the aborted inner journey are considered superfluous.

This battlefield psychology delights bureaucrats concerned with cost-effectiveness tables. But the result is usually a confused patient, terrified by his recent exposure to the unbridled and unfamiliar power of the Ground, with no understanding of the life events that overwhelmed him. What motivation remains for him to reach out for the meaning of his experience is further compromised by high doses of long-acting neuroleptics that dull sensory and psychological sensitivity.

Clearly, the decision to so profoundly disturb the brain and body chemistry of a person in a psychotic ASC should not be made with impunity. Rather, these medicines need to be used *artfully.*

ARTFUL HEALING

For any healer, *artfulness* implies a deeply empathic awareness of a patient's state of consciousness, especially a recognition that the days immediately following a first psychotic break are a critical period during which a healer's responses have long-term consequences. In the stormy early phase of a psychotic ASC, the patient makes a desperate attempt to orient himself to an unaccustomed opening to the Ground. This is an opening that he may experience again at some time in the future. He will actively seek meaning in this awesome life event, often by forming delusions cast in a religious or metaphysical context. Judgments and interpretations given by surrounding helpers and healers go a long way in determining how he feels from that time on about himself in relation to his Source. At that moment he needs to maintain sensitivity and awareness by retaining access to all his psychological resources.

During such a crisis, it is easy for a physician to use chemicals to alter consciousness. But in some cases, this may interfere with a patient's ultimately learning to use consciousness to alter chemicals. Artfulness therefore requires giving antipsychotic medicines only to those patients whose psychotic ASC renders them unable or unwilling to benefit from higher-level interventions, and respectfully soliciting feedback from them about the effects and side effects. The artful use of any psychoactive agent means knowing when to reduce the dose as well as having the courage to stop all medicines so as to reassess the original need.

Signs of excessive doses are easy to recognize. Patients know these as the "zombie effect"—inattentiveness to one's surroundings, diminished ability to think abstractly, loss of spontaneity and creativity, emotional numbing, indifference to the future, clouding of consciousness. In other words, overmedication causes exactly what we would expect from a severely contracted self that had been abruptly cut off from the enlivening energies of the Spiritual Ground.

Therefore, an artful healer recognizes that neuroleptics should be given at the lowest dose necessary to reduce the ASC to manageable proportions. This usually requires risking a temporary return of symptoms as the healer seeks to determine the minimum effective dose. It also means educating the patient to adjust his own dose according to his fluctuating needs, which may change weekly, or even daily.

Authoritarian hospital administrators recoil in horror from such a patient-centered approach, fearing a return to the days of Bedlam. Some argue that the ASC must be zealously eradicated, a goal that is often inconsistent with the patient's felt needs. The patient may desire only a *partial* return to the consensus state, wherein active fantasies and feelings are preserved until they can be integrated. Of course, in some cases a patient desires immediate relief from intense discomfort, and this should also be respected.

There is little basis for the common belief that giving medicines is incompatible with higher-level therapies, for the two interventions can often go together. People seized by extreme shifts of consciousness are often too confused, frightened, or combative to be reached by even the most sensitive efforts to help them integrate their ASC. Sometimes just "a kiss of Haldol" is all that is needed to reduce paranoia a notch or two, thereby enhancing receptivity to psychological or spiritual therapies. These, in turn, can prepare these people to stop the medicine well before they become withdrawn, apathetic, and depressed.

Fortunately, heavy-handed pill pushing is growing unfashionable among younger psychiatrists, especially those who keep up with their profession's journals. Research confirms that we can boost the odds for a lasting restoration of the self if we go light on antipsychotic medicines for the sake of gradual integration of the psychotic experience. For certain patients, no medicines are necessary at all. Even for chronically psychotic people, research has demonstrated time and again that in many cases psychotic symptoms actually *improve* when medicines are reduced.

During periods of stress—say, from changing apartments or starting a new job—dopamine activity increases in the brain. In predisposed people, disruptive psychotic symptoms may increase along with it. But if an individual learns to recognize these signs early on, he can then adjust his neuroleptic dose upward according to his level of comfort. Conversely, signs of the "zombie effect" mean that the dose is too high; it can usually be safely reduced by an increment or two. An artful healer makes an alliance with those patients who can assume the risks and responsibilities of managing their own states of consciousness as he teaches them how to cope with the expansions and contractions of their psyches.

For example, one of my patients, a junior-college student, found that he could tolerate occasionally hearing voices while studying, and he preferred this symptom to the dulling of mental acuity and memory caused by neuroleptics. But as final exams neared, his auditory hallucinations grew intolerably distracting, so he called to ask my advice. I suggested that carefully measured doses of Mellaril at bedtime might keep the voices in check while not causing the same degree of psychic dulling as when there was less stress. Because he was athletic, I also suggested that he slightly increase his daily running mileage to help him discharge excess psychic energy and to help maintain a regular sleep pattern. After he successfully finished the semester, he and I again conferred and agreed to cut back on his neuroleptic dose.

Yet it would be simplistic to assert that all people in psychotic ASCs can make such responsible decisions about starting and stopping medicines or adjusting their doses without input from a psychiatrist. When this was tried at a research hospital, patients tended to greatly underestimate their need and often relapsed, with disastrous personal consequences. Some people become violent or suicidal without their medicines, and courts often judge their psychiatrists to be legally responsible for their patients' actions if they withhold neuroleptics.

So the role of a healer who works with antipsychotic medicines is to balance their positive and negative effects from an objective position unavailable to his patient, being attentive to the patient's personal estimation of the quality of his life. Like insulin, neuroleptics are only symptom-relieving agents; they are far from curative. Reducing delusions and hallucinations may be more important to the community, but avoiding negative symptoms—often undervalued in thinking about dosage—may be much more important to the patient.

There is also a significant minority of people experiencing psychotic ASCs for whom neuroleptics are definitely harmful. These are people who have reached a relatively advanced stage of personal development and are struggling against inner or outer barriers to the next step forward. A temporary psychotic regression gains time for the psyche to "regroup." Here the therapeutic task is not to force conformity to society's norms, but to help the person learn to maintain awareness of those norms while not surrendering his advance. We return to this idea in chapter 12.

At the opposite end of the spectrum, there are many people who undeniably benefit from taking neuroleptics in the long term. These are: (1) those whose regression has followed a malignantly disabling course; (2) those who prior to regressing had not mastered a workable stage of personal or spiritual development; (3) those who lack the will or resources to withstand the rigors of higher-level therapies designed to foster liberation; and (4) those whose ASC is so disruptive of self-control that they pose a violent danger to society or themselves.

The statistics for people who fall into the latter four categories are impressive. Dozens of studies comparing relapse rates for schizophrenics who take neuroleptics versus those given placebos indicate that as many as 80 percent of placebo users relapse within two years, compared with as few as 20 percent of schizophrenics on neuroleptics. Alternative therapists ignore such evidence at the peril of those in their care. Yet a second look at these numbers reveals their flip side: 20 percent or more—an important minority—of people whose psychotic ASC is persistent enough to warrant that most dreaded of psychiatric diagnoses *do not* benefit from neuroleptics. If they do not benefit from them, it is safe to conclude that they are harmful for this group. For people whose psychotic ASC does not meet the stringent criteria for schizophrenia, the numbers would be far higher.

LITHIUM: THE EARTH ELEMENT

Alternative healers who condemn synthetic medicines such as neuroleptics as "unnatural" have trouble including lithium on their list of artificial bad guys. Lithium—from the Greek word for *stone*—is one of the basic metallic elements of the earth's crust, more common than lead or zinc, and allied to sodium and potassium. It is found in tobacco, sugar cane, and seaweed, and it has been identified as existing inside the sun.

Lithium carbonate, the salt of this highly reactive element, has been used since the late 1960s to dampen the extreme mood swings of the manic-depressive ASC, for which it is about 80 percent effective. More recently, psychiatrists willing to experiment with alternatives to neuroleptics are finding that lithium also has a general antipsychotic effect in some, but not all, schizophrenic ASCs. Like the neuroleptics, lithium cuts with a double-edged sword.

Millions of manic individuals whose careers and marriages have been wrecked by flights into the rarefied air of hyperaroused consciousness are grateful for lithium's grounding effects. Although most predisposed people would give up their milder "hypomanic" inflations of self only under protest, most are happy to forego episodic excursions into bankruptcy or jail brought on by full-blown manic attacks. Administered under carefully controlled conditions, lithium has the power to ground a manic episode as it takes wing and also to quash subsequent episodes. Each genetically predisposed individual faces the portentous question of whether this induced stability is worth the price.

About half of all people who have manic ASCs decide at one time or another that it is *not* worth it, and about a third stay with that choice for life. For unlike its cousins sodium and potassium, with which people impetuously dust their food, lithium can be toxic to several systems of the body. Natural or not, lithium must be used only with precise awareness of these effects.

Some of lithium's side effects are mental, others physical. The mental disturbances occur first and are what manic patients complain about most. Unlike most people in schizophrenic ASCs, manics feel great—*really* great—and they resent anything that deflates their high.

They complain that lithium makes them feel dull and uninspired, that it interferes with memory and spontaneity and deadens creative urges. Some, whose manic ASC led them to believe that they had acquired telepathic abilities, feel that lithium seals off that partial opening to the Ground. Sometimes they find that their friends and spouses don't enjoy their company as much. They tell them that they've lost their spark.

Yet when people in the ordinary state of consciousness take lithium, they usually don't notice very much at all. This is quite different from the neuroleptics, which induce an ASC characterized by indifference, loss of abstract thinking, and dulling of emotions no matter what the state of consciousness of the person who takes them is. Because the manic opening is initially to higher levels of Ground consciousness, in sharp contrast with schizophrenic openings to lower levels, manics fondly remember their glimpse of life beyond the mundane. Ordinary consciousness seems prosaic, empty, and—least tolerable to manics— boring. Although the sweet nectar of early mania may ultimately turn bitter, the prospect of never sipping it again proffers stagnation of self and depression, feelings with which most manics are all too familiar.

The postmanic state is one that especially calls for spiritual practice of a kind that offers a real prospect of reorienting oneself to the vitalizing energies of the Ground. In contrast to a majority of schizophrenics, whose ASC arrests personal growth, many manics have achieved a level of development in which involvement in advanced spiritual practice is feasible. Each time an *artful* psychiatrist reaches for his prescription pad, he also encourages some form of spiritual practice as compensation for a disheartening loss. If he is unable to point the way toward eventual reconnection with the Ground himself, his task is to find others who can and to solicit their help.

If he neglects this task, his patient's depression, which naturally follows an abrupt closure to the Ground, will soon remind him. The depression that follows a manic episode is of the worst sort, a hellish contracture of self that darkens the light of consciousness to the point that suicide seems to offer the only hope of surcease. Because lithium is not very effective in damping the depressive phase of the ASC, simple mercy compels psychiatrists to prescribe a second drug, an antidepressant. Antidepressants afford relief from the worst symptoms of depression, but they have their own side effects and can trigger another manic episode.

Any substance powerful enough to alter consciousness so dramatically must somehow affect brain function. Although its precise metabolic alchemy is obscure, lithium seems to reset the brain's internal clocks. These regulate our rhythmic sleep cycles, the daily ebbs and flows of various hormones, and our seasonal fluctuations of moods. In a way yet to be discovered, the cyclical rhythms of the bipolar ASC are tied to these biological metronomes.

Although lithium when carefully monitored is less physically toxic over the long run than neuroleptics, even its most fervent advocates would be hard pressed to call it health food. In some patients it disrupts kidney and thyroid functioning, so these must be regularly monitored. Some people taking lithium gain weight, lose hair, and develop acne. Because of its harmful effects on a fetus, it is strictly forbidden for pregnant women and for anyone who is trying to get pregnant.

For these reasons, many people at risk for mania try to tough out their mood swings. The helplessness that a psychiatrist might feel in this situation may lead him to give up on these patients, for experience has taught that psychotherapy is impotent to halt a manic attack once it gains momentum. In addition, the first mental capacity forfeited in early mania is *insight* that trouble is brewing. Manics are notorious deniers.

Nevertheless, there are opportunities to help in other ways. If a healer is actively involved in his patients' lives, he can teach them or their families to recognize a manic spiral in its early stages. He may then—with great difficulty—convince his patients to try lithium "just for the duration." He also can teach manic-prone patients to protect their regular sleep rhythms, for even one night of sleep deprivation can precipitate a vicious circle that leads to a manic ASC. Jet lag following east-west travel is also notorious for resetting the brain's internal clocks and triggering mania. Manic patients must shun the use of amphetamine and cocaine, which are especially hazardous for people predisposed to psychotic ASCs.

Facing the obvious drawbacks of inducing chemical conformity to accepted norms of consciousness, psychiatrists have searched for alternative physical methods to manipulate psychotic ASCs. Several have come into vogue in recent decades, from enemas to kidney dialysis, but most have quickly faded into history. Of the three that remain, two—electroshock and lobotomy—are badly outdated, and one—megavitamin therapy—holds continued promise.

ELECTROSHOCK AND LOBOTOMY: THE DARK AGES REVISITED

During my psychiatric training at a large California state hospital in the early 1970s, I once witnessed burly attendants dragging a protesting patient down a long, bare corridor toward the electroshock chamber. As the young man frantically dug his heels into the slippery linoleum, I saw him gesturing toward a small, framed sign on the wall, titled "Patient's

Rights." Of the ten rights listed, the eighth clearly asserted: "You have the right to refuse electroshock therapy."

When I pointed out to the elderly physician in charge that his patient was clearly exercising one of his rights, I was met with a cold stare and a response that epitomized what frustrated younger psychiatrists called "that old bughouse mentality": "Listen, this is for his own good. And besides, after we zap him a couple of times, he won't remember whether he gave consent or not."

In the decades since then, California has tightened the rules under which this artifact from a less enlightened era is forced upon unwilling people in psychotic ASCs. (Although ECT may be helpful in cases of recalcitrant biological depression where gentler methods have failed, it has no place in the treatment of people in psychotic ASCs.) But the memory of its abuse lingers on, and it is still widely used in institutions where manipulation and control take precedence over humanistic values. Even where it is restricted, some hospital staffers use it covertly as punishment for breaking institution rules, or to induce docility in "difficult" hospitalized psychotics.

Using electroshock to treat a psychotic ASC is like fixing a malfunctioning radio by kicking it or overloading its wiring. The marginal reduction in surface symptoms is offset by the sometimes permanent memory loss and the feelings of helpless fear that it incubates in patients unable to resist. The simple sight of the "black box" induces a standing wave of terror on any chronic mental hospital ward, and the use of electricity plays into the most fearsome paranoid delusions of control.

Another gruesome artifact undergoing a resurgence of sorts is *prefrontal lobotomy*, a form of psychosurgery that mutilates nondiseased brain tissue by cutting out those parts of the brain that mediate abstract thought, thus eliminating the need for symptom formation. Many of its past victims linger in a vegetative existence in the back wards of mental hospitals, mute testimony to the medical model run berserk.

MADNESS & MEGAVITAMINS

It would be a pleasant surprise if a single toxic substance turned out to be the cause of schizophrenic or bipolar ASCs. Scientists certainly find it tempting to search for such a neurotoxin, and many have done so. One of the first was J. W. Thudichum, regarded as the father of modern neurochemistry, who in 1884 advanced the idea that "many forms of insanity" are caused by "poisons fermented within the body."

The search is still on, and while the elusive toxin has not yet shown its face, one group of psychiatrists believe they have exposed it. These are exiles from orthodox psychiatry who call themselves orthomolecular psychiatrists, advocates of administering to psychotic patients massive doses of vitamins that essentially act as drugs. The theory is that the vitamins will correct an inborn deficiency of certain nutrients that schizophrenics require in vastly greater proportion than other people.

Enthusiasm swelled for orthomolecular techniques two decades ago after Abram Hoffer and Humphrey Osmond published a highly technical account of their research, replete with anecdotes of dramatic cures of chronic cases of schizophrenia. Hopeful patients flocked to the few psychiatrists willing to master the intricate metabolic charts necessary to use this method.

Briefly, orthomolecular theory is based on the chemical likeness between the natural hormone norepinephrine and the cactus hallucinogen mescaline, which induces an ASC that has a passing similarity to acute schizophrenia. Orthomolecular theorists believe that schizophrenia is a brain disease caused by aberrant genes or unrecognized allergy. The road to madness begins with *taraxein*, a toxic substance that misdirects norepinephrine into forming another wayward chemical, *adrenochrome*, said to be even more potent than mescaline in causing hallucinations.

The orthomolecular antidote to this internally generated hallucinogenic trip is to give niacin (vitamin B_3) and ascorbic acid (vitamin C) in amounts impossible to obtain through diet alone. Adherents believe these vitamins quell the overproduction of taraxein, thereby alleviating symptoms. For patients who do not improve, a four-day fast precedes another trial, just in case the patient has a covert allergy.

The medical establishment has never been fond of the idea that mental or physical symptoms might be relieved by substances anyone can buy without a prescription, and neither are wealthy pharmaceutical companies who generously support medical journals with their advertisements. Just as the orthomolecular movement seemed to be catching on in the early 1970s, the American Psychiatric Association appointed a task force to pass judgment. To no one's surprise, the APA found megavitamin therapy to be "essentially without value." From that time on, orthomolecular psychiatrists have had their own "outlaw" specialty with separate research agendas and journals.

Despite its probable bias, the APA task force made a few telling criticisms of orthomolecular practice. The main flaw it found was that most of the experiments indicating benefit from megavitamins used electroshock treatment along with the vitamins. When this obviously confounding variable was eliminated, the results were not so assuring.

Although alternative healers are naturally attracted to vitamin therapy, they may find that the orthomolecular approach is anything but "holistic" in any meaningful sense of the word. At least in its founders' view, it is purely a *physical* theory, and they discount psychological factors as playing a role in either the cause or cure of psychotic ASCs.

For instance, in typical orthomolecular practice very little of a doctor's time is spent getting to know his patient in a personal way. Instead, a written diagnostic test is administered and the subsequent treatment is based on the results. Other physical measurements, such as laboratory analysis of a patient's hair, blood, urine, and fingernails, are factored in. Patients then must swallow dozens, even hundreds, of pills a day, and electroshock may still be administered as a supplemental treatment.

Given the destructive potential of schizophrenia, even this combination might be worth a try if there were firm assurances that megavitamin therapy really works. But the verdict is still out, and the issue will remain clouded until university research departments thoroughly reexamine orthomolecular theory without preconceptions. What they will likely find is that a small but significant percentage of people in schizophrenic ASCs benefit from these methods, a percentage easily obscured in research with large numbers of subjects.

In the meantime, the relatively harmless orthomolecular therapies are worth a try for people facing a lifetime of taking far more toxic medicines. There is no reason that the orthomolecular approach cannot be combined with psychological or spiritually based therapies not included within its original paradigm. For more information, the reader is referred to the original sources.

PSYCHEDELICS: INSTANT EPIPHANY OR INVITATION TO MADNESS?

At about the same time that neuroleptics were discovered, a family of drugs with diametrically opposite effects also made their epochal debut in the consciousness of the Western world. As psychedelics began cleaving society into "straight" versus "hip," they shook loose a whole generation from its death grip on a single consensual reality.

Of all the ways human beings have devised to open the self to the Spiritual Ground, to become "subtle energy aware," psychedelic trips are the most dramatic and immediate. The power of the psychedelic ASC to forge the widest generation gap in history is in its unpredictability. Some people experience instant epiphany, a transformative journey to usually veiled but inexhaustibly resplendent worlds unmatched by the most sensuous of earthly charms. Others feel that they unwittingly accepted an invitation to dine with the Mad Hatter, his table set with a rich fare of pathological symptoms reminiscent of the early stages of insanity.

The excesses of the sixties and the aggressive buzz of cocaine have now made psychedelic trips as fashionable as beads and bells. Lucy in the Sky sprinkles her diamonds only on underground cadres of intrepid consciousness explorers who keep a studiously low profile. Left in the wake, however, is a residual mass of confusion as to whether these agents model mystic enlightenment or temporary insanity. The answer: both.

Take, for instance, one young man's favorable experience with LSD.

> At first the effects were merely interesting—paisley patterns wriggling across blank walls, birds leaving colorful trails as they flew overhead. But when I closed my eyes, something remarkable happened. I was able to see the whole of my worldly ego *from a distance.* I could examine objectively all the games I play to get what I want, the feelings I usually ignore, all the ways that I sell out. It was easy to forgive myself, though, because I knew I'd be more authentic from now on. Then all that melted away and then I was confronted by an awesome presence that filled my being— no, it *is* my being, and it is also divine and infinitely loving. It was as if I had known of its presence inside me all along, but somehow had forgotten.
>
> It's impossible to put all that in words so you can understand, but it was one of the peak moments of my life and a lot more real than this chair I'm sitting in. You know, I've never been the same since then. I've lost my fear of death, and I'm a lot more tolerant of people, even when they act mean and petty. I feel more connected to humanity, but maybe less bound to society and its conventions when they don't make sense to me. I try harder to help other people, and I even think I'm more intelligent in some ways. But I've never much wanted to take acid again, because now I know what's on the other side, and I don't mind waiting a while to meet it again.

Contrast that to one young woman's brush with madness after taking the same drug:

> My God, it was awful, like going to hell with no exit. I was dissolving, and there was nothing but an emptiness that had no end in time or space. I was sure I was dead, or at

least permanently insane. Nothing was in any way familiar, and I was cut off from everyone and everything I cared about. I was spinning in space with no center, nothing I could hold on to or trust.

Later the hallucinations just kept coming and coming. There were mostly big spiderwebs, and sometimes spiders would fall off and crawl around on my body. Then there were grinning faces that would melt and turn into other faces, like demons in a horror movie I saw once. It didn't matter if my eyes were open or closed, the hallucinations kept throbbing in my head. For a while I felt that I was being punished for the sins of humanity, the way Jesus died on the cross. When my friends tried to comfort me, I was sure they were all laughing at me because they gave me poison and were planning to kill me, but only after they tortured me for a while first. It finally wore off, but it took me days to get to the point that I felt safe in the world again.

Both of these personal accounts bear witness to the power of a *physical* substance—and not very much of it at that—to dissolve ego boundaries and expose the self to the awesome energies of the Spiritual Ground. It may be tempting to make value judgments about the quality of these kinds of experiences, thereby widening the polarities that confound contemporary discussions about psychoactive drugs. But although capricious recreational use by unprepared people can lead to severe problems, plant substances with psychic effects similar to LSD have been used for millennia by tribal shamanic physicians who recognized their benign power to spiritually awaken carefully selected individuals in ritual settings. Conscientious observation of the effects of psychedelics on informed adults who voluntarily seek out the experience can enrich our knowledge of how individuals respond to openings to the Ground and of what the subjective world of people in certain psychotic ASCs is like.

THE PSYCHEDELIC EXPERIENCE

Three psychedelic drugs captured the fancy of youths in the Western world two decades ago: LSD, psilocybin (from the *stropheria* mushroom), and mescaline (from the peyote cactus). Although each is unique in its chemical makeup, they affect the mind in a like way. Recent years have seen a proliferation of "designer" psychedelics, some with specific and easily controlled effects, created in response to the universal urge to extend personal awareness beyond the ego into ordinarily obscure areas of the Ground.

Because the psychedelic experience differs greatly from the *chronic* schizophrenic ASC, some theorists have abandoned it as a model to study psychosis. But in the first stages of an *acute* psychotic ASC—when visual hallucinations are as prominent as auditory ones, when senses are keen rather than dull, when emotions are enhanced rather than deadened, when a person prefers the company of an understanding friend to solitude, when simple confusion has not yet crystallized into delusions—the resemblance to a psychedelic trip is unmistakable.

The ASCs of both psychedelic trips and acute psychosis stretch self-boundaries into unfamiliar areas of Ground consciousness, for better or worse. As awareness expands outward, it creates a kind of "mental vacuum" in which either manageable psychedelic or intoxicating psychotic experience takes form. Conscious energies that have never been modeled by past experience rush in to fill that empty space. This can be like throwing open several windows in a stuffy room, or it can be like suddenly stripping away one's shelter against a raging storm.

Whether such abrupt dilations of the self are felt to be uplifting or horrific depends on the preparation a person has had to tolerate expansive ASCs, how he explains them to himself, the setting in which they take place, and the duration of the ASC. People in self-expanding ASCs notice a radical broadening of *meaning*, an increase in significance underlying ordinary events. Commonplace objects suddenly appear exquisite and profoundly important. An ant crossing a fallen leaf symbolizes the perpetual struggle of humanity toward enlightenment. A bottle of catsup is discovered to be a strategically placed instrument of divine grace. Previously obscure song lyrics coyly whisper their universal messages. Psychedelic trippers find it hard to answer simple questions because they simultaneously grasp several levels of meaning in every event, and they cannot decide which of them to address.

But the beatific sometimes harbors the seeds of the diabolical. The same flowering of hidden significance lurks at the genesis of the paranoid solution to any such confrontation with the uncanny. Like the psychedelic tripper's, the paranoid's world is full of shrouded intentions, covert meanings. "What did the man on the bus intend when he looked at me and scratched his ear?" "What was my boyfriend *really* saying when he told me 'Good-bye' instead of 'Good-night'?" And what if these cryptic ambiguities become a regular facet of daily life? Even during the most vexatious psychedelic trip, most people remember that they have taken a drug that induced an ASC, and they know that it will wear off after a few hours. (Bad trips emerge from the fear that it won't.) Subtract that expectation, or extend the experience for days or weeks, and it is certain that the outcome will be far from "trippy."

WAKING DREAMS

The physical structure of a molecule of LSD bears a strong resemblance to the inhibitory neurotransmitter *serotonin*. Serotonin plays several important roles in a normally functioning brain, including regulating mood. But its main contribution to psychotic ASCs may be its role as latchkey for our dreams. As long as serotonin is active in a brainstem center called the raphe nucleus, a sleeper will not dream. However, when neurons within this center slow their firing, higher brain centers in the limbic system and visual cortex shake loose from serotonin's inhibiting grasp, and a vivid dream unfolds in the sleeper's awareness.

The dreaming ASC is a normal and necessary opening to Ground consciousness, one of enhanced receptivity to telepathic input and premonition. Nature provides us this nightly opportunity to reconnect with our Source, but protects us from harm by immobilizing our bodies during dreaming and screening most dream content from memory. When we dream, our center of neural activity relinquishes its station in the reasoning cortex and descends to the fantasy-based limbic system. If we were forcibly prevented from dreaming for just a few nights, we would rapidly develop a waking hallucinatory ASC as dream pressure builds and intrudes into waking consciousness. At first, we might be fascinated by these intriguing chimeras. But after several days or weeks they would overwhelm consensual reality. How would we cope with such unmodeled experiences, and how would we explain them to ourselves?

Every major hallucinogenic drug slows the firing of serotonin-rich neurons in the raphe nucleus. In other words, they *inhibit an inhibitor* and free neurons downstream to fire without constraint. In this case downstream means directly at the heart of the limbic system, in the midst of centers mediated by dopamine and implicated in many psychotic ASCs. This demonstrates that if the balance of one chemical is knocked askew, the effect ripples through innumerable nerve networks that produce other psychoactive hormones. The entire network of resonating synapses is vulnerable to any changes anywhere.

Therefore we might reason that several intrinsic brain chemicals influence the expansions and contractions of self-boundaries that define the ASCs of schizophrenia and mania. Here is a compelling link among psychedelic experience, dreams, and psychotic ASCs, a link that ties serotonin to excess dopamine activity. Because we know that psychedelics lead some people to confront deep areas of their psyches, they are an important clue as to why other people are literally bombarded by subconscious ideas and images during everyday life.

Unfortunately, research that might unravel these interlaced threads is caught in a sticky web of government hysteria. In deference to the administration's abhorrence of the counterculture ethos during the Vietnam War, the U.S. government forbade even the most conscientious research scientist to possess *any amount* of the common psychedelics, which a curious adolescent can purchase for a few dollars from his local dealer. Perhaps it was easier to ban these mysterious drugs without debate than to oppose alcohol or tobacco, both of which are far more toxic. But in the current climate, any scientist showing interest in psychedelic research risks being professionally censured, a situation analogous to the medieval churchmen's refusal to look through Galileo's telescope.

We know that psychedelics can mimic madness. But could they also point to a path away from it? We could find out if we revivify the promising research into their potential as therapeutic agents for selected people whose symptoms indicate a troublesome blockade at certain phases of their development. Natural psychedelic herbs were tools of ancient shamans, who used them to manipulate consciousness for healing a variety of ills. In our own culture, there are some tantalizing case histories left over from less repressive eras. These hint at the therapeutic usefulness of psychedelics to resolve carefully selected psychotic ASCs. Of course, such powerful techniques require intensive therapy by skilled and specially trained practitioners.

It may well turn out that the currently known psychedelics are too unpredictable to be generally useful for treating psychotic states, even in the deftest of therapeutic hands. But disciplined research could lead to other healing tools of greater efficacy. Establishment medicine has not come up with a single advance in treating psychosis since lithium was introduced in 1969. We can do better if—true to the theme of this book—we "leave no stone unturned" in our search for alternative and humane solutions to these forms of human suffering.

CHAPTER 8

Brain Holograms & The Seven Chakras

◆

Even so large as the universe outside is the universe within the lotus of the heart. Within it are heaven and earth, the sun and the moon, the lightning and all the stars.
Whatever is in the macrocosm is in the microcosm also.
CHANDOGYA UPANISHAD

We should look not for rules, but for images of the human that have the breath of life.
ALBERT CAMUS

BENEATH AND BEYOND the brain's anatomical and chemical strata, another more mysterious domain remains to be explored. This is a level on which *consciousness is a primary force,* one that must be fully accounted for in all descriptions of reality. And it is a level to which science must next turn in its search for the physical shadows of our thoughts, the links between mind and brain, madness and sanity.

This is the territory described by quantum physics, a zone of indistinct location and built-in uncertainty. Here, shadowy particles suddenly transform into energy and back into matter again, objects leap from place to place without ever traversing the space in between, things vibrate together rather than touch, events act in synchrony at "impossible" distances, chaos imperceptibly gives birth to order, and information is at once everywhere and nowhere.

If we accept the compelling evidence that the human mind is influenced by the brain's visible hardware and by the stream of chemicals pulsing through its synapses, then we must accept that it is equally molded by brain events at the quantum level, as "magical" as those events may seem. When we look at the brain ever more closely, we find only myriads of tiny particles that result from the interplay of still smaller particles, until we eventually find there are no particles at all, only interaction, vibration, process.

Although the science of quantum mechanics is in its infancy, the submicroscopic realities we see frozen in its cloud chambers correspond far better to what we know of mind and spirit than do molecular movements at the synapse. Studying quantum effects within the brain will be the next wave in science's quest to understand how physical deviations lead to altered states of consciousness.

In this chapter, we explore how the consciousness of the Spiritual Ground interacts with the brain to give rise to the unique entity that we know as the human mind in both its consensual and psychotic forms. Considering the brain from the quantum level allows us to arrange consciousness into a hierarchy, with specific levels based on frequency of subatomic vibration. From here, we can construct a working model that helps clarify the crucial distinctions between regressed and transcendent states. This model—here cast in the ancient system of the seven chakras—forms the basis for the following seven chapters.

THE QUANTUM BRAIN

A visual image helps introduce the bizarre world of quantum events occurring in and among the neurons of the brain. On the gross anatomical level—the only level understood at the time Freud formulated his structural theories—the brain/mind can be visualized as a large, windowless mansion with stout walls, its interior containing dozens of capacious rooms with only a few doors and branching passageways connecting them. Some of these doors are shut tight; others are partially open; still others allow free access to the flow of biologic energy that continuously seeks the path of least resistance.

On the chemical/synapse level, the brain/mind also can be pictured as a windowless mansion, but one filled with an intricate maze made up of billions of narrow hallways and curving crawl spaces, each with thousands of tiny doors leading to ever more hallways that branch again and again and occasionally double back to meet themselves. The labyrinth doesn't stay put, but grows more complex with time. Varicolor bursts of electrochemical energy pulse through these slender pathways, sometimes breaking free and creating new connections as they go.

The brain/mind of quantum physics bears scant resemblance to either of the above images. The mansion is still large, but has open windows on its exterior. Its walls and roof are flimsy, leaky. There are no rooms, hallways, or doors inside. Instead, the entire structure is filled to bursting with vibrating energy, shimmering waveforms of shifting color and intensity in perpetual interaction, everything resonating with everything else within the building. These resonances are sometimes harmonious, sometimes discordant, but there is a continuous multitonal hum of activity, of process. From time to time organized patterns take shape within portions of the field, interact with other patterns, then dissolve into new combinations.

Within this quantum mansion, the familiar anatomical structures of the brain are but shadowy outlines, barely perceptible within the more compelling reverberation pattern. Neurons and synapses are springs of fresh energy pulses within the field. The external walls of the building are only slightly more substantial than the wave fronts constantly forming and dissipating within the interior. Numerous exterior windows, some more open than others, allow vibrating packets of information from surrounding fields to squeeze into the building, while swirling thought-forms leak into the external world, where they influence nearby fields and the less dense background field that supports all this activity.

Data are stored within this quantum soup neither in neat rows of boxes, as in the anatomical model, nor in complex circuitry and feedback loops, as in the chemical model, but in *phase relationships*. Here we find intermingling wave patterns of diverse frequencies and amplitudes distributing each bit of information evenly within the whole so that anything that alters a relationship in any part simultaneously alters all relationships everywhere. Patterns associated with thoughts, feelings, memories, intuitions, drives, and impulses appear much like the translucent "ghosts" circling visitors of the Haunted House at Disneyland, figures of pure vibration constructed only of holographic relationships. We see these ethereal specters clearly. Are they *things*? Are they *real*?

THOUGHT HOLOGRAMS

Numerous theorists have found it irresistible to make analogies between the mind and the far simpler three-dimensional holograms sold in novelty shops and adorning our credit cards. If not overextended, these analogies hold true, and they point to new theories of how variations from consensual thinking and feeling might take place in altered states of consciousness, both psychotic and transcendent.

Briefly, holograms are created when two beams of coherent light, such as those generated by a laser, intersect before striking a photographic plate. One of these beams is first reflected off the object to be photographed, while the other is projected directly onto the plate. As the beams cross, their light waves interfere with each other, in some places adding to each other's energy, in others canceling it. What falls on the photographic plate, then, is not a picture of the object to be photographed, but an *interference pattern* that captures only the relationship between the light waves of the two beams. Viewed directly, there appears to be no more on the film than a jumbled mass of wavy lines. The original object is reconstructed from this encoded pattern when another laser beam passes through it, rendering a precise three-dimensional image of the original.

A remarkable feature of holograms is that the photographic plate containing the interference pattern can be broken into tiny fragments, each of which contains the *entire original image*. Some clarity and resolution is lost as the plate is cut into smaller fragments, but the whole picture remains encoded in every part, recalling an ancient Hermetic axiom: "what is here is everywhere; what is not here is nowhere." Looking at holograms in another way, they are *memories* in the most exacting sense of the word. It was this characteristic of holograms that led the neurophysiologist Karl Pribram to make his now-famous analogy linking holograms to the mind.

Pribram studied under Karl Lashley, a scientist who tried for thirty years to pinpoint the location of memory in the brain. Working with trained laboratory animals, Lashley selectively cut out parts of their brains, expecting to remove the memories stored inside. When this didn't work, he removed larger portions, finally removing all but a tiny nubbin of sensory neocortex, only to find that the entire memory store could be retrieved intact from the little that remained. As he struggled with the unfamiliar idea that learning and memory involve a *field* of activity that cannot be reduced to individual physical processes of the brain, Lashley wryly exclaimed that learning must not be possible at all. It was left for his articulate student, Pribam, to make the connection with the emerging science of holography and to spread the word.

Incredibly large storage capacity in a compact space, diffusely distributed information, instant scanning of a lifetime of experience—these are just three properties of the brain accounted for by the holographic analogy. It is only a minor conceptual leap to extend the analogy to include altered states of consciousness and the shifting conceptions of reality that accompany them.

Holography requires energy in the form of waves—or vibrations—such as the force field surrounding a magnet; it is inconceivable in terms of particle mechanics alone. Rather than reducing the human mind to chemical activity at the synapse, the holographic model traces mind to *interactions* of dynamic fields within and surrounding our brains. These encoded interference patterns gain coherence through millions of synchronous impulses traveling in parallel pathways along tracts of neurons. If the frequency patterns of these impulses is altered, the state of consciousness also shifts, and vice versa.

Although we intuitively accept that our thoughts and feelings take up time, the hologramatic analogy confronts us with the unfamiliar idea that they also *take up space,* and so exert a primary effect on the physical world and directly on other minds. Occultist notions of mental forms, or "spirits," without physical bodies become less incredible. So does telepathy, psychokinesis, and other extrasensory phenomena that suggest that the individual mind has a permeable boundary.

All systems in nature have their own particular way of vibrating—for example, the swing of a pendulum in an antique clock, the notes on a guitar string, waves in the ocean, signals from a radio tower, beats of a heart. When vibrations in two or more systems coincide, they begin to *resonate* in a way that allows energy to be exchanged between them. It is for our imaginations to grasp how many resonating interference patterns might emanate from millions of electrical pulses coursing through the neurons of our brains. These, in turn, resonate with fields "external" to our brains, bringing us into subliminal contact with other centers of consciousness and with the ever-present power of the Ground.

Physicists know that there are at least four kinds of fields in nature, from infinitesimal fields within the atom to vast gravitational and electromagnetic fields of galaxies that exert influence over immense distances. Spiritual disciplines describe even finer, nonphysical fields of influence, known to us only through the medium of intuition. Ultimately, all fields within the universe interact, resonating and exchanging energy with each other.

The arbitrary *outline* of our selves within these fields is the *inline* of everything else, but the boundaries are indistinct. Energy constantly flows in both directions, inward and outward. This exchange is directly experienced as much by the mystic who transcends his ego as it is by the madman whose ego fragments into the chaos of psychosis.

Perhaps it was a similar image of resonating fields within fields that led Pribam to join with the physicist David Bohm in expanding the original hologram idea. This blending of perspectives led them to suggest that the entire universe might be holographic in its ultrastructure, being eternally guided by a hidden realm of frequencies underlying an illusion of concreteness.

A key point is that under the right conditions, any *part* of the universal hologram has instant access to the *whole.* A universal mind is reflected within an individual by resonating interference patterns, an endless dance of inner and outer in which, when in harmony, both move as one. But when they are in disharmony, the shrill discord of madness reverberates to the roots of the soul.

An ancient Buddhist sutra captured the feeling of this pattern poetically.

> In the heaven of Indra there is a network of pearls so arranged that if you look at one you see all the others reflected in it. In the same way, each object in the world is not merely itself but involves every other object, and in fact is every other object.

To carry the thought a step further, Jung's idea of the collective unconscious—usually interpreted as a passive force encoded into our genes—may be recast as an active principle of energy exchange. This implies a planetary field of consciousness, a resonant field of all human minds present now, in the past, and perhaps in the future. The idea would be similar to viewing ants or bees as participating in the single mind of the hill or hive, rather than being a collection of individual minds.

From this image, the idea emerges that the healing of psychotic ASCs is less a matter of administering from "without" than of creating a fusion of minds, a direct exchange of energies through the medium of the Spiritual Ground. The healer's state of mind is as critical to the healing process as the patient's. Yet orthodox psychiatry considers any such experience of merged ego boundaries to be typical only of borderlines or psychotics.

The layered nature of our triune brain suggests that we can extend inward the idea of mind as an orchestrated array of individual resonances. At the quantum level, each brain layer operates as a hologram with its own unique frequency that is more or less in phase with higher and lower structures. This can be likened to the field of sound that surrounds individual instruments in an orchestra, each single field merging with nearby fields to make a whole. We might empathize with what it would feel like if one of our brain's "instruments" were consistently out of harmony with its neighbors because of aberrant chemistry or early emotional trauma. Mental dissonance would follow—an ASC of inner turmoil, confusion, and loss of coherent self-boundaries.

Scientists know that a distorted hologram results when they disrupt the coherence of the original constructing beams, or shift the angle of the *re*constructing beam. In terms of the analogy with mind, this is like saying that these disturbances induce an ASC, a phase shift away from consensual reality. Distorting influences can arise from within the light-projecting apparatus (analogy: electrical fields surrounding the main nerve tracts and synapses of the brain), or from interference from nearby light sources (other minds, etc.).

How, then, might an imbalance of dopamine or norepinephrine, affect the brain's field structure to induce an altered state? Several complicated theories have approached this elusive connection. The technically inclined reader is directed to the notes for two original sources. Although it is beyond the scope of this book to describe these theories in detail, they have in common the idea that the constant activity of neurotransmitters at the synapse generates trillions of tiny electromagnetic fields that, by resonating with each other, coalesce into a river of synchronously vibrating energy.

The cumulative power of these tiny fields sets the overall state of consciousness. Woven into this whole-brain hologram are minor interference patterns surrounding smaller clusters of synapses. These may be likened to crystals, each having a unique vibratory structure that we experience as a memory or perhaps an idea. Under certain circumstances these vibratory mental patterns directly resonate with patterns in *other* brains, allowing for telepathic exchange of information.

Different neurotransmitters—or their psychedelic and neuroleptic pretenders—change the frequency of the minor fields, which in turn influence the overall state of consciousness through resonance. "Higher" states of consciousness vibrate at higher frequencies, allowing more information to be encoded into the resulting hologram in a given unit of time. We may speculate that the specific frequency also determines the nature and "direction" of any psychic openings to the Ground, with higher ASCs resonating with energies from subtle planes and psychotic states exposing the self to coarser demonic realms.

What emerges from these visionary theories is a picture of a brain redolent with diverse and commingled energies—pulsatile wave fronts of electricity coursing along excitable neurons, slower ebbs and flows of direct current shifting like ocean tides within the background structure—combining to create a holographic pattern that transforms the nonmaterial energies of the Ground into the mysterious congregation of memories, thoughts, feelings, and intuitions known as the human mind.

In this new view, psychotic ASCs may be recast not merely as a prolonged civil war between ancient and modern brain structures, or as missteps in the chemical ballet within the synapse: to these valid but incomplete images we now add the idea of ASCs as variations in frequency, shifts in harmonic resonance within the whole-brain field. Any frequency shift may be toward higher or lower planes in the spectrum of consciousness. It may allow greater or lesser amounts of information to be processed per unit of time, as well as different kinds of information to enter awareness. And the accompanying ASC may be more or less in harmony with the frequencies of other fields in the environment.

History records that in every era the human brain has been compared to the most sophisticated technological system of the times: a telephone switchboard, then a computer, now a hologram. Actually, some brain processes do channel information along trunk lines; others operate with a computerlike linearity; still others conform to simultaneous holographic principles. If we alter any of these processes, the overall state of consciousness within the mind is also altered. These are interdependent processes; one does not change without the other.

Over the past century, society has confronted the problem of restoring something resembling the consensual state of consciousness to people locked into maladaptive ASCs. Some approaches focus on the crude anatomical level of the switchboard (lobotomy, psychosurgery); others aim at the computerlike chemical level (neuroleptics, lithium, megavitamins); a few employ arduous psychological tactics to restore equilibrium to the brain by balancing the mind and its relation to spirit.

The next wave of *physical* therapies will manipulate consciousness by intervening at the holographic-frequency realm itself. This is what esoteric disciplines have sought since ancient times through contemplative techniques. Tibetan Buddhist physicians, for instance, assign specific *mantras*—silently repeated sounds of specific harmonic frequency—as objects of meditation to treat physical and mental diseases.

We may count on Western science to search aggressively for efficient ways to achieve similar results. Recent experiments with the consciousness-altering properties of synchronous flashing lights and sounds, and with the induction of specific brain-wave patterns by passing microcurrents of electricity through the skull, hint at things to come. The physical architecture of asylums may eventually be reanalyzed with regard to the "vibes" so well known to both hyperaware paranoids and Chinese architects, who survey the geomagnetic fields of a site before determining the precise alignment of a building. Medicines with fewer side effects will be developed by focusing on the vibratory properties of molecules rather than on their gross chemical interactions. Ancient healing practices using quartz or other crystals of specific vibratory frequency are undergoing a renaissance of sorts, although their scientific basis is presently inadequate to the theory.

At this point it is wise to consider a thoughtful caveat from transpersonal philosopher Ken Wilber about the holographic analogy of the mind. Wilber cautions against *reductionism*—the error of defining a higher level of function in terms of a lower one. In this case, the error would be in asserting that the mind *is* a hologram rather than *like* a hologram. Because holograms are, after all, *material* constructions, which unlike the mind are fully constrained by the laws of physics, Wilber points out that the analogy is hardly different from the more common error of reducing consciousness to chemistry. Both confuse lower-level physical activity with the superior energies of the Ground. A higher level can never be derived from a lower, for each higher level has capacities not present in lower ones. Physics—even quantum physics—will never fully explain the meaning of *Hamlet* or why a terrified person in a psychotic ASC decides to commit suicide.

Nevertheless, the holographic analogy can be useful if it is not overextended. Thinking about the brain and mind in this way leads to fresh understandings of both higher and lower ASCs. It allows us to associate ASCs of regressive psychosis, creative inspiration, and mystical rapture with specific brain states, as well as with planes of consciousness. While these theories stretch the limits of conjecture, they could grant future generations a means to categorize stages of human development by frequency and to develop a technology of consciousness that may advance the spiritual progress of the human race. Instead of reducing the complexity of the mind to elementary atoms or molecules as we search for the roots of psychosis, we can now turn to *levels of activity* and the dynamic relations between them.

The idea of human consciousness layered into a hierarchy of frequency bandwidths is not new. In fact, it is one of the most ancient ideas known to humanity, reaching back to the origins of civilization. The fit between these ancient metaphysical systems and quantum physics is often uncanny, and it has been described in detail by several thoughtful authors. Although hierarchical models of consciousness at first seem esoteric to Western minds, their correspondence to everyday mental phenomena is too striking to ignore. At this point I will adopt one of these ancient systems to guide our exploration of mind and spirit as they relate to madness and transcendence.

THE SEVEN CHAKRAS: AN OVERVIEW

Originally intuited from the disciplined practice of yoga, the system of the seven *chakras* is a five-thousand-year-old way to integrate body, mind, and spirit. It elegantly maps the progress of personal consciousness from its first quickening within a living embryo to the highest stages of self-realization and ultimate reunion with the divine Source. This venerable system is a cornerstone of modern medicine and psychiatry in most Oriental countries and is taught as a "hard" science in many

Asian medical schools. It is integral to the practice of acupuncture, which, like the chakra system on which it is based, seems to tap into the quantum level.

In Oriental medicine, the chakras are considered to be real physical energy centers, characterized as lotuslike "wheels," each with a specific location in the human body. It is said that these centers are funnels for drawing vital life force, or *prana,* inward from a universal source, and are interfaces between physical and subtle realms. But for the purpose of this book, we will concern ourselves only with their psychological aspects.

In their psychological sense, the chakras are *archetypes,* comprehensive themes around which human life revolves, centers that create unique modes of experience, discrete stages of consciousness that guide spiritual growth throughout life. When Jung learned of the chakras, he recognized them as "intuitions about the psyche as a whole, about its various conditions and possibilities."

A comprehensive description of the chakra system is beyond the scope of this book. The reader is referred to several available sources. For our purpose—contrasting psychotic regression with transcendence—I will use the chakra system to address four essential questions that guide us as we explore the knotty problem of distinguishing between malignant regression, adaptive regression that precedes spiritual growth, and higher states of consciousness that may be confused with regression.

The crucial questions:

1. At what level of consciousness did psychotic regression begin?
2. At what level did it end?
3. What is the highest level of consciousness *ever* attained by the person?
4. Do the symptoms resemble those of emerging spiritual realization?

Using this expansive model of the psyche refines our ability to categorize psychotic ASCs in ways that surpass those currently employed in the Western world. Studying the way consciousness takes form at each chakra reveals stage-specific modes of thinking, feeling, and behaving, as well as values, logic, ethics, defenses, and ways of relating self to Ground.

The following is a brief description of the seven chakras, introducing their ancient Sanskrit names. This sketch is painted with a broad brush and is intended only as an introduction; each chakra will be characterized fully in the seven following chapters.

First chakra, the "root" chakra (Muladhara). The first chakra guides the development of a fetus and infant before it forms a bounded self. Pre-mental and pre-ego, it is characterized by free communion between individual-to-be and Spiritual Ground. Its primary mode is *survival* as it prepares an amorphous being for personal individuation. For people centered at this chakra, relationships with others are dependent and clinging, based on need. The Muladhara chakra is traditionally depicted at the base of the spine in the lower pelvis.

Second chakra, the "typhonic" chakra (Svadhisthana). The second chakra operates throughout early childhood as self-boundaries gradually wall off a separate identity within the Ground, but are still far more permeable than those of most adults. It is characterized by a magical world of wish-fulfilling fantasy and a relatively free flow of conscious energies between individual and Ground, which is gradually diminished by social living. The primary modes of the second chakra are unbridled *desire* and free-form *sexuality*. Relationships with others are idealized and tinged with fantasy. The Svadhisthana chakra is physically embodied below the naval.

Third chakra, the "power" chakra (Manipura). The consciousness of the third chakra infuses a young adult throughout his quest for a career and suitable mate as he establishes himself as an effective and competent force in the world. It is characterized by maximum individuation, maximum alienation from the Ground, and prideful striving to fortify the ego. Its primary modes are *power* and *control*. People centered at this chakra are uncomfortable in the company of anyone operating at higher levels. Relationships are competitive and manipulative. Many—perhaps most—individuals in industrialized societies never progress beyond the third chakra. The Manipura chakra is centered over the solar plexus.

Fourth chakra, the "heart" chakra (Anahata). The fourth chakra rises above attachments to the material and social worlds and toward an impassioned union with humanity, indeed with all sentient life. In its capacity to lift the self above the ego and initiate a gradual reopening to the Ground, it is the first spiritual level. It is characterized by compassion, empathy, and devotion to goals that go beyond self-aggrandizement. Relationships are selfless and magnanimous. Its primary mode is *universal love*. The Anahata chakra is located in the midchest.

Fifth chakra: the "inspiration" chakra (Visuddha). The fifth chakra further reopens the self-boundary to the Ground, allowing an influx of higher consciousness that seeks creative expression through an expanded self. This is the level of majestic wisdom, access to universal symbols, surrender to divine power, and partial detachment from specific worldly outcomes. Its primary modes are *grace* and *creativity*. Relationships are characterized by shared commitment to higher goals. Following Freud, Western psychology generally holds that this is the highest stage a person can reach in life, and it pathologizes the next two stages, which are recognized and valued only in Eastern thought. The Vishuddha chakra is centered over the throat.

Sixth chakra, the "shamanic" chakra (Ajna). The sixth chakra provides the means to gain control over influxes of Ground so as to alter consciousness and reality at will. This is the level of benign sorcery, visionary power, and prophesy. It is characterized by expanded vision and direct access to universal knowledge. Its primary mode is *insight*. Although sixth-chakra capabilities may "leak" into lower strata of consciousness—often disruptively—this level is fully realized only after prolonged involvement in spiritual practice, usually in the context of monastic life. Hence there is a partial withdrawal from worldly commitments and relationships. Sometimes called the "third eye," the Ajna chakra is traditionally located in the midforehead.

Seventh chakra, the "reunion" chakra (Sahasrara). The seventh chakra marks a return of self to Source, a voluntary dissolution of self-boundaries, a merger of a fully developed soul with its divine essence. It is the culmination of a life exceptionally well lived, the fulfillment of humankind's highest potential. At the present level of human evolution it is rare for individuals to reach this plane of consciousness, although many glimpse it transiently. Characterized by unconditional surrender to the Ground, its primary mode is *unity*. Occasionally, people centered at lower levels experience fleeting breakthroughs of seventh-chakra "mystical" consciousness. These are unforgettable moments, sufficient to permanently transform a life. Most traditional charts portray the Sahasrara chakra at the crown of the head, or a few inches above.

DEEP STRUCTURES

As consciousness develops upward through the chakras during each generation of human life, the same archetypal drama unfolds time and again within numberless people in diverse times and places. Although there is an endless variety of enactments, these are but variations on a basic plot that is specific to each level of consciousness, with only the setting and costumes changing. The chakras thus represent deep structures embedded within Ground consciousness itself. Each chakra may be thought of as an interface between individual consciousness and levels of the Spiritual Ground in which energies of a particular "frequency" flow through self-boundaries that have become receptive to—holographically resonant with—that specific level.

Spiritual growth through the chakras is a process of incorporating ever-larger areas of the Ground into the self. So it is incorrect to think of the chakras as "created" by the self. As archetypal structures eternally present in the Ground, they await our attunement through worldly experience and spiritual growth. In this vein, Ken Wilber points out that a deep structure is *remembered* in the Platonic sense, and emerges in personal consciousness only when it is remembered.

Just as the physical self-center—the governing focus of neural activity—rises through evolutionary layers of the brain during life, so, too, does the subjective self-center open into the chakras sequentially. This is not to say that only a single chakra is active at a time, but that the self identifies with the roles of each level, one by one, and is ultimately transformed by them. There are, of course, sublevels within each major level, but passing through these does not require the profound realignment of deep psychic structures that accompanies transition to a higher chakra.

An avant-garde way of saying this would be to regard the self as climbing a ladder of hologramic frequencies within a universal field of consciousness, itself structured like a hologram. As one ascends to each chakra's discrete frequency range, this activates a series of fundamental resonances that set the pattern for each stage of life: infant, toddler, young, mature, wise, transcendent, infinite. Secondary resonances within each stage remain within the limits of the primary pattern. When a higher-frequency bandwidth—a higher chakra—is reached, this grants access to a greater quantity of information of a more intricate nature.

Because they are each interdependent facets of a unified field of consciousness, the chakras do not act separately and can be divided only intellectually. Like a nest of Chinese boxes, each higher chakra contains all the capabilities of lower ones, but not vice versa. Lower levels never simply disappear from consciousness. For optimal spiritual growth, each lower chakra must be enfolded into the higher level, subsumed within its deep structures, but ultimately transcended as a person frees himself from exclusive entanglement in that mode of experience.

For instance, even the most accomplished fifth-chakra artist or philosopher seldom abandons his humanistic concerns (fourth chakra), or ceases to aggressively promote his or her creations in the world (third chakra), or stops fantasizing about sex (second chakra), or neglects to seek food when he is hungry (first chakra). It is just that these activities no longer constitute the essential focus of his life. The individual seeks unity at each chakra, but he must continually rise above lower forms of unity to discover higher unities, until there is only Unity. And at any stage of life, the subtle but irresistible power of the higher chakras "pulls along" a growing self, especially one that is spiritually attuned.

But life offers no guarantee that its stages will always march in synchrony. Sometimes there are precipitous breakthroughs of higher-chakra consciousness before a self has "digested" the lower chakras—"spiritual emergencies." When chakras open out of phase, trouble lies near. Abrupt openings to levels other than the primary location of the self-center, higher or lower, usually are experienced as psychotic ASCs.

Typically there are three kinds of derailment from the ideal progression through the chakras. At any stage of development, there can be *fixations* on a particular level, arresting growth of the self-center. For instance, if a person's growth is arrested at the first two chakras, he remains obsessed with issues and gratifications he ought otherwise to have "outgrown," such as keeping a teddy bear as an imaginary companion. As he confronts the demands of adulthood, he gradually appears more and more psychotic if he does not relinquish this childhood affectation. Such fixations set the stage for so-called borderline conditions.

Sometimes the self *represses* a task or trauma on a particular level, leaving unfinished business that sets the stage for later regression from a higher level. During times of stress, these persistent backward tugs can drag a predisposed self into a schizophrenic break during early adulthood. Sadly, the end result is not a charming six-year-old in an adult's body, but a mismatch of discordant elements. With this kind of regression, the self carries mutilated bits and pieces of higher-chakra consciousness back with it. For instance, a person whose schizophrenic ASC caused him to regress to the second chakra may be overcome with universal love, which, lacking appropriate outlets, leads him to give away his disability check to a stranger.

At any point of development there may also be sudden *intrusions* of energies from higher levels before the self can make useful sense of them. These can occasionally be uplifting, but are more often disorienting and frightening. Ideally, there can be no skipping of stages, for a growing self cannot maintain a higher chakra until the basic structures of the level below it have emerged and are integrated. A developmental leap that occurs before requisite foundations are mastered is dangerously premature and apt to precipitate regression.

For example, a college student may be overwhelmed by suddenly finding that he has confusing telepathic intuitions that prevent him from concentrating on his studies, or that lead him to conclude he is possessed by a demon. When such spiritual emergences arise, they confound both patient and healers if they hold to conventional models of consciousness. Because we tend to deny levels of awareness above our present focus, breakthroughs of higher consciousness are usually misdiagnosed and treated with methods that negate their potential for spiritual growth.

It follows that transition points from level to level are times of danger. Wilber graphically described these crises as demanding the "death" of the present level because the self must release its accustomed identity and attachments in order to be reborn into the higher order of the next level. This experience is invariably traumatic because it exposes the newly expanded self to previously invisible areas of the Ground, and so to realities that are as yet inconceivable.

These transformative crises feel like imminent psychic death, especially when the self overidentifies with a lower level. This may occur, for instance, when a naive adolescent inadvisedly takes a psychedelic drug and confronts the insubstantiality of his separate ego—a deathlike feeling that can trigger explosive panic in the unprepared person. Such fragmentations are always a peril during transition periods. In Western cultures, the self is especially vulnerable during transitions from the second to third chakras, a time when first signs of schizophrenic regression often become manifest. Precipitous fifth- and sixth-chakra openings similarly overwhelm people in manic ASCs. Crises that mark such openings produce terrifying symptoms laden with chaotic emotions, such as feeling the world collapse. For, after all, they are defenses against ego death itself.

An ASC, then, can be seen as a sudden opening to a level or levels other than the one containing the self-center. Through a process analogous to holographic resonance, the specific "frequency" of an ASC provides a gateway to a specific chakra, higher or lower. When the self prematurely opens to higher chakras, the influx of unfamiliar energies may be confusing and frightening, but not necessarily destructive. However, when a fragmenting self desperately seeks coherence by contracting from a higher to a lower level, the resulting ASC is catastrophic as the self confronts anachronistic areas of the Ground.

THE PRE/TRANS FALLACY

People centered on lower levels who experience spontaneous intrusions of higher-chakra consciousness have not yet acquired adequate models to express the uncanny feelings that derive from an expanded reality. They desperately struggle to match the consensus view by casting these higher-order experiences in the symbolism of a lower level.

The result is usually bizarre. For instance, a feeling of union with the Divine (seventh chakra) may lead them to conclude that they are Jesus. Or telepathic inputs (sixth chakra) may feel like witchcraft or thought control. Universal symbolism in a popular song (fifth chakra) may suggest covert personal messages that are part of a grand conspiracy. To most observers, such interpretations seem merely weird, but they also impart to many psychotic ASCs the paradoxical appearance of having both regressive and mystical characteristics.

The failure to recognize that *similarities* are far from being *identities* is behind what Ken Wilber aptly calls the "pre/trans fallacy," a common conceptual error that confounds efforts to champion spiritual experience as well as to pathologize it. The point is that because *pre*-rational consciousness (chakras one and two) and *trans*-rational consciousness (chakras six and seven) are in their own ways *non*-rational, they appear quite similar or even identical to the untutored eye.

In Wilber's words, succumbing to the pre/trans fallacy leads to

> a mixture of confusion of pre-egoic fantasy with trans-egoic vision, of pre-conceptual feelings with trans-conceptual insight, of pre-personal desires with transpersonal growth, of pre-egoic whoopee with transegoic liberation.

Wilber's point is that once the pre/trans fallacy confounds the situation, one of two dangerous misreckonings follow: manifestations of transpersonal ASCs are reduced to prepersonal regression, or prerational regressions are elevated to transrational glory. The former error is widespread in orthodox psychiatry, which accepts Freud's interpretation of mystical unity as a return to a womblike state. The latter error has been common within the antipsychiatry movement, which tends to interpret primitive religious-tinged delusions as impending mystical insight. Such mislabeling leads to counterproductive therapies for people who would better respond to healing strategies tailored to their specific level of consciousness.

Because the ancient chakra system divides states of consciousness by field effects and frequency levels, it corresponds to the insights of modern physics. The idea of viewing human consciousness as developing through sequential levels is by no means unique to Eastern thought. Hierarchical models were proposed by Margaret Mahler, Jean Piaget, Lawrence Kohlberg, and Abraham Maslow, to name a few. But with the exception of Maslow's hierarchy, most stop short of acknowledging stages beyond the fifth chakra. The chakra system is unique in that it accepts the first five stages of human development honored by Western thought, then adds two transpersonal levels intuited from spiritual practices widely encouraged by Eastern psychologies.

Each of the following seven chapters examines altered-state phenomena specific to a chakra level in the hope that we may better recognize their distinct features and avoid the well-meaning errors of both establishment and alternative psychologies, as each struggles to grasp the entire breadth of consciousness while tethered to models adequate for but one or two levels.

PART 3

MADNESS IN PSYCHE AND SPIRIT: THE SEVEN CHAKRAS

CHAPTER 9

First Chakra:
The Roots of Madness in Early Life

❖

What did your original face look like before your parents met?
ZEN KOAN

To be, or not to be, that is the question.
SHAKESPEARE

AS SPERM PENETRATES ovum, a soft whisper perturbs the eternal background hum of the Spiritual Ground. A new being has formed within its Essence.

As the cells of the tiny embryo multiply, they create a receptive vortex, neither in space, nor in time, but in *consciousness*. For these nascent cells are of life itself. Their inescapable nature is to partake of the Ground, to draw it into themselves in a way that is unique in all the cosmos. The rudimentary awareness of the Muladhara chakra now begins to condense within a fledgling soul.

The consciousness of the first chakra is the cornerstone of human life. During the three-year span from conception to transition into the second chakra, the foundations of selfhood form within an unbounded field of consciousness. As elementary psychic membranes gradually separate self from other, and self from Ground, they form a supporting grid that must bear the weight of human emotions, reason, and the consensual reality of society. The ability of these basic structures to create and maintain a stable state of consciousness is determined as much by early life events as it is by genes. By the time a toddler's psyche expands into the second chakra, the roots of future psychotic ASCs have already taken firm hold.

Several characteristics distinguish first-chakra consciousness from later stages: (1) an unbounded self that begins life in subjectless absorption in the Ground; (2) an open sensory system that is unselective and undefended as it receives all stimuli that come within its range; (3) an instinctive mode of reacting, with the focus of neural activity centered in the reptilian brain; (4) learning through imprinting, leaving traces in that which becomes the subconscious mind; (5) no sense of time—no past, no present, no future; (6) diffuse awareness that lacks cognitive categories; (7) in later stages, a slowly emergent sense of self exclusively identified with the body; (8) finally, a gradual consolidation of self-boundaries that blend with those of the mother.

In this chapter, we explore the way consciousness of early life can be distorted by physical and psychological events so that the foundations of selfhood become too weak to support a mature and stable adult ego. We shall see that by the time a two-and-a-half-year-old is ready to expand into the second chakra, the roots of madness or sanity are firmly anchored in the soil of his genetic and family environment, with only the surface branches and limbs yet to be determined.

MADNESS & LIFE IN THE WOMB

By its eighth week of life, an embryo is no longer an amorphous clump of identical cells. Form stirs within it—a differentiation of matter assuming the shape of a human body, a differentiation of consciousness assuming the field structure of its mind. One segment of the embryo is especially "magnetic" in attracting infusions from the Ground. Here the first neurons cluster into an intricate web as they migrate toward their destinations in the brain-to-be. The following ten weeks will be a time of peril as these delicate cells follow their genetic script and coalesce into the mysterious organ that is to be the lifetime home of a self.

Never again in life will such explosive cellular multiplication take place in the brain, and never again will that brain be so vulnerable to damage. Complex enzymes that operate for only a few crucial hours to achieve a particular task come and go, leaving no trace of their momentary presence. What effect do hormonal surges triggered by maternal stress, food additives, medicines, alcohol, pesticides, or radiation have on on these fleeting processes? Could they create conditions for neurochemical short circuits later in life that distort consciousness into psychotic ASCs? We do not know, but we are beginning to find out, and there is mounting evidence that they do.

By the eighteenth week of life, the growing brain stabilizes into a miniature version of its adult anatomical shape. By the twenty-first week, the auditory cortex begins to function, and the fetus becomes sensitive to sounds vibrating its liquid pillow. At this point the fetus begins to be affected by the world, by the emotional tone of its mother's voice and the voices of others with whom she converses in friendliness, passion, or anger. It hears the music she likes, hears the rhythms of her breathing and heartbeat. Of course, there is not yet a self that listens to these sounds—no subject, no object—only *hearing*.

Until recently, scientists believed that a fetus is unaware of even primitive sensations because its neurons lack the fatty layer of insulation, called *myelin*, that allows them to fire efficiently. However, research on premature infants reveals that their brains respond to a wide variety of provocations, some of which stimulate growth of specific synapses from early in life. The function of a brain is to learn, and the learning that takes place in the womb is of the deepest and most fundamental sort.

Because a fetal brain matures from its older evolutionary layers upward, it can feel pain—perceived in old reptilian centers—from quite early on. Limbic centers mature next. But the fact that a fetus is incapable of thinking about traumatic stimuli entering from the external world or expressing its reactions to them in words does not mean that their effects do not register on a deep level. And it is exactly those brain centers implicated in the most severe psychotic ASCs that are first sensitive to the external world. To whatever extent people learn to be mad, it is probable that they learn it from a very early age.

A fetus lives not only inside the body of its mother, but also inside her field of consciousness. Many sensitive women are aware of a subtle telepathic rapport with an unborn child, which surely operates in both directions. How this *sub rosa* conversation affects an unborn's basic feelings about itself is of course speculative. But it is certain that of the host of reasons for conceiving a child, only a few are based on an unselfish desire to produce a secure human being. Negative as well as positive feelings constantly resonate between them, setting the stage for their future life together.

In sum, as a fetus nears birth, it already has developed numerous characteristics that are derived from its heredity. Yet there are at least as many forces impinging upon it that have more to do with experience in the uterus than with genes. The quality of the mother-child communion during those nine months of gestation foretells the quality of their relationship after birth in ways that we can as yet only imagine.

MADNESS & THE BIRTH EXPERIENCE

What may be the single most condensed learning experience of a lifetime awaits the unsuspecting fetus. As the first chemical alarms disturb the peace of the womb, and powerful muscular contractions press in on it from all sides, the fetus responds by releasing massive quantities of the hormone ACTH from its pituitary gland. This in turn signals the adrenal glands to flood the system with the stress hormone adrenaline so as to activate the body's defense systems.

ACTH and adrenaline have an immediate effect on the brain, stimulating it to produce large amounts of proteins vital to learning. More importantly, these hormones trigger massive growth of new synapses, linking neuron to neuron in a way that organizes the brain to survive birth and subsequent life in the world. The hours of labor lay down specific nerve pathways that will, for better or worse, shape that person's experience throughout life. This is known as *imprinting*, a rapid kind of learning that establishes social attachments early in life.

Stanislav Grof has developed an important theory about how the pain and struggle of birth may be etched into psychotic experience later in life. While he stops short of asserting that birth trauma causes psychotic ASCs, he speculates that traumas specific to various birth stages *predispose* one to psychosis, as well as determine its content and coloration. He views many psychotic ASCs as desperate attempts to heal the preverbal anguish of the passage through the birth canal.

We know that emotionally painful childhood experiences can lead to irresistible compulsions to relive the trauma later in life, as if to undo the emotional damage. But the idea that imprinted *birth* traumas can have the same effect has always been speculative and often ridiculed by orthodox psychiatrists. However, several recent studies have documented a link between birth trauma and suicide, especially in adolescents. Moreover, one research project demonstrated a strong correlation between the *kind* of birth trauma and the *method* of suicide. From these correlations it is not farfetched to infer that birth traumas are imprinted as deep subconscious memories that are reactivated during crisis points in adult life. ASCs that throw open the psyche to the subconscious would be especially likely to tap into this realm.

One of my psychotic patients described in graphic scatological imagery an experience that is suggestive of reliving a birth trauma.

> I always have to watch out for shit-storms. I never know when one will hit—they come in waves. When a shit-storm hits, I have to make myself real small to keep from getting smeared. I live up the ass of a beast who knows I'm a smelly turd, so he tries to push me out with all the other

crap in the world. It's real dark and tight in there, so I close my eyes and roll up in a ball, a tiny turd-ball, to keep from getting squished. But I can't breathe when that happens, and I know I'm getting gored by hairy goats with giant horns that hurt me so bad and make me bleed until I'm covered with blood and shit so that I just want to scream. But nothing comes out, so I try to die. I just get stuck there in a world of shit. That's where I live most of the time, in a world of shit.

While we await research that clearly demonstrates correlations between birth trauma and psychotic ASCs we might join Grof in speculating that disturbances during this time of feverish synapse growth create risks for all sorts of adult maladies, from psychosis to depression to addiction. Subliminal memories of birth traumas may weaken a person's tolerance for stressful situations that resemble birth stages, and so trigger regressive ASCs. These, in turn, may be distress signals from a mind desperately striving to heal itself.

Grof believes that imprints from birth trauma become so deeply buried under years of accumulated worldly memories that they come to the fore only during profound ASCs that hurl open the gates of the subconscious. Birth symbolism may erupt during dreams, meditation, psychedelic trips, or psychotic episodes. Grof views these ASCs as unparalleled opportunities for discharging long-buried imprints that are an unrecognized source of suffering and maladaptive behavior.

THE INFANT-MOTHER BOND

Infused with the unitary consciousness of the first chakra, the infant tumbles into the world, and eventually into his mother's arms. This final step of the infant's biological birth sets the stage for the first step of his psychological birth as an individual. If up to this point learning took place through imprinting, now a new way of learning derived from the child's first worldly interactions with his mother comes to the fore. This is called *bonding*, an intuitive, nonverbal rapport that operates on an emotional level quite unlike rational ways of thinking and perceiving.

Still one with the Ground, the stressed and exhausted newborn seeks a point of focus in the world, a font of soothing love, and a secure object to sustain him as he begins the long task of making sense of things. He instinctively searches for these in his mother, her face pattern, her smell and taste, the nourishing softness of her breast, and her voice, which he has come to know throughout the last months in her body. The love of his mother and the omnipresent Ground flow together in a blissful unity that saturates him with an experience of aliveness. With no formed self-boundary enclosing his consciousness, he merges with these maternal sensations, enfolding his being into the feelings within her heart.

For better or worse, this dyadic bond forms the cornerstone around which the child's subsequent explorations of the world will be oriented. The bonding that occurs in the hours and days after birth is a vital physical and emotional link, a primary knowing that underlies and supports rational thought. The child uses the mother as a beacon of orientation to reality. In addition, the shared feelings that resonate between infant and mother guide the earliest stages of self-boundary formation, and determine how the "I" that is to dwell within that boundary will eventually come to regard itself.

If we accept the compelling evidence that aberrant genes predispose an infant to psychosis later in life, then we must ask what finishes the job. We know that not all predisposed people become psychotic—even identical twins are only about 35 percent concordant for schizophrenia—and of those who do, not all develop malignant or chronic types.

It is likely that a genetically predisposed fetus is *already* experiencing his developing self in a way that is different from his genetically normal peers. Then, as the mother-infant bond solidifies after birth, the child's subtle deviations from her expectations can set up runaway vicious cycles that disrupt normal bonding. The quality of the psychic bonds that form during first-chakra consciousness reverberates throughout the life cycle and influences the outcome of the infant's genetic potential. It is, of course, impossible to conduct ethical research on humans that would conclusively demonstrate this idea. But because psychosis, especially schizophrenia, disrupts selfhood in such a fundamental way, it seems reasonable to trace its roots to a time of life when the first sense of self comes into being.

For this to be true, the brain would have to register and store memories from very early in life. There is mounting evidence that it does. For instance, research on cats and monkeys demonstrates conclusively that the final "wiring" pattern of the mammalian brain is laid down during the crucial several months beginning with birth. This is especially true in the neocortex, where sights, smells, sounds, and handling by parents strengthen specific nerve pathways, while understimulated ones atrophy. The mind translates the feelings of early life into the architecture of the brain in a way that is as important as genetics in determining our individual differences.

Although the shopworn notion that an immature brain cannot support awareness or store memories is dear to many pediatricians, recent scientific observations of babies should lay that idea to rest. Using high-speed photographic techniques to study infants in their home environments, researchers captured on film extreme slow-motion records of subtle muscle movements. They found that every conversational sound, even individual syllables, evoked distinct muscular responses in the child. Although invisible to the unaided eye, these movements continuously vary with the intensity and emotional tone of any nearby conversation. This research suggests a vast, unseen dimension of family interaction operating on a microscopic level invisible to ordinary view.

SELF/NOT-SELF

Once bonded to its mother, the infant's task is to emerge from primal unity with the Ground into early stages of selfhood. He uses his mother as a stepping-stone for this transformation. Through the process of bonding, the infant's unshaped consciousness is surrounded by his mother's self-boundaries, which protect him from too much stimulation or frustration. A symbiosis develops from this merger in which child and mother temporarily become one. Yet the mother cannot always be physically or emotionally present when her infant needs her. When he is hungry, mother doesn't always notice; when he is playful, she may be weary. The child feels her absence within himself, feels his own subjective aloneness.

Then the infant discovers that when he bites his thumb there is pain, but when he bites his blanket there is no pain. When he feels movement, his hand waves before his eyes, but his teddy bear's arms remain still. From this early "I/not-I" split, there grows a rudimentary psychic membrane parting his fledgling self from the consciousness of its Source. He connects these first sensations of selfhood with his *physical body*, an identification that persists for the next several years. Once established, this self/not-self dichotomy enables his split-off portion of consciousness to define itself, and much later to reflect upon itself.

This first self-boundary is extremely vulnerable, and there is much opportunity for its consolidation to go awry. Its strength and stability will support the individual's relationships with others, and with the Ground, for a lifetime. Should it fail, there are no guarantees for emergency roadside repairs.

For instance, every time a stranger appears, the infant leaves the known and enters the unknown. A strange face triggers fear of abandonment—the greatest threat to survival that can befall an infant. Will his mother's emotional availability impart a reassuring sense of security in an uncertain world? Will she be an unshakable protector in the face of the unfamiliar, a soothing presence that empowers him to endure such intrusions without dissolution? Or will she plant seeds of paranoia by failing to salve his fear of the unknown?

Innumerable repetitions of what the child psychiatrist Margaret Mahler calls *separation-individuation* experiences slowly cleave the mother-child dyad from the fourth month of life through the transition to second-chakra consciousness early in the third year. If all goes well, the growing child gradually and contentedly forms his own self-boundary separate from his mother's. There will always be a good deal of overlap of these fragile boundaries, however, a shared area of the psyche where the feelings of one directly resonate with the feelings of the other.

SELF & SELFOBJECT

To emphasize this fusion of selves, the psychoanalyst Heinz Kohut coined the term *selfobject* to describe a person who has been incorporated into another person's self. In this situation, one's thoughts, feelings, and self-image are conditioned by the thoughts, feelings, and opinions of the fused selfobject.

For instance, a young child is so immersed in the body and mind of his selfobject mother that he feels he can control her in the same way he controls his own arms and legs. Kohut envisioned the supporting structure of a newly forming self as derived from selfobjects. While there may be more to it than that, it is true that the child retains bits and pieces of his parents' personalities as he splits off his own individuality. If these incorporated fragments fail to hold together within a stable self-boundary, regressive disorders of the self, including psychosis, follow later in life.

Kohut holds that there are three means by which a child incorporates selfobjects: mirroring, idealizing, and twinship. Failures in any one may render the child's maturing self vulnerable to fragmentation during stress.

Mirroring begins as little more than a worshipful glow in a mother's eye as she bathes her growing child in admiration and approval. The mother echoes her child's unfolding self in a way that affirms his adventurous explorations and confirms his basic right to exist. If all goes well, her child eventually incorporates the knack of praising and rewarding himself. From this he gains a sense of confidence and efficacy, as well as finding reasonable limits to his ambitions.

Subtract mirroring from a child's early life and he is left with a cold emptiness, a feeling of being dead inside, a sense of life's pervasive meaninglessness, a dreary existence bereft of pleasure or reward. If *some* mirroring takes place, but is distorted or inconsistent, he incorporates an unstable self-image, such as manic grandiosity alternating with guilt-ridden despair, or paralyzing ambivalence complicating minor decisions. These feelings are common in psychotic as well as borderline states.

Idealizing, the second self-building mechanism, occurs as the child looks up to and identifies with a powerful selfobject whom he perceives to be a wellspring of calmness, perfection, and strength in the face of uncertainty. The very idea of space and time as stable and reliable entities—a sine qua non of sanity—is derived from basic cause-and-effect relations learned while confronting and reducing uncertainty during early childhood. From these experiences, the child internalizes a capacity for self-soothing so conspicuously lacking in schizophrenics and borderlines as well as addictive personalities.

Self-soothing skills are especially important to an adult genetically predisposed to surges of brain dopamine during times of stress. A sudden buildup of dopamine in the limbic system is felt as an insistent but unfocused restlessness, an agitated push toward action as if some unseen danger were threatening. Without an acquired capacity to neutralize this pressure by self-soothing, the schizophrenic retreats into an omnipotent delusion that conceals his helplessness and vulnerability.

Twinship, a third means of acquiring a sturdy self-structure, is important later in childhood. At this stage, the child finds a role model and identifies with the skills, talents, and values of a mature individual who represents consensual reality. Optimally, the child incorporates from good role models a sense of group membership, agreed-upon reality, and affiliation with society and later with humanity. Lacking twinship experiences, a child may develop feelings of being a perpetual outsider or a defective specimen, or perhaps of not even being human. These can color psychotic experience later in life.

For these three self-building scenarios to create a coherent self that resists fragmentation, a single factor must be abundantly present in that child's mother or maternal surrogate: *empathy.* This is simply the capacity to think and feel oneself into the inner life of another person. Empathy alone inspires the mirroring that quickens the best of the child's talents and affirms his sense of belongingness in the world. It is empathy that emboldens a mother to allow her child just the right amount of character-building stress and frustration before she soothes him with her mature strength. It is empathy that stirs her ability to model society's values and realities, all the while empowering the child to courageously step beyond these when he is ready. And it is *lack* of empathy that enfeebles an emerging self, devitalizes its spirit, and undermines self/other boundaries so necessary for a sane life in a reliable world.

SELFHOOD EMERGES

A child who defines himself through an empathic mother who truly knows him will naturally and joyfully begin to separate from her and form a self-boundary of his own. According to Mahler, who spent years painstakingly observing children in various stages of development, this process begins at about the fourth month of life and continues through the third year. Early disruptions of separation-individuation set the stage for malignant psychotic ASCs, while late-phase disruptions lead to borderline selves that are vulnerable to benign psychotic episodes.

The conditions for a borderline outcome begin during the time of life known to harried mothers as the "terrible twos." Dauntlessly endowed with a newfound ability to walk about on his own and explore freely, the child grows intoxicated with his heroic omnipotence and the presumed hospitality of a benevolent world. With blithesome naiveté, he practices independence as if to avenge his earlier helplessness. However, an inevitable series of bumps, bruises, and abrasions follows as the material world asserts its well-known indifference to soft flesh. The chastened toddler repeatedly returns to his caretaking selfobject for soothing, ideally followed by a new round of age-appropriate mirroring and exploration.

Countless repetitions of these adventures followed by reunion with mother—*rapprochement* is Mahler's term—gradually consolidate the child's still-porous self-boundary. Rapprochement imbues the child with awareness of his own solitary mental space, personal selfhood, and vulnerability. With that realization, he surrenders his infantile delusion of omnipotence. Because rapprochement marks the transition between first- and second-chakra consciousness, the child faces his first "hero's journey," a trial of great significance and great peril.

Will the mother empathize with her bewildered child's feeling of vulnerability and respond by reaffirming his personal power and independence? If so, he will learn to love and accept the self he encloses within his boundaries. Or will the mother's own unfulfilled need for a fused and dependent selfobject prevent her from easing her child into a separate existence equipped with a reliable self-boundary? In the latter case, the child's weakly enclosed self, fraught with guilt, painfully tears away from her with the harsh lesson: "To exist as a separate individual is to harm someone who needs me."

Such a traumatic separation leads to a deeply wounded self: the borderline condition in which an unstable self-boundary fluctuates from all-inclusiveness to empty nothingness. The borderline's self is so fragile that he depends upon the constant presence of a powerful selfobject in order to exist without dissolution. This selfobject acts as a lifeboat in a churning sea of chaotic feelings. In a poignant message to her psychiatrist, one adult patient described her desperate craving for merger.

> I felt like a moving picture you projected on the wall. I only existed because you wanted me to, and I could only be what you wanted to see. I only felt real because of the reactions I could produce in you. If I had scratched you and you didn't feel it, then I'd be dead.
>
> I could only be good if you saw good in me. It was only when I looked at myself through your eyes that I could see anything at all. Otherwise I only saw myself as a starving, annoying brat whom everyone hated, and I hated myself for being that way. I wanted to tear out my stomach for being so hungry.

The price of this illusory safety-through-fusion is a relentless threat of engulfment by a dominant selfobject on one hand, or abandonment and psychic death on the other. The borderline can perceive others only as wholly good (empathic, gratifying) or wholly bad (aloof, withholding). There is no gray area. Therefore he oscillates between chameleonlike conformity to the expectations of others, which affords a semblance of psychic safety, and sullen withdrawal, which temporarily affirms his charade of an individual self. But if the selfobject proves unable to tolerate the borderline's clinging dependency, what follows is panic, disintegration, feelings of being unreal, end-of-the-world sensations, and finally a psychotic ASC marked by ineffective suicide gestures. The one thing a borderline will *not* do is assert selfhood through independent action. To do so would stretch the fragile boundary separating self from other, and from the Ground, to the breaking point. This threatens dissolution into a psychotic ASC.

DO PARENTS CAUSE MADNESS?

Throughout the animal kingdom, only human beings develop manic or schizophrenic ASCs. A characteristic unique to the human race is a prolonged childhood with extended dependency on parents. Because this provides so many opportunities for a developing psyche to be derailed on its long journey to maturity, many theorists conclude that the genesis of madness is to be found in the way parents—especially mothers—raise their children.

In past decades, the term *schizophrenogenic* came into vogue to characterize mothers of children who later develop psychotic ASCs. Some describe these mothers as cold, cruel, obsessive, sexually repressed, semihuman sadists. Others more compassionately see them as overcome by difficulties caused by their own parents, an unstable marriage, social inequities imposed on females, or possibly their own genetic endowment.

Recently, however, there has been a powerful impetus to sweep away the idea that parents—no matter how aberrant their child-rearing techniques—have anything to do with psychosis. Led by crusading psychiatrist E. Fuller Torrey, this movement holds that we need look no further than one's genes, or perhaps a virus, to find the origin of madness. Torrey absolves parents of blame for their children's psychoses, which he views as primary brain diseases, nothing more. Because much parental guilt has been irrationally conceived, we might welcome this relatively more enlightened viewpoint, based as it is on important scientific verities.

Yet there is danger of smugness here, for the issue is far from settled. In their zeal to right a terrible wrong, Torrey and his followers lose sight of the fact that a genetic predisposition is just that—a predisposition, not an inevitability. Torrey seems victimized by the same kind of overinclusive thinking for which he pillories R. D. Laing and virtually every other advocate of psychological causation. Not all predisposed people become psychotic, so there must be nongenetic reasons that determine why some do, some don't, and a minority actually emerge from psychotic ASCs with stronger selves.

In other words, madness is as much a disorder of the mind as of the brain, if not more so. And because consciousness within a mind is on a higher order of being than the physical brain, it can never be completely determined by lower-order events. Mind is, however, *influenced* by physical events, which are, in reverse, even more profoundly influenced by consciousness. This great and enduring mystery will never yield to simplistic reductionism.

Torrey's unconvincing rejection of the possibility of schizophrenia being imprinted during early childhood turns attention away from another important likelihood. Even if parents do not actually cause madness in their children, there may be something they could do to *prevent* it once a child's genetic liability is established. We don't know this for sure, but there is reason to believe that there is hope.

To find out, it would seem simple to study how mothers of psychotics raise their children, and then avoid their practices. Descriptions of so-called schizophrenogenic mothers may be found in thoughtful writings by such intellectual luminaries as Harry Stack Sullivan, Melanie Klein, Bruno Bettelheim, Freida Fromm-Reichman, Gregory Bateson, Jay Haley, Theodore Lidz, Lyman Wynne, Alice Miller, Ping-Nie Pao, Harold Searles, Heinz Kohut, Otto Kernberg, and Silvano

Arieti, to name a few. But because most of these authors either wrote prior to the emergence of modern genetic research or seemed to ignore it, the fundamental idea of a schizophrenogenic mother seems ripe for revision.

By most accounts, a schizophrenogenic mother brings a sense of incompleteness to child raising. This does not mean that she rejects her child. Quite the contrary: she regards him as particularly close and significant for her. She *needs* her child in a distorted way as much as her child needs her. Because she cannot empathically differentiate her own anxieties, desires, and fantasies from the needs of her child—*her* self-object—she cannot set stable boundaries between them. By seeking to fill her own emptiness through him, she smothers his emergent sense of being the origin of his own thoughts and feelings. He lives with a constant threat of engulfment, of being absorbed into her being. Any movement toward autonomy leads him to feel that she cannot survive without him, added to his certainty that he cannot survive without her. For him to individuate would destroy them both.

The schizophrenogenic mother *owns* her child's inner world, and she governs her possession with scrupulous authority. In this way, the child comes to feel that his actions *originate* from his mother. The result is a child who can neither know the world he is in, nor orient himself in his own private existence. He feels that he is taking up too much space in the world, even with his thoughts. Like a slow virus lying quietly in wait for years, traces of this situation may intrude during psychotic ASCs later in life as feelings that he is dying, disappearing, or being kidnaped.

With such a psychic parasite for a caretaker, the child's vital energy is detoured into providing meaning for his mother's life, supporting her insecurity and fulfilling her frustrated fantasies, with scant remainder for his own development. Because he cannot distinguish which feelings arise from within, and which derive from his parent, a lack of correspondence between inner and outer reality is set in place. Small wonder that many psychotic ASCs revive feelings that someone is either stealing one's thoughts or implanting alien impulses within the mind.

The crazy-making conflicts have not yet ended, however, for the human élan vital is not to be denied. Because living beings naturally move toward greater independence and away from external control, the child continues for a while to angrily resist psychic annihilation, focusing his mounting hostility on his oppressor. But another deadly dilemma quickly emerges. The helpless child *needs* his mother, but he also *fears* her. The unfolding inner dialogue then becomes: "I need you. I fear you. I hate you. I hate myself because I need you."

Another checkmate. From here, the child can safely move neither forward nor back, nor is standing still possible. To hate someone necessary for survival is an irreconcilable predicament, but to hate oneself is worse. One defense may still be possible: projection, attributing one's hostile feelings to someone else. But if the recipient of this projected rage is the mother, the child experiences his own anger added on to her covert hostility toward him. He feels himself to be inescapably dependent upon a person by whom he feels persecuted. Vicious cycles set the stage for a lifetime of paranoia.

The child searches for a solution to this impossible circumstance. Instead of continuing the natural process of self-expansion, he contracts his own being to a minimum in order to accept his mother's identity as his own. But this fused mother-self cannot be other than freakish, self-hating, and ultimately dishonest. As the child approaches adulthood and once again reaches for his personal identity, his struggle with this grotesque false self forms the fault line of the schizophrenic cleavage. But for now, his problem is resolved. Having learned that self-initiated action harms those he most needs and fears, his false self resigns into docile compliance to the will of his maternal selfobject.

This temporary solution to a no-win separation-individuation scenario seems to work so well that the schizophrenogenic mother is fooled into believing that her approach is flawless. She may consider her child to be exceptionally good—no trouble at all. When one of several siblings becomes psychotic, it is common for parents to describe him as having been the "best one," the least likely to fall prey to mental disorder. Yet beneath this carefully maintained illusion, behavior that seemed so good is merely a leaden caricature of normal childhood vitality.

Years later we might encounter a still-fused mother-child dyad that has become lifelong in duration. After a series of increasingly regressive ASCs, the child (now a disheveled adult) is visited by his mother in a mental hospital. She sits indulgently, speaking for her son, scolding, overprotecting, rolling her eyes in mock tolerance when he intrudes with a crazy thought, treating him like an undependable child in need of control. At first, he slumps in his chair as he passively accedes to her usurping his selfhood. Then an unspoken threshold is crossed. With arms flailing, he leaps from his chair and bolts from the room, screaming that there is a vulture eating his eyes. Until one of them dies, neither will break this selfobject bond that devours the corpse of their individuality.

Like any prisoners, exiled feelings associated with the true self relentlessly seek escape by ferreting out weak points in the underside of awareness and tricking the guards with clever disguises. The true self becomes the shadow, in the Jungian sense. It is repressed and feared, but its clamorous presence is never to be denied. The incessant pressure from the endungeoned shadow threatens a lifelong danger of losing control.

My psychotic patients often exclaim that at the bottom of their surface symptoms is an omnipresent fear. What is it they fear? Although sometimes cloaked in projection, the answer is invariably "myself." Here is a deep dread of the *berserker* episode, of the true self's vengeful escape from its shackles, bearing with it ceaseless strivings for freedom and a life of its own.

After the evocative movie *The Exorcist* was released, there was a minor epidemic of people feeling possessed by intrusive "entities" threatening to set free their most unspeakable urges. Although healthy individuals with firm self-boundaries embrace such penetrating myths as opportunities to confront their own shadow natures, people struggling to fend off psychotic ASCs find them terrifying.

Some theorists extend the mothers-cause-madness idea to include manic states. They posit that mothers of manics have strong subconscious feelings of hostility coexisting with genuine affection for their child. The relationship has enough rewarding aspects to repeatedly whet the child's expectancies, only to frustrate their ultimate fulfillment. In other words, there is sufficient gratification to maintain arousal at a high pitch, but the child's need for consistent empathy is neither fulfilled nor totally ignored. The carrot is always in sight, but just beyond reach; the mother can neither reject her child nor allow him to be happy. The result is a child who oscillates between a grandiose "anything is possible" stance and hopeless despair—mania and depression.

Other investigators believe fathers of psychotics to be as disturbed and disturbing as their mothers. These men are alleged to be passive, insecure in their masculine identity, and ineffective in shielding their children from the pernicious influence of their spouse. These fathers are said to be submissively fearful of losing the approval of their dominant wives, behaving more as sons than husbands, and locked into a covert rivalry with their children for the affection of the mother.

If the above description of schizophrenogenic parents sounds suspiciously like the description of the borderline syndrome from chapter 3, it may not be by accident. One recent study showed that fully 75 percent of parents of schizophrenics who followed a malignantly regressive course were themselves borderline or frankly psychotic, while only 21 percent of parents of schizophrenics with mild or transient psychotic ASCs had such diagnoses. This suggests that the parents were themselves damaged at an early age—victims of a multigenerational family habit of poor child rearing. Or it could be that their psychopathology reflected a similar genetic endowment. That issue is far from settled.

DO FAMILIES CAUSE MADNESS?

A primary function of a family is to edit and interpret society's unwritten codes of conduct and transmit them to children. These lessons begin during infancy, and much of their content is subliminal, such as eye contact, facial expression, hand gestures, expressive tones of voice, and a sense of personal space. Because adult schizophrenics conspicuously fail to master these basic repertoires of their cultural heritage, family interaction is a logical place to search for the roots of madness.

Thomas Scheff once suggested a simple experiment to demonstrate the effect of deviating from our culture's unstated conventions.

> In your next conversation with a stranger, consistently focus your gaze on his ear rather than on his eyes or mouth. You will find the conversation to be dramatically askew for as long as you persist in this deviant interaction. The subject will contort his own gaze, or even move his body to realign visual contact. Most often, the discourse will be irretrievably damaged. Confusion, vertigo, and occasionally anger will emerge, not only in the subject, but oddly enough by the experimenter himself who will find it equally impossible to converse, or even think clearly, until he refocuses his gaze on more conventional areas of his listener's face.

Most societies insist on conformity to their unwritten rules and consider conspicuous deviations to be disruptive to the social fabric. A young adult who consistently ignores these conventions makes himself a target for derision. His peers consider him weird, untrustworthy, an outsider. What follows are obstinate vicious circles that wreath the life of a child whose family fails to prepare him for the social world.

A child raised in a healthy family not only develops a feeling for these prevailing norms, but also gains a more important insight—that these rules are only conveniences, that they are *relative*. He can later abandon those that do not fit his true self. But in schizophrenogenic families, this vital function breaks down: not only are the rules distorted, they are taught as *absolutes*.

More than twenty separate studies by at least ten different research teams have discovered wayward communication in families harboring children who developed psychotic ASCs, especially schizophrenia. Their results are consistent. Focusing on communication patterns alone, the researchers Lyman Wynne and Margaret Singer, who conducted at least six carefully designed studies, could predict which families would produce schizophrenic offspring after spending just a few hours in close contact with each family. Their conclusion: "communication deviance is a statistically significant 'predictor' of the severity of offspring pathology."

In a similar vein, Theodore Lidz, who led a Yale University family-research team, found his results to be so consistent that he wrote:

> Whatever segment of the family transactions we studied, we found something seriously amiss . . . All of the schizophrenic patients under my care came from disturbed or very peculiar families. Indeed, sometimes after spending an hour or two with one or both of the patient's parents, I would wonder just how long my sanity or anyone's sanity would withstand living with these people, to say nothing of being raised by them.

What these research teams consistently discovered in those families was communication that was blurred, inconsistent, amorphous, wandering, disruptive, and illogical. Questions were answered with questions, slips of the tongue went uncorrected, conclusions did not follow from premises, and neutral events were personalized. Vulnerable children did not occupy a definable niche in the family, but instead felt unliked and unwanted. Basic trust and cooperation were usurped by rivalry, undercutting of worth, threats of separation or rejection, and one parent conscripting the child into a power struggle against the other. The child lived in a battleground, frustrated in his efforts to satisfy either parent, locked into a losing situation at every turn.

Once a family oddity became apparent, members closed the doors to outsiders and presented a front of sham solidarity. Wynne and Singer described the confusion that a perceptive fly on the wall might experience during a family conversation.

> Instead of being able to follow and comprehend a line of thought and to visualize what the speaker is describing, a person listening to this type of [deviant communication] finds himself puzzled about what he is hearing and what he should think. The listener is unable to construct a consistent visual image or a consistent construct from the speaker's words.

Nothing generates suspiciousness more than ambiguity. If sophisticated researchers found themselves thrown off balance by the muddled syntax in these families, it is not difficult to imagine the impact it has on a tenuously structured child when it constitutes the predominant mode of relatedness in his life. If a child grows up never clearly knowing the intent of those who communicate with him, he is bound to invent his own strange explanations for things.

DO DOUBLE BINDS OR CONSTANT CRITICISM CAUSE MADNESS?

One particularly addled communication pattern—the double bind—is thought to unhinge children who are vulnerable to psychotic ASCs. Double binds were first described by the linguist and philosopher Gregory Bateson and his Stanford University coworkers, who pioneered the study of family patterns that lead to psychotic conclusions.

A double bind is simply a damned-if-you-do, damned-if-you-don't choice imposed by a strong person on a weaker one. Because the weaker person is forbidden to comment upon his predicament, this contradictory set of expectations allows no possibility of resolution or escape. In this way, a family might pressure a child to earn high grades, but then thwart his efforts to study by calling him a bookworm or making demands on his study time. To obey one command is to gainsay another. The following breakfast-table exchange is illustrative:

> Mother: Put some butter on this hot toast, Johnny.
> Child: (clumsily trying) Mommy, I can't.
> Mother: (impatiently grabbing the toast and buttering it herself) Johnny, you just must learn to be more independent!

In Bateson's view, such preposterous dialogues prevent a growing child from learning important social cues and distinctions. Double-bind theorists argue that it is exactly this cognitive cleavage, and the deeply ingrained confusion and ambivalence it engenders, that *is* schizophrenia.

One final theory of how families sow the seeds of madness is based on the way family members express emotions. Researchers have long known that some schizophrenic patients relapse shortly after returning home to live with their families, while others do not. They set out to identify what was different about these families. What immediately became apparent was that families, or halfway house proprietors, that promote relapse are highly critical, overinvolved, and intrusively concerned with trivial aspects of the person's life. Researchers named this combination "high expressed emotion" (high EE), because emotions are expressed with an acidic intensity that makes them especially difficult to swallow and digest without psychic dyspepsia.

For instance, a parent, in a high-EE family might say things like: "Johnny, you lazy bum, why do you stay in bed half the day? I know you're just doing it to spite me. You'll never make anything of yourself." Contrast this to a low-EE parent, who might say, "Johnny, if you try to get up a bit earlier, you'll probably get more done." This is not to say that families should be encouraged to keep their feelings to themselves. But they can learn to avoid criticism that induces guilt ("You're giving me a headache"), overinclusive remarks about personality ("You are an arrogant young man"), or declarations about what the child is thinking or feeling ("You enjoy being mean to your sister"). When high-EE families learn to control their vitriolic outbursts, to balance criticism with praise, to set realistic goals, and to include a bit of humor in their exchanges, the relapse rate of psychotic family members declines.

If such vulnerability to emotional overkill exists among adult schizophrenics, we might speculate that predisposed children would be even more defenseless. As yet there is no hard evidence to indicate that a high-EE environment throughout childhood actually *causes* psychotic ASCs. Yet several researchers have extended their findings to suggest that high EE is one of several factors that convert a genetic tendency for dopamine overactivity into a psychotic outcome. This idea gains credibility in light of cross-cultural studies that show that societies such as those of the Pacific Islanders, which frown upon passionate outbursts and temper emotionally charged bonding between family members, have low rates of mental disorders of all sorts.

THE ROOTS OF MADNESS: A SYNTHESIS

Just as all but the most creed-bound geneticists admit to a certain plausibility in the above accounts of crazy-making parents, so all but the most dogmatic of psychological theorists acknowledge that genes play an important role in some forms of madness. If we look at genetic and family influence together, we can study how to amend their interaction to reduce the likelihood of malignant regression.

A second look at the evidence that families cause madness opens the possibility of the opposite effect, that it is the genetically predisposed *child* who upsets the balance of his family, who in turn respond to him aberrantly. In other words, family theorists may have confused interactions that cause psychosis with those *caused by* psychosis. When they observe a fused mother-child dyad, they may be merely viewing a mother's instinctive efforts to compensate for a subtly deficient infant. As E. Fuller Torrey points out, clinicians who treat schizophrenics are acutely aware of the disruptions to normal family life that result from having a psychotic family member at home.

For instance, prepsychotic children who display "tactile defensiveness" engender a curious turnabout of the tails-I-win, heads-you-lose scenario. From birth, these children cry when picked up and show contentment only when set back down, thereby providing a neat but incalculable double bind for anyone trying to follow the rules of good mothering. The *interaction* between mother and child thus becomes mired in a cycle of poor mutual cuing and shared frustration and pain.

The counterpoint is that this argument assigns far too much power to a child surrounded by mature adults who are—or ought to be—able to compensate and adapt. Yet it does illustrate how each of the arguments for family causation can be reinterpreted in light of genetic research.

As we begin our quest to integrate nature and nurture, we must first acknowledge the sad reality of pure genetic forms of madness that take an inexorably malignant course even within near-ideal families. These make up the preponderance of chronic schizophrenics who have enlarged cerebral ventricles, thickened corpora callosa, atrophy of the frontal cortex, or abnormal electrical activity deep in the limbic system. Some have never fully developed beyond first-chakra consciousness, and others have permanently regressed to this primitive and weakly bounded level.

I have encountered families who produced one severely schizophrenic individual out of several children, the others being normal in every respect. When I compared how these children were raised, often by sensitive and empathetically attuned parents, I could find no difference that came close to explaining how one child could have acquired such a comprehensive failure of his core self purely from living with these parents. Although unrecognized birth trauma could not be ruled out, the parents were clearly not to blame, although some of them *felt* they were. In this regard, Silvano Arieti, one of the original proponents of the idea of schizophrenogenic mothers, eventually concluded that only about 25 percent of mothers of schizophrenics fit the image.

We can extend this reasoning to cases of recurring mania that arise within families with a strong genetic loading for that episodic malady. Unlike schizophrenic ASCs, stressful life events do not generally precipitate manic or depressive episodes, which follow an internally driven rhythm of their own. Observed between manic and depressive phases, the personalities of these people are often surprisingly well integrated— many better than average—despite cyclic disruptions of their life course that strain their capacity to adapt. We may reasonably assume that the core personality is a more accurate indicator of the quality of one's parenting than is a propensity for surges of norepinephrine and periodic states of hyperarousal.

In contrast, the disjointed and contradictory selves that emerge in multiple personality disorder can almost always be traced to traumatic childhood experiences, either perpetrated by deranged parents, or following their failure to protect their children from abuse. There is no reason to suspect a genetic role in MPD. Because the conditions underlying this disorder are rooted in second-chakra consciousness, they will be considered in the next chapter.

For psychotic ASCs that are less than malignantly regressive, but potent enough to derail the self's smooth progression through life's stages, I propose that traumatic perinatal and early-life events are at least partially responsible, more so than is currently acknowledged. When such ASCs emerge spontaneously, they can precipitate regression to lower-chakra consciousness during troublesome transition periods, especially when the self encounters a barrier to spiritual growth.

So in some cases there is an irresistible genetic push toward psychotic ASCs. In others there is a weaker genetic leaning that can be overridden by ideal parenting. In still others there is no genetic contribution at all, simply a frail self-structure that was held back by prolonged fusion with powerful but insecure selfobjects. In the latter instance, such damaging experiences would have to take place during first-chakra consciousness, when primal membranes that differentiate self from other, and from Ground, begin to encircle the self.

What is confusing about all this is that the end product may look the same. This suggests that researchers who found aberrant communication in families of schizophrenics may have measured the *residual effects* of damage—either genetic or psychological—that occurred much earlier in life, perhaps even before or during birth. Although errant communication—double binds, high EE, etc.—can make a child neurotic or confused about certain aspects of himself, it is not in itself sufficient to cause psychosis unless the self was undermined much earlier in life. Once the first chakra is successfully negotiated, it is too late to create a psychotic, no matter how diabolical the effort.

FIRST-CHAKRA REGRESSION

If first-chakra consciousness is the soil where the roots of madness take hold, it is also a level to which a maturing self might regress during severe psychotic ASCs. An adult whose self-center has descended to the first chakra for whatever reason is painful to behold. This is a level of oral and anal fixations, appropriate for an infant struggling to survive the first years of life. *Survival* is their primary purpose, but survival for an infant, not for an adult who carries back with him dislodged patterns of second- or third-chakra consciousness. These out-of-place cognitive sets inevitably cast his infantile strivings in a bizarre light.

When a malignantly psychotic ASC takes a person back this far, his consciousness is preoccupied with food, coffee, or endless cigarettes consumed obsessively, with little enjoyment. Occasionally he will obsessively drink water until he damages his kidneys, a hazard among institutionalized schizophrenics. Like a presocialized infant, he may be fascinated with feces to the point of smearing them on walls or placing them in his mouth.

Hoarding small trinkets, sometimes hidden in body cavities, is irresistible for a severely regressed psychotic, who may enhance his odd appearance by decorating his clothing with bits of colorful trash. Spontaneous speech, when it occurs at all, is directed toward immediate gratification of alimentary needs, both oral and anal. In severely regressed people, speech may be replaced by repetitive rocking motions, as if to recapture some dimly remembered pacification from long ago. There is a minimum of expressed feeling, except for an occasional tantrum when he is frustrated. He is dependent upon others for survival, but he never forms attachments to them.

People whose self-center operates predominantly from the first chakra do not respond to therapies appropriate for higher-level consciousness, such as intensive psychotherapy or spiritual techniques designed to enhance openings to the Ground. If these are attempted, as they sometimes are by desperate families and naive therapists, they are frustrating for patient and healer alike, and usually make matters worse.

Many severely regressed people can be helped to live functional lives through the artful use of antipsychotic medicines, but care must be taken not to overdo this perilous intervention, especially over the long term. A trial on megavitamins administered by a physician trained in orthomolecular psychiatry will probably be harmless and may benefit a minority of cases.

Although it is generally inappropriate for people centered at higher chakras, behavior modification is especially suited for first-chakra consciousness. If skillfully applied, simple stimulus-reward contingencies, do not tax the infantile coping skills of these patients and can improve social skills to the point where some can rejoin the community in sheltered homes. Recent research indicates that many of these people, if provided a humane environment with reasonable expectations, can improve markedly over the long term.

Although regression to the first chakra usually occurs only among people with malignant ASCs, it occasionally takes place as part of a *reparative* sequence during benign regressions. Unlike malignant ASCs, these "mini-regressions" almost always follow a catastrophic life event, such as being abandoned by an important selfobject, that rekindles infantile trauma. Emotions are retained, and there is confusion and agitation proportional to the velocity of the self's headlong retreat through levels of consciousness. Although thinking is disorganized, and speech may be little more than a delirious babble, there are also moments of lucidity and self-observation during which the individual recognizes his predicament and cries out for help. Hallucinations are poorly formed and indistinct, and there may be vague delusions referable to the stomach or bowels. We may contrast this to chronic first-chakra regressions characterized by passivity, pervasive lack of insight, and absence of hallucinations and delusions.

A self-center caught up in this kind of atavistic quicksand cannot gain a handhold even in second-chakra consciousness (where most manic and schizophrenic regressions arrest themselves), and is drawn downward to the most primitive level. The higher chakras are closed—nonoperative in consciousness—but they can be reactivated if matters are not forced, and if the person is sheltered from the stress that precipitated the breakdown.

If a person caught up in such a crisis is provided a safe environment, with ready gratification of his survival needs and a minimum of demands on his coping capacity, his predominant mode of consciousness will gradually ascend to the next level. He will need a temporary parent to empathetically guide him through this second infancy. An artful healer who assumes this role must follow his patient's progress with a discerning eye, and employ therapeutic strategies that specifically address each level of consciousness as the self-center haltingly moves upward.

FROM PREDISPOSITION TO PREVENTION

As we devise new strategies to minimize the chance of either a genetic predisposition to psychosis or toxic parents producing a lifelong invalid, we must include both genetic and family theories. Given this new synthesis, it is likely that as many as half of permanently disabling psychotic ASCs could be prevented, or diverted into favorable life path-ways.

For instance, we might imagine a child who inherited a tendency to experience the world and interpret its many realities in nonconsensual ways. We might also envision this child's hypothetically ideal parents informed in advance of his genetic predisposition by technology that will likely be available within the next decade.

As that child learns to live in the world, his frontal lobes are relatively unable to integrate sequences of ideas without specially structured cues or commands. Because communication between the left and right hemispheres of his brain may be partially obstructed, he has trouble placing his actions in social contexts, unless his parents devote extra attention to these skills. He finds it difficult to modulate his emotions when he is frustrated or confronted with uncertainty. During such moments, the dopamine centers in his limbic system become overactive, and he feels a discordant inner restlessness that requires extraordinary amounts of empathic soothing to still.

Now imagine that this child's parents intuitively recognize that he exists within a field of consciousness that includes their own thoughts and feelings. This enables them to compensate for the child's unique way of processing sensory information. During pregnancy, the mother is treated as special by her own loving selfobjects, so she finds it easy to maintain a placid inner state. Her pregnancy allows her extra time to meditate regularly, and through this practice she establishes an unspoken communion with her unborn and with the subconscious residues of her own early life experience.

As the time of birth nears, the mother rehearses breathing and pelvic exercises to facilitate her natural delivery. As the child enters the world, he is welcomed into a softly lit room, the predominant feature of which is his mother's warm skin and breast as she gently bathes and massages him. The synapses that are rapidly proliferating within his still-unfinished brain form a physical supporting grid for a psychic self that is primed to accept soothing, is ready to trust, and can intuit a sense of belongingness.

As the newborn's psyche begins to construct holographic patterns of the consensual world, his empathic parents instinctively anticipate his needs, neither overstimulating him nor leaving him wanting. Wordless harmonies resonate between him and his caretakers and condition his own fundamental vibrational patterns. These harmonies are periodically broken by inevitable frustrations and deprivations, but timely reunions with empathic parents quickly restore synchronous patterns within his psychic field.

As the child grows into a toddler, empathic mirroring enlivens his tentative explorations of a world apart from mother, followed by just a little extra soothing that directs his psychic energies along navigable neural pathways. This compensates for his inborn exaggerated stress reaction and enables him to incorporate his mother's self within his own without fear of engulfment. His self-secure mother joyfully encourages his wary independence and offers a fresh measure of support during what is a particularly lengthy rapprochement period. This insures that his slowly forming self-boundaries can withstand the social challenges that this unusual child will later endure.

As the child learns to communicate, his parents take pains to be consistent in their rewards and punishments. When he is excited and hyperaroused, they set firm limits on his behavior, and they teach him to cope with this and similar ASCs by monitoring his breathing and concentrating on his inner awareness, especially his feelings. They teach him to ask for a massage and also to give one back. Both calm a turbulent arousal. Kindly, they teach him to laugh at them, and at himself.

Finally, as the child approaches maturity, his parents encourage him to express his unique experience of the world, and all the ways it strays from the overtrodden path of the consensus, through creative expression—art, music, poetry, science. Nondogmatic religious rituals emphasizing universal love facilitate his ability to entertain openings to the Ground, so that these become a lifelong source of inspiration to a progressively *larger self,* rather than a source of dissolution and loss of selfhood.

The genetically predisposed child enters maturity not merely as a conforming member of society, but as one poised to express his unique endowment in a way not given to his peers. His capacity to reorder reality no longer catches him off guard, but instead inspires his progress through levels of consciousness that others find unapproachable through ordinary means. A firm core self at his center is prepared to shed the artificial boundaries of worldly ego so as to explore what lies beyond. The potential madman has grown into a potential sage, an uncommon traveler in territories off-limits to common humanity.

CHAPTER 10

Second Chakra:
Hallucinations & The Occult

◆

Incommensurable, impalpable, yet latent in it are forms;
Impalpable, incommensurable, yet within it are entities.
Shadowy it is and dim.
                                                    LAO-TZU

Ain't it just like the night to play tricks when you're tryin' to be so quiet?
                                                    BOB DYLAN

THE ESSENCE OF second-chakra consciousness is captured in a charming and popular comic strip, *Calvin and Hobbes*. Calvin is a free-spirited lad who chafes against anything that restricts his perfect liberty. His counterploy to the powerlessness of childhood is to mobilize an assortment of grandiose fantasies. In a flash, he transforms himself into a fearless space cadet on a cosmic assignment, a rampaging dinosaur who terrorizes the school-yard bully, a majestic eagle who soars high above his teachers and parents.

Hobbes is Calvin's stuffed-tiger doll, a loyal, intimately involved, but sometimes contrary companion with a mind of his own. Hobbes's special knack is to become a *real tiger* only when alone with Calvin. Together they invent games, plot adventures, and try to cope with adult authority and drooling monsters that lurk under the bed at night. Carefree but temperate, Hobbes is Calvin's only friend; he needs no other. It matters little that Hobbes appears to grown-ups as a limp and lifeless doll. To Calvin, his companion's vital reality far exceeds any need for confirmation.

The popularity of *Calvin and Hobbes* speaks for a universal longing to recapture our turbulent passage through the consciousness of the Svadhisthana chakra. We know that we left something important back there, some dimly remembered alchemy, something *magical*. Yet we also instinctively draw back from Calvin's enchanted world, for there is unspoken danger there. The whole of civilization stands united against our return. The danger we fear is of nothing less than madness.

We may imagine Calvin having matured into an adult. Would he be a psychiatric patient lost in a fantasy world of his own making, diagnosed as suffering from hallucinations and delusions about talking animals? Likely not. That irrepressibly imaginative lad would surely have grown into a novelist, an inventor of artful contrivances, or perhaps a maverick entrepreneur famous for his quirky promotions. Poor Hobbes, his stuffing straining through mud-smeared tiger stripes, his strength and spirit long ago absorbed into Calvin's own, lies crumpled in a forgotten trunk in the attic. Calvin's punishment for abandoning his best friend is to regard his own offspring with the same bewilderment he caused his parents.

But for Calvin to negotiate the slippery slope upward from second-chakra consciousness, he would have to pass through a several-year span when many of the symptoms of adult psychotic ASCs are considered *normal*. By the conclusion of this period, he would have radically altered his relation to his parents, consensual reality, and the Ground.

In this chapter, we explore the psychology of the phantasmagoric world of the second chakra in its normal childhood manifestations and in its pathological aspect.

THE TYPHONIC SELF

Ken Wilber refers to the consciousness of the second chakra as "typhonic," after the Typhon, a mythological being, half-human, half-serpent. This is an apt symbol for a time of life when the brain's center of control moves upward from reptilian to old-mammalian (limbic) levels, and when the mental self similarly ascends from instinctual to emotional and sexual realms. The task of the typhonic stage is to prepare the individual for his or her eventual next step to the neocortical rationality of the third chakra.

Once a child masters the crucial rapprochement tasks at the transition between the first and second chakras, and has grown comfortable with brief periods away from his mother, he gains an indispensable cognitive skill called *object constancy*. This is the ability to form a stable mental image of what is not immediately present to the senses. Object constancy is a faculty that most adults take for granted, but which people prone to psychotic ASCs struggle to maintain.

For example, if a toddler is to risk exploring the flower garden while his mother is in the kitchen, he must maintain a stable mental image of her. This image soothes him by assuring that she has neither disappeared nor turned into something else while out of sight. Without object constancy—learned from repeated goings-from and returnings-to a predictable selfobject—the external world does not stay put long enough for an enduring sense of consensual reality to take hold. A child who cannot master object constancy grows up with a fluid sense of reality and a vague paranoid feeling that things are not as they seem.

Besides object constancy, eight other characteristics distinguish early typhonic consciousness: (1) a fledgling self that cannot stand on its own without external support and, hence, is easily drawn back to the Ground, to which it is powerfully attracted; (2) a self that identifies with the physical body—that is, is not yet mental or located in the head; (3) self-boundaries shared with parents, although relatively less so than during the first-chakra stage; (4) self-boundaries that enclose a rudimentary sense of I-ness, but which are far more permeable to the Ground than those of a mature adult; (5) a creative but concrete cognitive life, dominated by emotions that are relatively untempered by rationality; (6) a vivid fantasy life that intermixes wishes with consensual reality; (7) the beginnings of a sense of linear time, with fantasy-tinged recollection of past and anticipation of future; (8) a logical system in which effects sometimes precede causes.

It may be obvious that these traits characterize adults caught up in psychotic ASCs as much as they describe normal toddlers. This is because most psychotic regressions eventually arrest themselves in second-chakra consciousness, often permanently.

For a child to emerge from this phantasmic level into a civilized world, he must gradually sever his once-blissful communion with the countless realities of the Ground and affirm the single reality of the consensus. This developmental process radically constricts awareness.

The child performs this task through a *second* rapprochement phase. If the first partially split him from his mother, the second wrests him from the hypnotic embrace of the Ground. In other words, just as he did during the earlier maternal rapprochement phase, the child tentatively "wanders away" from the Ground into the world of the consensus, supported within his parents' self-boundaries. He can accomplish this only if the first rapprochement phase provided him with a reliable sense of object constancy with his mother, and increasingly with his father. The child's mental image of his parents is a way-station that shelters him as he turns his awareness from its Source and replaces that connection with the worldly strength of his parents.

This creates an inevitable conflict between consensual reality, represented by his parents, and the fascinating energies of the Ground, now increasingly labeled fantasy or hallucination. So at this point the child must choose either repression or regression, with scant middle ground. If he sides with the consensual world, he forfeits a larger realm of emotion, creativity, and union. Conversely, if he does not sever his connection with the Ground, he surrenders will, autonomy, and any chance for a coherent ego. This is always a painful choice: there is loss in either case. Yet repression is clearly the better of the two possibilities, for it allows the self-as-ego to grow, and so bears hope for eventual reunion with the Ground. If his parents do not support him in this task, he will turn from their world back toward his original immersion in the Ground. This is usually temporary, but it sets the stage for later psychotic regressions.

There is a less obvious danger. The sealing off of self from Ground might be *too* complete. The Spiritual Ground is the wellspring of all experience, the vital power underlying sentient life itself. Although the growing self must turn away from the seductive allure of the Ground, that separation is ideally a partial and temporary one, a passage in exile that sets the stage for a triumphant return after certain tasks have been completed.

Only by virtue of its intimate relation with the Ground can the self live in grace, connected to its instinctual, creative, and spiritual roots. Without partial openings to this envitalizing power, a split-off self takes on an enfeebled alienation and forfeits inspiration to continue upward through the chakras and back to its Source. Such a closed-off self may have no trouble gaining third-chakra consciousness, but it will encounter great resistance if it is to develop spiritually beyond that stage.

THE BIRTH OF EGO

Children who see or hear things that others do not are quickly taught that their perceptions are inaccurate. For this reason, the second rapprochement phase that echoes throughout the early years of life presents a great dilemma to the growing child. The power of the Ground continues to imbue his weakly bounded self with an enchanted aura. Enough remains of the original connection to render the world awesome, mysterious, full of unplumbed depths and hidden meanings. Poised against this is the strength of his parents as representatives of consensual reality, enforcers of a narrow worldview.

Just as the child craves the blissful contentment of being submersed in his oceanic Source, so he is drawn toward becoming an individuated being who shares the world of his parents. Of course, his parents are ordained by the necessities of civilized life to win the battle, at least for a time. At first, the child merely keeps secret his rapturous moments of communion. But gradually the energies of the Ground grow ever more distant from awareness. What was once so close as a breath now takes on an eerie strangeness, a sense of being threatening, alien, *occult*.

As the child repeatedly affirms his worldly orientation, the Ground becomes a *deus absconditus*—an absent God. Remnants of its living presence are banished to the subconscious mind, sealed over and hidden from view by the overpowering glare of the sensory world. Just as the rising sun obscures the nighttime stars, so does the crude force of the material realm obliterate the Ground's subtle energies by dominating attention through the senses. If memories of its depth occasionally break loose from their subterranean chambers to reenter awareness, they make a frightening mismatch with consensual reality, which is reinforced again and again by the child's expanding social contacts.

Transpersonal philosopher Michael Washburn termed this obligatory splitting of self from Source, *original repression*. Although the task of forced forgetting spans several years, when it is complete the typhonic child is radically transformed into a socialized being locked into a single consensual reality. This change is as much physical as psychic. The repressed power of the Ground does not simply disappear; rather, it is confined within the lower regions of the body—the lower abdomen, pelvis and genitals. This, in turn, frees the self to find a haven in the mental space associated with the head.

The temporary "victory" over the the Ground, and the mind-body split that ensues, signals the end of the child's identification with his physical body. The body and its unruly emotions are demoted from self to object. Limited in feeling and awareness, the child begins to identify exclusively with the cerebral realm. No longer is the self a grand composite of body, mother, and Ground. To engage the social world, it must turn away from these greater identifications. The self then splits off and identifies with the *ego*. The ego is like a psychic circle drawn around a part of the self, so that everything outside seems dark and alien.

Originally merely a mediator between the typhonic self and the external world, the inflated ego comes to assume a central position in consciousness, which it jealously guards until it is (possibly) transcended much later in life. Although the mystical insight that the worldly ego is an instrument of illusion that blinds us to a greater reality is an important spiritual truth, this is far from saying that we would be better off without having formed an ego in the first place. In order to transcend the ego, we must first possess one that is well fortified and maintained in working order until the consciousness of the higher chakras prepares us to reclaim our whole selves. The path back to spirit never bypasses adulthood.

Taking up residence in the space vaguely located behind the eyes, the newly empowered ego disowns the body and the Ground. (Peoples of non-technological cultures often locate their sense of "I" elsewhere. The Pueblo Indians of the American Southwest believe the self to be centered in the chest, while some African tribes locate it in the belly.) It redefines itself as a disincarnate "thinking thing," and thereby nurtures the grandiose illusion that it is completely on its own. Of course, for it to exist at all, the ego must continuously draw sustenance from the Ground, but it develops a kind of amnesia about this essential reality. Without this forgetting, an independent and socialized existence would be impossible, along with any chance for significant spiritual growth. Yet the primal consciousness of the Ground, embedded in every neuron of the brain, every living cell of the body, is not to be denied. It lies in wait, sometimes assuming disguises to play tricks on the sane and psychotic alike, although in different ways.

Because original repression redirects the energies of the Ground toward the lower body—the sexual system—it marks the point at which genital predominance begins. This is the Oedipal period so well described by Freud. If the focus of first-chakra consciousness is on *survival,* the focus of the second chakra is on *sexuality,* energized by the submerged power of the Ground. Of course, the classic outcome of the Oedipal conflict is further repression of the newly sexualized Ground. Freud renamed this life force "libido," and although he believed that it is *only* sexual, he also recognized it as the source of all psychic energy.

Original repression represents a twofold gain. First, it allows the mental ego to command the split-off body from on high. This enables the ego to overrule the body's incessant oral, anal, and sexual urges so as to be "sane and socialized." Second, original repression selectively seals off areas of the self-boundary that permit influx of nonconsensual Ground energies (gateways that some psychotics never close). This prepares the ego to enter the competitive worldly arena of the third chakra.

Yet, at the same time, original repression brings about a profound loss. Half of the human endowment—the larger self that contains the wisdom of its Source—is exiled from awareness. If an individual is to avoid regression into psychosis, this split must be steadfastly maintained until the worldly ego is *fully prepared* to reengage its disowned larger self through conscious and willing surrender to the ever-present Ground.

THE FALL FROM EDEN

Original repression is a mythic theme that emerges symbolically during a variety of ASCs that reopen self to Ground. Western cultures express it as the Judeo-Christian myth of the Fall.

Eden can be likened to our innocent immersion in the Ground, a state of divine union far removed from the travails of the material world. Eve, our human mother bearing the fruit of worldly knowledge, is the instrument of exile from the Garden. The serpent—a potent symbol of the submerged Ground as an occult force—conveys this worldly knowledge to her, and along with it free will and responsibility. Primal humanity *must* turn away from both the serpent and God so as to suffer an alienated journey through the earthly realm and ultimately back to Eden.

Yet the serpent is the key figure in the tale, an exile from heaven that represents what must now be hidden. Dare we return the worldly apple to him and reown Paradise? No, to retrace our steps leads only to Hell, to *madness*. We must forge ahead at any cost, gaining awareness at each new level. The serpent is thus a complex symbol of our primitive evolutionary roots, of repressed sexuality, and of the forbidden power of the Ground mythically projected as an alien and occult force. But that same iridescent reptile is also a representation of the serpentine path through adulthood and back to the Garden.

It is in this latter aspect that the serpent is cast within the ancient chakra symbolism of Tantric yoga that forms the model for these seven chapters. Representing repressed and sexualized Ground energies— called *kundalini*—the serpent is depicted as a latent source of spiritual power coiled asleep in the first chakra, centered in the pelvis. Threatening the danger of madness if prematurely disturbed, the slumbering serpent must be awakened only through disciplined spiritual practice that gradually elevates awareness upward through these planes of being.

Once aroused, the kundalini serpent ascends upward through the chakras, opening each sequentially. If controlled, it elevates the seeker to joyful reunion with the Source at the seventh chakra. If uncontrolled, its untimely ascent sweeps the ego into chaos—a "spiritual emergency." The serpent is thus an emissary of occult power, a supremely debased bearer of madness if uncontrolled, but also a guiding beacon illuminating the path to ultimate salvation.

Not all people find that spiritual path easy to follow. Some halt at the late stages of the second chakra, their enfeebled ego suspended, able neither to master the consensual world nor to return to the Source. These are the "borderlines," who constantly depend on the support of stronger selfobjects to maintain their precarious hold on a constricted reality.

Others tentatively achieve the third level of consciousness, only to plummet back to the second chakra when they encounter an intolerable stress. This catastrophic outcome may follow a massive failure of the cerebral cortex to keep lower brain systems in check (as in schizophrenia or late mania) or abortive efforts of an immature self to expand into higher states (spiritual emergencies). In either case, the individual again opens to the Ground, not as an innocent toddler absorbed in harmless fantasies, and not as an accomplished seer provisioned for a triumphant journey home. Unchecked regression produces only a confused and floundering ego that vainly struggles to force consensual reality models onto the energies of the Ground as they percolate into awareness. What follows is an absurd mismatch of realities that leads directly to madness.

Any such resurgence of Ground energies can assume many forms in awareness. But because they were banished by original repression, they are perceived as not-self. Originating from "outside," they flood into the psyche as hallucinations, or as riptides of alien feelings and impulses. Plato captured the essence of this in his "doctrine of recollection": when the soul grows accustomed to the world, it forgets its vision of the divine light and so becomes mad to retrieve what it has lost.

Other than the pathological categories of modern psychiatry, technological cultures provide no models to help us integrate these uncanny experiences. So an individual confronting them often falls back on models provided by systems of the occult—a word meaning "hidden from view." The extensive literature of the occult, which reached its pinnacle during the Middle Ages, was largely created by people who encountered nonconsensual Ground energies. It represents their often bizarre efforts to communicate otherworldly perceptions to a secular society that was progressively locking into a single consensual reality.

THE SPECTRUM OF HALLUCINATIONS

It is virtually impossible to walk the streets of an inner city without meeting one of those strange, lost souls who oddly gesticulate and mumble to themselves in solitary conversation. We wonder what on earth they hear in reply, but few of us muster the audacity to inquire.

Even jaded mental-health professionals are unsettled when confronted by hallucinating people. Most hesitantly inquire, "Do you hear voices?" then hastily change the subject. It is not difficult to understand why. There is a natural reluctance in us all to enter private worlds populated by ghostly apparitions and unearthly presences of sinister intent. When one does cross that threshold, one is likely to return with an appreciation of why occult hypotheses of hallucinations have not vanished, despite the scorn they engender in the scientific establishment.

Consider this account by one of my recovering psychotic patients describing hallucinations that emerged during the acute phase of his ASC:

> It began gradually while I was spending a lot of time alone in my apartment. At first it was just a feeling that something was watching me, like a presence. Then I'd see something moving out of the corner of my eye, but when I'd look directly there would be nothing there. The voices began as kind of a background chatter too soft to make out exactly, like gurgles in a stream. I became convinced that someone was in my apartment, so I'd search from room to room and find no one. It really got scary when I heard something whispering my name over and over. I called a priest, but he just told me to go see a headshrinker.
>
> After a couple of days of this I started to hear whole conversations among individual voices: a woman, a man, then another woman, mostly laughing and poking fun at me. Sometimes they seemed good-natured, but at other times they would curse and insult me. One made jokes about my penis whenever I'd use the bathroom. Then people began walking around my living room dressed in different things—business suits, blue jeans, even glasses. One woman wore a pretty red dress. They would move around as if they were looking for something and enter closets and other rooms. I told myself I was just hallucinating, but the more carefully I looked, the more details I noticed, like unwashed hands, missing buttons, and braids in the woman's hair. One seemed to have a cold because he coughed all the time. I'm telling you, Doc, these people seemed just as real as you do right now!

Although not all people in psychotic ASCs experience hallucinations of such clarity, they are by no means uncommon and can take many grotesque forms. Every historical epoch has recorded accounts by individuals who see and hear things imperceptible to others. Some cast them as religious revelations or express them as art. But mostly—and for good reason—they keep them to themselves.

Yet there is evidence that hallucinations once held a more predominant place in daily experience than they do now. In ancient times, people did not "hallucinate"; they saw *visions* and received *revelations* that were sometimes prophetic and played an important role in daily life. In the *Iliad*, for instance, the Greek heroes of old seemed incapable of making decisions on their own without direct guidance from the voices of the gods. Early books of the Bible tell of people receiving direct verbal commands from their patriarchal deity as they sought divine guidance.

No less a figure than Socrates admitted to hearing a precognitive inner voice. In the *Theagetes*, Plato quotes him: "By favor of the Gods, I have, since my childhood, been attended by a semidivine being whose voice from time to time dissuades me from some undertaking, but never directs me what I am to do." The historian Xenophon, in his *Apology for Socrates*, attributes these words to the martyred philosopher:

> "The prophetic voice has been heard by me throughout my life:it is certainly more trustworthy than omens from the flight or entrails of birds. I call it a God or daimon. I have told my friends of the warnings I have received, and up to now the voice has never been wrong."

Socrates spent his days as a teacher and did not establish a religion based on what his inner voice told him. But our most venerable religions were based on the teachings of people overwhelmed by what would now be considered a hallucinatory psychosis. Saint Paul, (Saul, before his conversion) for instance, was notorious for his anti-Christian polemics. One day he was traveling on the road to Damascus when

> suddenly there shone round about him a light out of heaven, and he fell upon the earth and heard a voice saying unto him, "Saul, Saul, why persecutest thou me?" . . . and he was three days without sight, and did neither eat nor drink.

Similarly, Mohammed, founder of Islam, experienced a complex hallucination while fasting and meditating in a cavern.

> Wrapped in his mantle he heard a voice calling upon him . . . He beheld an angel in human form which displayed a silken cloth covered with written characters. "Read," said the angel. "I know not how to read," replied Mohammed. "Read," repeated the angel . . . Upon this, Mohammed instantly felt his understanding illumined with celestial light and read what was written on the cloth.

Whether revelatory or psychotic, hallucinations occur in states of consciousness that are outside of clearheaded wakefulness, such as dreaming, psychedelic drug trips, prolonged sensory deprivation from solitary confinement, delirium from fever or alcohol withdrawal, epileptic seizures in the limbic system, deep hypnosis, religious ecstasy brought about by fasting and repetitive prayer, and the near-death condition. Each of these ASCs weakens self-membranes and opens awareness to unfamiliar patterns from the Ground.

However, not all hallucinations are solitary events. Anthropologists have reported simultaneous group visions during shamanic rituals in primitive societies. Even modern cultures provide anecdotal accounts of simultaneous hallucinations among group meditators and communal psychedelic users, suggesting that there is a latent human potential for recontacting the Ground by these means. Because such collective visions are open to consensual validation, they conform to the social definition of reality. Nevertheless, most psychotic hallucinations are private and unwelcome.

Hallucinations during manic states, melancholic depression, and other psychotic ASCs differ little from those of schizophrenia. There is one important distinction, however. People with multiple personality disorder (MPD) often hear the voice of an "alter" for weeks before it first acquires power to enter the body at will . They perceive the alter's voice coming from *inside their head,* in contrast to voices heard by schizophrenics and manics that originate in the external world—a ventilator duct or electrical appliance. Even after the alter gains the ability to take command, some MPD sufferers can hear it speaking while it is not in the body, but "nearby." Alters usually lack the threatening quality of schizophrenic voices or the grandiose tone of manic voices.

Common wisdom has it that visual hallucinations are associated with acute brain diseases, such as meningitis and fever delirium, just as auditory hallucinations occur in schizophrenia and mania. However, some manics and schizophrenics see vaguely formed bodies or faces speaking to them before they fall asleep or during moments of relative sensory deprivation. Complex hallucinations can arise in which a person sees, hears, touches, and even smells an apparition, a most discomfiting experience.

Most psychotics perceive their hallucinations as unequivocally *real,* and they cannot distinguish them from normal vision and audition. For instance, if a visual hallucination follows one's shifting gaze, moving to wherever the eyes fall, it would be reasonable to conclude that there is a disturbance in the visual cortex of the brain. The flashing lights known to migraine sufferers fall into this category. However, psychotic people commonly hallucinate humanlike figures that appear in a corner of a room, disappear from sight when they look away, then are waiting in the original position when they look back. These spectral figures conform to mundane physical laws, becoming obscured when something passes in front of them, reappearing when it is removed, and themselves blocking from view objects in the room that are behind them.

Visual hallucinations may be of ordinary people wearing workaday clothing, but may just as readily be fantastic monsters. Lilliputian humanoids may appear, like the dwarfish figures encountered by people sensitive to certain medicines. One elderly gentleman, who developed a sensitivity to an antiulcer drug, suddenly encountered gnomelike creatures strolling around his retirement home. These clownish apparitions mimed the gestures of the old folks, performed cartwheels, and entertained him with foolish facial expressions. These hallucinations occurred in an otherwise clear state of mind, and apart from their outlandish appearance seemed as real as ordinary perceptions. He lost contact with these small folk when the medicine was withdrawn.

Like Alice stepping through the looking glass, some psychotics who regress to second-chakra consciousness live in a dual world of fluid boundaries where spectral figures continuously blend with consensual perceptions. These people spend their lives in a realm so removed from ordinary reality that hospital attendants and other consensual beings are but vague presences in their total field of perception, sometimes intermingling with hallucinated entities, but never interacting. Their hallucinated voices sound the same as ordinary human voices, although they emanate from household pets, potted plants, even stuffed animals.

Some schizophrenics unknowingly subvocalize the words of their auditory hallucinations as they hear them. This was demonstrated by researchers who held sensitive microphones near the patient's larynx when voices were perceived. Theorists seeking to attribute hallucinations to disturbed brain metabolism find this observation challenging, because the areas of the brain associated with hearing are quite separate from those that regulate speech. Some patients can quiet the voices by holding their mouths wide open, but most are curiously reluctant to use this technique, even though they are sincere in wishing to rid themselves of their tormenting voices.

Command hallucinations—a hallucinated entity actively directing a person's behavior—often lead to destructive or suicidal acts, although most psychotics are capable of ignoring such commands. Nevertheless, some vulnerable people eventually succumb to their voices. The results are unfailingly grim. Schizophrenics have cut off their genitals or plucked out their eyes in response to insistent voices. Arsonists, random assassins, and serial killers frequently attribute their crimes to hallucinated commands, often from a perceived "devil."

Typical of these, David Berkowitz, the "Son of Sam" serial killer who terrorized New York City for two years, made a chilling statement to interrogating officers.

> It was a command. I had a sign, and I followed it. Sam told me what to do, and I did it . . . Sam is really a man who lived 6,000 years ago. I got the messages through his dog. He told me to kill. The situation had to be perfect. I would find a parking place for my car right away. It was things like that which convinced me it was commanded . . . I always found the perfect spot. Everything always fell into place . . . [Asked if he felt remorse for murdering seven strangers]: No, why should I? It was commanded.

Perhaps the main difference between Berkowitz's aberrant experience and that of, say, Joan of Arc, whose voices and visions instructed her to inspire an army to war, is the social outcome.

CONVERSATIONS WITH HALLUCINATIONS

Because the voices and visions of psychotic people confirm a "crazy" stereotype, few investigators make systematic efforts to uncover their true nature. An exception is psychologist Wilson Van Dusen, who worked for seventeen years at a California mental hospital, where he devised a way to converse directly with his patients' voices. His technique exposed in unusual detail the character of these apparitions, which seem to be suspended in a strange netherworld between being and nonbeing.

Of course, Van Dusen could not himself hear what his patients' inner voices were saying. But he discovered that the "entities" behind the voices could hear what he said to them. They would then respond as if they were independent centers of personality and will. Van Dusen selected patients who felt they could distinguish between their own thoughts and what they heard as voices. He instructed his patients to give a verbal account of what the voices said. At all times, he treated the voices as real, because that is what they were to his patients.

Most psychotic patients remember quite vividly when they began hearing voices. They usually heard a solitary voice, sometimes familiar, calling their name repeatedly from a distance. When acknowledged, the primary voice gains power, and others soon follow. Curiously, the voices recall only events that occur *after* the date of their arrival in the patient's psychic life. They are unable to access memories of events prior to that time unless newly recalled and spoken aloud by the patient.

Carrying his investigations one step further, Van Dusen administered standard personality tests separately to his patients and their voices. He was surprised to find that the hallucinated entities displayed more psychopathology than did the patients themselves. Even though the voices always perceived exactly what the patient said or did, they would often disagree with the patient's interpretation of the test questions or inkblots, chiming in with versions uniquely their own.

Following Van Dusen's tactic, I have also established conversational rapport with hallucinated voices perceived by a number of patients under my care. Once trust is established, this technique is easier than it would seem, because most of these people are willing to relay their voices' answers to questioning. (Some therapists argue that this technique only intensifies the hold that the voices have upon the patients. But it also affords the therapist valuable information about the subjective experience of his patients, and so facilitates empathy. It would be antitherapeutic, however, to dwell on hallucinatory experience to the exclusion of other therapeutic techniques.) Like Van Dusen, I found these dialogues to make compelling late-night stories, but most were encounters with extremely unevolved personalities. My experiences will be interwoven here with those of Van Dusen, with which they have a remarkable concurrence.

The voices are sometimes frightened and in need of reassurance. They frequently use words not in the patient's vocabulary, and affect a manner of speaking quite unlike that of their host. During conversations with the voices, some patients are unable to follow the gist of what is taking place and say they feel like a third party.

Two "orders" of hallucinatory voices consistently emerge. The more common, lower order are, in a word, stupid. They direct their dull-witted malevolence to insults and threats that are obscene and sacrilegious. They display a pervasive lack of general information. It pleases them to call attention to bowel and bladder functions, upon which they comment with cackling profanity. A favorite trick is to direct attention to sexual or scatological matters, then sternly criticize the patient for noticing them.

Lower-order voices are usually attached to schizophrenics, although there are exceptions. Rarer, higher-order voices mostly occur during manic ASCs, and can enter the lives of people who fit no diagnostic category, many of whom turn to their "inner voice" for guidance and inspiration. They make up a tenth or less of all psychotic hallucinations. Some are friendly, supportive, and even strikingly prescient. The higher-order hallucinations may appear in visual as well as auditory form and are often creatively symbolic in their communications.

On occasion, higher-order voices demonstrate power over the lower order and can even banish them. Many people in touch with higher-order voices also hear the lower order and assign them individualized names, such as "the Whisperers" or "the Eavesdroppers." The higher-order voices are usually more gifted and imaginative than the patient, but the degenerate lower order always have less talent and creativity. Not surprisingly, many nonparanoid patients attribute these voices to beings from other worlds. Paranoids tend to form conspiracy theories around them.

One young psychotic woman whom I knew for several years divided her voices into helpful "Mentors" and malicious "Outworlders." The two competed for her attention and engaged in heated arguments about what was best for her. When her sewing machine broke and she was unable to fix it, the Mentors gave her detailed step-by-step directions for its successful repair: "Tighten that screw. Stretch the little spring over there." They sang songs to her when she was lonely, told jokes, and gave advice as to how to respond to the Outworlders, who would jealously tell her to disregard the Mentors and coax her to commit suicide. During times of her life when the higher order predominated, she functioned quite well in the world, painted, wrote poetry, and needed no medications.

Those unfortunate people caught in the exclusive grasp of lower-order voices fare less well. They find themselves beset by forces relentlessly determined to usurp their will and live through them as they please. The lower order may spend years working to control some part of the body, such as the ear, which then becomes deaf. One voice spent two years trying to possess a patient's eye, which gradually went out of alignment. Carl Jung, who paid a great deal of attention to his patients' voices, wrote of a woman who was plagued by countless voices distributed all over her body. He found one voice, located on the right side, that was reasonable and helpful. He cultivated a relationship with the voice and eventually freed that half of her body from other voices. But he was never able to halt the voices on the left side.

Lower-order voices threaten pain to control behavior, and sometimes cause real pain to enforce their power. One of my patients felt a hard slap across his face whenever he was slow to obey his voices' lewd commands. Lower-order voices are incapable of sequential reasoning and show no sign of having identities or memories of their own. Yet they fraudulently claim to be historical or biblical figures, either naming themselves after presidents or saints, or being named by the patient. When Van Dusen asked a group of voices if they were spirits, they answered, "The only spirits around here are in bottles," followed by raucous laughter. Such flashes of tawdry humor confirm the voices' intellectual vacuity. However, this does not negate their power to undermine the patient's already-fragile sense of self.

Consistent with their sordid nature, lower-order voices insinuate themselves into every corner of the patient's privacy, exploit every weakness, lie with feigned sincerity, claim powers of prophesy, make false promises, and command degrading acts. They are resolutely irreligious or antireligious; just the mention of religion provokes howls of anger or derision from them. This trait may lead them to disrupt the patient's spiritual practices, although one patient told me that the only time he could free himself from the voices was during prayer or in church. If the voices identify themselves as Christ or Satan, they give commands commensurate with those identities. Van Dusen reported one woman's hallucinatory voice that claimed to be Jesus. When the psychologist convinced her that the voice was an impostor, the woman came to regard it as sick and began to counsel it, a tactic which quickly caused the voice to exit and never return.

More frequently, the voices establish a credibility with vulnerable psychotics exceeding any granted to ordinary humans, and in so doing promote a variety of delusions. They may declare themselves to be aliens from other planets and then help construct elaborate belief systems founded in extraterrestrial realms (nonpsychotics can have similar experiences). Sometimes several voices cluster into "families," with each having its own role in the kinship hierarchy. Not surprisingly, hospitalized patients often find these hallucinated worlds preferable to institutional life and tend to withdraw into them, sometimes permanently.

During several conversations with my patients, I urged the voices to reveal more of their true nature and motivations, but they never gave straight answers to these probing questions. Instead, they defended their presence with vulgar sarcasm, as in this conversation with the voices of an elderly woman who survived on Social Security disability payments.

> Doctor: What have the voices been telling you recently?
> Patient: They've been scaring me again. They keep saying they are going to take my children to their island and perform surgery on them, then make me eat their livers.
> Doctor: Would you ask them where their island is located?
> Patient: (after a pause) They said it's in purgatory.
> Doctor: What name do they go by?
> Patient: . . . Friends of the Enemy.

Doctor: Please ask them if there is anything we can do to make them go away.

Patient: I've asked that before. They just tell me to try swallowing poison.

Doctor: (frustrated) Ask them why they pick on someone like you, and why don't they just go back to their island and leave you alone.

Patient: OK . . . Uh, they said they like me because I'm so rich and sexy.

Therapists who work closely with psychotics gather numerous anecdotes of apparent telepathy or precognition mediated through hallucinated voices. For instance, lower-order voices might announce what passers-by will do next, coupled with scurrilous references. One patient complained about voices spoiling a card game by revealing her opponents' hands. In contrast, higher-order voices may offer useful paranormal information and can be a means through which nonpsychotic sensitives gain insight into future events. Although most sensitives are reluctant to reveal the nature of their sources for fear of being considered crazy, they usually characterize their extrasensory perception in sensory terms: "A little voice told me," or "I saw it in my mind's eye."

Sometimes a person's hallucinations radically change in character, such as occurred to Melissa, a fifty-four-year-old Mexican-American woman who was distracted by voices for years, despite taking antipsychotic medicines. She regularly heard three voices: two males and a female, none of which resembled voices of people she knew in the consensual world. These unfriendly voices insulted and criticized her for the most ordinary actions. Once they spent days urging her to commit suicide, chorusing, "Do it, do it," until she took a small overdose of her medicines, after which they laughed and ridiculed her.

When I asked Melissa to remember how her voices began, she recalled vividly that

> it was the day my husband died. That night I saw him in my dreams and the next day I could hear him as if he were still at home somewhere. When I'd close my eyes, I could even see him. He helped me when I tried to figure out how to raise the kids and pay the bills, but sometimes he'd get mad and yell at me. For a while I had another boyfriend. My husband didn't mind at first, until my boyfriend started telling me how to raise the kids. Then my husband would argue with him, but of course only I knew what was going on.

One day I went to a *curandero* (medicine man) who my neighbor recommended. We never saw each other before, but when I walked into his room, he said to me right off, "Your husband has been dead for five years, but he's standing next to you right now." I was so scared I thought I would pass out, because I knew he was right. He said that my husband loved me so much that he didn't go to heaven. Then he rubbed some holy water on me and prayed. I felt strange inside. Then he yelled and waved his arms in front of my chest, and I passed out for a minute. When I woke up, he told me my husband went to heaven. I never saw or heard my husband again, and I could finally sleep and rest.

About three weeks later, the voices I hear now began. They came when I was trying to fall asleep, and they kept calling my name. I think if my husband didn't go to heaven, he would have kept them away from me. I don't know. I tried to find the *curandero* again, but they said he went back to Mexico. The only thing that helps when the voices scare me is reading the Bible."

SOME "RATIONAL" EXPLANATIONS

Because Western scientists are so successful in dealing with the physical world, they tend to limit themselves to theories consistent with the belief that all reality is reducible to physical objects or events. This has led to a number of theories, some quite sophisticated, that claim to explain hallucinated voices as products of disorderly brain metabolism. However, these materialistic theories fall short of accounting for the complexities of hallucinated voices and visions.

For instance, Princeton University psychologist Julian Jaynes proposes that the self-reflective capacity necessary for free choice came about only with the advent of modern civilization. Prior to that, hallucinated "voices of the gods" directed people's day-to-day activities in a semicivilized world. Jaynes offers a meticulous argument that these voices were a normal part of experience in ancient historical epochs. They now occur only in regressed states of consciousness like schizophrenia that extinguish self-reflection. This is a compelling idea. However, Jaynes overreaches his data by concluding that the voices are generated by the silent-speech area in the nondominant hemisphere of the cerebral cortex, a part of the brain known to be more specialized for music than kingly dictums.

Other investigators fare no better in accounting for psychotic voices. In his classic psychoanalytic study of schizophrenia, Silvano Arieti argued that hallucinated voices are abstract ideas that become "concretized" into perceptions during psychotic regression. For instance, a person has an idea that he is defective, then perceives a voice repeating, "On the blink." L. J. West took another tack with his "perceptual release" theory, holding that a state of relative sensory deprivation during psychotic ASCs creates "porous filters" that allow memory traces from earlier experiences to "leak" into awareness as hallucinations. Even the pioneer transpersonal psychologist Charles Tart explained away hallucinations as products of a malfunctioning cortex, "whereby stored information is drawn from Memory, worked over by Input-Processing, and passed along to awareness as if it were sensory data."

Medical literature is overflowing with these kinds of elaborate speculations that associate hallucinations with abnormalities in the brain's memory-retrieval or auditory-processing systems. Yet none of these come close to accounting for several characteristics of these voices: (1) the clear sense of "otherness" of psychotic hallucinations; (2) the distinctly separate and complex personalities of the voices; (3) their use of words foreign to the patent's vocabulary; (4) the ability of a voice or voices to "take command" in MPD, but not in schizophrenia or mania; (5) the voices' occasional ability to demonstrate paranormal knowledge; (6) their division into high and low orders; (7) the insatiable perversity of the lower order; (8) the higher order affording valid information not previously known to the hearer. These traits are consistent from patient to patient.

Just as it is insufficient to explain away telepathic or precognitive dreams as subconscious memories, it is equally insufficient to conclude that a repressed memory can disguise itself as a voice calling, "Hey, you" over and over for several days, or suggest suicide by sneaking a bomb onto an airplane. It is difficult to imagine how a malfunctioning auditory-processing system could spew forth a chorus of shrieking voices claiming to be messengers from Satan and incessantly commanding an otherwise nonviolent person to commit a series of hideous murders.

This is not to say that the brain is uninvolved in hallucinatory ASCs. Numerous alterations in anatomy and chemistry associated with psychotic ASCs were described in chapters 5 and 6. These could destructure a weakly bounded self that stays intact when not overstressed, leading to an exchange of energy patterns from the surrounding field of consciousness that do not ordinarily resonate with awareness. So West's idea of porous filters allowing "leakage" from the subconscious might be partially correct. But it is not "memory traces" that leak through, and it is not the *personal* subconscious that is involved.

This line of reasoning is consistent with Stanford University sleep researcher William Dement's suggestion that psychotic hallucinations are untimely intrusions of dreams into waking consciousness. In chapter 14 we will see how the dreaming ASC increases receptivity to extrasensory inputs. Like psychic events in dreams, hallucinations may be extrasensory in that they enter consciousness through the back door. Not only is the brain shut off from the external world during dreaming, it is also primed to process vast amounts of information. This includes subthreshold activity ordinarily obscured by the glare of waking sensory activity. Like psychotic ASCs, dreams bypass self-boundaries and open passageways to ordinarily obscure areas of the Ground.

Chapter 1 stated that the transpersonal conception of consciousness allows for, but does not prove, the existence of mind in noncorporeal form. Could the ever-mysterious depths of the Ground harbor aggregations of mind and will that penetrate weakened self-boundaries of people regressed to second-chakra consciousness? Because materialistic science fails to account for the rich variety of hallucinatory experience of both psychotic and nonpsychotic varieties, it is appropriate to take a fresh look at ancient occult systems to see if they match the experience of psychotic ASCs in ways that modern theories do not.

THE OCCULT HYPOTHESIS

The ancient occult hypothesis states that *there are other dimensions of reality and beings interpenetrating our own. These exist outside ordinary awareness, revealing themselves only through the medium of consciousness primed by inward reflection.*

Although events that appear only in ASCs lie beyond the reach of empirical science, this says more about the limitations of the scientific method than the reality of the events. We must therefore rely on the collective experience of human beings to gather data from this realm. These include the perceptions of millions of people who felt themselves to be out of their bodies during near-death events, or who perceived a "death apparition" in which the figure of a recently deceased person appeared as a vivid hallucination prior to their learning of that person's death. Efforts to wedge these experiences into narrow materialistic paradigms are no less absurd than fanciful occult explanations that accrue to them.

Although it is beyond the scope of this book to include the intricacies of occult lore spanning thousands of years, certain occult systems seem to account for the experience of hallucinating psychotics more accurately than do psychiatric journals. The following section briefly scans several such systems.

A Realm of Spirits?

With roots in Eastern Vedic teachings and Western Gnosticism, *eso-teric spiritism* posits a reality plane of nonphysical beings. Although the Catholic Church brands much of this as heresy, it continues to perform exorcisms on people thought to be possessed by demons. (Recently, the Pope publicly reaffirmed the Catholic Church's belief in angels and stated that they have played an important part in human history.) Modern-day mediums and trance channelers embrace variations of these teachings.

At the basis of spiritism is the perception that human beings have a number (usually seven) of subtle "bodies" or "vehicles," invisible in the ordinary state of consciousness, but perceived by clairvoyants or "sensitives" under special conditions. These bodies are hierarchically structured from the base to the divine. Each is said to operate on a "plane of existence" determined by a vaguely defined "frequency of vibration," an idea that anticipated modern holographic theories of consciousness. The physical body is the lowest of these vehicles; it operates on the grossest level, the material world. Higher levels represent aspects of consciousness that operate independently of physical embodiment.

Although different esoteric systems disagree on the terminology, the "body" nearest to the physical is usually called the *etheric*. It is said to be a subtle duplicate of the physical body, with which it interacts, controlling glandular and metabolic functions. Acupuncture meridians known to Oriental medicine, but absent from anatomy charts of Western medicine, lie within the etheric body. The etheric body dwells on a plane of reality only slightly higher in frequency than ordinary reality.

The next higher vehicle is the *astral* body, which interpenetrates both physical and etheric planes. The astral body is said to extend beyond the physical body by several inches. Clairvoyants call it the *aura*, a cocoonlike oval of colored light that is responsive to emotions. Some sensitives believe that the astral body can separate from the physical body, at which time it resembles traditional descriptions of ghosts. It is also like the "gray chiffon" body reported by people who have had near-death or other out-of-body experiences. The astral plane is thought to be an entire world to itself, existing between physical and spiritual planes. It is the abode of earthbound spirits of the dead and *elementals*—nature spirits less individuated than human beings, subrational but mimetic of human thoughts and feelings; they bring to mind the lower-order voices of schizophrenic hallucinations.

Subsequent higher planes are variously called the mental, the subtle, the causal, the ultimate, etc. Although esoteric teachings from different places and times are remarkably concordant in their descriptions of the etheric and astral levels, there is greater variance in descriptions of higher levels. Awareness of the lower three levels will suffice for our present discussion, but we will return to consider these higher levels in terms of the chakra system.

Esoteric disciplines agree that correct spiritual practice gradually elevates awareness through these planes of existence. Excessive attachment to earthly concerns—"low consciousness"—mires an individual within baser planes in life and death. At death, the center of awareness is said to detach from the physical body and assume the highest level it attained in life. Here it awaits either reincarnation or final judgment, depending on the belief system. Souls arrested at lower levels, and those too attached to earthly objects or people, do not transit to higher realms. These are said to become "earthbound." Such a predicament causes confusion and disorientation, so they linger near an overvalued worldly attachment, such as a house, money, or food. Alternately, they attach themselves to a living person for sustenance, gaining entry through weaknesses in the unwitting victim's aura, or astral body.

Astral weaknesses that invite unwanted possession are said to be caused by emotional trauma (especially in childhood), drunkenness, or unsound spiritual practices. For instance, some esoteric techniques for *astral projection* contain a chill warning that going out of the physical body creates a danger that "something else" might enter when the self is away. Elementals, demons, and earthbound spirits are said to attach to a person through this means, causing negative mental effects that resemble schizophrenia or MPD, and sapping the vitality of those so possessed. Exorcisms allegedly rid an individual of these "psychic parasites," sometimes redirecting them to higher planes or, if carelessly administered, merely releasing them to search for another vulnerable host.

Clairvoyants and sensitives as well as people in psychotic ASC's, seem to regularly commune with spirit-like entities such as those described in the occult literature. The following is a case from my own files.

> Joseph is an unobtrusive middle-aged man who has had several hospitalizations for hallucinations and out-of-body experiences. He decides daily how much antipsychotic medicine he will take, depending on how well he feels able to cope with "all those other things" he sees when he reduces his dose. He once advised me never to go to a particular grocery store because that was where a group of "spirits" congregated.
>
> "What on earth would they be doing in a grocery store?" I inquired.

"They eat," he replied. "They especially like the meat department. Sometimes I see them eating out of cans, too. They don't care that they can't open them."

"Joseph," I exclaimed incredulously, "You aren't going to tell me that spirits have to eat!"

"They don't *have* to," he replied, "they just *think* that they do."

Spirits in Tibetan Psychiatry

Technological cultures demonstrate great reluctance to accept theories of insubstantial beings and planes of reality that are not evident to ordinary people. In the Western world, these teachings are confined to the Theosophical and Spiritualist movements, which have relatively small followings despite their revival in the so-called New Age movement. However, throughout portions of Asia, ancient and highly effective systems of medicine—empirically disciplined and "scientific" in their own right—incorporate theories of subtle energy bodies and nonmaterial planes of reality.

Some of these teachings from long-isolated regions of Tibet are beginning to reach the Western world. Unlike post-Galilean Western doctors, Tibetan Buddhist physicians have never been constrained from integrating spiritual teaching into their healing practices. Tibetan medical students engage in rigorous training at long-established universities and hospitals. Their healing techniques are highly effective in treating physical and mental illnesses among ethnic peoples. Yet they use virtually no synthetic medicines, and their diagnoses include naming one of eighteen "elemental spirits" that cause neurosis or psychosis.

"Ghosts" or "demons" described in Tibetan psychiatric texts are essentially archetypal forms of negativity that overtake consciousness and provoke insane or maladaptive behavior. They are cast in eloquently symbolic language that is rich in meaning to members of the community. When I read the detailed descriptions of the eighteen elemental spirits responsible for mental illnesses, I was struck by their similarity to diagnoses in psychiatry's respected manual, DSM III-R.

Tibetan healing techniques readily fit a holographic concept of consciousness that is hierarchically structured on "vibratory levels," each with a corresponding "reality." Besides prescribing herbal remedies designed to harmonize the physical body with its environment, Tibetan physicians recommend meditation with individualized mantras chosen to resonate with consciousness at specific frequencies. Many of these practices are now influencing alternative healing systems in the West.

Compared with materialistic models, Tibetan spiritist cosmologies bear a greater correspondence to the experience of psychotics in hallucinatory ASCs.

Mediumistic Hallucinations

Although most psychotic ASCs open the psyche only to lower-order voices, we might wonder whether some people maintain contact *exclusively* with higher-order voices. If so, we are unlikely to learn of them by studying people who consult orthodox psychiatrists. Individuals who dare to communicate with hallucinatory voices and visions and can relay their messages coherently were once called mediums. A contemporary version of mediumship, in which a nonphysical "entity" allegedly speaks through the vocal apparatus of the medium, is called *trance channeling*.

The history of mediumship has been marred by theatrics and outright fraud—pitfalls to which some trance channelers have not developed immunity. Yet skeptics overstate their point when they assert that everyone claiming mediumistic abilities is knowingly fraudulent. Many are simply and sincerely reporting what they experience, however outrageous their subsequent explanations. At least some seem to be in contact with sources similar to the higher order voices heard by a minority of people in psychotic ASCs, as banal as their channeled pronouncements may be at times. Not everyone who hears phantomlike voices is psychotic, and some appear to be quite well adjusted.

Mediums express "channeled" information in one of two ways. Some, like schizophrenics, perceive their voices privately and unintentionally, then merely report what they hear. Others enter a hypnoticlike ASC in which a voice speaks out loud through them. The channel may or may not remember the event after returning to the ordinary state of consciousness. There is, therefore, an obvious similarity between trance channelers and people afflicted with MPD, whose "alters" irresistibly displace the core personality during spontaneous trancelike ASCs. However, most entities contacted by channelers are of a higher order than the often malevolent alters of MPD victims, and they do not enter unless summoned. Mediums and channelers usually describe being in contact with a single "spirit guide" throughout their lives, but some speak of occasionally having to stave off intrusive "negative entities."

Swedenborg's Hypnagogic Explorations

One of history's most intrepid explorers of hallucinatory ASCs was Baron Emanuel Swedenborg, a unique man who intertwined his spiritist experiences with the hard science of his time. Although many of his experiences properly belong in the realm of sixth-chakra consciousness, it is appropriate to consider them here because of their obvious relationship to the hallucinated voices of people regressed to the second chakra.

An eighteenth-century Swedish nobleman and member of parliament, Swedenborg published scientific papers on a wide variety of topics during his long life, including soils and muds, stereometry, echoes, calculus, blast furnaces, astronomy, economics, and magnetism. He was the first to expound the nebular hypothesis of the creation of the universe, and he founded the science of crystallography. Although his hallucinatory excursions might lead some to conclude that he was quite mad, he nonetheless became fluent in nine languages, built his own telescope and microscope, and designed a submarine, musical instruments, a glider, mining equipment, and the ear trumpet for the deaf.

By the age of fifty-six, Swedenborg had mastered the natural sciences of his time and devoted the remaining three decades of his life to exploring deeper realms of consciousness. He began with a diligent scrutiny of the hypnagogic ASC, that twilight reverie halfway between sleeping and waking. While in a hypnogogic state, he carried his introspection to regions from which some never return. Then he went even further by practicing yogalike breath-holding techniques designed to divert the mind's eye far from the physical world. The cosmology that this remarkable person meticulously described in his journals bears an uncanny relationship to the hallucinations that plague psychotics and inform mediums.

As Swedenborg intensified his introspections, he began to sense the presence of "other beings." Most people would reflexively pull back from such encounters, but the curious baron instead engaged in lengthy conversations with what he came to believe were angels and demons. His friends noticed him speaking with invisible figures, yet he was always able to return to mundane levels. By today's standards, Swedenborg could be considered insane at this point of his life; yet he otherwise showed no signs of incapacity, and he maintained his job as a government mining assessor. He also sustained a degree of mental discipline that enabled him to write sixteen books describing his inner explorations during this twenty-seven-year period. He insisted that most of his writings were dictated by an angel.

By conversing with his inner voices, Swedenborg devised an elaborate cosmology of spirits and the way they interact with humanity. He envisioned humans as existing in a "free space" between three orders of angelic spirits and three orders of demonic entities. There is, he believed, a constant flow of information among these six orders and humanity, but in the normal situation we are unaware of this interchange, taking it to be our own thoughts and feelings. Likewise, spirits do not ordinarily see or hear the physical world. But for each human experience there is a resonant event on either a higher or a lower spiritual plane.

Swedenborg described a natural barrier shielding spiritual planes from human awareness. He repeatedly warned others not to tamper with that barrier, for if it was broken, especially on the lower side, madness or death would follow. This natural obstacle that separates these dimensions fits in with reports by psychotics that their hallucinated voices act surprised and confused when they first appear. Swedenborg believed that the shield sometimes disintegrates spontaneously and is weakened by alcohol or morphine, by careless practice of certain rituals, and by habitual social isolation, such as occurs in the early stages of psychotic ASCs or during monastic life. Some of the entities that Swedenborg encountered closely resemble the voices heard during schizophrenic ASCs.

> When spirits begin to speak with man, he must beware lest
> he believe in anything; for they say almost anything; things
> are fabricated of them, and they lie . . .

Once broken, the barrier between human and spirit realms is not readily reestablished, a thought reminiscent of Pythagoras of Rhodes, who in the third century B.C. observed that the "voices of the gods" come at first reluctantly, then more readily once they form the habit of entering the same person. Although the concept of psychosis in Swedenborg's day was different from current thinking, he wrote of people who were possessed by entities from the lower realms. He also optimistically suggested that higher spirits could exert control over lower ones.

Occult notions of hidden intelligences who influence the affairs of humanity are found in one form or another in all major religions. However, Swedenborg's arcane cosmology would likely have been lost with countless other visionary phantasmagoria if he had not been such a paramount genius in other affairs, and if his description of the world of spirits did not strikingly correspond with the everyday experience of psychotics. Nevertheless, any cosmology of beings who dwell beyond consensual perception, and who likewise remain ignorant of us, resists any real test unless a means is devised to render the subjective world of psychotics and mediums open to all. A simple technique may be a step toward opening such sequestered worlds to scrutiny.

Raudive's Electronic "Medium"

The Raudive phenomenon, named after Dr. Konstantin Raudive, a psychologist who performed an unusual series of experiments in the Baltic state of Latvia during the 1930s and 1940s, may represent a replicable means of studying hallucinatory voices. The technique is easy to duplicate, and several researchers have subsequently experimented with it and written of their results.

Raudive began by conducting sensory-deprivation experiments on himself by attaching headphones to a source of "white noise," such as we hear between FM radio stations. He then listened to the headphones with eyes blindfolded for extended periods of time. Raudive found that he would occasionally hear intelligible voices mixed in with the obscuring sound. His curiosity piqued, he then connected a tape recorder to the source of white noise and continued his experiment. When he later played back the recording, he was surprised to find that the same faint but discernible voices he heard earlier were captured on the tape.

At this point, skeptical readers might point out that any magnetic tape head will pick up spurious radio transmissions if they are at the right wavelength. But Raudive noted that the voices on his tapes would address him by name, comment on conditions in the room, and even respond to his questions. Two voices identified themselves as deceased friends. Independent investigators who later followed Raudive's procedures reported hearing profanities in response to their more churlish questions, providing a refutation to the argument that the recorded words were from standard radio broadcasts.

Over the years of his experiments, Raudive collaborated with physicists, psychologists, and electronic technicians as he recorded and cataloged thousands of voices. Many of the recorded sounds were spoken at cadences faster or slower than human voices and were made intelligible only by altering the speed of the tape during playback. There were both male and female voices, speaking in several languages, sometimes in a curious mixture of tongues within the same sentence. One researcher reported that a taped voice showed signs of precognition when it told him to answer the phone during a taping session, only to have the phone ring a few seconds later. During another session, a voice provided instructions for setting up recording equipment so as to facilitate reception. Another experimenter, after demanding, "I want you to talk louder today," immediately heard the answer, "We always talk loud. Won't you please listen!"

Raudive's interpretation of these voices as disincarnate spirits of once-living human beings remains open to criticism. Yet the phenomenon has been repeated by enough independent and respectable investigators to reduce the possibility of fraud. Perhaps the best alternate hypothesis is that the voices originate in the mind of the listener and appear on the tape through a form of subconscious psychokinesis.

Despite my low capacity for tedium, I once spent an hour under the conditions of Raudive's experiment, hearing and recording giggling laughter after a few minutes, and later capturing remnants of a conversation that seemed to be about horses. These effects can be reproduced by any patient person with simple equipment. To date, no similar experiments have employed people in psychotic or induced ASCs. Yet it is commonly observed that people prone to schizophrenic ASCs begin to hallucinate intensely when they use a Ouija board or even enter an area where one is being used, suggesting that this popular parlor game may function in a manner similar to Raudive's electronic "medium."

Don Juan's Yaqui View of Madness

No one in modern folklore has done more to deepen our sense of alternate realities than the author-anthropologist Carlos Castaneda. In a series of nine books, he captures in exquisite metaphorical language the transpersonal field theory of consciousness, hierarchical levels of being, and the means by which reality is transformed by altering consciousness.

As a naively curious anthropologist trying to master the techniques of Yaqui Indian sorcery, Castaneda became an apprentice to a master *brujo*, Don Juan Mateus. Whatever their literal truth, Castaneda's works weave a rich tapestry of universal symbols illuminating the deepest mysteries of consciousness. His patient but demanding teacher taught him to enter ASCs in which he traveled to grotesque worlds populated by nonhuman beings, some composed of purely mental substance, others of inorganic physical matter. Finally, Don Juan explained to his student the secrets of free movement among these separate realities.

When one attains the clairvoyant ASC that Don Juan called *seeing*, human beings appear as "luminous cocoons" of swirling energy in horizontal bands. The layered consciousness within the cocoon originates from a cosmic source, symbolically known to Toltec seers as the Eagle, which continuously emanates "energy." Eddies within this radiant field condense to form individual human cocoons. Located in the midline of each cocoon is an *assemblage point* activating an area within its particular band—the portion that normally represents the ordinary world of consensus reality. At birth the assemblage point is mobile, moving freely along a vast continuum of possible realities. Only by repetitious learning experiences throughout childhood does it gradually come to be fixed at the consensus location.

According to Don Juan, sorcerers practice occult techniques to shift their assemblage points to specific areas within the cocoon, thereby inducing ASCs. With each shift, they travel to other worlds, some of which are populated by beings of radically different natures. Because great personal power and strength of will are necessary to realign the assemblage point at its precise original location, Don Juan cautions that these are extremely dangerous practices requiring adherence to an impeccably disciplined warrior's life.

For instance, slight deviations of the assemblage point from its original position illuminate worlds ordinarily invisible to the consensual eye, while at the same time causing familiar events to become distorted. Greater deviations cause the consensual world to vanish in an instant, as if it had been erased, stranding the unskilled practitioner in strange realms of unfamiliar dimensions. Spontaneous small misalignments of the assemblage point in people who lack the skill to realign it result in insanity, the extent of which is proportional to the degree of displacement. Misalignments are caused by constitutional weakness, unskilled sorcery, or being overwhelmed by a superior psychic power.

In response to Castaneda's skepticism about the "reality" of such altered-state perceptions, Don Juan countered that when seers shift their assemblage points, they are not confronted with illusion, but with *another world* every bit as real as this. Madness is not simply a propensity to participate in alternate realities, but a loss of power to move freely among them, along with the illusion that the consensus reality is the only reality. Don Juan would agree with R. D. Laing that we may be just as impaired by being stuck in the ordinary state of consciousness as in an altered state. So the task of a Yaqui warrior/sorcerer resembles the task of an enlightened modern-day healer: to maintain one's ability to move freely among as many realities as possible, the better to integrate them into a coherent whole and assist the "apprentice" to do the same.

WITHIN OR WITHOUT?

Minds conditioned by scientific-materialistic paradigms—including this author's—have great difficulty accepting without reservation the existence of spirit worlds as presented above. My purpose in including this perspective is to illustrate the superior "fit" of occult hypotheses with the inner world of hallucinating psychotics and to contrast it with modern views.

Beyond this, I would suggest that an open-minded agnosticism is the most reasonable approach to spiritist ideologies. We know that consciousness accrues to brains, but we don't know if brains are necessary for consciousness to aggregate into centers of intelligence and will, or that sentience is limited to brain-type physical structures. Because awareness can transcend brains under special circumstances, it is possible that it can operate independently. Jung recognized this when he wrote that most psychic phenomena could be explained better by the hypothesis of spirits than by the peculiarities of the subconscious: "In each individual case I must of necessity be skeptical, but in the long run I have to admit that the spirit hypothesis yields better results in practice than any other."

I would also like to enliven the materialist-versus-spiritist debate as to whether hallucinations arise from inside or outside the individual mind. If we accept the common view that the ego, or world-self, is identical to the whole self, then we are limited to two alternatives. Either we personalize these voices and attribute them to an external supernatural source, or we depersonalize them and reduce them to mischievous neurons or misplaced memory traces that are projected outward.

But a transpersonal perspective allows a third view: of the self *participating* in a universal field of consciousness, which includes partially bounded condensations of consciousness—individual minds—within a greater psychic pattern. This dissolves the self/other duality into an unitive realization that hallucinations are *outside* the constricted ego but *inside* the larger individual psyche, which merges imperceptibly with the Ground. In other words, it is only after a child identifies with the ego—originally merely a mediator between self and the physical world—that subtle aspects of the Ground are repressed and projected *outside*. In this regard, the famous medium Eileen Garrett once asked her spirit guide if she were actually seeing him or her own mind. The answer: "both."

In this way, transpersonal theory allows for a much-needed speculative reinterpretation of MPD, a malady that sharply challenges modern psychiatry's materialistic bias. MPD has its violent origins in second-chakra consciousness during a time when the self has not yet turned away from direct contact with the Ground. Imaginary playmates often accompany toddlers of this age; about 65 percent of all children and as many as 85 percent of MPD sufferers recall having them at some time before age ten. Like the comic-strip tiger Hobbes, these invisible companions have personal attributes that are initially quite unlike those of their worldly comrades. However, a healthy child gradually incorporates these characteristics into his selfhood, benefiting from them as he "forgets" his imaginary playmate.

Almost all children who later develop MPD were repeatedly physically and sexually abused, often incestuously, during their transit through second-chakra consciousness. There is no time for a weakly bounded self to come to terms with the effects of one sadistic event before the next takes place. This prevents integration. The child's self therefore remains open to the Ground well past the stage of ego formation. Under such brutal conditions, the lure of the parent's consensual world is no match for the comfort of the reliable phantom companion, who gains a permanent hold. What was once an invisible friend crystallizes into an alter, simultaneously maintaining an open passage that attracts less amicable energies.

It follows that therapists who successfully treat MPD reactivate the natural process of integrating imaginary playmates. First, the self extends its boundaries to include the alter; then the alter gradually loses its separate identity to merge with and broaden its host's personality. I will leave it for the thoughtful reader to decide if an alter's essence originates apart from the host's self, or begins as a split-off part of the host's self that later acquires boundaries of its own. Either conjecture fits transpersonal theory, and both highlight the paradoxical unity of inner and outer.

Hallucinated voices known to schizophrenics and manics, which are less fully developed "selves" than the alters of MPD, also invade the unshielded awareness of people regressed to the second chakra. These voices lie on a continuum with the unevolved "elementals" of esoteric spiritism, the archetypal "demons" of Tibetan Buddhist psychiatry, the recorded "voices of the dead" described by Raudive, the "lower- and higher-order spirits" of Swedenborg, the otherworldly "allies" of Don Juan's cosmology, and the "channeled entities" of modern mediums. Each of these hints at a world beyond the senses that is potentially accessible to all sentient beings under certain circumstances. They also confirm the enduring transpersonal intuition that consciousness is vastly more complex than materialistic notions allow.

CHAPTER 11

Third Chakra: Madness, Myth, & Logic

◈

If everybody contemplates the infinite instead of fixing the drains,
many of us will die of cholera.

JOHN RICH

Humankind cannot bear very much reality.

T. S. ELIOT

WHEN I FIRST met Beverly, she was a nineteen-year-old college student brought to a Los Angeles psychiatric hospital by police who found her loitering near a famous movie star's house. When police questioned her, she insisted that she speak to the star, who, she claimed, was her fiancé.

During my interview, I found Beverly to be an attractive but shy young woman who was obviously troubled and displayed a humorless mood. Her family told me that she had been an outstanding student until a year earlier, when she began to withdraw, neglect her studies, and accuse family members of reading her mail. She broke up with her boyfriend, telling him that he didn't understand her. Lately she had been spending long hours alone in her room, refusing to eat with her family because of what she felt were "toxic odors" coming from their food.

Beverly affirmed that she and the star were secretly engaged. She said that she met him at a gas station, and he invited her to dinner at an intimate restaurant, after which they made love. Although she had not seen him in person since then, she received phone calls from him that were sexually provocative. She told several of her friends about these calls, but they laughed and began avoiding her.

Then Beverly began hearing the star's voice speaking to her seductively from under her bed when she tried to sleep. She was sure he planted a "bug" there, but she could not locate it despite searching carefully. She concluded that her sister, who gave Beverly a "knowing glance" when she shared her secret, had planted the device in league with the movie star. Because she heard the star telling her that he wanted her to elope with him and live in his mansion "like a princess," she tried to telephone him, but could not get through. She then went to his home, feeling certain that he longed for her as much as she did for him.

Before choosing a course of action, I decided to observe Beverly in the structured environment of the hospital. When I found her in the hospital lounge the next day, she was distraught and agitated. She blurted out that she had discovered that the star owned the hospital, and that the nursing staff was following his directions, including planting another bug under her hospital bed. She said that the star was watching her, masquerading as another patient. When I asked her to point him out, she gestured toward a rather nondescript male patient watching television. As we walked toward him, I told Beverly, "Look, he doesn't resemble the star at all." Beverly smiled tolerantly and reminded me that Hollywood studios are expert at clever disguises; in fact, he was disguised when she first met him. She then approached the surprised patient and shouted, "Okay, you bastard, the game is over. Tell him who you really are!"

What strange twist of reason could lead a bright, physically healthy coed poised at the brink of maturity to arrive at such aberrant conclusions? This chapter focuses on how psychotic ASCs entangle the thinking and feeling of a young adult into mythlike delusions that can alienate him or her from consensual reality.

THIRD-CHAKRA CONSCIOUSNESS

As an adolescent self expands into the worldly consciousness of the Manipura, or "power" chakra, it reaches the level of the intellect—the rational, logical, and information-seeking aspects of the psyche. This mode of awareness permeates the science and politics of our civilized era. Through the emergent faculty of will, it provides us with power to manipulate not only our environment, but our own minds.

Yet despite the wonders that accrue to us through reason, our egos, split off from the physical body and from the Spiritual Ground, lack a purpose beyond the self. To regain that lost design, our passage through the third chakra must prepare us for even grander expansions of self-hood later in life. Many never reach those levels, however, and a few retreat to the typhonic consciousness of the second chakra.

It is in the early stages of reaching the ego-based third chakra that most psychotic ASCs first take hold of a vulnerable young adult's life. And it is deep in second-chakra consciousness that regression usually ceases and the self establishes a new and more primitive reality. At this point we might pause to take inventory of the consciousness of an adolescent as he navigates the treacherous straits of modern life between the second and third chakras.

As a healthy child's self expands beyond second-chakra identifications, original repression has already sealed off his intimate connection with the Spiritual Ground. His transit through the second chakra cleaved the unity of infantile consciousness into countless polarities: self/not-self, good/bad, male/female, reality/imagination, mine/yours, friend/foe. These dichotomies fuel the incessant tension of *desire,* a second-chakra legacy that intensifies as it carries over into the third. The exiled self craves its lost unity with the Ground and seeks to regain that bliss through symbolic worldly surrogates.

No longer having the Ground as an inexhaustible font of wonderment, and beginning to lose his parents as reliable sources of nurture, an adolescent naturally turns to the social world to gratify his desires. Of all levels of consciousness, the third chakra demands the most extroverted and socially involved stance. The device he relies on to gain membership in the social world is the *ego,* a mental mediator between internal and external realities. The ego keeps his psyche myopically close to the five senses and blind to spirit. He then identifies with the narrow awareness of the ego and comes to believe it represents the totality of his being.

This exclusive identification comes at a price, however, for the ego is far from being the whole self. All that is *not* ego must be banished to the subconscious. One of Carl Jung's great insights was his division of the human subconscious mind into two parts, the personal and the collective. The *personal* subconscious is composed of memories of events that have been forgotten or repressed during the course of an individual's life, a well as instincts and impulses that are forbidden by social conditioning. Together these make up what Jung called the Shadow.

The *collective* subconscious, in contrast, does not originate from individual biography. It consists of archetypes—universal patterns of thought and feeling that are embedded in the infrastructure of the Ground and are therefore shared by all human beings. Energies from personal and archetypal realms intermix to supply form and content to psychotic delusions and hallucinations.

It is not always a friendly world that greets an adolescent searching for a mature identity. Identified with an ego that insulates him from the power of the Ground, he must seek another kind of power, one that will divest him of childhood innocence. For this task he practices cunning to attain the only goals he can now visualize: mastery, wealth, power, control, prestige, sexual conquest. Again and again the modern world informs him that these are his best hope for salvation, and that he must aggressively redirect any residual desire for reunification with the Ground, or with his parents, toward these values. These become his grail, and third-chakra consciousness imparts a new way of thinking to aid him in his quest.

NEW LOGIC VERSUS OLD

Our ability to call upon a reliable system of logic to evaluate cause-and-effect relations in the material world emerges with third-chakra consciousness. The kind of logic at our command determines our view of reality, our ethical and religious systems, and the mythologies that give meaning to our lives.

Because higher logic is lost in most regressive ASCs, it is essential that we assess a psychotic person's capacity for reason before we choose our response. This enables us to gauge his depth of regression and communicate meaningfully at the specific level of his understanding. With this in mind, we can measure the retreat of a regressing psyche as it releases its grip on consensual reality and substitutes a delusional world of its own making. We can also distinguish expansive manic swings and benign regressions that precede advances to higher chakras.

Third-chakra logic has changed little since Aristotle formalized its rules at the dawn of modern civilization. Technological cultures adopted this legacy from ancient Greece as their preferred way of thinking, and they consider others to be inferior. Aristotelian logic makes for an orderly worldview. Certain rules of reason are taken as axiomatic, such as A is always A, never B; A must either be A, or not be A, with no intermediate state allowable; or A cannot be A and not-A at the same time and place. Therefore, six grapes do not make an apple, a frog is not a prince, and a mental patient named John Smith must always be John Smith, never Napoleon. Children are permitted to bend these rules, but when adults do so, they are thought to be softheaded at best, psychotic at worst.

Aristotelian logic is also called *neologic* to signify its relatively new position in human evolution, in contrast with *paleologic,* which was the predominant mode of thinking prior to modern times, and which reemerges during regressions to second-chakra consciousness. In terms of brain development, neologic emerges when the organizing center ascends from the limbic system to the neocortex as an individual transits into third-chakra consciousness. Paleologic, in contrast, is a broader, more capricious kind of reasoning that prevails in nontechnological cultures and preadolescent children whose self-center is still limbically based.

The basic unit of logic is the *syllogism*, a form of reasoning in which two statements are made, and then a conclusion is drawn from the way they relate to each other. For example:

> All leaves grow on plants.
> Mint is a kind of leaf:
> Therefore mint grows on plants.

This is a valid syllogism. Of sixty-four possible modes of syllogisms, only nineteen lead to valid conclusions.

It is important to note that if the premises of a syllogism are false, the conclusion will likewise be false, even though the reasoning is valid. Such is the basis of neurotic, but not psychotic, thinking. Neurotic thinking follows from faulty learning that feeds false data into syllogisms that are nonetheless valid. Here is how a neurotic person might find a way to feel guilty about a natural urge:

> Only bad people have sexual feelings. (a false premise)
> I have sexual feelings. (a true premise)
> Therefore I am a bad person. (a valid but false
> conclusion)

A neurotic person who arrives at such a conclusion has not forfeited his ability to reason. He is merely misinformed.

Now consider a classically *invalid* syllogism:

> All leaves grow on plants. (a true premise)
> Watermelons grow on plants: (a true premise)
> Therefore watermelons are leaves. (an invalid *and*
> false conclusion)

In this case, although both premises are true in their own right, they are coupled to draw a conclusion that is absurd. Once this kind of twisted logic is adopted, anything is possible. The imposing edifice of Western reason crumbles into madness:

Napoleon was a great man.
I wish to be a great man:
Therefore I must be Napoleon.

The FBI follows guilty people.
I feel guilty:
Therefore the FBI is following me.

Such confusion of similarities with identities is the hallmark of paleological second-chakra reasoning. It is the mechanism by which we form dream symbols, such as a sleek automobile representing the penis. Superstition—a kind of consensual delusion—is also derived from paleologic by keying in on the local and accidental, then identifying it with the universal through its similarities. Sometimes the similarities are no more than coincidental sequences of time. In the following examples, there is little difference between the way a superstitious person and a paranoid use paleologic to reach their conclusions:

I saw a black cat.
Then I tripped and fell:
Black cats bring bad luck.

A stranger walked by my house.
Then I felt weak and nauseated:
Strangers mean to do me harm.

When a person predisposed to psychotic ASCs begins to have experiences that clash with consensual reality, such as hearing voices, his efforts to discover an explanation through neologic only entangle him in contradiction. And when higher-level responses fail to cope with threatening circumstances, regression to the next-lower level takes place. Paleologic then takes over as the predominant mode of thinking, leading to a chain of conclusions that stray far from the narrow path of reason.

For a frightened person caught up in psychotic regression, paleologic confers a welcome relief of tension. Because there are a near-infinite number of statements available for syllogistic matching, the number of explanations he can construct to quell his uncertainty is almost unlimited. This is where his subconscious mind gets into the act.

When one listens carefully to a delusional person, it is usually easy to discern how his personal desires and fears shape his delusions. For example, a regressed woman bothered by intolerable sexual guilt can dispel that guilt though a series of paleological steps that restore her chastity by leading her to conclude that she is the Virgin Mary. If a man envies his neighbor, he can relieve that unpleasant emotion by concluding that the neighbor is the devil because he drives a red car. In the case history that introduced this chapter, Beverly, who felt unwanted and unlovable, followed a similar chain of misreckonings to conclude that a movie star wished to take her for his bride.

Paranoia comes in both psychotic and nonpsychotic varieties. A paranoid outlook is ingrained into the psyche during its passage through first-chakra consciousness, possibly during birth. But one does not have to be psychotic to interpret the world as a hostile place and maintain a lifelong stance of suspiciousness and exaggerated vigilance. Many paranoid people maintain their grasp of neologic and therefore do not form delusions. Some even acknowledge their paranoid tendencies and compensate by checking out their suspicions with others. But paranoia is most dramatically apparent when it underlies a psychotic ASC.

Paranoia and paleologic make a nasty combination. Projecting one's Shadow elements onto the external world renders them inaccessible to introspection or emotional release. The delusions that follow are therefore impervious to reason and can lead to explosive behavior. Further, if a healer becomes incorporated into a paranoid delusional system, he may be in danger of violence. Experienced therapists learn that it is best to dampen a paranoid's inner arousal with judicious doses of antipsychotic medicines before stirring up the psychotherapeutic cauldron.

Paranoid or not, we all construct our version of reality from the raw materials of the sensory world, using whatever tools of logic experience provides us. Consider, for instance, a craftsman supplied with a pile of wood and stone and directed to construct a home using only a hammer and chisel. The result would certainly be different than if he were given only a saw and plane, and different again from the edifice he would fashion using all four tools. Similarly, the reality of the neologician is radically different from that of the paleologician, and both appear crudely incomplete to a person who has transcended these levels.

Each form of logic—old, new, or transcendent—operates most efficiently at the chakra level where it comes into being and is maladaptive under other circumstances. Therapists who are unaware of pre/trans distinctions often confuse paleologic with poetic metaphors, which also couple objects and events in terms of similarities:

> Like Napoleon, I trudged confidently,
> across the snowbound steppes of despair.

In this case, the key word is *like*, which confirms the poet's recognition that he is not a diminutive French general on a misguided expedition into Russia. Good poetry employs the higher logic of the fourth and fifth chakras that transcends the strict linearities of Aristotelian logic, evoking universal meaning through symbolic associations. Although their delusions may have superficial symbolic or archetypal elements, regressed people are simply incapable of metaphoric thinking.

FROM THE CONCRETE TO THE ABSTRACT (AND BACK AGAIN)

The esteemed Swiss child psychologist Jean Piaget, who studied how cognitive skills develop throughout childhood, characterized the transition between second- and third-chakra thinking as moving from *concrete operations* to *formal operations*. To grasp how Piaget's insight relates to psychotic ASCs, we digress for a moment to examine the meaning of three terms: *connotation, denotation,* and *verbalization.* Each noun in our language may be considered in terms of this triad of meaning.

The *connotation* of a word is its abstract meaning, its definition as a class of like objects. For instance, the word *tree,* in its connotation, refers to all perennial plants having a woody trunk of considerable girth from which spring branches or fronds. All such definitions are abstractions that help us to understand objects not in our immediate presence. However, if a traveler were resting in the shade of a mighty oak, he might use the word *tree* to mean that particular oak, the concrete embodiment of the word. In so doing, he would be using the *denotation* of the word, its meaning in the present time and place: *this* tree.

In contrast, the *verbalization* of a word refers to its vocalized sound, independent of definition. For instance, we might laugh if someone called us a *putanini,* enjoying the word's amusing sound, but not knowing its Italian meaning. Severely regressed people commonly link objects or concepts because their names sound alike. For instance, someone might feel that he is the "prey" of conspirators whenever he kneels to "pray."

So connotation is an abstract concept, denotation is a concrete object, and verbalization is a sound. Most of us go about our affairs concerned with connotative and denotative meanings. Conversely, members of pretechnological cultures, children, and people in regressive ASCs mainly operate with denotation and verbalization. Although early connotative abilities appear in humans at about age three, enabling a child to postpone gratifications, it is not until his self expands into the third chakra at adolescence that he can take full advantage of abstract thinking. As long as we can connote, what is out of sight is not necessarily out of mind.

Connotation, then, is an advanced mental function that enables us to know what exists outside our immediate awareness and to make predictions about how things are likely to behave in the future. The idea of an impersonal but orderly force embodied in the laws of physics is a concept foreign to any who cannot access the connotative skills of third-chakra consciousness. During psychotic regression, this abstract force is often concretized and personalized into paranoid conspiracies.

Yet we pay a price for our ability to think abstractly. Those uniquely human feelings of anxiety and longing would not exist if we didn't fear what is not present or lament what we never had. For instance, my cat doesn't connote very well. He lives his laid-back life floating on a stream of present moments, blithely unconcerned with what is not immediately stimulating him. Once stimuli fall to a minimum, he promptly falls asleep. Consequently, he never gets anxious, because he doesn't make ominous predictions about the future. He shows fear if he sees an aggressive dog, but when no dogs are around, I suspect that he doesn't worry about them. Anxiety and longing arise from what is not here and now; both rely on connotation. So for my carefree cat, out of sight or out of time is out of mind. This is probably one reason there are no schizophrenic animals.

When a regressive ASC transports a person into a purely denotative realm, each perception opens a myriad of possible interpretations. Ideas adhere to specific incidents rather than categories, and awareness of the present is enhanced at the expense of past and future. Each moment is emotionally compressed. This prepares a person to deal with immediate threats to his survival. Living in the jungle with hungry tigers, our primate ancestors had more need for heightened present awareness than for leisurely philosophizing. Similarly, a person in a psychotic ASC who feels his selfhood to be constantly threatened desperately focuses his attention only on the present moment.

But day-to-day survival under these circumstances comes at the price of foresight, insight, and ability to focus on long-term goals. This loss of abstract thinking explains why patients in mental hospitals seldom organize themselves to improve their lot or to escape from token security arrangements unless led by a nonpsychotic like McMurphy, the misdiagnosed hero of *One Flew over the Cuckoo's Nest*. Similarly, regressed psychotics seem incapable of deception. For in order to lie, a person must foresee the results of his actions and visualize future possibilities. When a regressed person begins to fabricate for his own benefit, it is usually a sign that he is emerging from his psychotic ASC.

Therapists can estimate a person's level of regression by asking him the meaning of proverbs, which require abstract thinking to interpret correctly For example, when asked the meaning of "People in glass houses shouldn't throw stones," most regressed people reply, "If they do, they'll break the glass." Similarly, "Too many cooks spoil the soup," elicits an image of harried kitchen workers elbowing each other rather than the more abstract interpretation. When asked if he had close ties to his home, one patient innocently replied, "Yes, my father wears them around his neck." These kinds of concrete answers suggest that regression has been arrested at the second chakra.

The motley patterns of schizophrenic speech called "loose associations" are also a sign of paleological regression. Normally, each thought in our stream of consciousness is in some way connected to the preceding one by sequences of related memories or perceptions. For instance, a chain of thoughts might start with a rose we pick in the yard, progress to a rose we once admired in New York's Central Park, then leap to a Broadway show we saw while visiting that metropolis. In mild regressions, this way of linking ideas usually remains intact.

However, severely regressive ASCs disrupt these chains of reasoned associations. As regression sinks the self deep into second-chakra consciousness, and the neurological control center simultaneously descends to the limbic system, ideas adhere to each other not through incoming stimuli, or through logical association, but through a private *emotional* link that is generally inaccessible to an outside observer. One schizophrenic woman who had regressed to the typhonic level handed me a note that at first reading seems little more than an absurd series of non sequiturs. But with a second reading, a perceptive reader may discern a linkage of typical first- and second-chakra concerns.

> Doctor, why don't you tell me about these bad boys that are coming to me in bed and telling me about their carrots and sticks? My pain down below means that things in seventh heaven are looking up. When will you discharge me through my vagina, or will you get born again? Seven is the number that counts. Little girls like me are seven again, that is when my head turned around to see my behind. Help me please, show me the way back and I'll kiss your ass. Shit is for dinner again, so that's how it is for all of us down here.

In the above example, my patient was trying to communicate her concerns about her pelvic pain, her allied fear that she had become pregnant from a recent sexual assault by two male patients, and her desire that I discharge her from the hospital because the food was unsavory. Each discrete thought, however, became derailed by another thought linked by a subconscious association that is only partially discernible to an outside observer: discharge—vagina—born again. Only after I pondered her note for a while was I able to respond empathically to what was bothering her.

If regression continues unchecked, a new pattern of thinking emerges as the self contracts into first-chakra consciousness. Rather than associating related ideas, *sounds* of words make connecting links. In other words, verbalization replaces connotation and denotation. This completes the plunge from the abstract-conceptual, through the concrete-perceptual, into the preverbal realm of primitive sensation. Speech lapses into chains of incomprehensible "clang" associations, often rhyming, but otherwise making little sense—an infantile babble known as word salad. In the 1960s a popular motion picture, *David and Lisa*, sensitively portrayed a young psychotic woman who had regressed to this level and communicated solely in amusing but meaningless verse.

To return to Piaget's classifications, the term *concrete operations* describes normal second-chakra thinking. In this mode, a child manipulates objects through here-and-now denotative reasoning. This is not to say that a seven-year-old cannot grasp abstractions, provided that they apply to concrete objects available to his five senses. For example, if a child is asked how a chair and table are alike, he might answer that they both have legs, but not that they both are furniture. A severely regressed schizophrenic is likely to give the same answer.

Once a child develops an ego, and his primary reasoning mode becomes *formal operations*, he not only plays with objects, but also plays with *ideas*. He can compare classes of objects not immediately present, and use imagination to invent new combinations and test possible outcomes in his mind. From this, *free will* gradually emerges, enabling him to manipulate ideas and concepts, insert reasoning between a stimulus and his response, and feel responsible for his behavior. Free will is possible only for selves centered at the third chakra or higher.

The emergence of free will marks the end of childhood innocence and the beginnings of adult responsibility. At this point, the ego-based mind is just starting to transcend the physical brain and acquire power to direct the flow of conscious energies along desired neurological pathways. The mind can at last choose what, and what not, to think about. The dark side of this advance is that formal-operations thinking completes the adolescent's exile from Eden, from intimate communion with the Ground. With this blossoming of higher mental skills, the young adult gains membership into a world of aggressively competitive peers, courtship rituals, independence from parents, and success and failure.

These complex demands require efficiently operating frontal lobes capable of planning for an abstract future. To do this, the frontal lobes must mobilize the neurotransmitters dopamine and norepinephrine to override the roiling activity of the limbic system. Without these checks and balances, the ego cannot maintain its integrity against the onslaught of primitive emotions triggered by competitive stress. Unfortunate individuals who are genetically predisposed to schizophrenia cannot activate these brain functions, which are essential for third-chakra consciousness. And when a higher function is not up to a survival task, regression to the next-lower level takes over. During regressions to second-chakra consciousness, the newly emergent capacity for reasoned choice and will is forfeited, forming the crux of the legal-insanity defense.

The stresses of young adulthood also render certain individuals who are *not* genetically predisposed to schizophrenia vulnerable to regressions to second-chakra consciousness. These are the borderlines who never formed well-fortified self-boundaries during childhood. Leaving home and severing selfobject ties is especially stressful for these people, whose egos dissolve if momentarily unsupported. Independence from parents triggers a desperate search for surrogate selfobjects, who initially are flattered by the borderline's idealizing and engulfing "love," but who are soon put off by his clinging dependency and jealous rages. Inevitable rejections then fragment the borderline's ego and precipitate regression. Such regressions may be initially indistinguishable from schizophrenia, but they abruptly reverse when the borderline finds another acceptable selfobject, such as an empathic therapist.

Unfortunately, regression to second-chakra consciousness does not re-create a sprightly child in an adult's body, happily frolicking in a world of interesting fantasies. Once the self expands into the third chakra, it can never be the same. Formal-operations thinking outfits the ego with concepts and abstract ideas. If these are forced back into a primitive mode and suffused with paleologic, they become warped. A concept concretized in this way becomes like a *thing*, and so is manipulated by the same kind of magical thinking that children project onto their toys. Wishes and fantasies contaminate syllogistic reasoning, and delusions replace consensual reality.

A person's *ethics* also reflect his level of consciousness. Observing how an individual makes judgments about right and wrong can aid a healer in determining his level of regression. For instance, the ethical system of a preadolescent child, or a person regressed to this level, measures good and bad by conforming to authoritarian rules. Breaking rules seems wrong because he will be punished if caught. However, once he has activated formal operations, a sense of fair play—expressed by the universal golden rule—expands his ethical judgments into an abstract realm. So a healthy adolescent might avoid stealing a classmate's schoolbook because he imagines what the world would be like if everyone stole each other's books. This view is beyond the capacities of people regressed to the second chakra, who obey rules to avoid punishment, sometimes by a concretized deity.

MANIC LOGIC

So far we have considered forms of logic that emerge during schizophrenic ASCs, that most malignant form of psychosis. People caught up in manic ASCs, however, do not regress during the early stages of their hyperarousal. Mania is an untimely *inflation* of the ego into previously unexperienced areas of the Ground. Yet this is quite different from a mystic's *transcending* his ego. Ego inflation precipitously opens a person to the higher chakras before he is prepared to integrate these finer levels of consciousness. The result is an ASC very different from schizophrenic regression.

Mania follows cyclic surges of the excitatory neurotransmitter norepinephrine in the brain's arousal system. In contrast to the unbalanced qualitative shifts of schizophrenia, this initially induces a uniform, quantitative expansion of consciousness. When a manic ASC affects someone who has gained the third chakra, neological reasoning initially remains intact, although it is inadequate to meet the challenges of higher consciousness. Lacking adequate reality models, a manic casts these breakthroughs from higher planes in the symbolic, mythic, and logical elements of the lower level. This always results in distortion.

For example, an early manic ASC may suddenly infuse an immature young adult with feelings of selfless love (fourth chakra) that motivate him to give away his meager possessions indiscriminately, or to quit college in order to bring an end to world hunger. If the opening progresses to the fifth chakra, a sudden perception of archetypal symbols may inspire him to take on creative projects that he has no chance of completing. Or he may perceive how arbitrary and personally constricting are the norms of social comportment and recklessly flout the law. Sixth-chakra openings may impart confusing telepathic or other paranormal powers that he rationalizes in ways that seem wildly delusional to his peers. He may finally be overcome with waves of mystical rapture (seventh chakra) that render him unable to take food or water, or care for his hygienic needs, mimicking a first-chakra regression.

At any point along this progression the delicate balance among various neurological centers can go awry, precipitating a tumultuous regression to the lower chakras. This is always an ominous turn. During a manic ASC, volcanic upwellings of unfocused psychic energy infuse the self. This can fuel an irritability that tolerates no frustration and leads to explosive behavior. Hallucinated voices and visions grasp the painfully swollen ego with irresistible force, and they may command acts of violence directed toward anyone who thwarts the manic's impulses.

I was still in the first year of my psychiatric training when I met Cliff, who was transferred to a state hospital from the county jail.

Cliff was well on his way to becoming valedictorian of his college class. His scholarly aptitude throughout high school and college was remarkable in that he seldom needed more than three hours' sleep each night, but still had reserves of energy for long hours of study. A photographic memory was another of his assets, and he excelled at the piano, which he played in a campus nightclub to accompany his original folk songs.

Cliff's problems with the authorities began after three sleepless nights. He suddenly stood in the midst of a history class to give a long antiwar speech, then cursed at the professor, who insisted that he be silent. The next day, he began handing out anarchistic leaflets of his own production in the halls of the administration building, then lit a marijuana cigarette in front of a security officer who asked him to move outdoors. Police reinforcements were called when he resisted arrest, after which he broke every window in a patrol car before he was subdued by a blow to the head with a nightstick. Once in jail, Cliff refused to eat or wear clothes. He remained awake all night, shouting religious slogans through the bars of his cell, and accusing his captors of being Nazis.

When I met him in the hospital the next day, Cliff was in high spirits. He somehow perceived me to be an enlightened being who would soon liberate him from his unreasonable confinement. Dressed only in short pants, his body radiated an almost visible aura, and his eyes flamed with the certainty of his private truth. In the course of my interview, I asked him to interpret the relatively difficult proverb, "Still waters run deep," to which he responded with five separate interpretations of increasing abstraction and complexity. He then picked up a copy of the Upanishads from my bookshelf and read aloud, interposing astute explanations of those arcane texts. He told me that his insights were the result of his intimate intuitive rapport with God.

Awed by Cliff's extraordinary bearing, I was loath to apply a pathological diagnosis to what I felt was an appealing nonconformist in the throes of a spiritual awakening.

In my naiveté, I decided to observe him for a few days, certain that I could restore his reason through empathic understanding and by allowing his mind unfettered expression. However, the next morning I arrived at the hospital to learn that at 3 A.M. Cliff had leapt from a second-story fire escape, believing that God had chosen him to ascend directly to heaven.

As Cliff recovered from his broken leg, my supervising psychiatrist prescribed lithium. Cliff returned to his classes within a few weeks, wearing a cast as a tribute to my inexperience. Several years later, I received a letter from him. He had become chief engineer in charge of a major civic project. Following a second manic episode a year after the first, he learned to recognize the early signs of hyperarousal, and he used lithium only during these times. He fondly recalled his manic insights, as he felt that these had permanently changed him for the better, imparting a sense of "life's great mystery." He hoped that we both were the wiser for our brief encounter and concluded with, "Nice try."

Cliff's classically typical mania illustrates what follows when higher realizations abruptly impinge upon a self that is centered in third-chakra consciousness. Yet at first there was no regression, no retreat into paleologic, and Cliff retained a capacity for abstract thinking until the end stage of his ASC. However, neologic alone is inadequate to process higher-chakra infusions, which require whole-systems thinking to fathom. Because he could not integrate these glimpses of higher truths, they rendered him arrogantly impervious to feedback. Without a way to instantly inoculate an immature ego with the wisdom of a sage, lithium is necessary to shield an individual from harm until the manic cycle runs its course.

Yet the point at which lithium dampens the excesses of a manic ASC is the beginning, not the end, of the healing process. Psychotherapy is essential to help integrate higher realizations into the context of an individual's life. For people prone to mania, transpersonal methods are of great value in converting a disruptive ASC into an impetus for spiritual growth, but only after arousal is controlled. It is likely that mania will recur in a person's life, even if he takes lithium prophylactically. Practiced during intervals between manic episodes, spiritual techniques that gradually expand the self into the higher chakras can fortify a person to tolerate future openings without destructive consequences.

BENIGN REGRESSION

The ascent from the second to the third chakra is the time of life when most malignant schizophrenic ASCs shake a young adult loose from his moorings in the consensual world. Manic episodes also first occur during that perilous transition, although some strike later in life.

To get ahead of ourselves for a moment, transitions between *any* of the seven chakras can precipitate abrupt regressions to lower levels. These passages have a distinctive character at each level, but all can trigger a degree of atavism that precedes transcendence.

As a person transits from any life stage to a higher one, he realigns his values, his belief in a limited sphere of reality, his ethical and logical systems, his religious viewpoint, and his outgrown relationships. In other words he symbolically *dies* to his old life, to be reborn to a higher mode of functioning that subsumes the lower mode. As he endures these thorny transitions, disturbing images of his physical birth can emerge in veiled form as vivid dreams or hallucinations that color his psychic rebirth. These are wrenching experiences for which technological societies are ill equipped to prepare us, and which can be so extraordinary that they shatter a person's basic belief in the worldview of Western civilization.

Of course, there are some people whose ascent through the chakras is smooth and untroubled. They are indeed fortunate individuals whose passage through the first chakra laid down a solid foundation for a self that remains firmly "lashed to the mast" throughout life's turbulent tidal shifts. But few of us are so blessed. For most, normal expansions of consciousness are anything but linear. More often they are spiraling ascensions, consisting of regression, restoration, and higher integration. This is what the historian Arnold Toynbee called "the cycle of withdrawal and return" that has graced the lives of some of humankind's major geniuses.

Once an individual ascends to a higher chakra and then encounters a barrier to further progress, the psychic disturbances are usually brief and less spectacular than the dizzying plunge downward from third-chakra consciousness, especially if they take place in a supportive environment. This is because they usually do not propel the self deep into the second- chakra level, where no adult can remain if he is to be considered a sane and capable member of the modern world.

Michael Washburn aptly named these temporary retreats *regression in the service of transcendence*. Although potentially benign, such mini-regressions have enough power to strip away the ego's protective under-girding and expose it to the Ground, thereby overriding original repression. Recall that the ego crystallizes within a larger self in order to keep the Ground from awareness, to keep the self attuned to consensual reality. The ego rests on original repression, on negation of the Ground. It is a marvelous tool with which to cope with the tasks of the third chakra, but to do so it must insulate our day-to-day mind from the subconscious realm in both its personal and collective compartments. Therefore, the self that identifies with the ego fears annihilation when these repressed contents stream out of the underworld and flood into awareness.

Regression in the service of transcendence (RIST) is a natural healing process that lowers defenses against confronting unresolved impediments to higher consciousness. It can take place during transits from any chakra to a higher one. RIST is a clarion call from the larger self to the ego, proclaiming: "Old rules and habits no longer apply. Reality is not what you believed it to be. You must now reexamine and reorder your life. Nothing short of a radical transformation will suffice."

Arising from a stalemate in human growth, RIST forces a collision of atavistic and progressive trends. These upheavals at the very core of the self can be personally catastrophic, for they hazard a return of the repressed Ground in full fury. The outcome can be madness as well as enlightenment, disintegration as well as higher integration. Believing itself to be threatened by annihilation, the ego initiates a life-or-death struggle to free itself from the ominous force it confronts. It desperately tries to shore up old defenses and reseal the Ground. But this tactic can recoil upon the repressor as menacing hallucinations that render him unable to go on with ordinary life. It can destroy his ego and degenerate into malignant regression. This is the supreme risk of any spiritual quest, and it accounts for the many similarities between madness and mysticism.

Yet the ideal outcome of RIST is that the ego gradually discovers that its efforts are for naught. It realizes that its imagined adversary is not inherently alien and evil, but only a larger part of itself that was alienated and condemned. The ego can then choose to surrender to the underlying Source of its being, which saves it from further regression. This choice is reminiscent of Tibetan Buddhist deities who maintain both a peaceful and wrathful aspect. If the ego clings to its little world when the deity wants it to open up, the ego comes face to face with the deity's terrible visage. But if the ego surrenders to the process, the deity turns congenial.

Because of its similarities to early schizophrenia, RIST can be confused with that far more malignant ASC, especially when it occurs during third-to-fourth-chakra transitions. Unless there is physical danger of harm, antipsychotic medicines should generally be avoided in RIST, for they can freeze the process at a partially regressed level and foster long-term dependence on medicine to keep the Ground at bay. However, there are times when medicines must be used to ensure safety or because alternative treatments are not available. Even then, an artful healer administers doses sufficient only to ameliorate that danger, not to compel an abrupt return to a more constricted reality. Several studies have confirmed that certain subgroups of psychotic patients have better recovery rates following treatment with placebos—sham medicines—than with antipsychotic drugs.

When a healer recognizes such an untimely breakdown of original repression, he should help his patient arrange a retreat from the pressures of daily life. During these times, an empathic touch promotes integration of the subconscious energies flooding awareness. This strategy is reminiscent of what R. D. Laing envisioned during his noble experiment at Kingsley Hall. Laing correctly recognized potential spiritual openings in *some* of his patients. But Kingsley Hall's ultimate downfall followed from his failure to discriminate benign RIST from the far more common malignant regressions of schizophrenia, which yield to different tactics.

Several signs help us distinguish RIST from schizophrenia. ASCs associated with RIST begin abruptly, in contrast to schizophrenia's insidious onset. RIST is usually precipitated by a stressful life event, such as changing one's career or spouse, starting a spiritual practice such as meditation or yoga, or taking a psychedelic drug. Sometimes RIST simply occurs when a person reaches a degree of maturity in which he naturally begins to doubt the meaning and value of his present life, which he feels is flat or empty. For example, RIST can emerge when a person fails to achieve a worldly goal, or even succeeds in a worldly ambition only to make the depressing discovery that material rewards are elusive and transitory. In contrast, the disorganized thinking of schizophrenia is usually unrelated to specific life events, although nonspecific stress worsens symptoms.

In RIST, affect or feeling-tone is preserved and often wildly exaggerated. Moments of dark despair alternate with rapture, or feelings of being unreal give way to sudden insights. This is in sharp contrast to the bleak grayness of the schizophrenic ASC, in which affect is shallow or incongruent with what the person is saying. As RIST dissolves repression, a person confronts not only the Ground, but his personal subconscious—his Shadow. This divests him of his social persona and defenses, exposing him to a host of unwelcome insights. What can follow is a shock of self-recrimination and guilt, feelings notably absent from most schizophrenic ASCs. RIST may occur at any time of life and at any level of maturity, but the initial onset of schizophrenia is almost always during the second and third decades of life, at the opening of the third chakra.

Hallucinated voices that sometimes accompany RIST are of the higher order, and though they may advise, they never command. RIST may be dramatically extroverted in its presentation or take an introspective turn, but schizophrenia almost always leads to withdrawal. Except when it occurs during transits from the second to third chakra, RIST seldom completely deprives a person of his capacity for neologic and abstract thought, although paleologic may be intermixed with more advanced cognition. For this reason, a person experiencing RIST maintains some insight into his disordered state and tries to restrain his behavior, while impulsive behavior characterizes schizophrenia and mania.

Paranoid ideas seldom occur in RIST, or if they do, they reflect a global terror of the unknown rather than a specifically defined conspiracy. By projecting his inner terrors onto the outside world and imagining it to be everywhere on watch against him, a paranoid individual cuts short the defenseless inner exploration that is a hallmark of RIST. True paranoia is not the same as being frightened by awesome demonic images or by the unnerving experience of finding oneself in an unaccustomed ASC that cannot be explained in consensual terms.

Finally, RIST tells a meaningful story. A discerning observer can perceive archetypal or mythic themes acted out during RIST that are specific to the particular chakra level being left behind, or to the next higher chakra. Images of death and rebirth are prominent, and a person experiencing RIST may spontaneously assume a fetal position or postures that mimic passage though the birth canal. The mythic theme that emerges during RIST can inform a healer about the nature of the impediment to growth. The healer can then gauge his response in view of the actual life situation of the patient, his style of dealing with it, and his ability to integrate it into everyday life.

Images that emerge during RIST are more cataclysmic and less conspiratorial than in malignant regression. As the ego descends into a psychic underworld, it may generate visions of falling or being sucked into a whirlpool. Earthquakes, volcanic eruptions, raging floods, and other violent upheavals express a recognition that repressed forces are astir. Images of a colossal clash with evil or with ravenous beasts represent the ego's efforts to maintain repression, while bloody death-ridden images indicate that the ego feels itself to be losing that battle.

These dreamlike visions that infiltrate awareness during RIST have in common a motif of the self under siege by upsurgent forces of darkness that augur annihilation of the self, or of the world. Images of a descent into hell where one battles hideous entities are also common. As the inward turning continues, these images are woven into mythlike delusions in which are encrypted the hidden conflict behind the ASC. Buried deep in that archetypal code is the secret of redemption.

MYTHOLOGY IN MADNESS

The premier mythologist of our time, Joseph Campbell, once stated that there is a subtle plane of being that underlies and supports the visible plane and that provides the basic reality behind the great myths of all cultures and times. All socialized human beings must in some way relate to this subliminal plane.

Campbell was referring to what Carl Jung named the realm of *archetypes*—universal thought-forms embedded in a collective consciousness that is common to all humanity but is obscured by the glare of sensory stimulation. Campbell recognized that each great myth represents an archetypal theme that recurs again and again in different surface forms throughout history, independent of culture. The content changes from era to era and nation to nation so as to resonate with the specific concerns of the people who live by those myths, but the fundamental themes are changeless.

Myths instruct men and women not only in how to live their lives, but also in how to become comfortable in the divine presence. In his richly illustrative writings, Campbell cites numerous examples of how the mystery of creation, the drama of birth and death, the first stirrings of selfhood, the initiation into adulthood, the opening of the heart, the acquisition of cosmic power, and the reunion with the Source are recast into fairy tales, poetry, paintings, novels, and political movements. A well-told myth has a vital power to harmonize mind and body and express the living edge between self and Spiritual Ground.

Most psychotic ASCs, whether manic, schizophrenic, or RIST, dissolve the ego's defensive boundaries and open to awareness the subconscious mind cloaked in mythic symbols. Deep in the most deranged delusion is a personal meaning cast in a universal theme. These mangled myths are articulated by people desperately seeking to realign themselves with the collective consciousness of humanity.

The following case history is illustrative.

> Brian, a forty-eight-year-old mortgage-loan broker, was muscled into an urban emergency room at 3 A.M. by police who apprehended him striding purposefully, but stark naked, along a freeway divider. He refused to identify himself, saying only that names, like clothing, are meaningless social contrivances that keep us from knowing the truth about each other. He insisted that he be allowed to continue his mission before it was too late.
>
> Soothed by the gentle manner of a female psychiatric consultant, Brian proclaimed that he was in a life-or-death

race against the forces of Satan to found a new Jerusalem at a place where the four cardinal directions meet at a busy freeway intersection, and that this act will ensure the triumph of good over evil and ensure lasting peace on earth. He asserted that he was assigned his mission by a group of "advanced beings" who communicate with him through omens and dreams. He felt that these more-evolved beings prepared him for his task by granting him telepathic and other magical powers, such as moving physical objects with "beams of pure love."

A phone call to Brian's wife revealed that he had no previous psychiatric problems, but for the past year had been increasingly dissatisfied with his successful career, which he called "Mammon worship." After years of self-proclaimed atheism, he became involved with a fundamental religious group, but then quarreled bitterly with its minister over the concept of "God fearing," because he felt that there was nothing to fear from God. Following this, he did not sleep for several days, spending his nights pacing about his home, repeating that he was on the verge of an important breakthrough that would end war and unite all nations.

Brian was forcibly injected with sedating doses of antipsychotic drugs and committed to a psychiatric hospital, where he received more of the same. His psychotic ASC gradually subsided over the next few days, but he became so severely depressed and withdrawn that antidepressant medications were added to the chemical broth. When he left the hospital, he was "normal" by some standards, but he complained of a lack of vigor, feelings of emptiness, and an inability to make decisions about the future course of his life. He told his wife that he had "lost" himself. A week later he attempted suicide by taking an overdose of his prescribed medicines.

Brian's psychotic ASC meets many of the criteria for regression in the service of transcendence. Mythic elements of world renewal, salvation through love and understanding, inspiration from a higher source, a titanic struggle between good and evil, and acquisition of extraordinary mental powers gave coherence to his delusion. His lack of paranoia indicated that he had not projected his inner conflicts onto an imagined hostile world, and so was open to insight into his underlying motivations. Yet because he had reached a point of acting out his mythic task, there is little doubt that if left to his own devices his survival would have been even more imperiled than it was through standard psychiatric treatment.

We can only speculate as to Brian's outcome if he had been removed to a protective shelter where he could have lived through his myth in the company of empathic healers, themselves centered in the consciousness of the fourth chakra, which Brian's distorted "mission" indicated he was seeking. Instead of aborting his quest, the goal would have been to abet the process of disintegration and reintegration. As in Cliff's case, cited earlier in this chapter, judicious use of medicines to quell the surge of dopamine or norepinephrine might have been helpful for the first few days. But his suicidal depression certainly could have been avoided if he had found the understanding he was seeking in the company of healers comfortable with his solitary trek.

Although Campbell did not acknowledge a distinction between RIST and schizophrenia, his great insight was to view psychotic ASCs in terms of the myth of the "hero's journey." Here is its ageless theme:

> A hero ventures forth from the world of common day into a region of supernatural wonder; fabulous forces are there encountered and a decisive victory is won; the hero comes back from this mysterious adventure with the power to bestow boons on his fellow men.

Interpreted from this point of view, RIST is hardly an eternal loss of the soul; rather, it is a healing descent into the underworld to recover something missing or lost, so as to restore a vital balance. The hero's journey is one of *separation, initiation,* and *return.* Its theme is that in a death struggle with titanic supernatural forces, the self can be triumphant. The self is then reborn into a higher level of consciousness, maintaining access to the lower level when appropriate. But because this lower level is transcended, a more powerful self can operate upon it in a way that appears magical to those still below.

A great source of confusion is that mythological themes emerge from malignant psychotic ASCs as well as RIST. In either instance, delusions are drawn from the same archetypal source. Brian's case illustrates the difference: the high mythological theme of Brian's delusion, though superficially fantastic, was also purposeful and internally coherent. In contrast, typical schizophrenic delusions are unsystematic, grotesque, chaotic, and impossible to fathom. For instance, the following is a response given by a regressed schizophrenic to a picture presented to him as part of a standard psychological test (the picture is of a standing man near a reclining woman in an otherwise neutral setting):

"Oh God, he raped her. This is awful. I wish I didn't see this one. Oh, my goodness. This must be Vivian, and this guy is Damian [names of his hallucinated voices]. This Damian and Vivian decide to meet in an infinity room, and they set a date up in the past. They both want to be the Antichrist, and they want to prove who is the sexiest, and whoever is the sexiest is the winner. So they meet in this room in the present, and they make love, and it frightens Vivian, and she goes into shock. She figures out she has a body, and she is not really a double, but she is not good, either. Through the years of crucifying Christ, she became a baby sexually and this sex act killed her. And Damian thinks: I don't have the great Vivian to help me become the best, and he feels remorse because she died, and he never felt remorse before, and he has love for her, but the devil can't love or he'll die. It takes him two years to die. It kills something in his brain, and in the future he sets it all up and the world goes along with him, but he dies two weeks before he transforms the world. Christ comes back on the clouds. Two great Antichrists were not the answer.

In this incoherent admixture of the personal and the archetypal, ideas flow through a series of bizarre symbolic images that are internally disconnected. Because the sequence of symbols fails to speak to the universal mind, the reader finds it difficult to empathize with what is being communicated. Buried in the concretized second-chakra images are fragmented themes of an aborted upward journey and of being hopelessly lost or damned, which reflect this person's feelings about himself and his chronic psychosis. Confronted with such pervasive and long-standing cognitive disorganization, however, a healer would be ill advised to attempt purely psychological interventions.

In the case recounted at the opening of this chapter, Beverly formed a delusion of being courted from a distance by a famous movie star, who in truth was unaware of her existence. This *erotomanic* delusion was a projection of Beverly's disowned sexual urges and feelings of being unlovable. Through paleological thinking, it took the form of the Cinderella fable, an endearing myth of a handsome prince relentlessly searching among common folk for the orphaned object of his obsessive love, whom he desires to cherish and protect. Such myths are designed to resonate with second-chakra consciousness. A healer who recognizes this theme could help Beverly reown her natural sexual longings and need for an affirming selfobject by using tactics specific to her present concrete operational level. A longer-term strategy would be to gradually initiate her into third-chakra consciousness by activating myths and learning tasks that enhance power and self-reliance as she became ready to integrate these skills.

MADNESS & RELIGIOUS MYTHS

Death is present in an immediate way to a person experiencing a psychotic ASC. As his ego relinquishes its ability to stave off the repressed power of the Ground, he feels the self dissolving into a dark and seamless void, a helpless sensation that also underlies most psychedelic "bad trips." In response to this perceived death, there is a natural urge to seek solace in the myths and symbols of religion. Religious belief makes death palatable, or even nonexistent, by holding out the hope that the soul will survive physical death to enjoy a better life. This is a very appealing notion to someone poised on the crumbling edge of an abyss.

Because psychotic delusions are often cast in religious symbols, however bizarrely distorted, it is easy to confuse these with legitimate spiritual insights. Nevertheless, a discerning listener who is alert to pre/trans distinctions can separate the concretized religious images that emerge during primitive states of consciousness from the abstract symbols derived from higher states.

Traditional religions teach that there is an invisible force greater than ourselves that guides us during duress. How a psychotic person identifies that force reveals his degree of regression or readiness for transcendence. For instance, is his idea of God personified as a distant parentlike figure cloaked in wrathful retribution? Or is God felt to be a beckoning font of unconditional love drawing him toward higher commitment? In the first case, strategies appropriate to second-chakra consciousness are most likely to be helpful, while in the latter case, he might better be encouraged to overcome barriers against realizing fourth-chakra consciousness by plunging deeper into the mythic elements of his delusion.

Similarly, is the psychotic person's idea of Satan concretized into a cunning archfiend hell-bent on punishing his every shortcoming? Or is Satan viewed as an unevolved part of the self that resists higher strivings, an inner negativity to be reowned and overcome through self-knowledge? If a person says that he is Jesus, does he believe he is the historical figure of Christ, or is he expressing a feeling that divine consciousness dwells within him, as it does in his fellow men and women? And if he does express this literally, can he be guided into a more abstract way of integrating his inner realization? These distinctions direct a healer toward radically different treatment strategies.

254

If a psychotic person tends toward paranoia, he may contort his intuition of a pervasive universal force into a delusion that an insidious power wants to harm him. The basic intuition is roughly the same as that of a mystic, but the interpretation of it changes as the paranoid personifies the inpouring force of the Ground into a malevolent "they." To illustrate how close paranoia and mystical vision are, consider how a sudden unitive insight might be expressed by a person on the brink of transcendence:

> Everything is connected to everything else. There is much more to the universe than we know through our senses. A great power is at work in subtle ways. Nothing that happens is accidental or meaningless, but emanates from an unknowable divine will. I am an immediate and important instrument of that supreme plan.

Now the paranoid version:

> Everything is connected to everything else. There is more going on here than meets the eye. Something strange is happening just behind the scenes. No events are accidental or meaningless, because diabolical forces are pulling the strings. There are no coincidences; all is conspiracy! And I am the primary focus of this evil plan.

Both religious images and paranoia are ways of symbolizing the resurgent power of the Ground and attempting to cope with it by reducing it to human size. The paranoid's initial intuition is correct, but the threatening force is neither "out there" nor inherently evil. It is the wellspring of the self, shielded from awareness by original repression.

As a developing self naturally ascends upward to the third chakra, the Ground grows distant from awareness, and God becomes an abstract idea, sometimes a bad one. The person may then define himself as an atheist, a stance that seems reasonable during ego-based third-chakra consciousness, when the self is most isolated from its Source. As Jung pointed out, some religions actually shield a person against religious experience, against direct communion with the Ground.

Yet a more common third-chakra belief is of a "universal force" that is separate from the self. This reflects a frightened ego's effort to repress the ever-present activity of the Ground. Third-chakra minds tend to rationalize this universal force as operating through predictable laws. Once this third-chakra level of religious feeling is reached, regression to the second level produces a bizarre mix of concrete and semiabstract religious symbols, as in Brian's case presented earlier in this chapter. In contrast, if the self expands into fourth-chakra consciousness, communion with the Ground once again becomes a part of ordinary awareness. Immediate perception of universal love then supplants the *deus absconditus* of the third chakra, and awe replaces fear as the primary religious emotion.

LATE STAGES

Transpersonal philosophers such as Ken Wilber have shown that the collective consciousness of humanity is evolving in much the same way that an individual psyche expands through levels of ever finer awareness. A long view of history indicates that this is indeed the case. During our present era the most advanced cultures on earth identify their collective psyche with the late stages of the third chakra. People born into these cultures are more or less assured of developing the formal-operations thinking that third-chakra consciousness makes possible.

Just as our ancestors in early civilizations struggled to raise themselves out of the primitive muck of paleological superstition into the light of reason, humanity now poises on the threshold of another death and rebirth. The collective opening of the fourth chakra will be uneven, but there are sure signs that we are turning away from aggressive militarism, environmental exploitation, and scientific materialism toward a more compassionate and holistic ethos. Yet on both the individual and collective levels, the opening of the heart presents a hazard—regression in the service of transcendence.

Modern cultures provide hero myths with changeless themes to guide us through these arduous transitions. But the specific forms of these myths must be perpetually updated to reflect the higher strivings of evolving consciousness. Such revisions are normally the task of priestly vocations, but because the mythology of established religion grows more concrete and resistant to change as it becomes entrenched in a culture, the task of revising our myths lags behind our need for greater relevance.

The revising task is made more difficult because fourth-chakra consciousness requires a predominantly feminine mythology, in contrast to the aggressively masculine values of the third. Although they may initially seem strange to most, the new myths will exalt the receptive image of the Goddess as sensuous guide and emphasize nurture, compassion, affiliation, commitment, and cooperative effort, as opposed to conquest, dominance, competition, detachment, and individual achievement. The former, feminine images are anathema to our third-chakra-based power elite, who strive to suppress them as if their survival depended on it—which of course it does.

As the ego loosens its death grip on third-chakra consciousness, there is great resistance, and a lack of heroes to lead the way. Not everyone will advance even to the point of RIST. Many step back from this ego-threatening quandary into numbing addictions or flamboyant sexuality—the midlife crisis. Alcohol immunizes the heart to the feelings of awe and the call to selfless commitment of the fourth chakra. Cocaine blinds one to the path of the heart by amplifying the swaggering aggressiveness and grasping acquisitiveness of the third chakra.

Yet many people who cannot resist the call of the larger self are destroyed, or nearly so, by regression in the service of transcendence. Some become shipwrecked on the shoals of a psychiatric insensitivity that aborts their redemptive journey with heart-numbing medicines that are appropriate only for malignant regressions. These tactics may effect a simulation of the ordinary state of consciousness, but they also lead to depression and alienation of self from Source. Although regression in the service of transcendence draws the ego back toward its numinous origins, it does not necessarily permanently dissolve that ego, as do malignant ASCs. Its healing function is to open a channel to the Ground so that the self can be replenished by the rejuvenating power that issues from it.

CHAPTER 12

Fourth Chakra:
Madness as Spiritual Emergency

◆

Our greatest blessings come to us by way of madness,
provided the madness is given us by divine gift.
SOCRATES

AN EXQUISITE BLACK antelope in full gallop adorns the complex mandala of the Anahata chakra as depicted in ancient yoga texts. It is said that this shy, fleet, and graceful animal symbolizes spiritual experiences that move quickly from the ego's view, vanishing before it can grasp them.

The elusive antelope seems an especially well chosen symbol for the fourth chakra, which radiates the all-embracing consciousness of the heart. For once this level is attained, the self ever so warily slows its outward journey through the material world and timidly turns back toward the loving abundance of the Spiritual Ground.

At the heart chakra the growing self reaches a crossroads. Much of its work in the world is accomplished, yet much is left undone. Having mastered the mundane tasks of the third chakra, the self now begins to rise above its ego-based acquisitiveness to reaffirm its connection with the collective consciousness of humanity. The self stretches outward, once again opening to the energies of the Ground, allowing itself to be infused with what every major religion agrees is its essence: universal love.

The ancient Greeks recognized that Eros, their god of love, appears in two manifestations—the worldly and the heavenly. Therefore, *agape*—their word for universal love—was distinguished from the romantic raptures of the second and third chakras. Like its celestial counterpart, romantic love arises from a natural urge to fulfill the self by engaging the creative mysteries of life. But it is also characterized by seduction and jealousy, dominance and dependence, and attachment to an idealized object; the aim of lower-chakra love is to quell a feeling of emptiness.

In contrast, the universal love of fourth-chakra consciousness saturates the self with a perception of fullness, an inner abundance that is freely shared for the good of all. At the heart chakra, love is no longer tainted by need or craving. Instead, there is a joyous realization of a rightful place for all that exists in the world, an open receptivity that overrides possessiveness, a deep peace that grows from self-acceptance.

At this point in life, the urge arises for *commitment* to something beyond the ego—a social cause, perhaps, or a spiritual path, or even another person. An individual feels the upwelling energy of the Ground as a loving force, and he or she must grant that force free passage through the self and outward into the world, or it will be blocked and converted into physical and mental symptoms. But because a person whose self expands into the heart chakra leaves behind the coarser values of the majority of men and women, there will likely be scant support for his newfound goals. He must often travel this path alone.

Therefore, there is at this time a great temptation to step back, to reaffirm materialistic values, to regress *not* in service of transcendence, but in service of the *ego*. Such a retreat requires one to muffle the beckoning call from above, often with alcohol or other heart-numbing drugs. This leads to a higher-level madness that is arguably worse than regressions to lower chakras.

But once a fully prepared person opens to the heart chakra, there arises within a compelling sense of mission that restores a deeper meaning that was overlooked by an ego-based intellect. There is an eagerness to serve others and to share a sense of inner abundance. This new calling involves a labor of love, a compassionate effort to reduce the suffering of humankind. Every religion provides a symbol for this impulse. In Buddhism, it is the Bodhisattva, an evolved soul who is ready for nirvana, but who refuses to leave the world as long as there is suffering. Instead, he stays behind to heal, teach, and inspire. Saintly figures who dedicated their lives to selfless service, such as Mother Teresa of Calcutta, Mahatma Gandhi, Saint Francis of Assisi, Albert Schweitzer, and the Virgin Mary, epitomize the consciousness of the heart chakra in Western traditions.

Two personal attributes that are not possible at lower levels of consciousness emerge with the opening of the heart: *empathy* and its close companion *compassion*. Empathy is the ability to put oneself inside the mind and heart of another, to see, hear, and feel the world as he does, to experience that person's reality inside oneself. By itself, empathy is not exclusively a fourth-chakra attribute. It can even be used for greed or evil, such as when Hitler's propaganda minister, Joseph Goebbles, turned his intuitive feeling for the Zeitgeist toward manipulating his countrymen into embracing the Teutonic hero myths of the Third Reich. Similarly, modern advertising campaigns begin in board meetings where executives purposefully practice empathy to "read" the subconscious desires of potential consumers.

But when empathy is coupled with compassion, it becomes the most potent force of healing. Together they epitomize the consciousness of the heart. Compassion is a readiness to respond to another's pain without resentment or aversion, coupled with the impulse to dissipate the suffering. Unlike pity, which separates self from others and prevents sharing pain, compassion brings inward the suffering of another as a reflection of one's own pain. It embraces all who know sorrow and invites them into our life. "I truly understand that. I suffer with you. We share this as we would share our humanity" is the message of a compassionate heart. Yet this is not a passive or impotent suffering; it is one that mobilizes the healing love of the Spiritual Ground.

People who spend years in the medical professions know that some physicians, psychologists, and alternative practitioners are far more adept at bringing about healing than others, even though they use identical techniques or medicines. Research shows that healers most successful in curing disease and reducing suffering are those who are the most warm and empathic, who demonstrate unconditional regard for the individuality of their patients, who inspire trust by radiating confidence in themselves and in their patients' potential to recover. These are qualities that naturally accrue to people who are centered in the heart chakra or above.

As the self gains the fourth chakra, the brain's governing center of neurological activity also undergoes a transformation. You will recall that as the self expands from the second to the third chakra, the neurological center rises from the limbic system to the neocortex. This governing center then gradually advances to the most evolutionarily refined portion of the neocortex, the frontal lobes. Here it rules its kingdom from a position of great but despotic power, having at its command humankind's highest capacities for linear logic. If the ultimate potential of humanity were a single-minded mastery of technology to determine who is the most powerful warrior, the frontal cortex would be as lofty a neurological perch as we would ever need.

However, this seeming end point of physical evolution is far from the end point of consciousness evolution. Acting in isolation, no single part of the brain or mind is capable of achieving the wisdom inherent in the whole. Once ensconced in the frontal lobes—the topmost segment of the topmost level—there is nowhere for the governing center to advance but back downward and inward, to share its dominion with its forebears.

Just as the reasoning ego now reincorporates the heart, the neurological center broadens its locus of control to "reenfranchise" the limbic system. This is far from regression, however, for the seat of power does not merely relocate from a higher to a lower level, but *expands* to engage them both in harmonious discourse. Just as the substrings of an Indian sitar resonate with the primary strings to give a dimension of sound not possible in a simpler instrument, the field of consciousness within the brain resonates with a depth of meaning not possible from a single center. From this reunion of intellect and feeling arise the transcendent higher emotions of empathy, compassion, and selfless love.

THE OPENING OF THE HEART CHAKRA

As we saw in chapter 10, the worldly ego is a contraction within the whole self that was born in original repression. Original repression seals the psychic membrane that surrounds the ego and renders it relatively impermeable to the energies of the Ground. Once defended in this way, the tightly bound ego retains its supremacy in consciousness much longer than is necessary for most people, often for a lifetime.

The Italian psychiatrist and author Roberto Assagioli succinctly described the psychological status of the "normal" ego-based person prior to opening the heart chakra.

> One may say of him that he "lets himself live" rather than that he lives. He takes life as it comes and does not question its meaning, its worth, or its purpose; he devotes himself to the satisfaction of his personal desires; he seeks enjoyment of the senses, emotional pleasures, material security, or achievement of personal ambition. If he is more mature, he subordinates his personal satisfactions to the fulfillment of the various family and social duties assigned to him, but without seeking to understand on what bases those duties rest or from what source they spring. Possibly he regards himself as "religious" and is a believer in God, but usually his religion is outward and conventional, and

when he has conformed to the injunctions of his church and shared in its rites he feels that he has done all that is required of him. In short, *his operational belief is that the only reality is that of the physical world he can see and touch* and, therefore, he is strongly attached to earthly goods. Thus, for all practical purposes, he considers this life an end in itself. His belief in a future "heaven," if he conceives of one, is altogether theoretical and academic—as is proved by the fact that he takes the greatest pains to postpone as long as possible his departure for its joys.

Such a state of being falls short of satisfying the self's deep longing to regain its intimate relationship to the Ground. The first intimations of change begin with a nagging sense of emptiness, dissatisfaction, incompleteness. But what is lacking is not merely another material object to satisfy the senses; it is something vague and elusive, something that resists description. The real problem is that the self no longer needs its exclusive identification with the ego, and it ceases to benefit from being oblivious to the Ground. Original repression becomes a stubborn obstacle to one's higher destiny, the ego's way of holding off the rebirth of spirit by arresting growth and clinging to the trivial.

In other words, ego and Ground now lock in battle to determine which is to be the overlord of the soul. Until now the ego reigned easily as the exclusive sovereign of the psyche, and so it shunned direct contact with the Ground as an alien force at its borders that threatened to usurp its supreme authority. Accordingly, as a maturing person naturally opens to higher consciousness, the ego shores up its defenses in a desperate effort to keep one unaware of his real nature. Regression is one of the ego's key stratagems. Or the individual may seek shelter in the oblivion of addictions, or distract himself with sexual conquests and material wealth far exceeding any reasonable need. But these diversions are destined to fail in one way or another, for the ego is eye-to-eye with a resplendent force that is in all ways its superior.

Once a person opens his heart to the experience of compassion, he reengages the Ground in a way that he has not known since the second-chakra consciousness of childhood. Because of original repression, these sublime energies now seem unfamiliar. Effluences of rapture mix with waves of fear. He experiences the underlying unity of all sentient beings not as an intellectual abstraction, but directly as jarring telepathic intuitions or clairvoyant premonitions. He may be overwhelmed by sudden empathy with the great sufferings of humanity, and then choked by guilt and depression as he recalls petty and selfish deeds that arose from a narrower state of consciousness.

If a person is to withstand these higher realizations without regression in the service of transcendence (RIST) or worse, he must cease struggling against the eminence of the Ground and confront his resistances to it. He may then feel that he is courting death or madness. But unconditional surrender to a grander power, to his heart's impulse to regain Eden, is his salvation, not his executioner. Once he surrenders, regeneration in spirit commences on its own, and his larger self recognizes the Ground not as a menacing force, but as an intimate and beneficent power that heals his wounds and graces him with newfound potency.

If a person's passage through the first three chakras has successfully imbued him with an ability to trust his inner processes, to accept the wisdom of change and growth, he will integrate this infusion of higher consciousness as a benign *spiritual emergence.* But if his ego resists its destiny, or if his tentative efforts at regeneration take place in a hostile environment, a spiritual emergence easily becomes what Stanislav and Christina Grof have called a *spiritual emergency.* This overwhelms his ability to cope, and he will require assistance if growth is to continue.

SPIRITUAL EMERGENCE

An *artful* healer learns to distinguish between a natural and timely spiritual emergence and an uncontrolled and precipitous spiritual emergency. A spiritual emergence is an awakening into a level of awareness and insight beyond the ordinary capabilities of the ego. It heralds a passage into higher, transpersonal realms of consciousness. Although the self has not yet learned how to manage the power inherent in these breakthroughs, it recognizes them as important signs that guide it on its upward path.

A spiritual emergence may present itself meekly, perhaps as a sudden intimation of a deeper meaning in nature, a "runner's high" with a feeling of being at one with the environment, an appreciation of several startling coincidences, or a series of "hunches" that come true. For a fleeting moment, one feels selfless, boundless, beyond ego. In some cases it presents itself more dramatically as an out-of-body excursion, a near-death experience, or an awesome vision that inspires a new direction in life. Or it may momentarily overwhelm a person with a fully realized mystical experience, an ecstatic ASC that merges self with All. These latter events are unforgettable. Although they cannot be repeated at will, they leave in their wake a lingering sense of the unity of all things that becomes a vital source of energy sustaining the arduous journey back to the Source.

In any case, a person retains his grip on consensual reality during a spiritual emergence even as he opens to a larger sphere of nonordinary reality. This can render him stunned but intact, transformed but able to operate in the world. Although spiritual emergences are accompanied by a temporary suspension of ego-identity, they do not dissolve the ego as do regressive states. These fleeting glimpses into the higher chakras can take place at any stage of life, even in childhood, but they are best integrated when they arise in people who have reached the fourth chakra or above. When they occur prior to this level of development, they can confuse and frighten the recipient, who then judges the experience as being too far outside consensual reality for comfort. The tendency then is to quickly suppress or repress it.

In his famous allegory of the cave, Plato captured the feeling of people who have grown accustomed to living in the ego's shadow world and are then suddenly confronted with the light of truth behind the illusion. In the *Republic,* Plato wrote:

> At first, when any of them is liberated and compelled suddenly to stand up and turn his neck around and walk toward the light, he will suffer sharp pains; the glare will distress him, and he will be unable to see the realities of which, in his former state, he had seen but the shadows.

Occasionally, the first signs of spiritual emergence come to the attention of psychotherapists. In fact, empathic psychotherapy, even of an orthodox format, can remove impediments to the self's natural inclination toward higher planes of consciousness. Unfortunately, many therapists are unaware of the significance of such openings. Rather than celebrating these psychic advances as representative of humanity's higher potentials, they invalidate them as regressive and pathological. This invariably has a negative effect on a person's vulnerable psyche and engages him in combat with his higher strivings. The result is a worsening of symptoms, often expressed as vague somatic complaints for which no organic basis is found. Or he may experience unaccountable waves of panic when the incessant pressure of the Ground threatens to burst into awareness.

SPIRITUAL EMERGENCY

A healthy and mature person can tolerate a spiritual emergence without dissolution. But less-prepared people may be overwhelmed by the inrush of spiritual energy, which in extreme cases can temporarily disrupt the ego. This occurs when an individual lacks grounding in the lower chakras, when his emotions and imagination are undisciplined, or when his body and nervous system are unhealthy. Difficulties also arise when a person is exposed to advanced spiritual practice—prolonged meditation, repetitive prayer, or certain yoga techniques—before he is ready to withstand reimmersion in the Ground. In such cases there develops a crisis known as a spiritual emergency.

A spiritual emergency is an ASC of profound disorientation and ego disruption that sometimes accompanies spiritual emergence. The ASC is often of near-psychotic proportions, lasting minutes, days, or weeks, but it can end with a positive outcome if not interrupted. These upheavals bring to the surface unresolved aspects of the personality that impede spiritual growth. A spiritual emergency differs from both schizophrenia and regression in the service of transcendence in that the self neither regresses nor retreats in any other way, but actively engages the process even though it temporarily forfeits its ego-based ability to function competently in the social world.

A spiritual emergency may take a variety of forms, including ASCs colored by dramatic death and rebirth experiences, out-of-body experiences, extrasensory perception or premonitions, memories of what seem to be past incarnations, revelatory visions, and states of mystical union. Physical manifestations may include feelings of heat or electricity rising up the spine, spontaneous immobile trance states during which an individual is unable to communicate with others and feels he is receiving information from a "higher source," and feelings of pain or tension that are relieved when the individual assumes certain postures, sometimes resembling the classical positions of Hatha yoga.

Other characteristics that help to distinguish a spiritual emergency from regressive psychoses include: (1) onset precipitated by a stressful life event or involvement in spiritual practice, (2) ecstatic mood, although there may be attendant anxiety, (3) only mildly disorganized thinking; (4) hallucinations of the "higher order"; (5) intact reality testing, (6) good social functioning prior to the onset of the ASC; (7) insight that something within has changed; (8) absence of paranoia, although there may be appropriate fear; (9) positive and exploratory attitude toward the experience as relevant to one's life; (10) limited duration of the ASC; and (11) enhanced social and personal functioning when the episode is over.

The following accounts of two people who believed they had contact with an angel illustrate the difference between spiritual emergency and the schizophrenic ASC. It is important to note that it is not the *content* of the experience (seeing an angel) that makes the difference, but the way the individual integrates it into his thought and feeling. In the first case, Nathan, a twenty-eight-year-old resident of a board-and-care home, believes that he has been in contact with an angel since age sixteen.

Sheena comes to see me a lot. Sometimes she makes me laugh and sometimes she makes me cry. She flies round and round over my bed and drops pellets of particle mass on my body, and my body absorbs them, and this makes me extrasensible with telepathy. I can tell what's going on all over the universe then, in heaven and hell, and all the angels playing games and arguing with each other to see who sits closest to God, and the devils dancing on hot coals and breathing fire on the souls of screaming sinners. Sheena rides down from heaven in a flying saucer just to be with me. Even when I can't see Sheena, I hear her voice telling me what to do, like how to take a shower and when to pee, and telling me all the terrible things people are thinking about me. She says that when I die I'm going to be an angel like her if I don't let Satan eat me up. She says that I will be the prince of all angels because I am one of the chosen, but first I have to stop masturbating so much.

In the second case, Stewart, a forty-year-old social worker, encountered his apparition on two occasions:

I know this will sound crazy to you, but it sure was real to me. The first time I saw the angel I was lying in bed, and I couldn't sleep because I kept feeling there was something else in the room. I never felt anything like that before, and I usually sleep pretty well. Then I heard something like the wind blowing, and I opened my eyes. Well, there at the end of the bed was this figure just standing there looking at me. She—I felt it was a she—was all white and flimsy, sort of transparent, with a real peaceful look on her face. And, my goodness, she even had wings, just like a picture in my catechism when I was a kid. (laughs) Well, at least she wasn't holding a harp! Anyway, she said that she had something important to tell me, but I got scared and ran out of the room. I spent the rest of the night watching TV.

Boy, was I screwed up after that! I mean, I wasn't religious, didn't even believe in God, and here I was seeing an angel. I couldn't sleep for a week, worrying that she would come back. I felt so nervous that I couldn't concentrate on my work. My appetite left me, and I started getting migraines and dizzy spells. I thought I could hear a voice way off in the distance when I got these spells. I wasn't myself for a couple of months—way off center—and I even considered suicide during that time. I guess a part of me wished I had stuck it out and listened to what she had to say, though. My doctor gave me a checkup, but he couldn't find anything wrong. Of course I didn't dare tell him about the angel.

The next time I met her was three years later. I had taken up transcendental meditation, and she appeared to me during a particular meditation that felt so good that I didn't stop when the twenty minutes was up. There she was, just like before, but this time I didn't feel scared, just looked up at her and smiled. I felt full of love, and a strange wave of energy moved up through my body. She praised me for taking up meditation, told me that I would benefit from a particular psychology course I was thinking of taking, and that I should devote more time to the environmental group I was involved in. She even scolded me gently for drinking too much. Pretty worldly stuff for an angel, huh? Before she left, she told me that I could call her again if I needed her, but you know, I never have.

I now consider this one of the most important experiences of my life . It set me going in a new direction, and I'm more easygoing and tolerant of people now. More intuitive, too, and I guess I'm not an atheist anymore. The ulcer I was working on disappeared shortly after my experience, and my migraines stopped, too. Someday, somehow, I know that I'll met her again, and that is a real comfort to me. No one can ever tell me she isn't real, even though the idea of having a guardian angel still seems pretty weird to me. (With mock fear) Say, Doc, tell me you're not thinking of locking me up for all this, are you? Well, even if you did, I don't think all your medicines could take her away from me.

Both Nathan and Stewart had a visionary experience of meeting an angel. Professional training teaches most psychiatrists and psychologists to regard all such hallucinatory phenomena, accompanied by a conviction of reality, as deserving of antipsychotic medicines. In the first case, these medicines would be appropriate. Nathan spoke of his angel in a flat monotone, and he inflated his role in the story with grandiose images lifted from popular religion. He was oblivious to the effect that his fantastic account might have on others; he experienced it, and that was reason enough for everyone to accept it as genuine. The underlying structure of his story lacked internal coherence and exposed his profound conceptual disorganization, which had persisted for years. Without judging the ultimate reality of the angel, it is safe to say that Nathan's experience is typical of a person regressed to the second chakra.

In contrast, Stewart maintained clear insight as to the extraordinary nature of his experience, its conflict with consensual reality, and the unsettling effect it might have on a listener. In other words, he maintained his everyday common-sense mode of thinking. Stewart spoke with genuine feeling and a lively sense of self-reflective humor. Rather than inflating his ego with grandiose interpretations, he communicated a certain humility and wonder, and he accepted his experience as reflective of the mysteries inherent in human consciousness. His account was conceptually coherent and wholly integrated into his selfhood.

The spiritual emergency that followed Stewart's first encounter with the apparition was a result of resistances derived from his lack of preparation to encounter nonordinary reality. These were dissolved by the time of his second encounter, aided by meditation practice. His ability to surrender his resistances resulted in integration and genuine growth of his personality. This favorable outcome might have been aborted if he had encountered a powerful authority who invalidated his first experience, or insisted that he take antipsychotic medicines.

THE KUNDALINI SYNDROME

One special form of spiritual emergency has for thousands of years been known only to practitioners of a mysterious and long-secret form of yoga. It is only in the past decade that it has been gaining recognition among Western psychiatrists and psychologists. This is the *kundalini* syndrome, a cluster of peculiar somatic and psychic disturbances that are easily confused with mental or physical illness. Because the arcane teachings of kundalini yoga lie far outside Western reality models, they are best explained using the concepts of the original Hindu schools, which follow.

Distributed throughout all creation is a fundamental life force, called *prana.* Some yogis believe it to be a subtle form of physical energy related to the breath, but others say it has no physical manifestation at all. This energy is said to vitalize the body though subtle passages, called *nadis,* which the Chinese represent as acupuncture meridians. The *nadis* arise from three main vertical passages that parallel the spine and connect the seven chakras in their physical aspects, (see Figure 12–1).

At the base of these three passages, at the first chakra, lies the dormant spiritual power of kundalini, symbolically depicted in ancient texts as a sleeping serpent coiled three and a half times. Like Freud's

FIGURE 12-1 : *The seven chakras connected by the* nadis.

libido, kundalini is intimately connected with sexuality, which must be re-directed toward higher purposes. Tradition says that when the serpent is awakened, it provides the evolutionary energy of higher consciousness by traveling up the spine and sequentially activating the chakras.

According to yoga theory, the practice of certain breathing tech-niques clears the three spinal passages and galvanizes this latent force, which then rushes upward along the central axis of the body toward the crown of the head. As it rises, the kundalini pauses at each chakra, where it can be blocked, causing dramatic physical and psychic effects called *kriyas*. Upon reaching its destination at the crown chakra, it is said to give rise to a mystical state of consciousness characterized by inde-scribable bliss and unity with the divine presence. It is apparent that the Hindu conception of kundalini corresponds to the Christian image of the Holy Spirit, which when awakened appears as a tongue of flame over the crown of the head. The kundalini image also appears in the ca-duceus, the ancient symbol of medicine and healing arts, which depicts twin serpents entwined sevenfold around a vertical staff, (Figure 12–2).

FIGURE 12-2 : *A caduceus.*

Techniques for awakening kundalini in a controlled way are con-tained in the intricate texts of Tantric Hinduism, which cautions against casually unleashing this energy without the assistance of a guru—a trained practitioner who has mastered the means of channel-ing it along desirable pathways. These ancient teachings warn of grave physical and mental disorders should kundalini awaken prematurely; yet they also agree that the "serpent power" is a generous bestower of spiritual gifts, a force for psychosomatic healing, and a guide for the evolution of consciousness upward through the chakras. In their writings, such respected mystical adepts as Gopi Krishna, Swami Muktananda and Da Free John describe going through the typical kundalini syndrome prior to the awakening of their full psychic powers.

The San Francisco psychiatrist Lee Sanella has spent years accumulating case histories of people whose unexplained physical and mental symptoms correspond to ancient descriptions of kundalini awakening. Many of these people were initially diagnosed as suffering from a variety of disorders ranging from schizophrenia to delirium to multiple sclerosis. This is not surprising, for the effects of this potent psychic force resemble all of these. Yet it is an essentially benign condition that can lead to rapid personality growth and expanded consciousness if it is neither interrupted nor allowed to proceed too rapidly.

Most of Sanella's documented cases of kundalini awakening occurred in people in the early stages of spiritual practice, such as meditation or yoga study. Most had never heard of kundalini, and they feared that they were physically or mentally ill. Although the manifestations of kundalini are variable, there is enough uniformity to indicate that the experience is not illusory, but part of a predictable pattern. Because the experience may last from several days to years, the individual may pass in and out of several different ASCs, ranging from anxious confusion to superlucidity. This transformational process causes experiences too extraordinary to be considered "normal," but not so disruptive of the self that they are psychotic. Therefore, it could be seen as an example of, or perhaps an explanation of, spiritual emergency. It is an unfolding of an aspect of human potential that may be problematical, but is eventually desirable.

Typically, the first signs of kundalini awakening begin in the big toes or feet, as pain, tingling, or burning sensations. These migrate to the lower back and pelvis, where they may cause intense pain or unexplained sexual arousal. From here, powerful sensations of heat and energy stream up the spine, accompanied by spasms, tremors, writhing movements, unusual breathing patterns, or violent shaking. In some accounts, the progression then continues down the front of the body into the abdomen. A person experiencing this exquisite agony feels compelled to laugh or cry, or emit guttural vocal sounds that relieve the incessant pressure. Or he may assume the classic *asanas* of Hatha yoga, even if he was not previously aware of those positions, finding them to relieve his discomfort.

As kundalini reaches the head, there is typically an overpowering experience of an exploding fountain of light that engulfs the visual capacity. Intermixed with this display may be colorful geometric patterns and complex visions of archetypal figures, deities, or demons. A variety of sounds—buzzing, humming, drumming, popping, or even voices chanting—accompany the visual phenomena. In a true kundalini awakening, these sounds never include persecutory voices of the lower order, although some people experience higher-order voices that give helpful directives about what the person must do to clear out blockages. These voices are recognized as emanating from within the self and are not perceived as external entities.

Despite its benign nature, a kundalini experience can be quite unpleasant. As a young man, the Indian mystic Gopi Krishna, while engaging in lengthy, unsupervised meditations to the exclusion of other balancing factors in his life; experienced a series of uncomfortable symptoms that culminated in a stream of liquid light penetrating his awareness with a roar like a waterfall. He described the experience graphically.

> The moment my head touched the pillow a large tongue of flame sped across the spine into the interior of my head. It appeared as if the stream of living light continuously rushing through the spinal cord into the cranium gathered speed and volume during the hours of darkness. Whenever I closed my eyes I found myself looking into a weird circle of light, in which luminous currents swirled and eddied, moving rapidly from side to side. The spectacle was fascinating but awful, invested with a supernatural awe which sometimes chilled the very marrow in my bones.

This was followed by months of waning vigor, depression, insomnia, loss of appetite, and waves of unaccountable terror. When in a dark room Gopi Krishna would notice a red glow concentrated in his spinal region and followed by back pains so severe that he would become nauseated. He was sure that he had committed an unpardonable sin and was about to die. Fortunately, he then contacted an eminent yoga master, who recognized and validated what he was going through. Following the advice of this master, he shortened his meditations and altered his diet in a specific manner to allow the energy to flow in a more symmetrical way. From that point on, his distressing symptoms gradually cleared, and he began having blissful experiences that ultimately led to openings into the higher chakras and his eventual return to society as a spiritual teacher.

Although the several authors who have written about the kundalini syndrome disagree about details, they are unanimous in interpreting the symptoms as arising from the upward-moving kundalini energy, which meets physical or mental blockages at the various chakras. Differences in symptom patterns indicate which chakras are blocked. Once these blockages are overcome, progress through the chakras occurs far more rapidly than during normal development.

A CASE HISTORY OF AWAKENED KUNDALINI

Although Sanella has documented dozens of cases of kundalini experience, the phenomenon appears to be rare, at least in the Western world. In my twenty years of practice, I have encountered only one case that was unequivocally a kundalini manifestation. This occurred at a time when I was unaware of the concepts of spiritual emergency or kundalini awakenings, and it was a significant learning experience for me:

> Patricia, a twenty-seven-year-old artist and musician, was referred to me by her family physician for "vague, poorly localized somatic complaints suggestive of hysteria or incipient psychosis." Patricia said that her symptoms began shortly after she began practicing a meditation technique that required her to curl her tongue backward and hold it tightly against the roof of the mouth. As she adopted this unusual posture, known to experienced yogis as a potent way to alter consciousness, she also increased her meditation time from one to two hours a day.
>
> Patricia's symptoms began with a dull ache in the area of her anus. As the sensation gradually moved up her back, it turned into a fiery pain, "as if someone were running a blowtorch up my spine." (Indeed, it was easy to feel warmth radiating from this area as far as six inches above the skin.) She also described a peculiar feeling of being "tickled from inside," and she felt compelled to twist her neck and torso at odd angles to relive the inner itch. On occasion her tongue would spontaneously draw back in her mouth as in her meditation posture, and her hands would contort into odd positions, something like the mudras portrayed in statues of Hindu and Buddhist deities. At this point Patricia's physician tested her for colitis, epilepsy, pelvic inflammatory disease, and a pinched spinal nerve, with negative findings.
>
> Patricia reported that along with her physical symptoms she began having vivid dreams of jungle scenes with large boa constrictors winding themselves around her and slowly crushing her. Sometimes these images would appear while she was awake and frighten her. She also heard loud

hissing sounds, like those made by snakes. She reported other disturbing experiences that she called "imaginations," but she refused to describe these further. Despite her fear, she also expressed a strong feeling that something important was happening within her, something she preferred to keep private. Never having encountered such a bewildering and disconnected array of symptoms before, I naively feared that she might be developing a schizophrenic condition. After discussing the pros and cons with her, I decided to offer her a trial on the neuroleptic medicine Haldol.

This medicine did not alleviate Patricia's symptoms, but made her feel much worse—depressed, confused, unable to concentrate, more restless than ever. Just as I was about to inform her that I was unable to determine the cause of her symptoms and was therefore obliged to refer her to a university medical center for further tests, I attended a humanistic-psychology conference where Dr. Sanella described the symptoms of the kundalini experience. This led me to read the early self-published version of his book and to read Gopi Krishna's personal account of his similar experience. These prompted me to suggest that Patricia temporarily reduce her meditations to an hour a day, cease using the folded-tongue posture, and temporarily add some fish to her strict vegetarian diet. I also suggested that she take up running or swimming to balance her meditations. She conformed reluctantly, but enjoyed an immediate relief of the more unpleasant of her symptoms. We both agreed that she had little need for further psychiatric treatment.

I last heard from Patricia a year later. She happily reported that her music and painting had improved greatly during the interval, a fact that she attributed to a flood of new insights and intuitions that derived from her "illness." She also believed that she could handle stress more easily and felt that her posture had improved and that her body was less rigid. She told me that she tried to return to her extreme meditation practice, but stopped it when the same symptoms became apparent. She continued to meditate in a more moderate manner, and felt that she was making continued spiritual progress at a gradual, but acceptable, rate.

As in Patricia's case, the result of an uninterrupted kundalini awakening can be liberation from barriers to personal growth, as well as newfound sensitivity to the Ground. However, in some cases there may be an inflation of the ego, which comes to regard its enhanced powers as evidence of its superiority. The outcome following a kundalini awakening is largely determined by the degree to which a person can surrender to the feeling dimension of fourth-chakra consciousness.

THE DARK NIGHT OF THE SOUL

Following spiritual emergence, or a successfully resolved spiritual emergency, the self is bathed in the joy and illumination that characterizes the consciousness of the heart chakra. Ordinary tasks take on a new and hallowed meaning, enlivened by a growing awareness of their place in a larger scheme. There is an evanescent sense of a higher purpose, still not clearly envisioned, but compellingly near the heart.

Although still operative, the ego is no longer the sole repository of personal identity. There wells up a realization that all humanity, all sentient beings, share the singular consciousness of the Ground. The self now dwells within a larger sphere that encompasses a sense of identity with all of life. An outpouring of love flows through the newly awakened individual toward his fellow beings and the whole of creation. This abundance cannot be contained; it must be shared. There is a call to service as the self prepares to ascend to the fifth chakra.

But such an enchanted state of elation is not easy to sustain, for the individual now confronts a harsh world that somehow fails to partake of his personal transformation and is not always receptive to his altruistic strivings. The cold realities of greed, quotas, deadlines, limited resources, recalcitrant authorities, and narrow-mindedness are notoriously slow to yield to the idealism of the heart. Gradually the flood tide of exaltation ebbs as the individual becomes depleted of the energy he was so willing to radiate freely in all directions. He feels a push to reaffirm the primacy of his ego and revert to a lower level of being. His ego once again sets about its accustomed task of repressing the Ground as it reinterprets the recent spiritual awakening as sentimental fantasy or emotional intoxication.

Ideally, this fourth-chakra version of regression in the service of transcendence might serve as a splash of cold water in the face of one who is in danger of forfeiting pragmatism for a weak and quixotic utopianism. But there is another purpose. Any such tidal withdrawal of spiritual energies exposes the unresolved muck that was once concealed by the high water of spiritual emergence. In the midst of depression and despair lies a fresh opportunity to scour the stains of unresolved issues in preparation for the next cleansing tide.

Just as during regressions that attend transitions from the lower chakras, a person who has a vision of higher consciousness cannot peacefully return to his old state. The memory of the beauty and power of the Ground haunts him, despite the ego's halting efforts to suppress it. The ego is simultaneously drawn to, and apprehensive of, the great power it recognizes as its superior. The "reborn" individual, infused with a moral perspective that is more refined and exacting, acquires a thirst for truth that will not be slaked by banality. Feeling that he has fallen lower than ever, he looks upon his position with disdain and condemns his regression with vehemence. The customary world appears inhospitably desolate, barren of meaning, devoid of purpose.

That which Roberto Assagioli called "divine homesickness" haunts the individual and leaves him no peace. He feels a bleak melancholia that imparts a pervasive sense of unworthiness, self-depreciation, and a visceral fear that he has forsaken all that is sacred. His just punishment is permanent damnation. He feels paralyzed from within, as if his intellect has become dull and incompetent, his will passively impotent. Such angst can approach psychotic proportions if it imparts a sense of delusional guilt, of being personally responsible for everything wrong in the world. Not everyone survives this ordeal; suicide is an ever-present danger.

This retreat from the vitalizing energies of the Ground parallels the Christian idea of purgatory, a halfway station between heaven and hell, a place for inner cleansing, for expelling impurities so as to be worthy of completing the ascent to higher realms. When Saint John of the Cross traversed this subterranean route to spiritual realization, he called it his "dark night of the soul."

> As eyes weakened and clouded suffer pain when the clear light beats upon them, so the soul, by reason of its impurity, suffers exceedingly when the Divine Light shines upon it. And when the rays of this pure Light shine upon the soul in order to expel impurities, the soul perceives itself to be so unclean and miserable that it seems as if God had set Himself against it and itself were set against God.

Despite his torment, the Renaissance saint recognized a "light" that persisted through the dark night. This was a steady ray of hope for eventual spiritual regeneration. The light of recollection—sometimes but a distant memory—kept the vision of what he had accomplished alive, just as it shone on his "impurities" and fixed them in his awareness as he suffered through the purgative process. The message it bore was clear: "You who have gazed upon me must change your life." A return to an earlier state, so ardently sought by the ego, would have been his downfall.

The role of an artful healer in helping an anguished person living through such a "dark night" is to empathically affirm that his present state of mind is part of a natural process of renewal, and that others have descended before him only to resume their spiritual progress when they were better prepared. The healer must help him confront the shadowy aspects of his ego-based personality so that he can lovingly forgive himself as he makes himself over with greater integrity. He must also release what remains of original repression, and learn that he need no longer fear his inner being. It helps for an individual who has lost his way in the dark night to forgo his worldly responsibilities for a while and enter a retreat, where he can practice introspection and reevaluate his priorities without distraction. Once he completes this purifying process, he will have a reliable channel to his transpersonal Source, which serves as a navigational beacon to guide him through the arduous journeys to come.

REGENERATION IN SPIRIT

Years after resolving a spiritual emergency that resulted in psychiatric hospitalization, one person expressed her new state of being.

> Now, more than eight years later, I can look back and say, "I had this incredible mystical experience." It integrated and made sense of everything that had ever happened to me or that I had ever done. It showed me the meaning and purpose of life. It was a birth into a state of consciousness I did not even know existed, but which is now a permanent part of my life.

Another, now a professional writer and editor, put it this way:

> There is no doubt that I am better off now, in every way, than before. My relations with my family are infinitely more attuned, my writing much deeper, my friends much truer, my sense of self more steady, my clarity sharpened, and so on and on. In short, nothing bad, ultimately, came out of my "break with reality."

For these people as for many others, there was salvation at the end of purgatorial madness. Michael Washburn termed such emergences back into the light *regeneration in spirit*. These are moments of softer joy than the rapture that fills the self during the first stages of spiritual emergence, and they occupy a greater span of life, often unfolding over years. If uninterrupted, they lead to integration of what had previously been conflicting facets of the self: mind and body, spontaneity and discipline, work and play, sexuality and commitment, logic and creativity, giving and taking, will and devotion, ego and Ground.

From this point on, life is no longer an exhausting struggle between a tightly clad ego fixated exclusively on the senses and a grander world beyond the senses. As the consciousness of the heart chakra is integrated, the ego recognizes the Ground as a gentle and loving source of stimulation and inspiration. Whatever defenses it once erected to shield itself from its spiritual underpinnings it now allows to dissolve, and a new depth of feeling stirs within it. As the ego begins to dilate, it is infused with spiritual energies that bring it into accord with the higher self. Shedding its protective covering, it becomes a willing servant of spirit.

At this point, an individual expands his definition of "I" to include a more comprehensive center of consciousness. This act does not toll the death of the ego or initiate a lapse into madness as he feared, but actually strengthens his ability to function effectively in the world. He now values the ego as a tool for carrying out the dictates of a higher calling in the material world. In turn, the ego is free from bearing the artificial burden of self-identity and can focus on what it does best: mediating between the sensory world and the higher self.

This opening to the realm of deep feeling would have conferred a naked vulnerability—a "bleeding heart"—on a person who was centered at an earlier stage of consciousness. But the newly empowered individual now has a broader view of the world and can channel his emotions into constructive action. Far from being a weakness, this sensitivity allows him to be deeply moved without becoming overwhelmed. He learns to trust his emotions to provide useful intuitions rather than irrational distractions.

Relationships change accordingly. No longer is exploitation or domination his goal. Empathic merger with a kindred soul is what satisfies his heart. Compassion affords him greater tolerance of the shortcomings of others and teaches that what is most lovable about them is their vulnerability. And though he finds greater enjoyment in personal relationships, a spiritually regenerating person has greater tolerance for being alone. He savors quiet moments of communion with the creative energies that he increasingly locates within himself. He feels an unshakable desire to heal the wounds of the world, and for authentic self-expression. It no longer matters that there are daunting obstacles on the path, that human suffering is intractable; a steadfast commitment is an end in itself. Whereas his personal ambitions once felt like a "push" from the past to avoid poverty or powerlessness, his loftier goals now feel like a "pull" from the future, a calling toward a higher destiny.

Thinking also undergoes a radical shift from the linear to the lateral. The linear "first A, then B, then C" rationality of the third chakra yields to a loosely connected, sometimes zigzag flow of ideas, like the way a knight moves on a chessboard. Formal-operations thinking, considered by some to be the highest human capability, thrives on distinctions and polarities. But at the fourth chakra, this mode is transcended by reasoning that reaches beyond polarities toward reconciliation and synthesis. This higher logic condenses opposites into mutually sustaining unities. For instance, instead of seeing mountains versus valleys, unitive thinking conceives of a "mountainvalley" as a whole system, neither of its parts existing independently of the other. Other polarities—liberal/conservative, objective/subjective, and so on—gradually yield to this unifying logic of reconciliation.

When thinking and feeling conflict, thinking no longer automatically rules; but rather, feelings empower thought with an added depth. This reflects a finer resonance between old and new brain levels. This cognitive style is quite different from the emotionally based paleologic of second-chakra regressions, when feelings obscure and derail rational thought. Now the capacity for linear logic remains influential in reaching balanced conclusions. Thinking allows itself to be guided by feeling, while at the same time feeling becomes more "reasonable."

This wedding of head and heart leads to a higher ethical sense, a generosity of spirit that elevates the Freudian "pleasure principle" to the next level. A spiritually regenerating person no longer derives pleasure from "getting what's mine," but from distributing freely what he gathers from the endless abundance of the Ground. He transmits this manna through an empathic glance or a compassionate gesture of understanding that enlivens all who are its recipients. The Freudian superego is also ethically transformed. Originally derived from internalized parental and social values, the punitive superego is remolded into a self-willed conscience based on heartfelt assessments of what is authentically right and true. It is newly capable of compassionate forgiveness. The individual rarely experiences guilt, for he naturally desires and seeks only what is best for all concerned.

One consequence of original repression was that the ego-based self occupied a physical space vaguely behind the eyes. But now, as the regenerating individual reowns the Ground, he regains free access to his whole body. Ken Wilber calls this reintegration of mind and body the stage of the centaur, after the great mythological being with animal body and human mind existing in a state of wholeness. As the life force of the Ground courses through the individual without obstruction, his body takes on a sensuousness it has not known since childhood, before erotic feelings were exiled to the genitals. His entire body becomes a source of erotic wonder, which he may discover through noncompetitive athletics or dance. His personality turns less airy and cerebral, taking on a robust, visceral, and earthy cast. Rather than a quick source of relief from instinctive pressure, the sexual act becomes a lighthearted celebration of spirit, a playful way of expressing devotion, an unbounded merger of hearts.

This reclamation of the body as a vehicle for spirit may place the spiritually regenerating person at odds with Western religions that insist that instinct and civilized life are irreconcilably opposed, that social order can be maintained only when nature is contained, or that spirit is affirmed only when flesh is denied. This conflict is often resolved paradoxically; as the liberated person becomes more "spiritual," he simultaneously becomes less "religious." This is part of a larger shift in his personality. A spiritually evolving individual becomes relatively indifferent to superficial social appearances and the cursory judgments of others so long as his actions reflect what he authentically feels.

Regeneration in spirit resolves yet another polarity that splits off the subconscious mind from conscious awareness. Not only does the inner eye turn back toward its collective roots in the Ground, but much of what had been repressed from personal life as a result of parental and social training now reemerges. In Jungian terms, *persona* and *shadow* begin to fuse as the regenerating person feels his own pulse in what he abhors the most, feels the secret vulnerability that underlies his greatest pride. Life no longer unfolds as a series of disconnected events or irresistible impulses that seem to arise automatically. Instead, life feels like a meaningful journey leading from an intimately recalled past toward a definite—though still mysterious—destiny.

Once a person begins to surrender to the Ground and recognizes it as friendly rather than fearsome, miraculous rather than menacing, he is no longer obliged to pit the rigid defenses of his ego against this far more resilient power. Instead, he devises strategies for involving the Ground in his life in an immediate way. Some people are drawn to psychedelic drugs as a rapid means of exposing the naked energies of the Ground. But these powerful and sometimes capricious agents are certainly not for everyone. There is a far safer means of gradually opening self to Ground—the path of contemplation.

Once a person finds a comfortable home in his heart, regular meditation is essential for balanced progress. The consciousness of the fourth chakra primes him to benefit from this sublime art. Prior to this stage, meditation has little appeal and can be harmful for weakly bounded individuals. If a person centered in the third chakra is some-how motivated to take up meditation, he will usually find no use for it and cease to practice after a few weeks, saying that he finds it boring or that he doesn't have time.

Because meditation is a tool for observing the ego's strategies from an external vantage point, and therefore reducing its illusory power, it is contraindicated for people who have not progressed past the second chakra, or for people in psychotic ASCs who regress to that level. Their task is to fortify the ego so as to engage the tasks of the worldly third chakra. Any strategy that weakens the ego, no matter how beneficial it may be for people at higher levels, is bound to be harmful for those who have not yet mastered the tasks of the social world. Well-intentioned spiritual healers who recommend meditation for people in schizo-phrenic ASCs are simply not aware of essential pre/trans distinctions.

But for people who have successfully navigated the vicissitudes of the competitive world and who yearn to reunite with their higher selves, one of the several effective forms of meditation, yoga, or silent prayer is essential. These are proven means of freeing the psyche from its attach-ment to the senses so as to turn the inner eye toward the Ground.

As the self gains strength through its receptivity to the loving ener-gies of the Ground, it nears the point of its next transition. This further expansion of consciousness will mark its birth into the highest realm of human capability on the *worldly* plane. With the opening of the heart, the self has reached the pinnacle of its journey through the world, and it now begins in earnest the long trek back to the Garden.

CHAPTER 13
Fifth Chakra: Madness & Creative Genius

◆

*What if you slept? And what if, in your sleep, you dreamed? And what if in
your dream you went to heaven and there plucked a strange and beautiful
flower? And what if, when you awoke, you had the flower in your hand?
Ah! What then?*

SAMUEL COLERIDGE

*If there is a God we must see him, and if there is a soul we must perceive it.
Otherwise it is better not to believe.*

SWAMI VIVEKANANDA

LUDWIG VAN BEETHOVEN is famous for his heroic symphonies
that elevate the human spirit above its worldly attachments. He wrote
his most magnificent works after he became completely deaf, when he cultivated an inner ear that heard more than his worldly senses. Yet he had
another musical skill that no one alive today will ever fully appreciate.

Beethoven could *improvise*. The master took great delight in entertain-
ing his courtly friends for hours by sitting at a piano, casting aside his
written pieces, and playing what must have been a nineteenth century
version of progressive jazz. His favorite trick was to describe musically the
character of some well-known person. With eyes closed, he improvised
melodies that communicated personality traits so accurately that his audience could quickly guess the particular person portrayed.

The Indian classical musician Ravi Shankar plays an instrument so difficult to master that he spent two years learning how to hold it. When he cradles his sitar across folded legs to play a raga, something amazing happens. Shankar closes his eyes! Not a note of written music guides him through the ancient themes, nor has he memorized what he plays. Although he maintains an unwavering adherence to classic form, the intricate textures that flow from his instrument are improvised from beginning to end. Listening to Shankar coax such exquisite beauty out of taut strings and polished wood, one gets a feeling that his music is not originating from a mere human, but that the entranced artist is a conduit through whom celestial harmonies flow. Like most great improvisers, he would probably agree that his music originates from a source more exalted than his worldly ego. What is inside and personal, and what is outside and universal, become one in such an act of creation.

Both Beethoven and Shankar represent a minority of exceptional men and women who embrace the consciousness of the Vishuddha chakra. This is the chakra of archetypal vision and higher knowledge through willing surrender to the Ground. Traditional descriptions of the fifth chakra locate it in the throat, where it governs self-expression and creative inspiration. In this chapter we explore the way this chakra nourishes the creative impulse, as well as its confusing relationship to madness.

FIFTH-CHAKRA CONSCIOUSNESS

A fine balance of reason and intuition, self-control and surrender, discipline and freedom, individuality and unity characterizes fifth-chakra consciousness. It is the font from which flow universal symbols that vitalize art, music, and poetry. Here is the spring that feeds those vast rivers of insight that inspired the scientific breakthroughs of Copernicus and Newton, that awakened revolutionary philosophers like Plato and Kant, that empowered those rare political leaders who broke through the stagnation of their times to steer humanity toward ever greater freedom.

Although certain individuals centered at lower chakras can tap into the consciousness of the Vishuddha chakra, its full creative impact is realized only by those uncommon individuals who progress sequentially through the first four chakras, mastering the lessons of each. Once a person consummates the regeneration in spirit that is the final task of the heart chakra, he or she feels an irresistible thrust toward reaching life's full potential. The overriding goal is to become a person of wisdom, based not on faith, but on *experience*. To accomplish this, he naturally seeks to accelerate the process of transcending the ego that began in the fourth chakra. This requires that his life be lived intuitively, with greater openness to the Spiritual Ground.

To gain that opening, an individual identifies with a more comprehensive center than the ego, a *higher self* that reincorporates that which original repression long ago banished. As the enforcer of the Ground's exile, the ego is the enemy of intuition. To regain access to the archaic recesses of his subconscious mind, one learns to manipulate the ego at will, to put it to work when the situation calls for contact with the social world, and to suspend it when it is appropriate to look beyond.

The fifth chakra provides a person with power to control the ego through a kind of objective self-observation called *witnessing*. To make this clear, we must momentarily retrace the growth of consciousness prior to this stage. During passage through the third chakra, an individual identifies with purely rational faculties. From this position he observes and overrides childhood fantasies. But he cannot yet observe his own reasoning ego, with which he identifies. Once he reaches the fourth chakra, however, he transcends reason to identify with higher feelings—universal love, compassion, interconnectedness with all life—and can then objectively observe untempered rationality.

As he advances to the fifth chakra, he gains the power to witness thoughts *and* feelings objectively, to grasp how they fit into the unfolding pattern of his life and the larger patterns of history. This is not to say that he no longer has rational thoughts or compassionate feelings. If anything, these faculties deepen as he integrates them into a more inclusive sphere of control. Ken Wilber compared this giant step to an earlier stage of transcendence.

> At the moment the child realizes that he has a body, he no longer is *just* the body: he is aware of it; he transcends it; he is looking at it with his mind and therefore he cannot be *just* a body any longer. Likewise, at the point the adult realizes he has a mind, he is no longer just a mind—he is actually starting to perceive it from the subtle regions beyond mind. Prior to those points, the self was more or less identified with those structures and therefore *could not realize it*. The self could not see those structures because the self *was* those structures.

Once an individual looks upon his ego and its worldly cravings from the standpoint of a detached witness, he becomes a student of his own nature. He reowns subconscious shadow elements that were repressed earlier in life, and he grows aware of the exquisitely subtle movement of the Ground within him. But rather than recoiling in fear, as he would have earlier in life, he cherishes an enriched inner life as an endless source of fascination. With this key to a half-forgotten world of imagination, an individual unlocks the secret passage to the realm of the archetypes, the *prima materia* from which creativity is alchemically brewed.

At first glance this step forward appears to be regression pure and simple. Skirting the boundaries of madness, the creative person has a flair for suspending abstract thought so as to immerse himself in the concrete "nowness" of raw experience. This is his way of grasping reality by "soul-knowing"—neither by reason nor by demonstration, but by immediate contact, as he would know the taste of a ripe plum in his mouth. Yet unlike a regressed psychotic, the artist's witness stance conserves his ability to think abstractly, which he suspends only until his inspiration is complete.

As a witness, the artist watches himself seeing, thinking, and feeling, watches the world in a way that is at once personal and universal. This enables him to blend his own unique vision with the ordinary—to produce the extraordinary. The existential psychiatrist Eric Fromm called this "full awareness," which momentarily unites observer and observed.

> If we are fully aware of a tree at which we look . . . then we have a kind of experience which is the premise for painting the tree. In conceptual knowledge the tree we see has no individuality; it stands only as an example of the genus "tree"; it is only the representative of an abstraction. In full awareness there is no abstraction; the tree retains its full concreteness, and that means also its uniqueness. There is only this one tree in the world, and to this tree I relate myself. I see it. I respond to it. The tree becomes my own creation.

Trees were among Vincent van Gogh's favorite subjects. In his paintings we see them vibrantly aflame with life, their uniqueness locked in by the single-minded intensity of the artist's manic absorption. Van Gogh did not simply *see* generic trees lost in lifeless landscapes, nor were trees merely a concept for him. The passionate artist fused wrinkled wood and fluttering leaf with his own receptive heart, risking descent into madness time and time again, but returning with a vision of the highest abstraction that communicates the timeless essence of "treeness."

FIFTH-CHAKRA THINKING & LOGIC

Having gained the fifth chakra, a person slowly grows accustomed to free communion with the Ground, which he actively solicits as a source of inspiration. No longer threatened by his own creative wellsprings, he finds that the more he embraces this inexhaustible source of novelty and wonder, the stronger he grows. He learns to conduct worldly chores at an elevated energy level that constantly seeks an outlet.

Such heightened awareness promotes another advance in thinking. In the previous expansion, the fourth chakra added new depth of meaning to the formal-operations logic of the third chakra. That advance to the logic of the heart was one of synthesis rather than separation, of discovering ways that things are alike rather than different.

Fifth-chakra thinking adds a dimension of reason that transcends, yet includes, the holism of the fourth chakra. What now emerges is *synergy*—a word for situations in which the whole exceeds the sum of its parts. Once synergistic thinking is in gear, relationships among events or ideas are no longer proportional, nor are they additive; rather, they are seen as part of an emerging global order. Meaning no longer emerges from definition, but from interaction. Events are caused as much by a pull from the future as a push from the past. And the very act of playing the game has an unsettling way of changing the rules.

Like a rocket boost into high orbit, fifth-chakra thinking enables a person to mentally soar above any system of which he is a part. Once there, he contemplates the whole from a vantage point inaccessible to any component of the system. This allows him to devise ways to manipulate that system once he is back inside of it. From this panoramic view of reality, there is truth-seeing at a single glance. He places each idea alongside numerous others, envisioning how its truth or falsity influences the truth or falsity of the others. This whole-systems view broadens even the wide-angle perspective of the fourth chakra. It enables him to encompass a network of ideas and coordinate their internal relationships to achieve a specific purpose. He no longer interprets events in terms of his personal feelings about them, but in terms of where they fit into the grand scheme.

For instance, a person centered at the heart chakra might feel compassion for undernourished people in famine-ridden areas. Grasping how all humans share a common destiny, he dedicates himself to gathering food to feed the starving masses. In contrast, a person at the fifth chakra intuitively realizes that all stable systems tend toward repetitive patterns. Instead of swimming upstream against the natural flow of events, he fathoms where vicious circles are operative, and where these might yield to outside intervention. In turn, this insight reveals something about long-term causes of famine—perhaps uncontrolled reproduction or inexorable climatic changes. He then devotes his efforts not toward short-term palliation, but toward interventions that redirect long-term trends. Having mastered the lesson of the heart, he does this lovingly, with full compassion for those who are suffering, so that the totality of human misery is permanently reduced.

NONATTACHMENT

A particular form of intellectual and spiritual freedom that Zen adepts call *nonattachment to specific outcomes* flows from fifth-chakra consciousness. This is an act of submission to the wisdom and power of the Ground—which has been called the Tao—and an alignment of oneself with its incessant flow. From this perspective, when something seems wrong, we are challenged to discover how it fits into the larger picture, how it may be right on another level of meaning. Emerson affirmed this mode of consciousness when he wrote: "All things are friendly and sacred, all events profitable, all days holy, all men divine; for the eye is fastened on the *life* and slights the circumstance."

Our greatest artists and scientists all possess, at least for a while, this receptivity to a guiding hand, the nature of which they do not generally comprehend. Their hard-earned realization is that the Ground cannot be commanded, but if invited will reveal its immense bounty to those who are prepared to receive it.

This attitude of surrender, of "flowing with it," is far from careless indifference. Nonattachment is an act of higher love, of responsibility free from pride or guilt. When a person transcends the expectations of others, he is free to confront his own reality and respond to it for what it is. He then placidly withstands callous criticism, for he knows the worth of his creation and its place in history. His commitment to his art or science is an end in itself, executed in the fullness of the moment. But if he is addicted to specific outcomes, his focus is limited to what "should be" rather than to the infinite possibilities inherent in any creative act.

Exemplary fifth-chakra figures include Socrates, Albert Einstein, Abraham Lincoln, Confucius, Charles Darwin, Leonardo da Vinci, Thomas Edison, William Shakespeare, Benjamin Franklin, and—at first glance—Mikhail Gorbachev. These are people of extraordinary creative vision who broke through the customary way of looking at things, and who possessed the sinew to convert that vision into a new reality that altered history.

Of course, not all people who gain the fifth chakra are known for their outstanding accomplishments. Other factors, such as talent, intelligence, opportunity, and physical health determine how much a person achieves, no matter how acute his inner vision. Nevertheless, individuals who reach this level of development strive to fulfill and express their highest potentials. The humanistic psychologist Abraham Maslow called this the stage of self-actualization, in recognition of the drive to advance the evolution of the human spirit in both its individual and collective aspects.

However, a simple look around us reveals that people who have fully actualized the fifth chakra are rare at our current level of evolution. The time-honored association between madness and genius suggests that many of our most creative artists were far from integrating fifth-chakra awareness. Yet this did not prevent them from being privy to stunning inspirations. Although these breakthroughs are common, they as easily torment their unwary recipients as enlighten them.

THE "MAD" ARTIST

At this point, the reader may wonder what the exalted consciousness of the fifth chakra has to do with the subject of this book, psychotic ASCs. The answer: by itself, very little. Yet the idea that genius and madness are intimate bedfellows is one of history's most venerable notions, too prevalent to discard in favor of theory alone. The English poet John Dryden reflected this popular viewpoint when he wrote:

> Great wits are sure to madness near allied,
> And thin partitions do their bounds divide.

We may wonder if Shakespeare was speaking from experience when he wrote in *A Midsummer Night's Dream:*

> The lunatick, the lover and the poet
> Are of imagination all compact.

Two thousand years earlier, Aristotle held that "all who have been famous for their genius . . . have been inclined to insanity," a viewpoint that he may have acquired from his teacher Plato, who wrote in the *Phaedrus:*

> But he who, not being inspired and having no touch of madness in his soul, comes to the door and thinks that he will get into the temple by the help of art—he, I say, and his poetry are not admitted; the sane man is nowhere at all when he enters into rivalry with the madman.

Plato's notion that lunacy and creativity are linked seems validated every time we encounter another eccentric artist or inventor. Like madness, originality is spawned in collaboration with disorder. The artist flirts with the nonrational, communes with things mysterious. This is why the psychological literature linking creativity to insanity is staggering in its volume. But although we expect people centered at the fifth chakra to appear out of step with the majority of people in third-chakra societies, this alone is not sufficient to account for the scores of great artists and inventors whose lives were tormented by the most vile personal demons.

So far I have treated the creative impulse as arising after an orderly ascension through the chakras in their natural sequence. Yet it is well known that many prodigies and geniuses are inspired by a creative vision in childhood, and some gifted children manifest capabilities from chakras even higher than the fifth. This suggests that the progression through levels of consciousness can be erratic. Just as there may be uneven regression in psychoses, there may be uneven progression in normal development. Breakthroughs of higher energies into the awareness of people centered in the lower planes of consciousness cause most of the confusion between higher and lower states of consciousness.

People with weakly bounded selves—borderlines, schizophrenics, and some manics—are undefended from intrusions of Ground energies into awareness. Like the human mind that it supports, the Spiritual Ground itself is complex and multilayered—roughly analogous to the frequency bandwidths of the electromagnetic spectrum, which lie on a continuum, with low-frequency radio waves on one end, visible light in the center, and high-frequency X rays on the other end. When self-boundaries weaken, the individual is vulnerable to surges of exotic energies from one or another of the Ground's "bandwidths."

These untimely openings may be confined to a specific part of the spectrum—for instance, a schizophrenic who hears only lower-order voices—or include a wider array of energies, such as telepathy or precognition. During manic ASCs, visions of archetypal figures embedded in the "bandwidth" of the fifth chakra may enter. What a given individual *does* with these universal symbols rattling around inside his head is another matter, determined by his intellect, ego strength, self-concept, and so on. Occasionally, these incursions merge with extraordinary talent, a combination that can produce great art, but also great personal turmoil.

People centered at the fifth chakra often experience archetypal visions. These bear scant resemblance to the grotesque and threatening hallucinations of schizophrenia, which are second-chakra based. Instead, they instill a sense of wonder and awe that kindles an irrepressible urge to cast them in a material form that matches the person's particular talent. As long as self and Ground are still disunited, these images are felt to originate from somewhere *exterior*, and often surprise the recipient. One of my creative patients, for instance, saw a picture he was about to paint so vividly in front of him that he would request anyone standing between him and the hallucinatory scene to stand aside.

The reflexive habit among orthodox psychiatrists of pathologizing visionary experiences probably came about because professionals usually see only disorganized mental patients, not a Blake, Mozart, or Picasso. A healthy ego can withstand and integrate unannounced visitations of Ground energies, and then become a willing transcriber for its muse. The poet Amy Lowell described the fine line between hallucination and inspiration:

> Some poets speak of hearing a voice speaking to them, and say that they write almost to dictation . . . I do not hear a voice, but I do hear words pronounced, only the pronouncing is toneless. The words seem to be pronounced in my head, but with nobody speaking them.

Virginia Woolf also heard voices, which, in her inimitable words, "stir the long hairs that grow in the conch of the ear and make strange music, mad music, jangled and broken sounds." Yet she also was able to cultivate these disquieting intrusions into a garden of original ideas that blossomed into her most sensitive poems.

The romantic composer Robert Schumann could not sleep for a week during a manic ASC because he kept hearing high A reverberating in his ear, a note that suddenly changed into mysterious music, which he described in his diary as "more wonderful and played by more exquisite instruments than ever sounded on earth." He leapt from his bed to write down the melody immortalized as the slow movement of his Violin Concerto in D minor. When he tried to recapture the inspiration during a different mood the next morning, the single note exploded into a chorus of demons howling at him, joined by visual apparitions of menacing hyenas and tigers.

Of all poets whose inspirations flowed from otherworldly perception, William Blake stands foremost. Blake insisted that "mental things alone are real . . . this world is all one continued vision of fancy or imagination." The ethereal floating bodies that populate his meticulously crafted woodcuts were a prominent dimension of his everyday experience. He claimed that his poetry arrived with no premeditation, but was "dictated." Blake spoke of having conversations with the long-dead poet Milton and drew spectral heads to show his friends the supernatural visitors he received daily. Blake continued to write on his deathbed, feverishly recording his last bits of poetry. When his wife pleaded with him to put aside paper and pencil lest he exhaust himself, he exclaimed of the verse that poured forth, "It is not mine; it is not mine!"

FROM WITHIN OR WITHOUT?

Once a person reaches the fifth chakra, he is in the curious position of being alternately tormented and titillated by his creative illuminations, which he projects as external to him. But as the submerged contents of his personal subconscious become fully aired, and he becomes convinced of the Ground's benign nature, these apparitions transform into genuine visions from deep within, laden with myriad meanings and possibilities.

Such visionary raptures led the poet Rilke to fear that if his devils were to leave him, his angels would also take flight. But as the creative muse sheds its guise as an external entity, these visions transform from demonic to angelic. The realization grows that angels and demons are metaphors for Ground energies that either guide or afflict the self. By the later stages of fifth-chakra consciousness, these are reincorporated into an expanded self, which acknowledges its lifetime communion with the Ground and has little need to repress its instincts or shadow nature.

This blurring of subjective and objective is common to both madness and high inspiration. An artist can forfeit his individual identity during moments of intuitive absorption, feeling that he is less an inventor of his creations than a *discoverer* who "tunes in" to higher sources, the way a radio tunes in to invisible sources of information. Rilke, for instance, wrote that his mystical sonnets were "dictations" that had been "entrusted" to him. The composer Schumann also wrote music "under dictation," and felt that "gods were coming out of my fingers." In this same vein, Amy Lowell described the poet's role as

> something like a radio aerial—he is capable of receiving messages on waves of some sort; but his is more than an aerial, for he possesses the capacity of transmitting these messages into those patterns of words we call poems.

Bob Dylan described *finding* his most prophetic songs.

> It's usually right there in my head before I start. That's the way I write. But I don't even consider it writing songs. When I've written it I don't even consider that I wrote it when I got done . . . The song was there before I came along. I just sort of came and took it down with a pencil, but it was all there before I came around.

Picasso felt inspired by a similar nudge from an "external" source, then gradually reowned his creation once it was in material form.

At the beginning of each picture there is someone who works with me. Toward the end I have the impression of having worked without a collaborator.

The common thread among these accounts of inspiration is a passive waiting until something stirs in the deep collective layers of the psyche, then rises into awareness only when it is complete. The artist is swept along on a subterranean current, a passive observer of events unfolding in the dark. The spark of inspiration is struck at the interface between the realm of archetypes and personal awareness, just out of view of the ego, which is too enraptured by the senses to notice all that is happening beyond its narrow sight line. The ego is important only to craft vision into a form that can be meaningfully shared with others.

This way of looking at creativity invites us to rethink Jung's idea of the collective unconscious. Adopting the idea of universal mental forms from Plato and Saint Augustine, Jung viewed the archetypes—mental structures with universal symbolic meaning—as an inherited birthright, a passive tendency toward uniform ways of thinking that is "hardwired" into the mind/brain. But modern field theories of consciousness suggest that the collective unconscious is an *active* process that continuously operates at a subliminal level, affording access to a deep level of awareness in which all human beings participate in a give-and-take fashion.

Rather than a static force that shapes our ideas about reality, the collective unconscious evolves in synchrony with the evolution of consciousness within sentient beings. It contains information not only from our collective past, but also from our collective future. In the act of creation, an artist prospects for communal links with his fellow men and women at this deepest subterranean level, mining from the mother lode a synthesis of the yearnings, sufferings, and joys buried in the hearts of all people. Only in this way can a work of great art transcend the historical epoch of its creator and hint at immortality.

The deeper the artist penetrates into his own psyche, the higher the peaks of consciousness he ascends. By tapping into the wealth of common human experience stored in the chambers of the collective unconscious, the artist confers universal significance upon his work. His lack of adaptation to social norms, his outsider status, is his secret advantage. Finding no safe haven in the consensual world, he retreats into the terra incognita of the Spiritual Ground, where he commingles ancient and future knowledge, a thirsty wanderer dipping his cup into the stream of cosmic wisdom.

THE ARTIST VERSUS SOCIETY

Our most creative artists demonstrate that the universe of the senses is infinitesimal in comparison with the one awaiting discovery in the depth of the psyche. Like madness, the creative act is a headlong plunge into the forbidden, where fierce guardians of original repression lie in wait. Both madness and creativity uproot the consensual world structure, and with it the artist's idea of what is stable and reliable in his own consciousness. He cultivates mental states that disrupt the surface gloss of ordinary reality and scythe to the core of what is "unreal" yet intensely meaningful.

This is hardly a formula for conformity to comfortable social mores. Blake, for instance, railed against the "mind forg'd manacles of a life-denying civilization." Troublesome questions nag the artist's peace of mind. What is it all for? Should I spend my life competing with my fellows for social approval, for power to rule, to make millions? Or should I risk it all for the chance to make my vision real, to reveal my own essence as it encounters the essence of the universe? Is it worth being thought mad to inquire into our nature, our fate, the purpose of life, or simply to walk down a crowded street blowing a trumpet?

Such an antiauthoritarian attitude contains limitless possibilities for giving offense. The first reaction to any revolutionary breakthrough is not that it is difficult, but that it is *crazy*. Society's entrenched powers react to this threat as they would to madness, by attempting to regiment our artists and realign their models of reality safely within the consensus. During past eras the church harnessed them to "safe" subjects and methods. Capitalism tries to buy its artists, and Communist societies shut them away in asylums.

Yet art that is revolutionary enough for society to condemn often returns to set a new standard. Picasso's early paintings were pilloried as "grotesque creations of a deranged mind," and Stravinsky's masterwork *The Rite of Spring* touched off a full-scale riot in the music hall where it debuted. Even Beethoven's symphonies, which define what is conservatively acceptable to twentieth-century ears, provoked as much dismay at first hearing as the dissonant work of any modern master.

Like the madman, the artist cancels his membership in consensual society in favor of an outsider's role. Yet there is a world of difference between people who are incapable of social membership and those who transcend it, between *pre*social first- and second-chakra consciousness and *trans*social higher-chakra modes. Because both presocial and transsocial modes are *non*social, it is easy to confuse the two. But whereas presocial people replace consensual reality with a muddled mix of fantasy and fear, transsocial individuals reach an unseen reality and give it earthly form.

Albert Einstein's life demonstrated the power of a maturely creative mind that isolates itself from the mainstream. Although he was known as balanced, gracious, and personable, Einstein insisted on prolonged periods of detachment. He did not speak until past the age of three, and one of his teachers complained that he was unsociable, mentally slow, and "adrift forever in his foolish dreams." In his later years, he often withdrew into his attic room for days at a time. Of this custom he wrote, "I live in that solitude which is painful in youth, but delicious in the years of maturity."

What flowed from Einstein's penchant for solitude—some might call it "schizoid"—was a deluge of insights about hitherto unobserved and unimagined laws of the universe. He discovered these by *thought alone,* unsupported by experimental evidence that he might be proceeding in the right direction. In order to overthrow the conventional assumptions of physics, he detached himself first from the realities of society and then from the prejudice of dwelling on a single planet as he mentally measured the universe while streaking through space at the speed of light.

At first glance, Einstein's exercise in cosmic empathy seems little better than the twisted logic of the insane: empty space is curved; time can slow down or even stop; if you look through an infinitely powerful telescope, you see the back of your head. After he published his theory of relativity, it took orthodox science years to confirm its awesome truth. Later recalling his inspiration, he wrote, "When I examine myself and my methods of thought, I come to the conclusion that the gift of fantasy has meant more to me than my talent for absorbing knowledge."

CREATE OR GO MAD

Like psychotic ASCs, the consciousness of the fifth chakra opens the self to areas of the Ground that are ordinarily off-limits. Yet few of the great poets were truly psychotic, perhaps because they produced at white heat to keep their unquenchable vision flowing through them without impediment. And because they neither regressed nor retreated from the naked power of the Ground, they found within their battered egos a way to breathe life into their visions before they drove them mad. The fury of their pressurized state of consciousness found an outlet in an equal fury of expression, vented through talent and discipline.

Once allowed entry, the force of the Ground seeks release through the path of least resistance, be it art or madness. It is the strength of the ego that determines which will prevail. After a walk in the forest, Picasso described this compulsion for release as an "indigestion of greenness," a sensation that he felt obliged to "empty into a picture." Similarly, Amy Lowell described the creative urge as

> an imperious insistence which brooks no delay. It must be written down immediately or an acute suffering comes on, a distress almost physical, which is not relieved until the poem is given right of way.

Bob Dylan expressed it another way.

> I see things that other people don't see. I feel things that other people don't feel . . . My songs speak for me. I write them in the confinement of my own mind. If I didn't write, I think I'd go insane.

The symbols and metaphors of poetry are not merely white sugar frosting; they are the poet's way of expressing the inexpressible, of interlacing high fantasy with consensual reality, of merging the comfortably familiar with the darkly mysterious. The poet suffers to find the words of common expression too cramped, too encased in everyday design to give voice to the beauty, the terror, the love, and the unexpected flash of truth that disturbs his peace. His great challenge is to find a language more universal than human tongues and thereby wrest from his ineffable vision a way to impart its truth to his fellow men and women.

One of the fundamental attributes of creative people is their ability to make productive use of ASCs such as depression and mania, which cripple others. The critical problem is to master the discipline of a medium complex enough to express their high vision. "Execution," said Blake, "is the chariot of genius."

But meaning that is clear on a higher plane may be unfathomable at lower levels, where reality rests upon coarser space/time meridians. No one can fake knowledge of a higher strata of meaning. If someone has not experienced it, he simply will not believe in it or try to express it in any form. But once he has a clear perception of higher truth, he desperately searches for a way to bring it to his fellows. In this way, the artist is like a shaman who, having been given a magical vision, must translate it into rituals comprehensible to his tribe.

CREATIVITY & SCHIZOPHRENIA

Like many enigmas of the mind, the distinction between the schizophrenic ASC and creativity is difficult to fathom. For the artist is at once crazier and saner than the average person. Schizophrenia and the creative disposition are, on the surface, enough alike that it is easy to see why they have been equated. Nevertheless, a deeper look reveals that most artists who at one time were thought to be schizophrenic were probably misdiagnosed.

Some theorists call attention to the troubled lives of such creative lights as Vincent van Gogh, Robert Schumann, Edgar Allen Poe, Virginia Woolf, Sylvia Plath, Thomas Wolfe, Ernest Hemingway, and Winston Churchill. Yet a deeper study of their biographies quickly reveals that none was schizophrenic by the modern definition of that word. Instead, it is evident that all were manics, depressives, or both. In this section we take a look at the similarities that have confused historians, the better to see the essential differences.

Like the poet who casts about for metaphors worthy of his vision, the schizophrenic tells us of an unfamiliar reality, of hidden meanings that lie outside consensual language and logic. But with an ego too weak to sustain the discipline of the artist's craft, and a psyche regressed to childlike second-chakra consciousness, the schizophrenic is creatively impotent. As he tries to share his inner vision, his language contorts into bizarre forms, and his images degenerate into an incomprehensible order of symbol and meaning. His poetic muse, if he knows one, has gone mad.

In common with the schizophrenic, the artist curves in on himself, relying on feelings and intuitions for guidance rather than community standards. Both artists and schizophrenics tend to shift in and out of dreamlike and trancelike states in which the Ground reveals itself. The artist, however, gathers buried treasure from these labyrinthine caves of inspiration and returns enriched to the ordinary state of consciousness, while the schizophrenic misplaces his map and stumbles about in the dark.

Both artist and paranoid find meaning and relationship first, similarities and differences later. Challenged by the contradictory and unpredictable, they delve into the dark underside of awareness looking for the unexpected. Meaning lurks hidden in insignificant events, and mystery underlies the commonplace. If offered two "reasonable" alternatives, they devise a third. But although both see the world as others *do not*, the artist alone also sees the world as others *do*.

Because both are weakly repressed beings, the artist and the schizophrenic confront the world with an extremity of feeling that makes social adaptation difficult. Both tend to be moody, introverted, impulsive, careless with their bodies, and vulnerable to self-destructive rages. Always outsiders, they fashion personal realities disconnected from the consensus view. Like the fiery-eyed schizophrenic who talks to himself as he walks down a crowded street, the artist reminds us of our potential for being dominated by unseen worlds.

Both schizophrenic and artist confront us with what lies at the source of consciousness itself, sparking a timeless fear that original repression may not be so permanent after all. Lifetime fugitives from the consensus view, they show us what is conspicuously absent from everyday reality. The artist launches a vocation as agent provocateur, a subversive operative of the Ground, undermining original repression. He is unafraid to give voice to the treasures from this universal Source because he knows they are something we *already* share. But for the schizophrenic, the loss of consensus reality forces exile to a distant island cut off from society's channels of communication.

Such a prolonged quarantine teaches an individual to search for significance in *things* rather than people. The less satisfaction a person gains from interacting with people, the more he turns to his private world within. But because most creative activity is communicated on the artist's own terms, an artist's life is an ideal way for an inwardly tuned individual to express himself. The whole situation remains under his control, allowing him to choose which of his visions to reveal or keep secret. And the end products neatly protect their creator from madness by damping out extreme tendencies to withdraw, because the reward for a successful creative act is *company*.

So rather than originating from psychopathology, much of what we value in the world emerged from the efforts of an inspired and disciplined soul, not a regressed and fragmented one. It is unreasonable to pathologize the artist's delight in uncertainty, openness to unlikely possibilities, receptivity to the Ground, empathy with the minds of his fellows, and ability to use these traits to move and inspire others. The schizophrenic ASC, on the other hand, allows only ready access to the Ground. And without a mature ego to integrate this opening, the Ground only intoxicates the schizophrenic's psyche and initiates a regressive spiral that limits the individual to second-chakra functioning. This is in sharp contrast to the creative person whose contact with second-chakra consciousness is but a small part of his total awareness.

In other words, no matter how enraptured an individual may be with Ground energies, he cannot dedicate himself to an act of creation unless he possesses a working ego. At any moment, the Ground presents an infinite number of possibilities to awareness, all hypothetical. The ego's role is to subject these to critical evaluation regarding their appropriateness to the task at hand. Thanks to the ego's worldly nature, it can employ reason to check out its envisionings and decide which deserve to become manifest. A mature ego realizes that a new idea at odds with established fact requires a special burden of proof, and it has at its disposal the means to blend the rigor of reason with creative intuition, to the advantage of both.

For instance, the eccentric artist Salvador Dali was thought to be schizophrenic by some who use that word loosely. It is true that Dali's erratic mind did not run parallel to conventional lines of thought. Dali's gift was to seek out the miraculous, which he then blended into everyday life. Timepieces melting over tree limbs, grotesquely mismatched body parts, massive objects impossibly suspended in air—all make up Dali's preposterous worldview, which included his unshakable belief that his lifelong companion, Gala, was his dead brother reincarnated.

Yet the condition of Dali's sturdy ego was such that he combined his outlandish tastes and antic lifestyle with a remarkable ability to amass and manage fabulous sums of money as he exalted himself into a national hero in his native Spain. That same powerful ego consistently exerted such a masterful control over his paintings that they stun the observer with a near-photographic exactitude that not only strikingly contrasts with their absurd content, but mingles with it in a way that unsettles the observer's very notion of a dependable reality.

Dali demanded of himself and his audience what the poet Coleridge called "willing suspension of disbelief"—an ability to suspend consensual reality, to put it on hold. In contrast, the person in a schizophrenic ASC simply *denies* any data that do not fit in with his personal needs. The same fluid uncertainty that Dali elevated into an intriguing series of mysteries behind mysteries only unsettles the schizophrenic, who transforms every grain of ambiguity into paranoid conviction.

MADNESS OR METAPHOR?

Some theorists maintain that the second-chakra logic of the schizophrenic ASC is like creative thinking because both convert similarities into identities. For instance, a schizophrenic might argue that he is a rattlesnake because he feels venomous. This is an odd idea to be sure, but not so different from the one that inspired Franz Kafka to write *Metamorphosis*, the story of a man who awoke one morning to find that he had turned into a human-sized cockroach. Yet Kafka was able to relay his buggy idea as a *metaphor*, a high abstraction that communicates ironic insight, while a schizophrenic paleologically concludes that because he feels like a loathsome reptile who repulses people, he actually is one. Kafka was a master of metaphor, but the schizophrenic is its slave.

A good metaphor touches upon a special truth that cannot be told by other means. Even as it subtracts from ordinary reality, it adds depth to relationships and confers esthetic value. In metaphor we recognize a glimmer of schizophrenic reasoning: an object is *identified* with another because of common traits. When Robert Burns identified the object of his love as a "red, red rose," he knew that the flower and the particular woman had in common, among other things, that they appeared beautiful to his romantically primed sensitivities. However moonstruck, the poet certainly did not intend to communicate his undying affection for an actual flower. But when a person in a schizophrenic ASC asserts that he is a skunk cabbage, we can be sure that he is not striving for esthetic rapport with his listener.

Creative imagination reaches beyond the literal to *trans*verbal symbols—exactly the opposite of regression to *pre*verbal fantasy. Vision and high fantasy are not lower but higher modes of reasoning, involving a magical synergy that goes beyond paleologic *and* neologic. If the emotion-drenched symbols of the abstract painter are more than concepts, the fear-driven images of the schizophrenic are less. While the evocative metaphors of the poet are universals that succeed in being particulars, the concrete identifications of the schizophrenic are particulars that fail to be universals.

For example, Isaac Newton saw an apple falling from a tree and equated the apple's attraction to the earth with the attraction between the heavenly spheres. At that point he harnessed the unruly nature of paleologic and gained a universal insight. Had Newton's *only* tool been paleologic, he would have identified moon with apple and concluded that the moon could be eaten. It was quite another matter for him to compare the rate at which bodies fall to earth with the rate at which the moon deviates from the path it would follow if the earth did not exist.

Another source of confusion is in the schizophrenic's apparent capacity for witty expressions. For instance, I once asked a patient on a back ward of a state mental hospital to "lend me a hand" in moving a piano to prepare for a holiday party. He shot back, "It won't come off." I laughed spontaneously at what I thought was a sign of good humor until I noticed his ingenuous expression. He had taken my request concretely, believing that I was asking him to remove his hand from his arm. I, not he, created the joke by elevating artlessly literal thinking into humor.

Nevertheless, it is true that the poet retreats from neologic as he searches for inspiration. Rationality is a prison from which he struggles to be free. The unconfined rules of paleologic free him to grasp enticing potentials excluded by neologic. All things are possible, nothing is forbidden, and if anything can in some obscure way be identified with anything else, it is permissible to do so. The possibilities are infinite, but the poet chooses which to bring to life through metaphor. If he is to maintain his creative impetus, however, he must temper paleologic with the skills of a craftsperson. If the schizophrenic regresses to childhood, the artist must bring his childhood forward to join him in maturity.

So there is good reason to distinguish between the schizophrenic form of madness and the high vision that precedes great art or poetry. Yet we must also acknowledge the distant kinship between these two states of consciousness. By reason of their journey beyond the pale, both artist and schizophrenic risk the fate of outcasts, and they will either repent or pay dearly for their rejection of what is comfortably normal. But although the artist abandons his certainty that the world is the way he has been taught it is, he also accepts a mandate to bind his new vision to the old idea of reality. At this crucial point he parts company with those who follow only the unrestrained path to madness.

CREATIVITY & MANIA

Wild mood swings—sometimes disguised as alcoholism or addiction—have troubled many of our most creative artists throughout history. Modern writers who committed suicide include Anne Sexton, Sylvia Plath, Ernest Hemingway, Virginia Woolf, and Hart Crane. Others, such as Dylan Thomas, Thomas Wolfe, and F. Scott Fitzgerald, seemed content to drink themselves to death rather than confront their wrathful inner demons.

Although an affinity between madness and creativity is rarely found in schizophrenia, there is good reason to look for it in the manic ASC. In the early days of a manic episode, or in the nonpsychotic state of hypomania, there is an evenly distributed amplification of brain activity, and with it an inpouring of vitalizing energy from the Ground. Like the psychedelic experience, this has an unpredictable way of opening the higher chakras to awareness. It also makes for the tempestuous character structure so ubiquitous among manics of any stripe.

Ideally, the self expands gradually as it masters the tasks of each chakra, then undergoes rapid and dramatic transformations once it is strong enough to confront the next phase of life. A manic episode disrupts this schedule and can cause sudden breakthroughs into higher levels, regressions to lower levels, or both. When mild versions of these breakthroughs reach the fifth chakra and are absorbed by a healthy and well-bounded self, they can produce a *prodigy*. Mozart, for instance, wrote music with fresh and original imagery while he was still a preteen. Similarly, Isaac Newton discovered the laws of classical physics before the age of twenty-eight.

A manic ASC may be thought of as a kind of genetically programmed spiritual emergency . Ordinarily, as a maturing person edges close to a higher-level chakra, he experiences a sudden breakthrough as a benign spiritual emergence that motivates him to explore his intuitions even further. But in less-prepared individuals, such a lurch forward can precipitate a crisis state marked by a psychotic ASC. Such a crisis is likely to occur if the opening is more than one chakra removed from the location of the self. For instance, a person whose life is centered around conventional rationality (third chakra) may suddenly begin having out-of-body experiences during which he receives accurate information from a "spirit guide" (sixth chakra). This type of spiritual emergency is common in manic states.

At the onset of a manic episode, an individual is jolted into levels of awareness that he cannot fully integrate but may have a limited capacity to withstand. If he contains this force, it may fire the hearth from which great art is forged. Why some people have a greater tolerance for expansive ASCs than others is determined by a variety of factors, including the severity with which the self was isolated from the Ground during original repression. However, if original repression was not too harsh, and a person maintains a cordial relationship with the Ground, his ego will be less brittle when it bears the sudden impact of a manic episode. When he later returns to the ordinary state of consciousness, he can cast his vision in a form that strikes a resonant chord with others—in contrast to the schizophrenic, who is stuck in a lonely world that he lacks the means to share.

A review of biographies of artists and geniuses thought to be eccentric or mad reveals patterns of extreme mood swings, rather than the inexorable regression of schizophrenia. This holds true for van Gogh, Nietzsche, Schumann, Hemingway, Balzac, Handel, Goethe, Churchill, Theodore Roosevelt, and many others. Virginia Woolf, for instance, experienced episodes of frenzied activity during which she created her finest works. Sometimes she seemed to be experiencing kundalini effects: "my brain went up in a shower of fireworks," she once wrote. Like many people who experience manic ASCs, she highly valued these episodes and, despite bouts of severe depression, refused psychoanalysis, fearing it would drain her creative wellsprings and transform her into a contented, well-adjusted and drearily unproductive person.

> As an experience, madness is terrific I can assure you, and not to be sniffed at; and in its lava I still find most of the things I write about. It shoots out of me, everything shaped, final not in mere driblets, as sanity does.

Van Gogh was hospitalized on three occasions for what would now be diagnosed as mania. While confined at the asylum at Saint-Remy, he saw stars as swirling vortices floating above the stately cypresses near his room, a vision that led to some of his most sensitive works. He spoke of "furies of painting" when he would forgo food and sleep for days. But his manic flights also escalated into paranoid rages that led him to violently attack his friends and to mutilate himself. Paralyzing depressions followed, during the last of which he shot himself, leaving a message that asked, "What's the use?" We might wonder about the effect that lithium would have had on this great artist's personal torment and creative intensity.

One of my patients described his creative furor during a manic ASC.

It began with a delicious feeling of well-being and high spirits that seemed a little like smoking good pot, only with far more clarity of mind. Sleep seemed to be a ridiculous way to waste time; besides, there was a volcano inside me that was looking for a place to erupt, and I wanted to be awake when it happened. So I plunged myself into writing. My imagination soared, and words poured out nonstop, day and night. One long day followed another, and the pages piled up—about two weeks' worth, and I was just getting started.

I felt that I was chosen to write a book that would help others to understand the depth and truth of what I was realizing, the way everything fit together into a whole, like a divine plan. For a break, I'd get on my bicycle and pedal around Los Angeles, which seemed enchanted, like a fairyland. This would give me more ideas to write about. What joy there was in the smallest experience, like washing my hands in warm water! I'd have to hurry back to write it all down: the special way the soapy water swirled when I pulled the plug, the rough texture of the towel on my palms.

After a while I began to feel strange rumblings in my pelvis, sweet sexual feelings at first, but sometimes these were too painful to bear. Little fingers seemed to be walking up my backbone, tickling me from inside so that I laughed and rolled around the floor, even though I was alone. The first hallucinations followed—a big throbbing red face staring at me, sometimes laughing, too. There was a small earthquake that week, and I thought I caused it. At that point I couldn't write anymore. I got scared and paranoid, and I thought my neighbors were playing tricks on me. One of them finally called the cops when I phoned him in the middle of the night, and I ended up in a hospital.

Someday I'm going to read what I wrote then. It's about eight hundred typewritten pages. I suppose it is pretty wild and rambling, but I bet there's some pretty good stuff there, too.

Many people who inherit a predisposition to manic ASCs are blessed with healthy personalities prior to their first episode, with egos comfortably nested in third-chakra consciousness. This is in contrast to most schizophrenic ASCs, in which the self either is arrested in the late stages of the second chakra, or falls to that level from a shaky handhold in the early third chakra. Unlike schizophrenia, mania usually affects personalities that have not been eroded by years of aberrant experience during childhood and adolescence.

Nevertheless, a full-blown manic episode is considerably more than a benign spiritual emergence when it strikes a young adult trying to master the third-chakra tasks of finding a career, a mate, and a stable identity. A sudden infusion of higher-chakra consciousness overwhelms the ego under these conditions. Serious legal problems or forced hospitalization are sure to follow. Yet there are two conditions under which such a genetically programmed rush of energy actually enhances creativity.

The first is when the self has already expanded beyond the third chakra to integrate the fourth or fifth chakras. For people experiencing milder manic or depressive ASCs, such progress is possible because most do not have to take consciousness-contracting antipsychotic medicines in quantities sufficient to make severe schizophrenic ASCs livable. The self can continue to grow in between episodes. For many manics, the Ground is neither a stranger nor an enemy, for they have already reowned it to some extent. Rarely, a mature individual can learn to recognize a manic ASC at its onset and "ride it through," resorting to lithium only if things get out of control. This is, however, a hazardous strategy.

Yet mania can enhance creativity when it is mild enough to affect a manageable expansion of awareness. In other words, the ASC remains in the hypomanic range, where the inflowing power of the Ground supercharges rather than overwhelms the ego. This fuels the feverish absorption necessary for the creative act, as well as intensifying feeling and accelerating thinking to an extent that surpasses what is possible in the ordinary state of consciousness. It also allows prodigious amounts of work to be accomplished, usually at the expense of sleep. Yet it spares enough ego strength to supply the discipline and concentration necessary to complete the task.

The chief danger of the hypomanic state is that an immature self is vulnerable to bombastic inflations of self-esteem. The dancer Nijinsky, for instance, demonstrated the grandiosity that follows when an immature ego is overinflated with infusions from the Ground. In *A Social History of Madness*, Roy Porter quoted Nijinsky:

> "God is in me." Through his dance, states Nijinsky, he is the bringer of God, of divine fire, into the world, for "I am God in a body," possessed of grace, which comes of God. Civilization is built upon history; all that is just dead weight. "I am God's present." For God is life, God is movement. " I am a man of motion, I am God in flesh and feeling . . ." "I am the Savior." Like Christ he will redeem; but he will redeem through dance. Inevitably, he will be persecuted, he must be "a martyr." "I suffered more than anyone else in the world." Why? "Blinded by reason, the world cannot, will not understand . . ."

As overblown as Nijinsky's ego may have been, he demonstrated the sublime confidence that the manic ASC imparts to any enterprise. The manic's unquenchable thirst for outrageous adventure, quirky sex, restless relocations from place to place, exotic drugs, erratic friendships, uproarious parties, precipitous changes of spouses and jobs, all provide a naturally gifted artist with endless grist for his creative mill. The intermittent depressions that follow manic burnout supply the passionate quality of "soul" and deep empathy that characterizes great art.

It is no surprise, then, that recent research suggests that the antimanic drug lithium has a squelching effect on creativity for some artists. It especially blunts the richness of word associations on which poets and writers thrive. In one study, a group of people in creative professions who had taken lithium for several years were tested for creative associations while temporarily switched to a placebo, then again when lithium was restarted. Researchers found a significant increase in creative and idiosyncratic thinking while the subjects were on the placebo, an effect that decreased when lithium was resumed.

This is not to say that all manics are creative, or that all creative people are manic—far from it. People who naturally grow into the fifth chakra are even more abundantly creative without all the distracting turbulence attendant upon the manic ASC. They also maintain a consistent level of critical judgment that helps them to winnow out good

ideas from bad ones, which is conspicuously lacking in both schizophrenic and extreme manic ASCs. Also, that elusive quality called
talent has far more to do with creativity than extreme psychosis of
any type.

Psychiatrist Nancy Andreasen recently published an update of her
fifteen-year-old survey of faculty members at the prestigious University
of Iowa Writer's Workshop. Students and faculty of this program have
included Philip Roth, Kurt Vonnegut, John Irving, Robert Lowell,
Flannery O'Connor, and John Cheever. Because well-known writers are
brought in each year as visiting faculty, the workshop represents a reasonably valid cross-section of contemporary American writers.

Andreasen originally designed her research to test for a link between schizophrenia and creativity, not even suspecting a connection
with mania. However, she soon realized that schizophrenic ASCs were
conspicuous only for their *absence* among the talented writers. What she
found instead was that 80 percent of the writers had an episode of mania
at some time in their lives, compared with 30 percent of control subjects.
The writers also had higher rates of alcoholism to complicate their
mood swings. Andreasen's conclusion was clear.

> Earlier hypotheses about a relationship with schizophrenia
> were based on the recognition that schizophrenia often
> leads to unusual perceptions that predispose to creativity;
> in most instances, however, perceptions in schizophrenia
> tend to be more bizarre than original, and many schizo-
> phrenic patients suffer from cognitive impairments that
> are likely to inhibit creativity. Schizophrenia also tends to
> be a chronic illness, while [manic-depressive illness] is
> usually episodic, leaving more people with long periods of
> normality. Most writers reported that they tended to write
> during these normal periods rather than during highs
> or lows.

CREATIVITY & THE BRAIN

The opening to fifth-chakra consciousness is mirrored by a change
in the way the brain processes information. Earlier, as the self opened to
the fourth chakra, the organizing center of neurological activity expanded from the frontal lobes to reincorporate the limbic system and
embellish rationality with depth of feeling. Now, as fifth-chakra consciousness enriches the self, the neurological center again broadens to

include the reptilian brain as its helpmate. At this stage, the brain starts to act like a hologram, each of its parts blending into the whole.

From this point on, the brain operates as a resonating instrument, each of its fine-tuned "strings" vibrating in sympathy with the others. No part is repressed, and there is little remaining internal censorship. No longer is there warfare among instinct, feeling, and reason, each of which assumes a respected place in awareness. This internal alliance allows a person to access data of greater complexity, and then scrutinize them from several angles simultaneously. Once he integrates fifth-chakra consciousness, he balances reason by attending to his feelings before they get abstracted into thought. Then he consults his primitive archetypal roots, recalling a time when self and Ground rejoiced in intimate communion. And he does this without sacrificing any higher faculties.

In this way, fifth-chakra consciousness resembles early manic states. We know that alternating mania and depression follow from instability in brain areas that regulate mood cycles and arousal. The extent of arousal, and the depth of the ASC, is roughly proportional to norepinephrine activity in the brain. We may speculate that the inherited trait linking mania and creativity is a propensity for surges of norepinephrine that specifically arouse the limbic system, *without* loss of frontal-lobe functioning. So the balanced activity of early manic or hypomanic ASCs allows creative inspiration to percolate through excited emotional areas, while equally stimulated frontal lobes stand guard. These act as a censor that keeps a vigilant eye cocked toward consensual realty, allowing entry to the universal, but rejecting the trivial and bizarre.

So it is the *ratio* of activity among brain levels that establishes whether a state of consciousness is beneficial or maladaptive. The schizophrenic ASC is one of intense limbic arousal, mediated by dopamine. But in schizophrenia, the frontal lobes are *underactive*, abdicating reasoning power and with it their authority to keep lower brain regions in check. Normal frontal lobes keep time and space stable within awareness, and thereby enable us to plan sequential steps toward a goal. If these falter, the regulating center retreats to levels equipped to cope only with the present moment, making sustained creative effort impossible. Similarly, *extreme* manic states produce a schizophreniclike imbalance after lower brain activity overwhelms the frontal lobes.

The following table contrasts the effects on the psyche of a hyperaroused limbic system balanced by frontal-lobe feedback, such as in a hypomanic or early manic ASC, and a hyperaroused limbic system lacking this essential balance, such as in a schizophrenic ASC.

HYPOMANIA & EARLY MANIA *(balanced limbic and frontal arousal)*	SCHIZOPHRENIA *(limbic arousal/frontal inhibition)*
Enhanced visual imagery and ideation with insight into its nature	Hallucination, loss of discrimination between fantasy and consensual reality
Enhanced access to the personal subconscious	Projection of one's repressed traits onto others
Fluent flow of original and novel connections	Distracted by irrelevant ideas; loose associations
Relaxed openness to new experience	Anxiety, agitation, thought blocking
Sensitivity to emotional nuance	Easily overwhelmed by emotions
Impulse to share beauty of the sensory world	Lost in "a world of his own"
Absorbed in esthetic matters	Spaced-out; preoccupied with trivia
Insight intact; able to see through false solutions and erroneous data	Paranoid delusions; thinking distorts data
Reduced inhibitions; avoids premature negative judgments: "open mind"	Loss of critical discrimination
Desires to express insight in material form	Tasks of "this world" seem trivial
Feels attuned to "higher sources"	Delusion of control
Interconnectedness and meaning found everywhere	Delusion of personal reference

In sum, hyperaroused limbic or reptilian levels create little of value when they are isolated. But if tempered by an equally aroused neocortex, these same primordial centers turn into cauldrons of creativity. The neocortex is at a similar disadvantage when isolated. Left to its own devices, it produces endless chains of logically connected thoughts, but to follow them would be pure drudgery, like reading an outline for a college term paper.

Jung seemed to be referring to the wordless contributions of these lower brain centers to creativity when he wrote:

Primordial experience is the source of creativeness; it cannot be fathomed, and therefore requires mythological imagery to give it form. In itself it offers no words or images,
for it is a vision seen "as in a glass, darkly."

GENES & GENIUS

Families haunted by madness are also apt to produce artistic or scientific talent. This holds true in families with either manic or schizophrenic offspring, a link confirmed by modern studies.

For instance, Andreasen's research at the Iowa Writer's Workshop,
described earlier, showed that families of the writers she studied were
riddled with both creativity and mental illness in unusually high proportions. Furthermore, the type of creativity in the relatives was not
confined to literary talent, but included other fields, such as art, music,
dance, and mathematics. This suggests that whatever is transmitted genetically is not simply a specific gift for writing, but a flair for tapping
into novel forms of consciousness. Other studies confirm similar links
with creativity in families of schizophrenics.

Genes set up conditions within the brain that affect the way it interacts with the Ground to form the human mind. A reasonable speculation is that there are several genes involved in transmitting a predisposition for either schizophrenia or mania. A significant number of artistic
individuals have only a sprinkling of these unique genes, which cause
modest alterations that promote creativity. These allow periodic influxes
of Ground energy, but not so much that the artist is stripped of his capacity to make unusual states of consciousness meaningful, or to interpret symbolically what arrives unbidden into his awareness. If the affected person has a self-boundary flexible enough to withstand partial
penetrations of the Ground, he can then turn his genetic endowment
into creative vision.

In this way, creativity is a kind of safety valve allowing individuals
to cope with a predisposition to madness. Until humanity's collective
consciousness someday evolves to the fifth chakra, we might wonder if
the self-destructive excesses of the manic ASC and the burned-out victims of the schizophrenic ASC are the unavoidable price we pay for the
luxury of creative genius. If so, is it worth it? The poet Rimbaud answered this question, at least for himself, as he confronted the choice
made by all artists.

The poet makes himself a seer by a long, prodigious and
rational disordering of the senses. Every form of love, of

suffering, of madness; he searches himself, he consumes all the poisons in him, and keeps only their quintessences. This is an unspeakable torture during which he needs all his faith and superhuman strength, and during which he becomes the great patient, the great criminal, the great accursed—and the great learned one!—among men. For he arrives at the *unknown!* And even if, crazed, he ends up by losing the understanding of his visions, at least he has seen them.

And despite his personal knowledge that madness is far from a psychedelic paradise, van Gogh would surely have agreed:

Ah! My dear comrades, let us crazy ones take delight in our eyesight in spite of everything, yes, lets!

CHAPTER 14

Sixth Chakra:
Madness, ESP, & Dreams

❖

In order to see, you have to stop being in the middle of the picture.
SRI AUROBINDO

There is superstition in avoiding superstition.
FRANCIS BACON

ANCIENT EGYPTIAN MASKS of royalty and priesthood were cast in gold, with the head of a cobra protruding from midforehead at the location of the Ajna chakra. To the Egyptians, this symbolized the opening of the "third eye," the illumination of an awakened spirit, the life force ascending to the domain of secret knowledge. Once a person achieved this inner wisdom, he or she gained power to alter consciousness, and therefore reality, at will.

The ancient Egyptians are said to have been especially adept in spiritual matters and in controlling arcane forces by methods long since forgotten. In modern Western cultures, such powers are rare. From the modern perspective, once a gifted person learns to creatively manipulate the physical world through art, science, or technology, he has reached the pinnacle of human potential, the ultimate and final stage of evolution. There simply is nowhere else to go, and our cultures neither provide tools for further exploration nor encourage their members to develop their own. Anyone who insists on exploring more deeply is thought to be a "flake" who flirts with madness.

The idea of humankind's innate ability to understand its divine roots has waxed and waned in modern psychology, undergoing major revisions by Immanuel Kant, Sigmund Freud, and Carl Jung, who edged closest to the Eastern insight that the Source of consciousness—called in this book the Spiritual Ground—is accessible to all sentient beings. Because Jung kept this idea alive through the antagonistic era of behavioristic psychology, it could be revived in the works of Abraham Maslow, who affirmed humanity's potential for evolving to ever higher planes of consciousness. Novelist and consciousness explorer Aldous Huxley also popularized the idea under the name of the "perennial philosophy." Its most striking feature is that consciousness is structured into levels, from the coarsest and most fragmentary to the subtlest and most unitary. Huxley described the perennial philosophy as

> . . . a metaphysic that recognizes a divine Reality [within] the world of things and lives and minds; the psychology that finds in the soul something similar to, or even identical with, divine Reality; the ethic that places man's final end in the knowledge of the immanent and transcendent Ground of all being . . .

The power of the perennial philosophy is now being explored by the rapidly growing school of transpersonal psychology, led by Ken Wilber, Stanislav Grof, Frances Vaughan, Roger Walsh, and Michael Washburn. By applying the perennial philosophy to a widely misunderstood source of human suffering, this book attempts to find a practical application for it.

In this chapter, we explore several paranormal phenomena that accompany the self's expansion into the shamanic consciousness of the sixth chakra, with an eye toward distinguishing these from confusingly similar symptoms of certain psychotic ASCs.

SIXTH-CHAKRA CONSCIOUSNESS

H. G. Wells once wrote a story about an isolated land populated by a species of beings without eyes. If a sighted traveler were to trespass into such a country, he would certainly find its inhabitants to be skeptical of his outlandish claims of perceiving distant objects without the benefit of touch or hearing. If they were to believe him at all, they would surely explain his magical gift of sight as extrasensory perception.

Imagine life in a similar society in which the sense of sight were just beginning to evolve in a few individuals, the remainder groping along with the other four senses. Those "mutants" with the mixed blessing of sight would surely be thought of as abnormal and threatening to the established worldview. They would likely be confined in isolated areas, and the brightest among them would learn to keep their deviance a carefully guarded secret. This is not so different from modern societies in which a sure way of being seen as psychotic is to punctuate a conversation with personal references to experiences of telepathy, channeling, or communication with extraterrestrials.

This is why the transition to the sixth chakra is the most difficult of all. Opening the "third eye" requires painful detachment from objects and desires of the social world, a displacement of selfhood from the ego onto the Ground itself. A person crossing this threshold finds that his former patterns of living are no longer adequate, and that they must be purged. The extreme self-mortification practiced by religious ascetics is designed to rid them of their old connections to consensual reality. Because the sublime awareness of the sixth chakra differs markedly from everyday experience, the cost of this advance is self-imposed exile from the ordinary world of human affairs. The reward is knowledge of mystery.

If transit through the fourth chakra leaves the gateway to the Spiritual Ground ajar, and the fifth chakra flings that corridor wide open, it is for an individual whose self has expanded to the sixth chakra to boldly walk through. Just as the fifth chakra brings self-actualization, the sixth confers *self-realization*, an ability to rise above the ego to regard one's own divine nature. In this dilated state, the self reowns and identifies with all that was previously subconscious. This includes its instincts and repressed shadow elements, and the archetypes embedded within the Spiritual Ground. Previously unrealized levels of the Ground now become part of the self, conferring a visionary vocation driven by powers that to most people are confined to the realm of magic.

But if such an expansion of consciousness were to occur precipitously, even to one who had mastered the tasks of the first five chakras, the result would be a spiritual emergency of the first magnitude, a devastating regression as the ego makes its last stand. The reason such crises are uncommon in the Western world is that few individuals ever attain sixth-chakra consciousness, or even risk approaching it. It is far more likely for people centered in the lower chakras to experience *partial* openings to this realm. These are usually unplanned and uncontrolled, and they can cause people who experience them to fear they are going crazy, or can actually make them that way by severely fragmenting the ego.

In contrast, Eastern cultures take pains to prepare their members for this transition. In India, for instance, people traditionally organize their lives into four stages. In the first, the youth concentrates on his studies and self-mastery. As he matures, he devotes himself to family life and work. By middle age, he partially withdraws from worldly concerns as he begins spiritual practice. The fourth stage brings about a more thorough renunciation as the seeker withdraws and walks the solitary path of contemplation. The Indian culture provides him with support and validation for this final stage, and Hindu traditions supply a wealth of contemplative techniques to aid his journey into the higher chakras.

Once a highly evolved individual opens to the sixth chakra, he disidentifies with the ego, which he recognizes as a tiny fragment of human nature, merely a subset of capabilities with a limited purpose. Ego functions are still available if he needs to deal with worldly matters, but most of the time he finds that he has better things to do—namely, invest his energies in dismantling the last residues of original repression and reestablishing an intimate relationship with the Ground. This is an inwardly directed task, and he must turn his back to his attachments in the world if he is to proceed. The powers that follow appear so far beyond the pale to people centered at lower chakras that they are usually denied as categorically impossible or labeled fraudulent.

NO BOUNDARIES

Although the consciousness of the fifth chakra endows the self with intuitions of universal symbols that humans express as art, the sixth chakra grants *direct* access to archetypes embedded in the Ground. These are not objects of the senses; they preexist in consciousness as the first created forms upon which all subsequent creation is patterned.

Once a person enters this subtle realm, it is but a small step to learn to manipulate these archetypal "blueprints" that underlie reality, and therefore to alter reality at will. Here is the rarefied atmosphere of the shaman, the Gnostic high priest, the yoga master. It is a stratospheric plane of consciousness in which the magical is commonplace and there are no boundaries or limits. These powers seem miraculous to our everyday mentality, but to the sixth-chakra adept, they are just another skill. The really miraculous lies even further beyond reach.

To an average person, a sixth-chakra adept appears aloof, abstracted from human concerns. This reflects the detached introspection necessary to remain constantly open to the Ground. Remote though he may seem, the adept is far from indifferent. His has a higher compassion that includes but transcends the worldly compassion of the fourth chakra, and even the commitment to humanity of the fifth. The high compassion of the sixth chakra is not limited to the human condition, but extends to all sentient beings, indeed to all of creation within the infinite embrace of the Ground.

The concern of the sixth-chakra adept, however, goes beyond sentimentality and maudlin expression, for he has risen above his ego to the point where it matters little to him if others mistake him as cold or aloof. They need only observe his actions to realize the extent of his commitment to the evolution of the human spirit. This dedication may not be expressed in worldly actions; he may decide that his talent is to remain quietly involved from *within*. Of course, charm and charisma are not beyond such a person; he can mobilize these traits in abundance if he concludes that they are necessary for a higher purpose.

Also, the adept's detachment does not turn him away from creative pursuits. However, he has a different purpose in mind than the scientists and artists of the fifth chakra. Because many of the higher archetypes he perceives have no visible expression in the world of form, he may feel that it will further the spiritual strivings of humanity if he gives them form. Many of the great cathedrals, as well as the deities and mandalas depicted in spiritual iconography, are representations of such archetypes, which otherwise would not have found expression in the sensory world. These are minutely detailed representations of deep mysteries revealed in transcendent states of consciousness. More than individual statements by an artist, they are a means of communicating a wordless experience of the archetype to others who seek initiation into higher realms.

Up to this point in the development of consciousness, thinking has progressed from paleologic to neologic to synthesis to synergy. Sixth-chakra consciousness occasions yet another advance. But it is not simply another form of cognition. Thinking as we know it is at odds with the psychic activity of the sixth chakra, and the adept practices methods to *stop* his mind from thinking. He finds logic inadequate to process the subtle energies he confronts, so he cultivates *intuition*, a way of directly "reading" the Ground. Intuition is a finer kind of reason that takes in the seen with the unseen in an unfiltered apprehension of reality. With time, the adept finds intuition to be a more reliable means of gathering information, and it eventually becomes all he needs.

As introspection deepens, the adept begins to discern metapatterns, organizing principles underlying the unity of the cosmos, "archetypes of archetypes." This allows him to control reality in a way that transcends the laws of physics. Through his willingness to rise above the sensory realm, he grows exquisitely sensitive to events invisible to people deafened by the clamor of worldly affairs. The subtle energies of the Ground gradually yield to his will, and he becomes capable of telepathy, precognition, psychokinesis, psychic healing, out-of-body travels, and "channeling" information from nether regions of the Ground.

Because these kinds of paranormal powers come from *outside* the ego, they are sometimes noticeable in people who have regressed to pre-egoic levels. This is why second-chakra regressions are often confused with spiritual emergencies that manifest sixth-chakra capabilities. To consider them identical, however, is to lapse into the pre/trans fallacy. During second-chakra regression, original repression fails just when it is most needed. But in sixth-chakra expansions, the self *outgrows* original repression when it becomes a superfluous barrier to its spiritual growth. During the in-between period, however, partial repression of the Ground from awareness is a requisite for sanity.

Virtually all major religious traditions recognize psychic powers, although each interprets and values them in different ways. Eastern religions call them *siddhis*, and view them as signs of spiritual progress. They also warn that if the *siddhis* are overvalued, they can fascinate and ensnare the seeker, keeping him from enlightenment. Christianity is ambivalent about these powers. Although Catholicism values miraculous abilities for their own sake and even cultivates them within religious communities, fundamentalist sects view them as demonic and forbid their practice. All major religions agree that attention to these powers before the self reaches a certain level of spiritual attainment risks a descent into madness.

A recent poll indicated that a significant majority of Americans believe they have had a psychic experience of one sort or another at some time in their lives. Given that even half of these were actual paranormal events, it is clear that they are not the exclusive province of people centered in the sixth chakra. Indeed, children and animals occasionally demonstrate extrasensory perception, which seems to break over ordinary consciousness like an occasional rogue wave that surprises sunbathers relaxing above the tide line.

What is unique about people who have gained the sixth chakra is that they have cultivated an internal technology that enables them to alter consciousness at will and therefore master the *siddhis*. This is not to say that some people at lower levels do not have a measure of control over these forces. The gift of "second sight" may even run in families. But a sixth-chakra adept not only has greater command over a wider range of powers, he also uses them exclusively for higher purposes, such as healing or shamanic divination, and never flaunts or exploits them for self-gain.

In earlier chapters we saw that the neurological center of control ascends from the old reptilian brain during the first chakra, to the limbic system in the second chakra, to the cortex and finally the frontal lobes in the third chakra. Then, as the self expands into higher chakras, the control center broadens to reinclude first the limbic system in the fourth chakra, then the lower brain stem in the fifth chakra. At that point, inputs from the whole brain are reincorporated within the self. It is obvious that there is no place left for further expansion within the confines of the brain.

But just as the higher awareness of the sixth chakra is trans*personal*, it is also trans*physical*. At this point in the evolution of the psyche, consciousness asserts its ultimate superiority over the physical realm. Whereas in the lower chakras, self-awareness emerges from the brain's interaction with the Ground, at the sixth chakra the self begins to operate *from within the Ground itself,* and so transcends its lifelong connection with the physical brain. This is not to say that the brain is inoperative, only that its governing center is located above and beyond it, and therefore manipulates it for its own ends. In some esoteric traditions, it is believed that the sixth-chakra adept so thoroughly transcends the physical plane that he can choose to abandon his body and exist henceforth on a noncorporeal plane of being.

The emerging power of mind over brain is the ultimate assertion of free will, a faculty that emerges weakly during the final stages of the second chakra when a maturing child tentatively learns to override his impulses. Although will is "free" relative to physical laws, it is limited by the mental capabilities of each particular chakra. As the self expands, free will grows steadily stronger, reaching its zenith in sixth-chakra consciousness. The demonstrable power of human will is everyday proof of the primacy of the mental over the physical, of the ability of consciousness to govern the activity of its earthly caretaker, the brain.

Occasionally a person centered in the third chakra somehow steps "out of sequence" and acquires paranormal powers. These Rasputin-like forces can be quite unreliable in unskilled hands and are sometimes turned to dark purposes, something that virtually never occurs with people who have first integrated the empathic consciousness of the fourth chakra.

Most ASCs that render self-boundaries more porous (hypnosis, dreaming, deep reverie, meditation, psychedelic trips, and certain psychotic ASCs) temporarily foster ESP. Extreme duress or life-threatening situations also enhance ESP, which is more likely to occur between people who have close emotional bonds. Such openings are unplanned and fragmentary, and the person exerts little command over them. When an incompletely developed personality finds itself in partial command of paranormal powers, the best that can be expected is that these powers will be used for entertainment. They often abruptly disappear without warning.

SCIENCE & THE PARANORMAL

Extrasensory perception is one of the common threads linking psychotic, creative, and mystical states of consciousness. People who do not fit into any of those categories are also occasionally blessed (or cursed) with this latent human capability. Because the very idea of ESP turns conventional worldviews topsy-turvy, there are few phenomena more likely to raise the hackles of materialist scientists, who rush to fortify their paradigms by flatly denying its existence. This creates the odd situation of an incontrovertible body of evidence accumulated by one group of scientists being actively ignored by another group of scientists. Most of the objections may be summed up in the statement that because ESP is a priori impossible, all the evidence, no matter how compelling, must be either in error or fraudulent.

There are now several paranormal phenomena that are established beyond reasonable doubt. They have been tested to standards of statistical accuracy far exceeding those readily accepted by scientists everywhere for more mundane information. *Not* to believe that these phenomena occur implies a gigantic conspiracy involving hundreds of university departments and thousands of scientists of impeccable reputation in virtually every civilized country in the world.

Until recent decades, most evidence for ESP was anecdotal. Although anecdotes fall short of scientific proof, the thousands of well-documented incidents of ESP accumulated over the centuries make up an impressive body of evidence. Even in technological cultures that discourage such experiences, countless people have had precognitive dreams or other psychic occurrences. Any therapist who regularly attends to the dreams of his patients will attest to the widespread nature of these phenomena. In my twenty-one years of psychiatric practice, I have personally heard dozens of credible accounts. This one is typical:

> While we were on vacation, my husband was on an all-night deep-sea fishing trip. About 2 A.M I awoke feeling damp and very cold, although it was warm and dry in the room where we were staying. A few minutes later I heard my son crying in the other room. I went to comfort him, and he said that he had a nightmare about daddy. When I went back to bed and tried to sleep, I heard my husband's voice calling me. I couldn't rest for the rest of the night. The next morning I got a call from the Coast Guard saying that my husband's ship had sunk and that he had drowned. It happened at the same time I woke up and my son had the dream.

Another had a better outcome:

> I was sleeping soundly, but I awoke with a start. I couldn't
> see or hear anything, but I knew, *really knew*, that I should
> check on my child. Just as I arrived at her room and opened
> the door, I saw that a night lamp had short-circuited and
> was throwing sparks at the curtain.

In the past half century, dozens of highly regarded scientists in the United States, Great Britain, and the Soviet Union have successfully applied the hard tools of statistical analysis to demonstrate the existence of ESP. Because it is beyond the scope of this book to present their work in detail, the reader is referred to several excellent sources. However, it is worth taking a brief look at four paranormal phenomena that have been validated by rigorous scientific methods so we can recognize them when they occur in psychotic ASCs or spiritual emergencies. These are telepathy, clairvoyance, precognition, and psychokinesis.

Telepathy: Regression or Transcendence?

Telepathy is direct mind-to-mind communication that bypasses the sense organs. Because it does the least violence to conventional notions of space and time, telepathy was the first psychic phenomenon to be studied by J. B. Rhine at his now famous ESP laboratory at Duke University. Rhine's carefully controlled card-guessing experiments demonstrated an accuracy in gifted subjects that exceeded the laws of chance by several million to one. Rhine's early results were so amazing that he was attacked by the scientific community, which called him incompetent, a fraud, and worse. Yet those critics who later took the trouble to investigate his methods were unanimous in apologizing to him for their rash judgment. Since then, his experiments have been successfully repeated hundreds of times in various scientific settings.

There is evidence that ESP can occur outside the awareness of an individual affected by it. In an experiment conducted in a Moscow obstetric hospital, mothers housed in a remote wing of the building, well out of sight and earshot of their newborn infants, were continually monitored for physical signs of anxiety, such as increased heart rate and galvanic skin response. Researchers found that the mothers' *bodies* reacted dramatically at the precise moments when their infants were disturbed by doctors taking blood samples or performing medical tests, even though the mothers were not aware of any subjective change. Another, more grisly Soviet experiment involved recording brain waves of a female rabbit in a laboratory while her progeny were being killed, one at a time, deep beneath the ocean in a submarine. The recording show-edmarked arousal in the mother simultaneous to the death of each baby rabbit.

A clever experiment that skirts the borders of black magic added another twist to the question of whether psychotic "delusions of control" are always so delusional. Experimenters successfully used a third party to influence ESP scores of a standard sender-receiver pair. Two subjects were performing the usual card-guessing experiments in separate rooms of a laboratory while, unknown to either, a third person in another room alternatively attempted to interfere with, or assist, their guesses by mental imagery alone. This voodoolike experiment showed that the third party could strongly influence the scores of the original pair. This suggests that telepathy takes place within a field of consciousness, and challenges the idea of scientific objectivity. Perhaps this is why virtually every researcher who sets out to prove the existence of ESP does so, while virtually every researcher who tries to disprove it reports similar success.

Scientists have been unsuccessful in finding a physical medium for telepathic transmission. But if we look at it from the point of view of the perennial philosophy, whose most striking feature is that consciousness is structured into levels, we see that a physical medium is unnecessary for telepathy because consciousness is its own medium. Given that all sentient beings participate in a unitive Ground of consciousness with a structure analogous to a hologram, there is no difficulty in explaining how data from a distant source can instantly appear elsewhere. Just as information stored within a hologram is evenly distributed throughout its field, telepathically received information is *already present*. Under certain conditions, this information reaches an intensity sufficient to resonate across a threshold into awareness. People in psychotic ASCs, sensitives, and people who sharpen their awareness through spiritual practice all have lower thresholds for perception of this ever-present reality.

As schizophrenics describe the feeling of dissolving ego boundaries, they often speak of telepathy. "Someone is tampering with my thoughts" or "I know the awful things you are thinking about me" are common laments that cause therapists to nod their heads knowingly and write "delusions of control" on their notepads. A related fear is that angry thoughts harm others. Orthodox psychiatry explains away such feelings as "magical thinking," prima facie evidence of malignant regression.

Manic ASCs also trigger feelings that one is tapping into a vein of cosmic knowledge, or accessing the innermost thoughts and feelings of others. As mania propels an ego-based individual into higher planes of consciousness, he deems himself omniscient, imbued with inflowing wisdom of such magnitude that there are no limits to his prowess and invulnerability. Unfortunately, consensus reality sternly reasserts its limits with a heavy hand.

Although psychotherapists regularly collect anecdotes of ESP in their psychotic patients, research demonstrating telepathy during psychotic ASCs has been sparse. The few reports are inconsistent, and the experimental methods lax. Interest in this research has waned; at the time of this writing, a computerized literature search revealed that the last study was published in 1977, and only six preceded it, using widely different methods. These generally show that schizophrenics are no better at laboratory card guessing than anyone else. But at least two studies found that people in manic ASCs scored significantly above chance.

If we contrast the relatively balanced arousal of mania to the sensory disorganization of schizophrenia, the disparity in ESP performance is not surprising. Psychiatrist Jan Ehrenwald, who worked with a number of psychotic individuals who demonstrated telepathy, suggested that the ordinary state of consciousness keeps telepathic inputs outside awareness. But the weakly bounded schizophrenic self is continually deluged by a torrent of telepathy that Ehrenwald called "psi pollution." Paranoia is but one defense against being engulfed by this confusing buzz of random psi inputs. In Ehrenwald's theory, schizophrenics perform poorly on formal psi testing because they cannot select the targeted input out of a churning background sea of psi activity, including "static" from the examiner's prejudices. Ehrenwald concluded:

> Thus the schizophrenic's defensive posture toward psi is merely an exaggerated version of Western man's prevailingly hostile attitude toward it . . . Still, despite the schizophrenic's allergic reaction to psi pollution, he cannot help but maintain the reality of the uncanny powers that threaten to overwhelm him. To him their reality is not just one of new insights or conceptualizations . . . Regressed as he is to a prelogical level of experience, he regards telepathy not merely as a metaphor, nor as a faint echo of an intrapsychic type of communication reverberating from the past. Telepathy to him is a persistent psychic reality, blissful and terrifying at the same time.

During manic ASCs, on the other hand, a rapid inflation into the higher chakras allows the individual to at least partially integrate influxes from the Ground. Manics are generally less frightened and more welcoming of the Ground than schizophrenics, all of which allows for greater coherence. One of my patients described telepathy that accompanied her manic ASC.

> They were little impressions that jumped into my head from nowhere, not at all like thoughts or feelings that follow one another. I'd be thinking of what I was going to do next, and a stranger would walk by, and I'd flash: Hey, he's wearing red underwear, or he has a headache, or she has a child with leukemia. When I was with my friends, I'd know what they were going to say before they said it. If the phone rang, it would tickle me to tell them who was calling before they answered. At first, I didn't believe what was happening, so I checked out my impressions several times, and they were always right. Well, this upset a lot of people, so I stopped, but after that I knew my intuitions would be correct. After I began taking lithium, it stopped happening to me. I guess it's good riddance, but it was fun while it lasted.

Although telepathy can occur randomly at any stage of life, it is common during childhood before self-boundaries solidify, and during mildly regressive ASCs such as dreaming and hypnosis. This led many theorists, Freud among them, to argue that telepathy is a primitive form of preverbal communication that was superseded and subsequently repressed as humans came to rely on more reliable verbal means of communication. Because ESP is mediated by older regions of the brain, this point is valid as long as it is recognized that there is an essential difference between occasional telepathic breakthroughs and the refined powers of the sixth chakra.

So a healer must assess his patient's stage of development prior to the onset of disturbing symptoms. A deluge of ESP easily overwhelms the weak ego of a person centered in the second chakra, contributing significantly to psychotic confusion. When ESP occurs to people centered in the third chakra, it is sometimes helpful, sometimes frightening, but there is virtually no control over its manifestations. Nothing in modern life prepares an individual for such a metamorphosis. He may be so disoriented that he appears more psychotic than he actually is.

But by the time the fourth chakra is attained, the self begins to recognize extrasensory inputs for what they are, and to greet them as helpful intuitions. By the fifth chakra, these expand into a welcome source of inspiration, and the self gains a measure of control over them. But it is only when the transpersonal consciousness of the sixth chakra is integrated that the self operates within the Spiritual Ground itself, and therefore masters the extrasensory realm.

Nevertheless, it is easy to confuse second-chakra regressions with authentic spiritual emergences in which the sixth chakra exposes an unprepared person to unfiltered Ground energies. Both cause people to feel they have become telepathic or precognitive, or have acquired some other paranormal ability. But the underlying reality is quite different. Malignant regressions to the second chakra almost always begin from an early third-chakra base, rarely higher. This is in contrast to premature sixth-chakra openings, which usually affect people who have reached at least the heart chakra, have attained a measure of personal achievement in life, and have taken up a spiritual practice like meditation. An exception might be an adolescent who is naturally "sensitive," and who manifests verifiable ESP without regressive delusions or loss of ego functions.

Although second-chakra regression opens self to Ground, its inputs blend with personal wishes and fears so that the original perception is distorted beyond recognition. In contrast, higher-chakra ESP can be verified through reality-testing. If a person feels he is telepathically reading someone's thoughts, it is usually a simple matter to ask the other person if this is correct. Precognitive dreams can be tested by careful recording and confirmation. If a person reports traveling to other locations during out-of-body experiences, he might try to notice certain details or events, then confirm these later. If guidance arrives as inner voices, the healer might ask what they say to determine if they are of a lower or higher order. Pathological hallucinations occur repeatedly, while paranormal guidance is usually an isolated event. Genuine intuition can be distinguished from delusion by the calm feeling of resolution that follows, along with a quiet humility that prevents ego inflation.

In my work with people in schizophrenic ASCs, I developed the habit of testing reports of telepathy in hope of finding a true instance, but I have found most to be projections of inner fears. The following conversation with a hospitalized schizophrenic patient is typical:

Patient: You know, doctor, I can tell what everybody here is thinking every second.
Doctor: How can you be sure?
Patient: Oh, I'm sure all right!
Doctor: What do you think that person sitting over there is thinking?
Patient: Sex. He's planning how he's going to rape me.
Doctor: Rape you?

Patient: Every time I look at him I hear a voice saying, "Lust, lust, lust!"

Doctor: OK, let's test it on me. I'm thinking of a number from one to ten. Can you guess it?

Patient: (closes eyes and appears to concentrate) You're fooling me, doctor. You're not thinking of a number at all. You're thinking of how you're going to *help* him rape me.

In only one case do I recall a schizophrenic patient who demonstrated what appeared to be true paranormal abilities. This was a woman who heard both higher- and lower-order voices. Her reclusive lifestyle in a small California town allowed her to live without antipsychotic medicines. The higher-order voices occasionally gave her tips on winning racehorses whenever she genuinely needed to supplement her meager disability income. When she won, which she usually did, the lower-order voices would also try to give advice, but their predictions were invariably wrong. In fact, they usually picked the horse that came in last. She quickly learned to discriminate, and followed only the advice of the higher order.

Discernment is another faculty that is retained during spiritual emergences, but lost during second-chakra regressions. Malignant ASCs cause confusion between the inner world and consensus reality. During spiritual emergence, however, the individual recognizes that his experiences are nonconsensual and worries about this—a sure sign of basic sanity. As long as discernment is intact, the individual can distinguish what is coming from the ego—impulses, wishful fantasies, and so on—and what is coming from elsewhere. He may not be able to say *how* he knows, but he is certain that there is a real difference.

If we respond to psychotic people by automatically negating the reality of ESP when they feel they are experiencing it, we risk invalidating one of the few verities inherent in their lives. This pushes them even further away from "reality." If we do the same to nonpsychotic people, we risk cutting them off from an important aspect of their spiritual growth, thereby aggravating any spiritual emergency that accompanies the onset of these powers. Even if such a belief is obviously delusional, an artful healer still validates it as the patient's attempt to translate the sensation of an uncontrolled opening to the Ground into terms of consensual reality, which itself offers no better explanation.

This is not the same as encouraging someone in a psychotic ASC to dabble in occult practices, which are virtually always harmful. I have known three recovering schizophrenic patients who, while "playing" with a Ouija board, were beset with threatening inner voices that were extremely difficult to manage. The goal of a healer must be to affirm freedom of feeling, thought, and action as he or she reconnects a patient with a more reliable reality.

Clairvoyance, Precognition, & Psychokinesis

Besides telepathy, three other paranormal abilities have been scientifically demonstrated. Although none of these is specific to psychotic ASCs, all do occur during those states, especially during mania. More frequently, they accompany spiritual emergences and emergencies, so much so that their demonstrable presence can help to distinguish these benign conditions from malignant psychotic ASCs.

Clairvoyance is a kind of ESP in which the receiver does not "read" the thoughts of another person, but rather the state of some object. For instance, when parapsychology researchers tried standard card-guessing experiments without a "sender" actually seeing each card as it was turned, they were surprised to find that the "receivers" scored nearly as high as during telepathy experiments. Early in my career when a patient told me of his newfound clairvoyant faculty, I thought he was entering a manic episode. Only later did I realize he was in the midst of spiritual emergence. He related this experience:

> I was hiking in the mountains when I felt this peculiar surge of energy flow through my body, and I could see things with special clarity, as if everything around me was alive and aware of me. I noticed a boulder that seemed to be glowing. I had an irresistible urge to pick it up, and when I did there was a fine, unbroken Chumash Indian arrowhead under it. Later, I got the same feeling, only this time I felt an urge to leave the trail and hike cross-country. I must have come across an old Indian campground, because I found several pieces of pottery, bone fish hooks, and a stone axe head. At one point something told me to dig in a certain place, and I uncovered a string of beads several inches below the surface. For the next few weeks I found myself dreaming about the Chumash and what their life was like. [This person now has assembled one of the finest private collections of local Indian artifacts in Southern California.]

Despite its demonstrable validity, many scientists who reluctantly accept telepathy refuse to accept the possibility of clairvoyance. This is because it is easy to imagine an undiscovered radiolike energy that relays information from one brain to another, but the notion of receiving accurate information about an object of which no one else is aware does violence to our ideas of cause and effect. Lawrence LeShan put his finger on the reason that anyone experiencing clairvoyance might question his sanity.

> If [clairvoyance] is possible, then anything is possible and nothing is impossible. I may find myself living in a universe in which I understand nothing and can predict nothing. A world gone mad!

Even more disruptive to the materialistic worldview is *precognition*, which refers to the paranormal ability to predict future events. It is impossible for materialistic models to explain how events that have not yet occurred could transmit information back in time to affect us in the present. Yet precognition has been demonstrated in careful laboratory experiments, during which subjects were asked to intuitively guess which of four colored lamps on a computer panel would next turn on. The specific color was determined by one of the most random events in the universe, the radioactive decay of strontium 90, which follows a pattern that is unforeseeable by scientific means. After thousands of trials, researchers found that several subjects could predict the unpredictable against odds of more than 10 billion to one. As is true for most ESP research, some subjects consistently showed extreme sensitivity to future events, while others demonstrated no ability at all.

Precognitive information often infiltrates awareness as warning premonitions before disasters, a sort of mild but nagging "paranoia." Studies of railroad accidents show that significantly fewer passengers board trains that later crash than would be predicted by normal passenger flow patterns, indicating that some potential victims are somehow forewarned. Not surprisingly, premonitions often arrive in dreams. I have heard more accounts of this kind of ESP from my patients than any other, and I have learned to take them seriously. The following is an example.

> Gary, whom I had never before met, called me for an emergency appointment. When he arrived, he appeared extremely frightened. "My family thinks I've gone crazy, so if I tell you this story you must promise you won't commit me. Nothing like this ever happened to me before."
>
> After I offered my assurances, he told me about a vivid dream he had six months earlier in which he was driving

his car. A yellow Volkswagen shot out of a side street and slammed into his fender. He abruptly awakened in a cold sweat. A few days later, he was slightly injured when a yellow VW crashed into his car exactly as he dreamed it would.

"I didn't know what to make of that, so I just put it out of my mind until I had another dream two nights ago," Gary said. This time a big truck crested a hill and hit me head-on. I don't know, but I think I was killed, or hurt real bad. Since then I refuse to drive my car. My family told me they're not going to taxi me around forever, but I'm too scared to try it myself. What should I do?

After getting to know him a little better, and not finding any other reason for him to fear driving, I asked, "How long was the time between the first dream and the accident."

"Three days," he replied.

"Well, I'd suggest that you wait twice that long before you drive again, then see how you feel about it. Come see me again when the time is up."

Gary called a few days later to cancel his appointment. "My wife says you must be nuttier than your patients," he said, "but I think you gave me good advice. Last night I had another dream in which I saw that same big truck disappearing down the road. I think I'll go back to driving now."

Of all psychic phenomena, *psychokinesis*—the ability to mentally move an object or alter a physical substance—is the easiest to demonstrate. Most of the successful experiments were performed with dice-rolling machines. The subject simply wishes for a particular number to come up, and the results are compared with those expected by chance. As with other ESP experiments, physical variables, such as the distance of the subject from the dice, do not affect results, but psychological variables do. For instance, if the subject believes that standing far from the table gives better results, then allowing him to do so usually improves his score.

Psychokinesis seems to be most prevalent during puberty, especially in teens with repressed anger or sexual conflicts. The Israeli psychic Uri Geller's TV demonstrations of metal bending may or may not have been genuine, but following his shows hundreds of teens phoned in to the studios claiming that watching his performances stimulated them to discover similar powers in themselves. Sometimes the onset of psychokinesis in a disturbed adolescent leads to a diagnosis of psychosis, such as in a twelve-year-old boy I met during my psychiatric training:

> Ralph was assigned to my care during morning rounds, where his case was presented as "compulsive lying and vandalism with incipient psychosis." When I first entered his room, Ralph was sitting on the edge of his hospital bed fingering a steel house key. When I asked what was troubling him, he spontaneously broke out crying and denied doing the things he had been accused of. "They said I ruined all the silverware and broke glass figurines around the house. I never touched any of that stuff!"
>
> As I became familiar with the case, I learned that Ralph recently was punished by restriction to his home after his parents caught him masturbating. Feeling restless and frustrated about not being able to join his friends, he read a magazine article in which there was a description of psychic metal bending. A short time later, he heard a loud rumble in the kitchen drawer and found the entire set of the family's silverware twisted out of shape. An iron fireplace poker was similarly bent. During the next few days, several pieces of glassware mysteriously fell off shelves while he was home alone. Because he consistently denied causing any of this destruction, he was hospitalized for psychiatric evaluation.
>
> Over the course of several conversations, Ralph admitted that he practiced bending metal objects in the way described in the article. Once I pledged not to speak of our talks to his family, he agreed to demonstrate his ability. Ralph then rubbed the thick doorkey lightly with his fingers, and I was aghast to witness it slowly deforming out of shape. He then set the key down on a table, and it continued to bend for a few moments more, even though he was not touching it. Despite this convincing demonstration of psychokinesis, Ralph steadfastly maintained that he was not aware of destroying any objects in his home, only feeling frustrated and angry at his parents. He insisted, "Ghosts must have done it."
>
> After several family therapy sessions in which Ralph's parents were instructed about normal adolescent sexuality, and Ralph learned to assert his frustrations ver-

bally, he went home. A year later, his family reported that there were no more occurrences of these "poltergeist" phenomena.

MADNESS & PSYCHIC "SENSITIVES"

Parapsychologists recognize the existence of *sensitives*—people who consistently possess telepathic and other paranormal abilities, sometimes through inwardly perceived voices and visions. Psychic sensitivity often runs in families, although it follows no predictable pattern of inheritance, sometimes appearing spontaneously for the first time, sometimes following a multigenerational history. Although many sensitives are quite well adjusted, university studies reveal that a significant percentage have specific personality quirks.

One study of sensitives justified some general conclusions about their personalities. Researchers described them as overreactive, histrionic, disorderly in thinking, "inadequate in will," and having "disintegrative personalities." They were more likely than the average person to hallucinate under conditions of sensory deprivation. Other studies revealed them to be more emotional than rational, vacillating in mood, easily distracted, unconcerned with logical inconsistencies in thought, suggestible, and ready to accept new ideas without criticism. The majority are female and tend to be vivid dreamers, readily hypnotizable, and easily overwhelmed by psychic eye-openers like LSD and marijuana, which they generally learn to avoid. As children, they were likely to have had a menagerie of guardian angels, imaginary playmates, and toy animals, which they regarded as intimate friends.

Although these studies were performed before the diagnosis of borderline personality was recognized, the character traits attributed to sensitives appear similar to those of that weakly bounded condition. It must be emphasized, however, that many people with natural telepathic sensitivity demonstrate no psychopathology at all, and some use their intuitions to help others. Sensitivity follows openings to the Ground from whatever cause. It may be an aspect of a healthy and unconstricted personality, a harbinger of spiritual emergence, or the result of years of spiritual practice that gradually open the sixth chakra.

At this point an important question arises. If ESP occurs regularly during crisis states, such as when a family member is endangered, could it operate within us at a subliminal level *all the time?* The question strikes at the heart of the inside/outside distinction so vital to understanding psychotic experience. When a schizophrenic tells us that "aliens with laser beams" implant ideas in his head, or a manic tells us he is guided by "cosmic forces," are they describing glimpses into an aspect of consciousness shared by us all? Can any of us be sure which thoughts are authentically "ours," and which originate from the "outside?"

If indeed we are constantly influenced by subliminal extrasensory inputs, there must be a threshold of awareness that differs among various individuals, and also within the same individual according to his moment-to-moment state of consciousness. We might speculate that the range of this threshold is set during original repression, partially influenced by one's genetic endowment. Throughout life, the threshold varies within this range according to the integrity of one's self-boundary, the level of stress, one's willingness to explore altered states of consciousness, and perhaps other unknown factors.

Psychotics and others with permeable self-boundaries remind us that we may be more affected by telepathic impressions than we realize. Most are probably of an undramatic nature, which we experience as hunches or subtle feelings of attraction or revulsion toward others— good and bad "vibes" of common parlance. These blend with memory fragments to emerge partially masked, an amalgam of self and nonself. The implication is that telepathy is deeply rooted in human nature, but is repressed by the ego during the third chakra. It is then gradually revived, with the addition of willful control, as one gains the higher chakras. In the other direction, the breakdown of original repression that follows psychotic regression reawakens ESP, for better or worse.

TRANCE CHANNELING & MULTIPLE PERSONALITIES

Channeling, a kind of paranormal information transfer that seems outrageous to many, is a contemporary expression of what used to be called *mediumship.* Channeling bears a close relationship to multiple personality disorder, as well as to hallucinations that occur in psychotic ASCs. Jon Klimo, who wrote a comprehensive and objective book on the subject, offers this definition:

> Channeling is the communication of information to or through a physically embodied human being from a source that is said to exist on some other level or dimension of reality than the physical as we know it, and that is not from the normal mind (or self) of the channel.

Although entering a trance ASC to make contact with unseen sources of prophetic wisdom is a practice at least as ancient as the oracle at Delphi, there is no other paranormal phenomenon that elicits such howls of derision from materialist scientists, who single out channeling as a prime example of New Age buffoonery. The fact that a few channels earn large sums of money from theatricalized presentations of revealed wisdom from long dead "entities" does little to enhance its credibility. Just as was true during the heyday of mediumship earlier in this century, there is little doubt that some of these modern mediums are outright frauds with a cleverly staged act that convinces only the credulous.

Yet there is also little doubt that many modern channels are sincere about the experiences they report, whatever the actual nature of their sources of channeled information. Few knowledgeable people call MPD victims fraudulent, but the idea that a discarnate entity can temporarily speak through a channel is not a bit more incredible than an "alter" abruptly elbowing aside the core personality in MPD. It is well known that many MPD victims have among their alters "helper selves" that are similar to channeled entities. These give guidance and comfort, and may persuade other alters to join together for the common good.

Just as hypnosis can bring out alters in MPD, a channel enters a self-induced trance during which an entity speaks through him. Also like MPD, the channel may or may not later recall the experience. Some channeled entities claim to be extraterrestrials, others identify themselves as beings from "other dimensions," and a few even claim to be God. But most say they are spirits of the dead, usually from ancient cultures with advanced mystical traditions. Despite this impressive lineage, much of what comes through is no more than vaguely spiritualized psychobabble. The following is illustrative:

> I am Ramtha, the Enlightened One, indeed, that which is termed servant unto that which is called Source, to that which is termed the Principle Cause, indeed, unto that which is termed Life, unto that which is termed Christus— God experiencing that which is termed Man, man experiencing that which is termed God—am I a servant unto also. And who be He that be divine enough to be that which is termed the tranquillity of all things within His being? You!

Yet some channeled material goes considerably deeper, exceeding the personal capabilities of the channel. Although often cast in Christian imagery, most channeled messages simultaneously reflect an Eastern point of view in which human beings are godlike participants in a universal mind, evolving through a series of lifetimes or planes of existence toward eventual reunion with the Divine. Other common themes are that we create our own realities from which we learn and evolve, that the ego is a small part of a higher self, and that the universe is inhabited by sentient beings on nonphysical planes of existence.

The following excerpt from *A Course in Miracles,* a lengthy tome channeled by a Columbia University psychologist, is illustrative of the mixture of Christian symbols and the perennial philosophy.

> There is nothing outside you. That is what you must ultimately learn, for it is the realization that the kingdom of Heaven is restored to you . . . The Kingdom of Heaven is the dwelling place of the Son of God, who left not his father and dwells not apart from Him. Heaven is not a place nor a condition. It is merely the awareness of perfect oneness, and the knowledge that there is nothing else; nothing outside this oneness and nothing else within.

Channeling sharply challenges the prevailing closed model of human consciousness on which current explanations of MPD are based. This closed model holds that individual self-boundaries are inviolate; nothing gets in or out without passing through the senses or organs of communication. Alternate personalities in MPD are created de novo from an individual psyche and are wholly contained within it, although generally beyond awareness. In contrast, channeling implies a personality entering from *outside* the channel's self-boundaries. There are even some channels who are unable to control the process and are at the mercy of the whims of their entity. In these cases the distinction between channeling and MPD is quite weak, although some differences remain.

For example, unlike the alters of MPD, the majority of entities channeled throughout the long history of the phenomenon come across as benign, helpful, and loving. On the whole they seem to be more spiritually evolved and self-aware than the average man or woman. Although three-fourths of MPD subjects have alters who are under age twelve, no reported channeled sources have been children. Also, most channels contact one entity, while most MPD subjects have more than one alter. By and large, channels do not demonstrate conspicuous psychopathology, and have endured childhoods no better or worse than ordinary people.

These differences are understandable if we adopt an open model of the mind as suggested by the perennial philosophy. Almost all MPD victims were physically or sexually abused during their passage through second-chakra consciousness, a time of normal permeability to the Ground. To cope, they escaped into dissociative ASCs much like a hypnotic trance. The closed model suggests that at this point a second, third, or several psychic membranes form around split-off parts of the self—just as the original ego membrane did—creating a series of alters. However, this fails to explain why many alters are complete, complex personalities with their own religious and food preferences, talents, allergies, and even languages.

In contrast, the open model recognizes that any trancelike ASC renders self-boundaries unusually permeable to outside influence. The dissociated self of an abused child might then act as a "beacon" within the Ground, attracting clusters of conscious energies specific to its level of development. These could solidify around the core self and "stick," acquiring identities of their own through their association with an embodied human self. Alters then take on personal traits by crystallizing around the core personality's unmet needs, such as aggressive defense, expression of rage, or passive dependence. The implication is that alters are coherent nonphysical centers of intelligence, will, and sometimes wisdom who must be dealt with in their own right. As an artful healer teaches the core self to meet its needs on its own, the alters gradually dissolve their self-boundaries and unite into a composite whole.

We know that consciousness accrues to brains, but that does not prove that brains are *necessary* for consciousness to aggregate into willful and intelligent forms, or that selfhood is always limited to brain-type structures. We take for granted the association of mental activity with the physical brain, but that may be merely one way for consciousness to organize itself. In the open model of the psyche, our individual minds are part of a vast and deeply mysterious sea of consciousness, with which they interact. Such theories may initially seem fantastic to people whose sensibilities are accustomed to closed-reality models of technological cultures. But are they more farfetched than the orthodox idea of several complex personalities, complete with their own identities, agendas for living, and physiological responses, being instantaneously created and then coexisting within the same brain?

The open model suggested by channeling and MPD also encourages us to rethink current theories of the hallucinated voices that accompany a variety of psychotic ASCs. The presence of lower-order voices in schizophrenia suggests a general permeability to the Ground that allows beings of lower evolutionary status to collect like parasites around a damaged and vulnerable self in much the same way that alters adhere to an MPD victim. Of course in schizophrenia, these voices speak *to* the individual, whereas in channeling and MPD they speak *through* him. However, the difference is more one of degree than of substance. So we might speculate that channeling is a voluntary and higher-level manifestation of the same mysterious process that underlies psychotic hallucinations and MPD.

As yet there is no way to conclusively prove the superiority of the open model of the psyche over the closed, or vice versa. Perhaps there never will be. But the stubbornly demonstrable facts of telepathy and other paranormal events, bolstered by the age-old phenomena of channeling and MPD, strongly suggest that human minds are relatively open systems, some more so than others. They also suggest that consciousness is far more than a passive by-product of the brain, and is more complex and universal than any of us can know. The challenge is to come up with new theories that fit *all* the data, rather than ignoring important aspects of human experience simply because they don't fit in.

DREAMS & MADNESS

There are few statements made by people in psychotic ASCs that would not seem reasonable if preceded by the phrase, "Last night I dreamed that . . . " Whether dreams are called "messengers from the gods," "the royal road to the unconscious," or "the last natural channels of communication with the supernatural," they have been recognized from the dawn of history as radical departures from everyday reality. As we stroll through our sometimes delightful, sometimes terrifying dream landscapes, we gain a personal glimpse of the everyday reality of people in psychotic ASCs.

Each of us enters a dream ASC several times a night. During the first period of twilight sleep, we might see fragmented visual images passing through our awareness as it gradually opens to the Ground. Although these images can be quite vivid, unlike a full-fledged dream they lack a plot, and we take no part in the play of events. As sleep deepens, our brain waves gradually slow. Then, from four to six times a night, at about ninety-minute intervals, a dramatic event "wakes up" our brain, despite a near-paralysis of body movement. During this period, our eyes dart about under closed lids, our heart-rate surges, breathing speeds up, penis and pelvic organs become congested, and blood is shunted toward our brain. This is called REM (rapid eye movement) sleep, and it lasts up to twenty-five minutes. If we are awakened, we will usually report being in the midst of a vivid dream, typically with a plot and often in color.

In intensity of arousal, REM sleep resembles excited wakefulness. Yet the dreamer is far removed from worldly events and is difficult to awaken. Not only does the brain shut off the senses, but it gears up to handle vast amounts of information, especially those barely audible rhythms of subthreshold ESP that are obscured by the raucous din of waking activity. The fact that REM begins early in fetal development, and that newborn infants spend about half their time idling in the REM state, suggests a special openness to the Ground from the first stirrings of life. We might wonder what mysterious events populate the un-molded consciousness of a fetus and newborn during his prolonged immersion in the REM state.

Our dream experiences afford us a unique view of what life is like in psychotic ASCs in which the limbic system dominates brain function without much input from the cortex. In our dreams we feel strong primitive emotions such as anger, fear, frustration, and lust. But softer adult emotions like compassion and empathy are less prominent. The sense of free will so characteristic of ordinary waking life is notably absent. Although thinking of a sort does occur in dreams, long-term planning is nonexistent, concentration is fleeting, and we cannot shift attention flexibly among several objects as when awake. We accept bizarre and improbable events without the least doubt or surprise at what is taking place. Never do we compare dream events to consensual reality, nor do we say, "Hold on here, this is just impossible!" In other words, our emotions, cognitions, and reality testing are virtually identical to what occurs in severely psychotic ASCs.

Recent research suggests that the link that led Freud to liken the dream to a "model psychosis" is that psychotic hallucinations and delusions are partially triggered by dreams intruding into the waking state. At these moments, the subject is flooded with images from his personal subconscious and from the Ground. During schizophrenic ASCs, a person may wander about in a kind of permanent somnambulistic dream.

This idea gains credence from research in which volunteers were deprived of sleep for several days at a time. The experimental subjects entered a floridly psychotic ASC, as did Peter Tripp, a New York disc jockey who staged a "wake-a-thon" as a publicity stunt. After a few days with no sleep, Tripp developed vivid hallucinations and paranoia. He saw spider webs in his shoes, worms crawling on his tweed suit, and flaming auras surrounding his furniture. After eight days of sleeplessness, he accused his examining doctors of being undertakers and fled from them to escape being buried alive. Thirteen hours of sleep rid him of his psychosis, but he complained of depression for months afterward.

Similar psychotic symptoms afflict people who are allowed to sleep but are awakened at the onset of each REM phase. This induces a "REM pressure" that results in nearly twice as many dreams the next night. This "REM rebound" has important connections with psychotic ASCs. During waking hours, dream-deprived subjects begin to have cyclic feelings of persecution, difficulty concentrating, irritability, and mounting anxiety. These cycles run at intervals of ninety minutes, just as normal REM episodes do during sleep, and they are accompanied by brain-wave changes identical to those of REM sleep.

The connection between psychotic experience and dreams was further reinforced when sleep researchers discovered that schizophrenic patients who are deprived of REM sleep show no REM rebound the next night. This strongly suggests that schizophrenics discharge accumulated REM pressure while awake as dreamlike hallucinations and delusions. The fact that antipsychotic medicines like Thorazine increase REM activity during sleep adds even more credence to this idea.

People in manic ASCs are similarly vulnerable to REM intrusions during wakefulness. Both acute schizophrenic and manic ASCs can be triggered in vulnerable people when they skip even one night of sleep. Once a manic ASC gains momentum, it sets up a vicious cycle that causes an individual to forgo sleep altogether, setting the stage for ever more intrusions of dream consciousness into the waking state.

From ancient times, dreams have been recognized as a source of precognition, as would be expected from any ASC that opens self to Ground. Many people today have had experiences, such as in the case of Gary, presented earlier, in which they received advance warning of a calamitous event. Experienced psychotherapists hear dozens of stories of dreams that later took place in waking life. One from my own files is typical.

> Marie is a mother of five who told me of a vivid dream in which she was in a stark white room with a man and a woman. The woman was dressed in a pale green outfit, and the man was wearing a dark blue suit, maroon tie, and black wingtip shoes. They told her that her youngest son was killed in a bicycle accident.
>
> Marie and I explored possible covert sources of anger toward her son that might have shaped the dream image, but nothing special came up. She decided on her own to forbid her son to ride his bicycle for a while.
>
> When Marie arrived for her next appointment a week later, she was in shock and grief. Her son had disobeyed her and took his bicycle to school. When she learned that her son had been injured in an accident, she went to the local hospital, where she was told of his death by a man and woman who fit her dream description exactly.

The link between dreams, ESP, and psychotic ASCs may eventually be found in the limbic system. We know that the limbic system is highly active during dreams and certain psychotic ASCs, when it is also freed from the control of the cortex. Spontaneous telepathy is associated with strong emotion and with people who are closely bonded. Similarly, psychic sensitives are often highly emotional ("limbically predominant") people who tend to ignore intellectual explanations in favor of feeling their way to understanding. Conversely, intellectuals and other "cortically predominant" people who have trained themselves to devalue their emotions, or even block them from awareness, consistently score low on ESP tests. Admittedly, this evidence is circumstantial, but it points the way for future research. It indicates that each of us has a latent potential for reconnecting with the Spiritual Ground and the collective soul of humanity through the medium of our own dreams and deep feelings.

MADNESS AS A SHAMANIC VOCATION

One of the ways a sixth-chakra adept controls the paranormal is through lucid dreaming, a technique wellknown to shamans in pretechnological cultures. Many shamans *dream* their preternatural skills, but their definition of dreaming includes far more than ordinary sleep dreams. Lucid dreams are ASCs in which the dreamer is fully aware that he is dreaming. From this watchful stance, the shaman controls the events of his dream, and therefore its capacity to predict or even *determine* the future. Some older shamans profess to have begun lucid dreaming in their mother's womb, a process that they continue throughout their lives to master their tribal roles as prophets and healers.

Thus the Yaqui *brujo* Don Juan Mateus initiated his apprentice Carlos Casteneda into the sixth-chakra consciousness of the shamanic sorcerer through a technique he called *dreaming*. Castaneda learned to accomplish *dreaming* by striving to locate and control his hands in his ordinary dreams, then extending this power to choosing all his dream actions as he would make any other choice in life. As Don Juan told him, once this is accomplished, "there is no difference between what you do when you sleep and what you do when you are not sleeping." The puppet strings connected to the archetypes of reality itself then fall within the grasp of the shaman.

Compared with modern cultures, pretechnological societies not only are more tolerant of individuals who spontaneously enter ASCs, but actively seek them out for shamanic training. Shamans are found in nearly all archaic cultures, where they are accorded revered positions as prophets, healers, and intermediates between society and the supernatural. A novice shaman studies paranormal techniques of proven efficacy within his tribe, but he earns his full shamanic status only undergoing a spiritual emergence of an intensity that would cause it to be regarded in modern cultures as an acute psychotic ASC.

This is not to say that all psychoses in archaic societies result in shamanism, or that all shamans have been psychotic. Most aboriginal cultures clearly distinguish between shamans and chronically deranged people. A shaman must be able to handle everyday reality *better* than his fellow tribesmen. He must know how to enter nonordinary states of consciousness for the sake of prophesy or healing, and then return at will. Truly regressive mental states with pointless delusions or inexplicable behavior, such as a man persistently roaming about his village conducting himself like a hungry dog, would be even less accepted in a subsistence society than in an affluent one.

Joseph Campbell clearly outlined the difference between a regressed psychotic and a shaman engrossed in a visionary trance.

> What is the difference between the predicament of the [schizophrenic] and that of the trance-prone shaman? The answer is simply that the primitive shaman does not reject the local social order and its forms; in fact, it is actually by virtue of those forms that he is brought back to rational consciousness. And when he has returned, furthermore, it is generally found that his inward personal experiences reconfirm, refresh, and reinforce the inherited local forms; for his personal dream-symbology is at one with the symbology of his culture. Whereas, in contrast, in the case of a modern psychotic patient, there is a radical breakoff and no effective association at all with the symbol system of his culture.

Yet there are many similarities between the shaman's calling and a psychotic ASC. First, the shaman's position is traditionally inherited, suggesting a genetic predisposition. An adolescent considered suitable for shamanic initiation is usually markedly introverted, apt to spend long hours in self-absorbed solitude during which he engages in a life-and-death battle with his unmastered psychic energies. He tends to be seized by mysterious illnesses, such as epilepsy or catatonic episodes. Despite his aloofness and introversion, he can be emotionally explosive, which increases his social estrangement. During adolescence he is progressively absorbed in a narrow circle of ideas and shuns sleep to the point where the boundaries between sleep and waking are unclear.

The onset of shamanic power is marked by a spontaneous trance ASC in which the youth experiences a hallucination, usually auditory, but sometimes also visual, repeated several times. This is seen as a "spirit voice" from an animal guide that gives specific instructions about the path he must follow. The future shaman's family believes that he is acutely ill, but the elder shamans know better, promptly diagnosing the symptoms as the onset of shamanic power and predicting cure as soon as certain "adjustments" are made. The novice then joins the exclusive company of other shamans, whose task is to train him to explore and ultimately master the spirit world. If this makes him seem a bit crazy to his old family and friends, so much the better.

Shamanic training sharply contrasts with the treatment accorded people having spiritual emergencies in technological cultures. Here such people are deemed unable to tolerate the stark terrors of their inner world and are prematurely forced to redirect their attention back to the world of the senses. Modern cultures offer few guidelines for using such altered perception to advantage, and their demands for an unnatural conformity only intensifies the individual's anguish over and above the original anxieties of the crisis situation. When people in spiritual emergencies are prevented from working through their inner chaos, any resolution will be incomplete, often fostering a lifelong spiritual constriction.

Shamanic training proceeds in the opposite direction, which could serve as a model for artful healers in our culture to respond to confirmed spiritual emergences. The shamanic aspirant is encouraged to *go toward* his inner vision, to strike up conversations with higher-order voices, to embrace his fear, the better to familiarize himself with his subjective world. He may then be ritually given psychoactive herbs to propel him even deeper into other realities. All the while, he is afforded emotional support by teachers who draw upon traditional tribal knowledge to assist his inward journey. His adjustment is made easier by virtue of the respected social position awaiting him when his training is complete.

So the goal of shamanic training is not to restore a "sick" individual to "normal," for once a person emerges spiritually, he can never be like most others. Instead, he learns to cope with an expanded reality by developing the internal technology to enter and return from the far-flung reaches of the spirit universe. He conditions himself to withstand states of extreme mental acuity in which his sensitivity to the Ground is many times greater than normal and entire areas of his being that were previously inaccessible are exposed. He becomes a powerful and flexible member of his society, a "healed madman" rather than the cowed and fearful conformist he might become in another time and place.

The sixth-chakra capacities of ESP, shamanic powers, and channeling indicate that materialism can no longer claim to be a complete or even a "scientific" philosophy. To be true to its own methods and observations, science can no longer assert that the universe is a mechanical system determined from top to bottom by laws that govern physical matter. This inelastic model may be contrasted with the cosmology of the ancient Greeks, who retained the idea of a stable physical universe but included unstable gods as part of it. The gods could intervene miraculously in specific situations, but never in the universal pattern. Ultimately, even the gods were subject to Logos, the underlying order of the cosmos. This maintained equilibrium, but there was also room for the miraculous, which was the work of the residents of Olympus. We may rejoice that it is still possible to petition Olympian heights for hidden wisdom.

Each of us maintains a degree of forgetfulness of our identity as a dweller within a common consciousness. This holds us back and causes us to hold others back from reuniting with our larger selves and our Source. The first glimmerings of remembrance begin with the opening of the heart at the fourth chakra and quicken as we integrate the sixth. We are then ready to return from our exile out of Eden and reach for the unitive consciousness of the seventh and highest chakra.

CHAPTER 15

Seventh Chakra: Madness & Mysticism

◆

Ah, but a man's reach should exceed his grasp,
Or what's a heaven for?
ROBERT BROWNING

Be of good cheer.
It is I.
Be not afraid.
MATTHEW 14:27

THE JOURNEY HAS been long, and the trials many. The time for homecoming is near. As a mature individual expands into the unbounded consciousness of the Sahasrara chakra, he or she completes the long journey through the world of material form. Now he *remembers* the infinite abundance that was his before original repression closed his inner eye. He bears within him the accumulated wisdom of a lifetime lived among his fellow men and women. He gratefully returns this hard-won knowledge to its oceanic Source for safekeeping.

The seventh chakra represents the crowning evolutionary goal of humanity, the culmination of our long and painful exile, and our triumphant return to Eden. It has been said that within the seventh chakra there are seven more chakras representing ever higher levels of transcendence and nearness to divine perfection. However, few of us ever reach the stage where we need be concerned with such otherworldly enigmas.

Unless we do, we might better focus on the ultimate worldly epiphany and the hallmark of seventh-chakra consciousness: the experience of *mystical unity*. Although mystical experiences come in great variety, the following story told by a physician is typical:

> I had just finished my medical internship and was hiking alone for several days in the Sierra Nevada Mountains, trying to unwind, when I awoke one morning feeling especially exhilarated. Everything around me seemed perfect just as it was. The air was crisp and cool, the sun played with the wispy high clouds, and a songbird piped away in the giant redwood that gave me shelter during the night. Joyfully, I packed my gear and began hiking toward my next camping place. My feet seemed hardly to touch the ground, and my pack was never lighter. Then something told me to stop and sit under a pine by the side of the trail.
>
> When I closed my eyes to let the sunshine warm my face, I suddenly felt myself jolted out of my physical body. It was as if I was floating near the treetops. Nothing like that had ever happened to me before. But instead of being frightened, I knew that I should just go along with what was happening, that nothing would harm me. I don't know if I could have seen my body back on the hillside or not, because I didn't look. That's because I immediately felt myself drawing near to a brilliant golden-white light that radiated such perfect love that I could only bask in it in awe. There was also a deep, resonant humming sound that filled me with its vibrating energy. Words fail me here, so I can't tell you of the immense glory of the light or the wonder of being near it, but I recognized it as something I have always known, but somehow forgotten. It and I were one and had been from eternity, although at the same time it was more—infinitely more—than what I feel myself to be.
>
> Time and space were irrelevant during this experience, but I felt that I was not ready to go forward into the light, and it slowly retreated into the distance. At that point, I mentally looked back and saw the pattern of my life as a whole, all the little pieces of my personality, some in harmony, others conflicting. I felt that I had a choice of changing any part of myself or leaving the whole thing alone. There was even the choice of not coming back at all, but I was young and healthy and just starting my medical career,

so that didn't seem right. Finally I got a feeling that my bladder was full, so I'd better decide right away.

Well, here I am telling you about this, so you can see I came back, though I haven't been the same since. Before that I was an atheist. That sure ended fast, but I still can't find a religion that makes me feel the way I felt that day. I mean, it was so *real* . . . I think I am more loving and considerate toward others now, and feel more a part of humanity, although it's easier for me to see through all the little social games, too. In medical school, all I could think about was making lots of money, but that's not so important to me anymore, and I give my patients better care. Life is easier, not so serious, but with a lot more freedom and purpose. All in all, I consider the experience a moment of grace that started me on a higher path. That was fifteen years ago, but it still stands out as the most important day of my life!

Although similar mystical experiences can occur during any stage of development, when they are fully integrated they signal the self's expansion into the seventh chakra, the fulfillment of a life exceptionally well lived. When such experiences break through to people centered at lower chakras (the person in the above example was in the late stages of the third chakra at the time), they usually elevate them to the next-higher level of awareness and start them firmly on a spiritual path.

This chapter describes the mystical experience and its confusing relationship to schizophrenic and manic ASCs. We will also explore the roles of meditation and traditional religion in spiritual emergencies and other psychotic ASCs.

SEVENTH-CHAKRA CONSCIOUSNESS

The lifetime of spiritual growth that separates a fully evolved psyche from an infant's preevolved consciousness readies us to return to our Source. Recall that our task as we pass through the first three chakras is to consolidate a semipermeable psychic membrane separating self from Ground, and then to form an even more tightly bounded structure—the ego—within this outer boundary. If successful, we become hearty third-chakra warriors, emancipated, courageous, and rigorously competent as we compete for wealth, security, and a mate. Ideally, as we master these skills we also retain enough awareness of our larger selves to chip away at original repression and begin the long trek back to the Garden.

Our third-chakra worldliness, fortitude, and independence serve us well during that journey.

As we traverse the fourth, fifth, and sixth chakras, our task is to dissolve those timeworn and obsolete psychic boundaries. This takes place sequentially, first between our ego and other egos (fourth), then between our ego and the larger self (fifth), and ultimately between the larger self and the Spiritual Ground (sixth). The term *larger self* is just another way of describing the whole of our personal bit of consciousness in communion with the Spiritual Ground from which it arose, within which it is sustained, and from which it has never been separated. The essence of this union of self with Ground is captured in an ancient Hindu scripture, the Chandogya Upanishad, which tells us, "An invisible and subtle essence is the spirit of the whole universe . . . *Thou art That.*"

If our journey away from and back to the Garden is successful, we become wise sixth-chakra seers, compassionate and committed in heart, creative and spontaneous in mind, open and generous in spirit. Ideally, we have mastered the skill of suspending our egos to commune freely with the Ground as we shift away from and back to the consensus state at will. Our vision, self-control, and readiness to leave behind our six earlier identities empowers us to reopen the gates of Eden.

The sage consciousness of the seventh chakra is characterized by an absolute "withinness" that paradoxically encompasses the entire sweep of creation. Whereas the lower chakras are bursting with uncountable bits of information about the physical world and its endless circles of cause and effect, mystical consciousness is nothing if not *simple*. No longer is there an ego, or even a separate self, to keep us from the All. No longer does time split the present moment from eternity, nor does space part here from everywhere. What remains is perfect unity that pervades all being with its sublime presence. For the self that confronts this presence, all that remains is to surrender, to *die*.

This death may be literal or symbolic. The story is well told by the Zen parable of ten bulls—progressive steps toward enlightenment depicted in a series of ten drawings framed by hand-brushed circles. In the first, the naive oxherder perceives only the tracks of his lost bull, which symbolizes the ego's resistance to self-awareness. He tracks the bull through rough terrain until, nearly exhausted, he eventually sees the bull, and then tries to tether it. The great beast puts up a violent struggle, but the herdsman's persistence prevails, and the bull, finally docile, follows. The seventh circle, titled, "Bull Transcended," depicts the herdsman finally at home absorbed in serene contemplation. The eighth, titled, "Both Bull and Self Transcended," is simply an elegantly brushed circle with nothing inside, a perfect void, unmarred by figure or form.

The story could well end here, but there are two more frames that depict the oxherder returning to his village as a sage to walk once again with his fellows and share the truth of his illumination, his every action an expression of surrender to that ideal.

This parable tells us that mystical experience, although permanently transforming, is itself impermanent. While it lasts, its intensity is such that it renders a person unable to function in the world, so lost is he in rapturous regard of the divine. Our ego-based sense of duality in which an "I" encounters a "world out there" is necessary for worldly living, but absent during such epiphanies.

The sixteenth-century mystic Saint Teresa of Avila poetically described this feeling of merging self with All.

> It is like rain falling from the heavens into a river or a spring; there in nothing but water there and it is impossible to divide or separate the water belonging to the river from that which fell from the heavens. Or it is as if a tiny streamlet enters the sea, from which it will find no way of separating itself. Or as if in a room there were two large windows through which the light streamed in: it enters in different places but it all becomes one.

Because the essence of the mystical experience is unity, it transports us far beyond the distinctions necessary for language, logic, and ordinary communication. With ego suspended, thoughts, actions, perceptions happen of themselves, with no doer, no see-er, no hearer, only *doing! seeing! hearing!* There is an obliteration of the senses and a suspension of personal selfhood, which is replaced with a much larger identification, that of the entire universe. This state is one of pure consciousness, empty of content, in which the individual directly experiences the "Ground of the Ground," which transcends even the archetypes of the sixth chakra. The contemporary mystic Da Free John described a moment of illumination.

> In an instant, I became profoundly and directly aware of what I am. It was a tacit realization, a direct knowledge in consciousness itself without communication from any other source . . . There was no thought involved in this. I am that Consciousness. There was no reaction either of joy or surprise. I am the One I recognized. I am that One . . . Then truly there was no more to realize. Every experience in my life had led to this.

During a mystical experience the psyche acts as a conduit for new insights, new meanings, new understandings, all of which are ineffable—utterly beyond the power of words to express. Intoxicated with its transcendent vision, the logical mind trips over paradox after paradox as it gropes for words of sufficient clarity and grandeur. The psychiatrist Stanley R. Dean once tried to characterize the ineffable.

> An intellectual illumination occurs that is quite impossible to describe. In an intuitive flash, one has an awareness of the meaning and drift of the universe, an identification and merging with creation, infinity and immortality, a depth beyond depth of revealed meaning—in short a conception of an over-self, so omnipotent that religion has interpreted it as God. The individual attains a conception of the whole that dwarfs all learning, speculation, and imagination, and makes the old attempts to understand the universe elementary and petty.

In this state of all-knowing, there is a paradoxical childlike innocence, a freshness of vision in which truth rings clear and self-evident, beyond need for justification through ordinary reason and language. There are no goals, because there is no future in which to attain a goal; only the eternal here and now exists. The Sanskrit term for this state of consciousness is *sat-chit-ananda:* pure being, pure consciousness, pure bliss.

Needless to say, being in the midst of a mystical experience makes it rather difficult to give a luncheon speech or drive on the freeway. But a person who is centered in the seventh chakra does not live in a state of perpetual rapture, unable to function in the world because he is busy merging with the cosmos. Far from it. Because the higher chakras subsume the lower ones, a seventh-chakra sage commands the full range of human potentials, which gives him a distinct advantage over people who can call upon only a fraction of those potentials. What is different about him is that he has *integrated* the mystical experience and identifies with the Spiritual Ground itself, not with a split-off part. From this vantage point, he can choose to operate from the whole, or from any part.

The relationship of self to brain also undergoes a final shift as the seventh chakra is integrated. Recall that during the passage through the fourth chakra, the neurological control center—the governing locus of "mind" in the brain—extends downward from the cortex to reengage the limbic system. As the fifth chakra is integrated, this expansive process includes the lower reptilian brain in a synergistic whole. Having gained the sixth chakra, the self—still identified with an individual mind—transcends biology and operates from a center within the Spiritual Ground itself. The seventh and final step leaves the limited mind behind altogether as the self identifies with the All in perfect unity. This is the final transcendence of duality, the healing of the myriad splits between inner/outer, I/not-I, self/God. At this point there are no remaining distinctions; nothing is separate from self as pure Being.

Although such peak experiences are naturally fleeting for human beings, they leave behind residues that transform the self forever. Withdrawal from society in favor of a life of contemplation is an option that some mystics take, but most renew their practical involvement in humanity with a vitality and gusto that affords them greater effectiveness in the affairs of everyday life. Some Western mystics have even become known for their proficiency in business.

For the mystic sage, there is no longer a need to renounce the world—only his ego's attachments to it. Once free from these, he lives within society with unblemished integrity, no longer experiencing its customs and rules as obstacles to self-fulfillment. A prime example is the Buddha, who, after finding enlightenment under the bodhi tree, returned to live and teach in the social world that he had relinquished many years earlier. It is said that such people live *in* this world, but are not *of* it, meaning that they have renounced their identity with social roles and are free to live like a joker who can assume any role in the deck, or to quit the game altogether.

MYSTICISM & PSYCHOTIC ASCS

A surefire way to earn a diagnosis of psychosis at a modern psychiatric clinic is to punctuate a conversation with references to losing one's identity so as to become one with all creation. In a determined effort to purge any residual connection with spirituality, Western psychology takes pains to reduce mystical experiences to infantile states of consciousness, or to equate them with madness. Freud, for instance, equated the mystical experience with the "oceanic" state of being undifferentiated from one's mother, a "restoration of limitless narcissism." Similarly, the eminent psychoanalyst Franz Alexander referred to Zen meditation as "training in catatonia" and "a sort of artificial schizophrenia." More recently, the trend is to reduce this most sublime aspect of human consciousness to abnormal discharges in the temporal lobes of the brain.

In response, the regrettable counterreaction among antipsychiatrists has been to elevate schizophrenia to transrational status by casting it as a kind of twisted mysticism. Many of these theorists also consistently confuse schizophrenia with manic ASCs. Others ignore the role of the brain in inducing malignant psychosis. Some argue, against all evidence, that first- and second-chakra regressions are breakthroughs of sixth- and seventh-chakra consciousness without the individual having first traversed the intermediate territories. If the psychotic works through a few hang-ups caused by poor parenting and social oppression, they argue, he will quickly realize his hidden potential as a seer.

On the surface, it is easy to see why this error is perpetuated, for *pre*rational schizophrenia and *trans*rational mysticism are both *non*rational states. Both are openings to the Ground in which nonconsensual realities penetrate awareness. The essential difference is that the schizophrenic collapses into prerational consciousness and no longer has a working ego or command of logic to process this influx of unfamiliar energy. In contrast, the mystic transcends linear logic in favor of holistic means of processing information, although he is fully capable of linear thinking when a situation demands it. His expanded reasoning enables him to restructure nonconsensual realities into an expanded worldview that includes the old as a special case.

Although the mystic becomes temporarily imperceptive to the sensory world, this is hardly an infantile or psychotic state. Far from being lost in pointless fantasy or hallucination, he voluntarily enters into deep contemplation of consciousness itself, then returns to share his insights. Socrates, for instance, was known to stand in motionless self-absorption for hours, but would then emerge to offer brilliant dialectics conceived during his intense introspection.

Another erroneous argument points out that withdrawal from society is common to both transcendence and psychosis. However, the mystic *willingly* turns his back on worldly concerns in search of a greater good, while the schizophrenic has no choice because his chaotic ASC renders him too disorganized to cope with the complexities of modern life.

Mystics commonly proclaim that their most exalted experiences are indescribable, leading some theorists to suggest that they are preverbal. But there is a world of difference between lacking command of language and confronting realities for which language has no words. By its very nature, language requires that we divide things into distinct categories. When we assign a word to an object or action, we emphasize its differences from other things. But the mystical experience of unity resolves all distinctions. It is therefore beyond conventional language, which is designed to follow the logical development of one idea at a time and is inadequate to express a kind of awareness that encompasses a large number of concepts simultaneously.

Despite these difficulties in finding words for mysticism, many experiences that are now ineffable may not always be so. As more people evolve into the higher chakras, we can expect them to invent words for subtle shades of consciousness. The essence of the mystical experience may be ineffable, but certain people have managed to translate its immeasurable depth into such literature as the Tao Te Ching, the Upanishads, the Koran, the books of the Bible, and the teachings of the Compassionate Buddha. We find in these scriptures a remarkable similarity among the experiences described, which suggests a potential for ever-greater consensual validation in the future.

Another source of confusion is that once a mystic penetrates the veneer of consensual reality, he and the psychotic are alike in their unconstrained freedom to re-create reality models, which may follow their personal quirks or repressed needs. This is an ever-present danger for those on the mystical path, who often encounter subconscious "dragons" lurking in ambush. This is why a spiritual teacher, or guru, is helpful as one reaches higher planes of consciousness. Ideally, disciplined spiritual practice, having first broken through consensual reality, then provides broader, more flexible models to replace it.

Like the madman, the mystic discovers that ordinary sensory reality is one of many possible realities, a "thin veil of illusion" that is easily penetrated into deeper realms beyond. But the schizophrenic rejects consensual reality only to confront an incomprehensible universe, which he recklessly rearranges into chaotic or paranoid patterns. Endowed with the power to re-create reality, both madman and mystic feel themselves to be godlike creators of the world. At that point, the mystic surrenders the last vestiges of ego and recognizes that all sentient creatures are also godlike, even if they don't yet know it. The schizophrenic, however, desperately clutches his ego and expresses his power over reality as the quintessence of madness: "I'm God, but you're not!"

Ever since Freud wrote that "in the id [primitive, instinctual consciousness] there is nothing corresponding to the idea of time," the mystic's sense of timelessness has been confused with regressed ASCs. It is true that in both seventh- and first-chakra consciousness there is a feeling of perpetual nowness, a living of life in an infinite present moment. This is because the Spiritual Ground is timeless, eternally present. Yet it misses the point to interpret the mystic's apprehension of eternity as a throwback to an infantile state in which the self has not transcended time, but is merely ignorant of it. As the mystic immerses himself in eternity, he retains full awareness of linear time passing on another level. Far from involving a resurgence of the timeless id, the mystical experience unfolds in an eternal present that transcends duration.

Mystical insight has been falsely equated with paranoia in the sense that it feels absolutely real, beyond need for logical demonstration. Paranoia, however, is a defensive projection of disowned feelings onto others.

In contrast, the mystic accepts all his feelings and impulses as his own. Both paranoid and mystic share a portentous intuition of hidden purpose, a discovery of unseen relationship that is not apparent in the ordinary state of consciousness. This insight that "everything is connected to everything else" may equally turn out to be beatific or diabolic. The two possible interpretations are complementary expressions of a single feeling—being the center of a pattern. Because he has integrated each of the lower six chakras, the mystic evaluates and tests his intuitions in ways that are not possible for people centered in the second or third chakras, where paranoia is generated. Ever aware of the premises underlying his thoughts, he processes his conclusions on all seven levels of meaning at once, not just two or three.

Both paranoid and mystic inhabit a world in which every coincidence bears an intended message from beyond the range of the senses. For both, the smallest event explodes with hidden significance, revealing a divinely inspired order (or a devilish plot) that exposes the macrocosm in the microcosm. The mystic, however, blends a lifetime of living in consensual reality with advanced logic to meld diverse events into a sacred synthesis. This is what Andrew Weil called "positive paranoia," the insight that there is no such thing as coincidence, that all events are part of a divine plan. But having only paleologic at his command and fear in his heart, the paranoid vainly clings to his faltering ego, which distorts the Ground's unifying structure into a fantastic system of conspiracy.

Finally, the mystic's suspension of personal identity during peak moments superficially parallels the ego loss of a regressed schizophrenic. The mystic, however, tolerates this experience with equanimity and reengages the ordinary state of consciousness with a deepened perception of self in the context that all selves are one. This strikingly contrasts with the schizophrenic's inability to manage his life without a functional ego.

Joseph Campbell summed up the essential difference between seventh-chakra transcendence and second-chakra regression with a characteristic metaphor.

> The difference—to put it sharply—is equivalent to that between a diver who can swim and one who cannot. The mystic, endowed with native talents for this sort of thing and following, stage by stage, the instructions of a master, enters the waters and finds he can swim; whereas the schizophrenic, unprepared, unguided, and ungifted, has fallen or has intentionally plunged, and is drowning . . . What I am saying is that our schizophrenic patient is actu-

ally experiencing inadvertently that same beatific ocean deep within that the yogi and saint are ever striving to enjoy: except that, whereas they are swimming in it, he is drowning.

MYSTICISM & THE MANIC ASC

The situation of a person immersed in a manic episode is quite different from that of a schizophrenic, so much so that it seems certain that many cases on which antipsychiatrists based their opinions were not schizophrenic at all, but people in manic ASCs who were misdiagnosed. This would explain these patients' spontaneous recoveries and penchant for discussing their psychotic experience in glowing superlatives. Mania sets in motion a dual process in which the self expands to higher chakras while simultaneously being inundated by energies from the lower chakras. The problem is that crucial intermediate stages are bypassed, which prevents the higher inputs from being integrated and eventually allows the lower to predominate.

In this way, mania is a spiritual emergency of a special kind that is determined by the vagaries of brain chemistry. Those who view mania as pure regression overlook its spiritual dimension, and therefore forgo an opportunity to help the manic integrate the higher aspects of his experience when he returns to the ordinary state of consciousness. In common with other spiritual emergencies, a manic episode can destroy leftover impediments to growth. Although the rapid inflation of self-boundaries during mania rarely reaches the level of mystical union, this does occasionally occur. When it does, it can have lasting positive effects on the individual's life if he is fortunate enough to encounter an *artful* healer who recognizes the potential for growth inherent in his experience and helps him integrate it after the extreme phase of the ASC subsides.

Such a favorable outcome is likely if a manic ASC occurs in a person who has already integrated the fourth chakra or above. When a mystical experience occurs to people centered lower than the fourth chakra, they are usually unable to process information of that magnitude, which usually gets written off as a product of a disordered mind. The lessons tend to be quickly forgotten after the ordinary state of consciousness is restored. The same is true when a mystical experience emerges during a psychedelic trip undertaken by a person whose life has not yet prepared him for higher realization. On the other hand, some recovered manic patients are compulsively drawn to psychedelic agents in an attempt to revive the ecstatic elements of their manic ASC. This is in contrast with people recovering from schizophrenic ASCs, who usually look back upon their psychotic experiences with extreme distaste and avoid risking a return at all costs.

One recovered manic patient described his struggle to retain the significance of his ASC after he returned to ordinary consciousness.

> Throughout those periods it was my best self that was dominant, something strong and deep and tender and intense, which was, I still believe, more than just myself. My great difficulty in the period of "normality" is to remain true to the vision which came to me then. I must recognize that in this present life of active participation in the world of men, I am very far from having maintained the mystical identification which I felt so keenly during the disturbance.

Fortunately for the significant minority of people who have spontaneous flashes of mystical realization, there are proven methods for preparing the self to integrate this pinnacle of the human potential.

THE ROLE OF MEDITATION

Maybe human beings have always known how to meditate. Or possibly at some time in distant history one of our ancestors—perhaps a forlorn prisoner in some ancient dungeon—discovered that if he sat still, concentrated on his breath rising and falling, and faithfully repeated this tactic until his mind was perfectly still, some extremely interesting things happened. How he later convinced others to attempt this initially difficult technique is unknown. But the practice of meditation spread throughout Asia to become the cornerstone of the Hindu and Buddhist religions, which refined their techniques over millennia to serve as well-marked trails through the wilderness of inner experience. Western religions generally find repetitive prayer more suitable, and reserve powerful consciousness-expanding meditation techniques for an elite few who enter monastic life.

As the popularity of psychedelics spurred interest in ASCs during the 1960s, meditation became a fad among the young people of that turbulent era who sought to break away from what they felt were stale religious and social rituals. Eager to explore consciousness "on the natch," they joined the Beatles and other celebrities who followed the guru Maharishi Mahesh Yogi. Millions of disaffected youth outraged their parents' sensibilities by assuming grotesquely uncomfortable postures, chanting odd-sounding Sanskrit phrases, and rhapsodizing about "divine bliss" and "cosmic consciousness"—which, however, they rarely experienced.

Like all fads, this one soon faded, its passing hastened by overstated claims by some meditation groups that their initiates could acquire spectacular preternatural abilities like physically levitating their bodies. Efforts to popularize meditation without esoteric embellishments, such as that of the Harvard researcher Herbert Bensen, who renamed it "the relaxation response," seemed only to strip the ancient discipline of its unique spiritual value. At its peak of popularity, meditation became so faddish that some advocates hailed it as a panacea for a wide range of physical and mental maladies, including the major psychoses. The idea was that if the person in a psychotic ASC is pushed a little further into his subconscious mind, he will emerge out the back door to a higher sanity. Unfortunately, this often had disastrous effects.

Although meditation promotes an ASC of great stillness and calm, reduces the effects of stress, and promotes longevity, these are but a small part of its complex effects on the psyche and, taken by themselves, can be misleading. Practiced regularly and with discipline, meditation has the formidable power to break down original repression and reopen the self to the Spiritual Ground.

There are two basic techniques of meditation—*concentration* and *contemplation*. Both are deceptively simple. Concentrative meditation requires no more of the meditator than to sit quietly, relax, and silently repeat a sound with a specific psychological effect, called a mantra, over and over. After a short while, the meditator notices his mind wandering, at which point he takes mental note of the distraction and then returns to the mantra. Transcendental meditation is a popular form of concentrative meditation practiced for twenty minutes twice a day.

Contemplation, or receptive meditation, is an advanced technique in which the meditator uses no specific object of concentration, but intently watches the shifting contents of his awareness as an unmoving witness. The task is to vigilantly observe whatever comes to mind while remaining detached from the repetitious melodramas of the lower chakras. When the meditator inevitably gets lost in thought rather than observing it, he simply notes his distraction and returns to "mindfulness." As he lets go of each fascination, he sees beyond it, and then lets go again to see beyond that. With practice, he finds it possible to observe thoughts and feelings just as they take form in awareness. This hones self-observation in a nonverbal, noncognitive mode. The image of the ideal meditator's mind is of a polished mirror that reflects clearly, itself unchanged. Buddhist "insight" meditation (*vipassana*) and Zen "just sitting" are forms of receptive meditation.

Whatever the form, meditation gradually dissolves the ego to lay bare the primordial contents of the subconscious in both its personal and universal aspects. Practiced regularly, it permanently alters the relationships between the ego, the self, and the Ground. I cannot describe this better than did the Catholic priest and contemplative Thomas Merton.

> [Contemplation] is a vivid realization of the fact that life and being in us proceed from an invisible, transcendent, and infinitely abundant Source. Contemplation is, above all, awareness of the reality of that Source. It *knows* the Source, obscurely, inexplicably, but with a certitude that goes both beyond reason and beyond simple faith. For contemplation is a kind of spiritual vision to which both reason and faith aspire, by their very nature, because without it they must always remain incomplete . . . In contemplation we know by "unknowing." Or, better, we know *beyond* all knowing or "unknowing."

The psychologist Robert Ornstein aptly compared the meditative process to an eclipse of the sun. He pointed out that the stars are present in the sky all day long, but are obscured by the sun's glare. When the moon passes across the solar face, it obliterates that glare, and we become aware of these more subtle sources of energy. Similarly, after meditation diverts attention away from our involvements in the sensory world, the blinding glare of our inner dialogue gradually ebbs, baring the primordial contents of older and deeper brain/mind levels.

Deep meditation first exposes repressed emotional memories and archetypal imagery, but the meditator may also notice subthreshold extrasensory inputs and signals from the body's glands and viscera. Finally, even these are transcended as the meditator disentangles himself from the world of form altogether. At this point he starts to experience moments of "no-thought" as he regards the pristine consciousness of the Ground itself, devoid of content, uncolored by ego, unmixed with particular thoughts, feelings, or instincts: being as being. This pure consciousness ceaselessly flows from a center of measureless energy that dwells at the core of the self. These moments are rare and fleeting, but are shot through with unparalleled bliss.

When such intense introspection is practiced diligently over time, the meditator cannot help but shift his identity away from the ego and recognize his once-taken-for-granted self-boundaries as arbitrary creations of the mind. It is important to recognize, however, that his ego is not fragmented as in psychotic regression. The ego is transcended, but left intact to function when it is appropriate for it to do so. His self-sense becomes fluid and transparent, and encompasses ever-larger identities:

first with other people, then with consciousness itself, then with the entire universe. These expansions are naturally expressed as compassion, universal love, and commitment to the spiritual growth of all creatures.

MEDITATION & SPIRITUAL EMERGENCIES

For most psychologically healthy people, it takes months or years of practice before meditation unravels original repression and permanently opens self to Ground. Ideally, this takes place only after the individual builds up "mental muscles" to withstand such radical expansions of consciousness without regression. Before confronting the Ground, he must first confront and master the contents of his personal subconscious—buried psychic wounds and shadow elements cast out by an ego that found them unacceptable to its image. Facing these can be quite unsettling, causing some people to prematurely cease practice. Orthodox psychotherapy is well designed to deal with the shadow and can be quite helpful during this stage, although it will be inadequate for what follows.

As a constantly watched ego loosens its defenses and grows more permeable, the consciousness of the higher chakras starts to infuse it. Untying the knot of original repression has dramatic effects, which may or may not be in the direction of spiritual growth. Ideally, as the process unfolds, compassion deepens one's relationships, archetypal images inspire creativity, ESP becomes a comfortable fact of awareness, and finally the self merges with the Ground from a position of strength and joy. Along the way, the meditator learns to transcend the painful aspects of everyday life and lives with a serenity that characterizes the lives of the great mystics. Ken Wilber described this process when all goes according to plan.

> It is the natural and orderly unfolding of successively higher-order unities, until there is only Unity, until all potential is actual, until all the ground-unconscious is unfolded as Consciousness.

This ideal progression is not guaranteed, however. A sudden influx of unitive consciousness may catch one unprepared, triggering a spiritual emergency. This can be quite dangerous, challenging an artful healer to distinguish malignant regression from regression in the service of transcendence. If he suspects the latter, the healer must determine what precipitated the crisis. Was the person engaged in traditional meditation, or was he free-lancing and immoderate in his practice? Did he confront a disowned element from his personal subconscious, or was he frightened by an unaccustomed paranormal event or a surge of empathy that precipitated guilt for past insensitivities? Next, the artful healer assesses the degree of regression. Did the person take a half step backward out of fear of the unknown, or is the regression more profound? What was his chakra level prior to the crisis, and what is it when regression is arrested?

Any regression accompanied by ego fragmentation or predominant second-chakra elements—hallucinations, delusions, and so forth—is a definite signal that meditation should be immediately stopped, sometimes permanently, depending on the self's ability to emerge from the psychotic ASC. If this tactic quickly terminates the emergency, meditation may later be tried again, but only for short daily sessions under the guidance of an involved healer who helps the person deal with whatever arises. If the self is reconstituted only with difficulty, that person should engage only in spiritual practices that strengthen the ego. Not everyone needs to meditate to achieve a measure of spiritual growth. In milder regressions, temporarily scaling back meditation may be all that is needed to resolve the crisis, along with counseling focused on the specific obstacle that impeded progress. Sometimes switching from receptive to concentrative meditation will do the trick.

Many people who *never* meditate also develop spontaneous spiritual emergences or emergencies. In these cases supervised meditations may be beneficial once it is established that the problem has been precipitated by some unresolved personal factor, not a genetically programmed alteration in brain chemistry.

Meditation is most likely to help people who have already integrated fourth-chakra consciousness, or are on the verge of this expansion. In these cases, a mixture of orthodox and transpersonal psychotherapy can help clear impediments to growth from the personal subconscious, while preparing the person for symbolic death and rebirth into higher consciousness. However, people deeply involved in third-chakra scenarios seldom find any purpose in meditation. Because of their infatuation with the ego, they usually find meditation a waste of time or feel threatened by what they uncover within themselves. Needless to say, a healer who takes it upon himself to advise people in meditation should himself meditate regularly, preferably with the guidance of a self-realized teacher.

MEDITATION & PRAYER IN PSYCHOSIS

Perhaps Carl Jung was in an overcautious frame of mind when he warned Westerners against practicing yoga, which "in certain unstable individuals might easily lead to a real psychosis." Many successful practitioners of yoga and other meditative techniques in the Western world would today take exception to Jung's blanket admonition.

However, Jung's warning was on the mark for people who have an inborn or acquired tendency toward ego fragmentation. Such people are well advised to avoid these powerful techniques for expanding consciousness. This is especially true for people predisposed to schizophrenia, and also for "borderlines," whose fragile ego boundaries dissolve without constant selfobject support. Meditation is a reliable device for overcoming the limitations of the ego *only* after the ego has proved its ability to function in the world and is becoming an impediment to further spiritual advancement.

Practiced by individuals who lack a strongly bounded self, meditation can backfire and dissolve precisely what most needs to be strengthened. There are several well-documented cases of severe psychotic regression in people with a history of schizophrenia who participated in intensive meditation retreats. For these people, meditation triggered agitation, paranoia, messianic religious delusions, and suicide attempts. The lesson is that before anyone sets out to transcend the ego, he must have consolidated a strong ego in the first place. Or, as the transpersonal psychologist Jack Engler put it, "you have to be somebody before you can be nobody."

This does not mean that spiritual growth is impossible for people with unstable egos. Spiritual growth is a broad concept that simply implies that a person is making progress in mastering the tasks of the current chakra while steadily expanding toward the next. So for people who are completing the tasks of the lower chakras, or for people who regress to those levels, spiritual growth means *fortifying* the ego, not assaulting it. The final chapters of this book explore specific strategies to foster spiritual advancement at each level.

Although it draws scant attention in transpersonal circles, there is one meditationlike tactic that is quite suitable for people centered in the lower chakras. *Prayer* resembles concentrative meditation in that both require steadfast attention, and both can be soothing to mind and body. Yet prayer is not nearly as powerful a technique for altering consciousness. Because it assumes that there is a superior being *external to the self* that is somehow responsive to entreaty, prayer fortifies the ego's self/other discriminations rather than loosening its boundaries. Although people centered in higher chakras tend to view prayers of entreaty as external projections of the Ground—which they perceive as not outside the self at all—it must be remembered that regressed people do not do well with such abstract concepts, and need an externalized symbol to act as a stabilizing selfobject.

Many schizophrenics find that reciting a short prayer quiets their bothersome hallucinated voices, which have a way of shrinking from any suggestion of religion. For people who are not psychotic, but not yet ready for intensive meditation, the Catholic "prayer of simple regard" may be ideal. This resembles a mild form of contemplation in that the practitioner strives for a state of quiet alertness and inner poise as he waits to be touched by the "Holy Spirit." Because the source of the infusion is felt to be outside the self rather than hidden deep within, this technique seldom threatens original repression, yet it still has the power to help the person grow more comfortable with what may stir within his subconscious. One caveat: hypnotically repetitive prayer can easily be overdone, as it often is among fearful people in psychotic ASCs, who should be guided toward moderation.

In contrast, people predisposed to *manic* ASCs frequently benefit from meditation between manic episodes. By stimulating gradual self-expansion, meditation conditions the psyche to tolerate extreme ASCs precipitated by instabilities of brain metabolism. These unplanned infusions of Ground energies are not so disorienting to a person who is already familiar with his personal subconscious and with the Ground. It is unlikely, however, that a person in the midst of a manic ASC could be persuaded to sit still long enough to meditate, although it is not strictly contraindicated as it is in schizophrenia and borderline states.

By keeping the meditator in touch with his higher potentials, meditation also helps dampen the extremes of depression that alternate with mania. Meditation has an especially potent antidepressant effect if it precedes or follows vigorous physical exercise like running, swimming, or Hatha yoga. This combination alters brain metabolism in a manner similar to antidepressant medicines, without the bothersome side effects. Strenuous exercise is also a desirable way to divert the boiling-over energies of a person in a manic ASC, although such people often prove to be indefatigable and tend to overdo it.

THE PRE/TRANS FALLACY REVISITED

As we conclude our survey of the seven chakras, it is appropriate to take a deeper look at the lingering source of confusion between *pre*personal and *trans*personal states of consciousness. The elusive pre/trans fallacy seriously contaminates theories of both orthodox psychology and its radical alternatives. Each well-meaning system succumbs to it in its own characteristic way, and it thwarts efforts to develop a comprehensive healing approach that is of value in both psychotic ASCs and spiritual emergencies.

Because orthodox psychologists and psychiatrists are familiar with the way the ego dissòlves during psychotic and borderline ASCs, they tend to regard urges to rise *above* the ego as regressive homing instincts designed to revive a primal connection with one's mother. In assuming this stance, however, they divert many natural ego-death-and-rebirth sequences away from their natural course toward spiritual growth. The concept of a spiritual emergence or emergency is nowhere to be found in mainstream psychiatry; instead, anyone who demonstrates regression in the service of transcendence is automatically labeled as a "brief reactive" or "atypical" psychotic at best, and schizophrenic, manic, or borderline at worst. Such people are often given consciousness-constricting medicines that gainsay their chances of working through the crisis.

As Ken Wilber put it, this error is like equating rocks and rockets since both lack propellers. He continues:

> Pre and trans can be seriously equated only by those whose intellectual inquiry goes no further than superficial impressions. But until that type of mentality loses its appeal, orthodox psychiatry will continue to see saints as insane and sages as psychotic, thereby proving itself a proudly tenacious impediment to the growth and evolution of humanity on the whole.

On the other side, the antipsychiatry movement elevates premature and regressive openings of the psyche to the status of transcendent mysticism. In his influential book *Love's Body*, for instance, Norman O. Brown almost makes one wish to be schizophrenic.

> It is not schizophrenia but normality that is split-minded; in schizophrenia the false boundaries are disintegrating . . . Schizophrenics are suffering from the truth . . . The schizophrenic world is one of mystical participation; an indescribable extension of inner sense; uncanny feelings of reference; occult psychosomatic influences and powers; currents of electricity, or sexual attraction—action at a distance . . . Schizophrenics pass beyond the reality-principle into a world of symbolic connections . . . Schizophrenics pass beyond ordinary language into a truer, more symbolic language.

Following this tack, antipsychiatrists have applied to schizophrenics consciousness-expanding techniques that are suitable only for people with much stronger egos, while stubbornly withholding treatments that

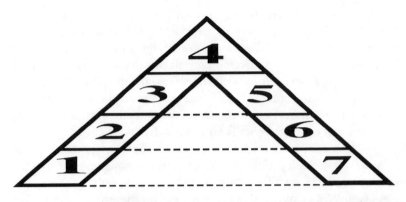

FIGURE 15–1 : *A graphic representation of the seven chakras and their relationship to the Spiritual Ground. Each chakra has its own unique tasks and learning experiences. Yet the pyramid's two sides represent vastly different stages of development. The steppingstones on the sevenfold path include three of progressive alienation of self from Ground (left-hand side), one of infusion of the self with universal love that marks the crucial turning point, and three of progressive reunion (right-hand side).*

halt regression and stabilize the ego. The results of the pre/trans fallacy are equally disastrous no matter which side falls prey to it.

In this book I have attempted to clarify the essential differences between: (1) severely regressive psychotic ASCs caused by inherited predisposition or early-life failure of self-boundary formation, (2) spiritual emergencies with benign regression in the service of transcendence, and (3) genuine spiritual experiences of people who have mastered the tasks of the lower chakras and are naturally expanding into higher consciousness. Figure 15–1 shows the superficial similarities between pre- and transpersonal states of consciousness:

The three higher chakras are superficially similar to the three lower ones by virtue of their relationship to the Ground. The first and seventh chakras appear alike because both the selfless infant and self-transcended mystic bask in blissful unity with their Source. In these egoless states, the unbounded self is open to the free flow of Ground energies. The difference is that the infant has no choice but to surrender to this immense power, while the mystic sage willfully regulates its flow so that he may function in the world in an uncommonly effective way. During his passage through the lower chakras, the mystic experienced the exquisite pain of separateness and alienation, both of which he finally transcends.

So the fully evolved sage incorporates the experiences of a lifetime, along with the joys and sufferings, passions and loves that imbue it with meaning. Through his arduous journey away from and back to Eden, he fulfills his highest human potentials and finally reclaims his divine nature. Because his individual mind is in a perpetual give-and-take relationship with its Source, an enlightened sage in turn enriches the eternally evolving Ground with the highest wisdom and love.

The second and sixth chakras bear a similar relationship. Both are stages of semipermeable self-boundaries, of constant communion with the Ground. The sixth-chakra adept and the immature toddler operate from a nonlogical stance, relying on intuition to guide them. This is where the similarities end. The toddler has no control over his emotions, instincts, drives, or degree of openness to the Ground. He uses paleologic as his exclusive means of processing information. The self-realized adept, in contrast, has mastered the logical forms available to humanity, and then develops a level of awareness in which reason no longer separates him from an intuitive grasp of reality. He can enter and emerge from ASCs at will, engage paranormal powers with precision, and assert his will over his emotions and instincts, which he nonetheless values as important sources of information.

We see that the third and fifth chakras also occupy similar levels. During the passage through the third chakra, the self identifies with its ego. In the fifth chakra, the process of transcending the ego has begun but is far from complete, as a short conversation with some of our most creative artists or accomplished scientists quickly demonstrates. Both the third and fifth chakras confer skill at manipulating concepts and objects. But in the former case the focus is on obtaining material security, while in the latter case creativity is a means of higher self-expression.

The fourth chakra stands alone at the capstone of the pyramid. It represents both the stage of greatest ego differentiation and the momentous turning point where the self tentatively reopens to the Ground, allowing its essence—universal love—to flow into it and alter its course of life. It is this love, first directed toward humanity, then toward one's own higher spiritual self, and finally toward all of creation, that motivates the journey back to the Source.

As psychiatrist M. Scott Peck pointed out, the path to sainthood always goes through adulthood, with no quick and easy shortcuts. Ego boundaries must be hardened before they can be softened. Personal identity must be firmly established before it can be transcended. One must cultivate and maintain a place in the world before one can abandon it without regression into madness. The release from ego boundaries associated with madness may provide a glimpse of nirvana, but not nirvana itself. Authentic spiritual growth can be achieved only through the persistent exercise of universal love that flows through the heart chakra at the peak of one's estrangement from the Source. This simply may not be bypassed.

Taken as a whole, the most evolved societies on earth have progressed to the upper reaches of the third chakra, although there are still many cultures that operate predominantly from second-chakra consciousness, just as did the Western world during the Dark Ages. The behavior of these theocracies is generally regarded as insane by third-chakra societies, which also define as insane individuals from their own culture who have regressed to the second chakra. Of course there are many people within any culture who are well above or below the mean of their culture's overall stage of evolution.

Pessimists may disagree, but it is possible that human consciousness evolution is gaining momentum. This is more noticeable on an individual level, in that once a person bridges the difficult gap between the third and fourth chakras, further expansions follow more rapidly. What is true for the individual is likely to be true for humanity as a whole.

MADNESS, MYSTICISM, & RELIGION

Mystical experience lies at the core of every highly developed religion. It has been sought after and treasured by the best of men and women throughout history. Descriptions of it were first committed to writing more than thirty centuries ago, and since that time its inexhaustible theme has emerged in the symbols and rituals of every religious tradition. Despite different forms of expression, each religion clearly describes the same expanded perception of reality, deepening of values and ethics, and altered view of humankind's place in nature that follows from a direct confrontation with the Divine.

We might, therefore, expect the great religious traditions to take the lead in categorizing the various ways that the self interacts with the Spiritual Ground, and in developing methods to direct these openings toward spiritual growth. Because people in psychotic ASCs are drawn to religious symbols in the hope of finding meaning in their chaotic confrontation with the Ground, organized religion is in a unique position to assist this forlorn segment of humanity. Unfortunately, Western religions have failed to meet the challenge. There are a few church-run mental hospitals, but these usually differ from state-run institutions only in that they pay somewhat more attention to cleanliness and sanitation.

In past eras, however, gurus, high priests, and shamans were also the physicians and psychiatrists of their societies, with mandates to administer to the ordinary and extraordinary symptoms of those in their care. In Europe during the Middle Ages, when bizarre or deviant behavior was observed it was interpreted as a mysterious manifestation of the Divine, which qualified a person more for the monastery than for the hospital. Monasteries were havens for the mad, who were treated with prayer, ritual, simple work, and an unambiguous environment. No records were kept, but we might wonder if this lifestyle was more effective in fostering adaptation than the grim secular institutions that followed, or the life on the streets that characterizes today's "treatment," even with the mixed blessings of modern medicines.

Times have changed since the monastic era, but Western religions have hardly changed with them. The sentimental themes of modern religions no longer speak to people in psychotic ASCs or spiritual emergencies. High religious symbolism is birthed from solitary and passionately received revelation by people who more or less vainly try to communicate their insights across several levels of consciousness to those who have not felt them. Idols, icons, sacred texts, prayers, and rituals fail in their purpose when they are passed off as expressing the essence of the religious experience itself rather than being metaphorical signs pointing toward the path. Such concretizations reduce the original awesome vision of a religion's founder from a raw, deeply felt, fluid experience into a cold and static institution, frozen in formality, offering placebo spirituality to those who would rise above their egos in order to be healed.

As the hospital gradually displaced the church as the archetypal Western institution, it added a measure of reason and science, but it also widened the split between ordinary consciousness and the means for expanding consciousness, between suffering people and the secret of ending suffering. As the church retreated, it abandoned its role in elevating consciousness in favor of peddling thinly disguised codifications of the economic and sexual preferences of an entrenched power structure. At their best, Western religions now operate as if the fourth chakra were the highest human potential, and at their worst, they stir up second-chakra fantasies and fears to maintain control over the spiritually gullible. The result is that effective treatments for spiritual emergencies are virtually unknown in the West, and people experiencing them are lumped together with others who have vastly different needs. (The opposite tends to happen in the East, where psychotic experience tends to be treated as if it were a spiritual failing of one sort or another.)

Techniques for fostering mystical knowledge that once flowered in the West were driven underground with the excommunication of the Gnostic heretics. Since then, we are asked to take on faith what once could be directly experienced through religious practice. The churchmen knew that face-to-face encounters with the Absolute exposed dogma for what it is and therefore threatened their authority. The result is that most Western religions discourage practices that lead to authentic religious experiences and offer nothing in the way of theory or practice to the mentally ill. Attempts to seek personal visions or revelations are met with open hostility, which places mainstream religions in the curious position of denouncing the kinds of sacred experience that inspired their founders.

If Western religions are to regain their relevance, they must get back into the business of developing and teaching *spiritual technology*—time-proven, culture-relevant techniques for expanding human consciousness. To achieve this, they must heal the split between East and West by incorporating both the language and methods of consciousness exploration from the richly introspective Hindu and Buddhist teachings. In these are found detailed maps of levels of consciousness that lie beyond traditional Western knowledge. Such traditions enable Eastern psychologies to teach virtuoso techniques for inducing and controlling mystical and other desirable ASCs.

This is not to say that Eastern systems should be adopted in the West without modification. Because Eastern psychology and religion remain synonymous, they tend to focus primarily on transpersonal levels—the sixth and seventh chakras—and so overlook disturbances based within the lower chakras. Eastern psychologies are clearly inferior to Western systems in understanding early childhood development, psychodynamics, defense mechanisms, and the chemical systems of the brain. This puts them at a disadvantage in developing a holistic approach to the major psychoses, which they regard as an exaggeration of the psychopathology of everyday life. Because their ideal of mental health is liberation from the constraints of the ego, they tend to ignore the fact that many psychological maladies first require strengthening the ego.

To temper the extremes of Eastern thought, Western religions must heal the centuries-old split between spirituality and science by subjecting their beliefs to rational scrutiny. This means developing a science of introspection that rivals the Eastern disciplines in its rigor, while taking advantage of the unrivaled ability of Western science to determine what works and what doesn't. In other words, religion should not reject science, only seek ways to transcend it. Science, in turn, should not usurp the place of religion, only seek to strengthen its foundation. If science and religion were to heal the split that keeps them from sharing their tools for healing, they would gain unparalleled power to reduce human suffering.

Such a healing requires a major revision of prescientific religious dogmas that clash with reason, as well as a new role for the clergy.

Priests must again don the mantle of physician and spiritual healer, just as psychiatrists, psychologists, and social workers must become more like shamans, gurus, and priests. This means sharing ways to assess altered states of consciousness so that the combined tools of spiritual and scientific technology can be applied at any level of development. Refined knowledge of shifts in the relationship of self to Ground must stand side by side with knowledge of genetics and brain chemistry if we are to address the horrendous plight of today's mentally ill.

The main point is that neither religion nor science alone can realign people in psychotic ASCs with the upward course of human evolution. The world's most accomplished mystics did not develop the medicines and vaccines that halted the scourges of smallpox, bubonic plague, and polio, nor did they invent those marvelous machines that lift us to the planets and beyond. But for all its wonders, science has found the solution neither for humanity's penchant for war, nor for directing more love and empathy to our child raising, nor for fostering compassion in our healers.

We have traveled far since that portentous day in history when physician and priest first took separate paths. The necessary healing between East and West, spirituality and science, requires that both traditional religion and mainstream science endure their own spiritual emergencies, with no guarantee that the outcome won't be temporary regression.

Yet there is hope. By affirming the universal love and compassion of the heart chakra, the most highly developed Western religious traditions are already one giant step ahead of our political and social institutions. They are thus at a crucial turning point in evolution, poised to move toward a wide-open spiritual affirmation, pulled forward by the most enlightened science of our time. The result may revive Socrates's definition of a true religion as any community of people who allow God to operate within their hearts, as well as reaffirm religion's sole justification for existence: to lead its followers on the evolutionary path to higher consciousness.

PART 4
HEALING THE SPLIT

CHAPTER 16

Artful Healing I: Schizophrenic & Borderline Conditions

◆

The cure of soul has to be effected
By the use of certain charms . . .
And these charms are fair words.
SOCRATES

"DON'T JUST *DO* something—stand there!" So goes an Eastern response to the West's irresistible urge to meddle with natural processes. In a similar way, an artful healer recognizes that at times nothing needs to be done for many people whose behavior deviates from the norm. The following personal experience is a case in point:

In a wild canyon in the foothills of California's Santa Ynez Mountains, a few miles from where I once made my home, lives a strange hermit. He was briefly my patient, but is no longer.

I first met the hermit—call him Olaf—when he came to my office and politely asked my secretary for an appointment. I had a last-minute cancellation, so I was able to see him right away. Because of his striking appearance, I had noticed him in the local grocery once or twice, but I had never before appreciated the piercing intensity of his eyes, which was so direct as to be unsettling. Tall, lean, and sinewy, with long hair and flowing beard, Olaf dressed in rough-cut suede, hand-stitched into a woodsman's outfit that made him look like Robin Hood. On his rare visits to town, children would follow and tease this strange man who talked out loud to himself. But when he turned to quietly stare at them, they would quickly run away.

Olaf told me he had just been released from a county psychiatric hospital, where he had spent the past three days. He had been committed there by the local police for little more than refusing to answer their questions when they stopped him for jaywalking and looking out of place. Olaf told me he had been living alone in the mountains for several years, coming to town only for groceries. Mostly, he lived off the land, setting traps for quail and rabbits and gathering pine nuts, edible roots, and wild berries. He said he had a small inheritance, but refused to elaborate further, deflecting my questions adeptly. He said that he came to me at the recommendation of the hospital psychologist, who told him I could give him medicine to make his "spirits" more tolerable.

Olaf went on to say that he had been hearing inner voices since he was a child, and that they were companions who kept him company throughout his solitary nights in the mountains. He clearly preferred them to human company. Sometimes he heard the voice of God, he said, along with several others of varying character, mostly friendly and sometimes amusing. These were okay, but there was one particular voice—Moloch, he called it—that tormented him with personal insults, blasphemous curses, and threats. He said that he was not interested in psychotherapy because "I talk only to God about my problems," but he wondered if medicine might keep Moloch at bay.

"Olaf," I replied, "there are medicines that can stop the voices in some people, but not in others. Unfortunately, if they work at all, they usually make all the voices stop, not just the bad ones, and they have some side effects you should know about." He listened intently as I explained about how neuroleptic medicines affect the mind and body. He then told me that no medicine was powerful enough to cut him off from God, and asked if he could try one. I agreed, and gave him a prescription for a minimum dose of Prolixin, one of the least sedating neuroleptics. Olaf thanked me and agreed to a follow-up appointment in two weeks, which he never kept.

I heard no more from Olaf until six months later, when I was jogging alone in the mountains and impulsively followed a seldom-used trail up a remote canyon. I came upon a crude but neatly kept campsite by the side of a stream—no more than a fieldstone hearth, a sleeping bag under a lean-to, and an odd hand-carved puppet of a skeleton hanging from a tree limb. Realizing that the campsite was occupied, I hurried up the trail, where I met Olaf. He looked even wilder than I had remembered, and although he was not hostile, he showed little interest in talking to me. "Olaf," I pressed, "I'm curious to know how that medicine worked for you." His eyes were aflame as they locked onto mine. "The medicine is death," he replied, with an incongruous smile. "It murders the soul. The spirits of the canyon took it from me before it sent me to hell with Moloch. Moloch lives in hell now. God banished him from my canyon forever. Thank you, but I don't need your help." Olaf abruptly turned away and purposefully strode down the trail toward his home.

Somewhat stunned, I continued up the increasingly overgrown trail, but I found the hermit's canyon to be inhospitable, for all its beauty. I could not shake an eerie feeling that I was being watched, though I neither saw nor heard anything to confirm that feeling. As I hurried back down the trail, anxiously looking over my shoulder, I spotted Olaf standing naked, knee-deep in the rushing stream below his homestead. His arms were raised, fists clenched, his piercing eyes staring at the sky through a break in the canopy of wild oaks. He was humming a wordless, repetitive chant while rocking gently to his inner rhythms, seemingly oblivious to my passage. I felt that he was communicating with a being or beings unimaginable to my sane and socialized sensibilities, a reality that was far more compelling than the treacherous lure of civilization. Realizing that I had trespassed in a place where I had no business, I quickly jogged home and left Olaf in peace.

Years later, Olaf still dwells with the deer, rabbits, coyotes, snakes, owls, mosquitoes, and spirit voices of his haunted canyon. He bothers no one, and no one bothers him, except with their curious stares and rude remarks when he makes his monthly trek to the grocery. Olaf is insane by all accepted definitions, yet he is not to be pitied, for he is not lonely, and he is free in a way that most madmen or sane men will never know.

Countless solitary folk like Olaf live quietly in small towns, or in modest apartments in central cities. They spend their days in private, nonconsensual worlds that, for all we know, may be richer and more peaceful than our own. Most of these people bother no one and ask only meager subsistence from our affluent society. For all the noble intentions of modern physicians, psychologists, and social workers, the best thing any of us can do for Olaf and others like him is *leave them alone.*

Yet many people who enter psychotic ASCs do not wish to be left alone. Others—agitated or severely delusional people who cannot tend to their personal needs—call attention to their predicament in a way that a compassionate society cannot ignore. In this chapter, we examine both orthodox and transpersonal strategies to deal with psychotic ASCs that induce regression to the first and second chakras—schizophrenia and the borderline syndrome. It includes a suggestion as to how we might replace our failing system for treating people with chronic psychoses with a more enlightened system of New Asylums.

The following discussion postulates what treatment for various psychotic ASCs would be like under ideal circumstances, which include adequate financial resources, modern facilities, skilled therapeutic staff, the patient's freedom from work and family obligations, and plenty of time to see the healing process to its conclusion. Yet we must recognize that ideal conditions are seldom possible, and compromises are inevitable. Although what follows may be somewhat utopian, I believe that it is not impracticably so.

ARTFUL HEALING & THE SCHIZOPHRENIC ASC

Making a diagnosis of schizophrenia is a grave matter, and a conscientious healer does not use that term lightly. Before he or she arrives at that diagnosis, spiritual emergence or emergency and manic-depressive disorder should first be carefully excluded.

By definition, a diagnosis of schizophrenia implies (but does not guarantee) a malignant course and requires that regressive symptoms be obvious for six months or more. The schizophrenic ASC causes regression to the first or second chakra, and there is emotional blunting, delusions, and hallucinations. Changes in the brain's architecture may be visualized with specialized X-ray techniques. In paranoid types, persecutory delusions are aggravated by lower-order auditory hallucinations.

When confronted with people in such a dismaying condition, an artful healer resists labeling them as hopeless, thereby consigning them to a lifetime of spiritless custodial care or harsh exploitation on the streets. Many will always be different from the norm, but that difference does not have to mean "defective" or "outcast." There is nothing that requires that increased dopamine activity in a person's limbic system lead to unremitting misery, destructive behavior, or social alienation. Instead, an artful healer compassionately helps these unique people to *become the best schizophrenics they can be.*

Therapy for schizophrenia aims at restoring conditions for spiritual growth to resume. In most cases, this means adopting strategies specific to the first two chakras, with the goal of helping the person to gain or regain the ego-based consciousness of the third. Methods to achieve this are radically different from the ego-transcending strategies appropriate for spiritual emergencies and manic inflations.

The excesses of the deinstitutionalization era have sapped the will of Western societies to provide for the 1 percent of the population who spend their lives in chronic schizophrenic ASCs. These people are disabled, although not hopelessly so, and they cannot be expected to fend for themselves in a competitive capitalist society. In recent decades, however, they have been treated as if they were schizophrenic by *choice*, or as if they were guilty of some unspeakable moral crime.

In the present assembly-line system, the patient makes a monthly pilgrimage to a community mental-health center, where he briefly visits a harried psychiatrist or social worker who is burdened with impossible caseloads. Patients are quickly given refills of their antipsychotic medicines and shunted toward social relief agencies for minimal financial support. Those unable to deal with labyrinthine bureaucracies, or unwilling to put up with this kind of degradation, sleep in alleys and scrounge for discarded food in trash bins.

NEW ASYLUMS

The time has come to resurrect the idea that chronic schizophrenics need a wholesome place that isolates them from the stresses of competitive society. The now-dilapidated system of state mental hospitals once provided a semblance of what I have in mind. In the midst of valid concerns about their conspicuously antitherapeutic conditions, it is easy to lose sight of the fact that they filled a crucial need for the chronically mentally ill. These imperfect institutions at least provided food and shelter, health care, respite for the patient's family, a social network, and asylum and sanctuary from the pressures of the world.

Conspicuously lacking though, were treatments that distinguished between the unique ASCs of schizophrenia and less-profound mental disorders. Patients of all diagnostic categories were lumped together, with "treatment" aimed at enforcing rigid conformity to hospital rules. This fostered total dependence on the institution, with each featureless day blending imperceptibly into the next. When farms and sheltered workshops that were once part of the hospitals were shut down in response to protests that patient work equaled patient exploitation, the residents were left with little to do other than drink stale coffee, chain-smoke, and watch TV, all of which fed their sense of restless indolence.

If we are to rebuild a more enlightened system to care for schizophrenics and other socially disabled people, a working start-up model could be the kibbutzim of modern Israel. Egalitarian communes, usually based on agriculture, in which members live and work together, sharing the fruits of their collective labor in a noncompetitive way, many kib-butzim are also places for scientifically raising and educating children through warm and caring collective parenting. They are known for pro-ducing happy, well-adjusted adults of extraordinary social competence. The knowledge gained from these social experiments could be applied toward a system of New Asylums for people in regressive ASCs. These would revive the old sense of the word asylum as a temporary, or in some cases permanent, sanctuary from the pressures of modern society.

A key feature of the New Asylums would be empathy for the particu-lar state of consciousness of their inhabitants. Consider the design of the Yorkton Psychiatric Center in Canada. The architect prepared himself for his task by ingesting LSD, then spending several hours in a conven-tional psychiatric institution to gain empathy as to the effect a building has on people in ASCs. He was able to appreciate firsthand the confus-ing effect of long echoing hallways, oddly shaped day rooms, glassed-off nurses' stations, and total lack of privacy.

To apply this insight, the architect avoided the clever ambiguities that designers so often try to achieve, such as making a space appear larger than it actually is. Junctions of walls to floors were clearly de-fined, and the illumination was arranged to avoid creating silhouettes of faces or bodies, while allowing sufficient contrast to sharply model fa-cial features and other elements in space. He also created circular forms for all the larger spaces, which reduced sudden undesirable person-to-person confrontations.

This same kind of empathy for unique states of consciousness may be directed toward other subtle aspects of the New Asylums. People in psychotic ASCs can be disturbed by low-intensity sounds unnoticed by the staff. Background noises from faulty fluorescent light fixtures or electrical appliances that are ignored by most people are irritating to hyperaroused people and can lead to behavior easily misinterpreted as responses to hallucinations. Many schizophrenics improve when they are moved to quieter environments with low-intensity lights. In one case, a patient thought to be mute when admitted to the hospital simply would not answer questions asked in a loud voice, but readily re-sponded when the same questions were whispered.

In the New Asylums, people would be separated according to their current level of function, using either the chakra system or a similar model. Under the old state-hospital system, a misguided egalitarianism subjected patients in a wide variety of ASCs to the same environment. The idea was that higher-functioning patients have an uplifting effect on lower-functioning ones. But in most cases the principle of the lowest common denominator asserted itself, and the opposite occurred: the more regressed patients lacked the ego strength to benefit from this unnatural intimacy, and the higher-functioning patients were distracted from their own recovery tasks by disturbed people begging for cigarettes, screaming, or even urinating on them while they slept. Only when people engage in treatment specific to their level of consciousness can they resume growth.

A prominent feature of the New Asylums must be to reduce the sense of humiliation that accrues to people made to feel like useless outcasts from society. All human beings, mad or sane, try to sustain an image of themselves as competent to attain their personal goals, including validation through group membership. The opportunity for productive work must therefore be a cornerstone of the New Asylums. This is a major change, for at present the potential of these unusual people lies fallow in a society that finds no use for them.

People in schizophrenic ASCs are no different from anyone else in that they feel and behave better when they have meaningful work that imparts a sense of usefulness and pride while giving them something to look forward to. In other words, work is an essential aspect of healing. Indeed, it is the only thing that could make economically feasible a system of high-quality treatment centers with competent staffs. Although it is doubtful that the New Asylums could ever be completely self-sufficient in a technologically based economy, patient labor could relieve the taxpayers of a significant portion of their upkeep.

Work should be tailored to the particular characteristics of the schizophrenic ASC, and divided into levels of difficulty. Schizophrenics fare better at clear-cut tasks that do not require a lot of improvisation, and at jobs with minimal social interaction in which they are left alone to perform their assignment, with a supervisor available to assist them should they request help. Because of their low stress tolerance, they feel overwhelmed in situations where there is time pressure, competition with other workers for advancement, or intrusive and critical supervisors. The schizophrenic ASC renders a person easily overstimulated, so clamorous work environments should be avoided in favor of placid ones.

The goal of the New Asylums would be to return a percentage of its residents to society as relatively higher-functioning individuals capable of independent living. Of course, this is not feasible for the many schizophrenics who are permanently regressed to first-chakra levels, so the New Asylums must also serve a custodial function. Yet even those who remain can learn rudimentary chores that afford a sense of usefulness, especially in agricultural communities. It is amazing how the most regressed individual can respond to sincere praise for a simple job well done and spend the rest of his day in a brighter mood. In such an atmosphere of nonexploitative industry, a sense of community pride would percolate through staff and patients alike.

TRANSPERSONAL THERAPIES
FOR SCHIZOPHRENIA

Given such an environment of usefulness and hope, therapeutic energy can be directed toward the five aspects of transpersonal healing: physical, emotional, intellectual, social, and spiritual.

Physical Healing

On the physical level, antipsychotic medicines can improve the quality of life in most cases of correctly diagnosed schizophrenia, especially when combined with a broad range of other therapies. In a setting free from the kind of stress that aggravates schizophrenia, these medicines could be prescribed in far lower doses then they generally are now. The patient should have a say in regulating his ASC by using neuroleptics as his ally, rather than having them forced upon him by an authoritarian institution bent on manipulating his thoughts and feelings.

The artful healer who prescribes antipsychotic medicines adjusts the dose frequently according to the level of patient-perceived stress. People who take these medicines often complain that they feel sedated and emotionally blunted—"zombified," as some put it. Others develop a feeling of inner restlessness and impending doom.

To avoid these troublesome side effects, the healer should assist his patients in adjusting their dose of medicines upward or downward to mesh with their unique neurochemical gears. This is not difficult if the healer respects his patient's subjective experience as the most important factor in determining dosage. If the patient feels sedated or emotionally blunted, this usually means that the dose is too high for his current level of stress. Should stress increase and uncomfortable psychotic symptoms like hallucinations break through, the dose may be temporarily increased while the healer seeks to understand the source of that stress. Sometimes perceived stress, and therefore dosage, changes from day to day.

To many patients, taking medication is a reminder that they are different from others and that their lives are far from what they or their families hoped for. But if the healer establishes a collegial relationship with schizophrenic patients rather than an authoritarian one, he can eliminate the common feeling that they are being force-fed mind-deadening drugs through no choice of their own. The goal is to establish medicines as useful tools at the service of each patient's will. Recent studies indicate that over the long term, as little as *one-tenth* to *one-fifth* of the usual dosages results in similar relapse rates and improved social functioning. Nevertheless, it is not possible for all people in schizophrenic ASCs to master the skill of managing their own medicines.

Where this has been tried without balancing input from a psychiatrist, patients took ineffective doses and tended to relapse.

Contrary to the widespread idea that all schizophrenic patients require antipsychotic medicines for a lifetime, a significant minority do better *without* routine medication, keeping it in reserve in case of a flare-up. The problem is that it is difficult to tell in advance who these people are. About 70 percent of schizophrenics who discontinue antipsychotic medicine relapse within two years. This, of course, means that about 30 percent are at risk of taking unnecessary medicines for their lifetimes. Given our current state of knowledge, the only way we can distinguish this important minority is by trial and error.

An artful healer who wishes to give his schizophrenic patients a trial off medicines is alert to the first signs of relapse, which usually appear about a week before the full-blown psychotic ASC takes hold. Typical signs are feelings of inner tension, difficulty sleeping and concentrating, restlessness, preoccupation with one or two ideas, and loss of interest in accustomed activities. People who have feelings that popular songs or TV shows are sending personal messages or that strangers are talking about them, or who begin to hear distant voices, are even closer to impending relapse. It is helpful to be alert to idiosyncrasies in individual patients. For instance, I learned to tell that one of my patients was about to become psychotic when she began decorating her clothes with feathers. Another patient would bring his guitar to my office and sing songs in the waiting room during the early stages of a manic episode.

There is much more to physical therapy for schizophrenics than giving medicine. Because the schizophrenic ASC disrupts self-boundaries, firming up the body image should precede other attempts at ego building. The New Asylums could research methods to reeducate self-boundaries by enhancing awareness of sensations, feelings, images, and urges associated with moving the body. Dance therapies are powerful tools to re-create the patient's sense of time as expressed in different cadences of motion, as well as teach postures associated with specific emotions. For more advanced patients, aerobics classes are excellent antidotes to the vegetative lifestyles of today's mental institutions.

Emotional Healing

On the emotional level, an artful healer conducts psychotherapy with schizophrenic patients in a way that is unlike therapy for neurotics, manic-depressives, or people experiencing spiritual emergencies. Research clearly shows that people in schizophrenic ASCs respond unfavorably to psychoanalytic therapies in which a disengaged therapist stirs up emotionally charged memories and offers theoretical interpretations as to their meaning. Yet the widespread conclusion that psychotherapy is useless for schizophrenics is equally unfounded. What *does* have healing power is a supportive personal relationship based on empathy for the chakra level of the particular patient. For severe psychotics, therapy is best undertaken once florid symptoms are reduced by antipsychotic medicines.

Psychotherapy with people in schizophrenic ASCs is a daunting task, and not every healer's forte. It takes a healer with near-saintly compassion to provide unforced empathy with someone whose basic sense of reality bears scant resemblance to his own. For instance, one of the pioneers in psychotherapy for schizophrenics, Freida Fromm-Reichmann, dressed in old clothes as she entered her patients' padded cells in case they smeared her with feces. Hannah Green wrote a novelized account of this charismatic therapist's work with a severely disturbed patient in the popular book *I Never Promised You a Rose Garden.*

In studies of healers who do well with schizophrenics, what emerges is that they seldom agree about technique. Yet they have several personal characteristics in common: (1) they cultivate nonprofessional sources of satisfaction, so they can be content with their patients' slow progress; (2) they do not feel threatened when their patients attempt to merge identities with them or display primitive rage; (3) they live close to their own subconscious minds and the Spiritual Ground; (4) they find nonconsensual worldviews fascinating; (5) they entertain images of odd, even absurd, realities within themselves; (6) they have a lively sense of humor and can appreciate the irony intrinsic to any psychotherapeutic situation; (7) they have experienced ASCs in positive ways, which helps them to empathize with people who perceive the world from a different perspective; and (8) they possess enough physical and mental stamina to make a long-term commitment even if the outcome is less than ideal. In other words, the optimal therapist for schizophrenics is—with full awareness—just a little crazy himself.

A healer endowed with the above traits has little trouble treating his patients as people of value and esteem who are struggling with problems not entirely foreign to his own. He is warm, optimistic, and accepting, but also balances closeness with distance when his patients confuse their identity with his. He does not insist on the exclusive validity of his own reality sense, but realizes that madness and sanity are complementary variations on the human condition, and that his position is superior only by virtue of his training. He does not insist that the patient always be responsible for making himself understood; instead he searches for meaning through empathy. He observes and tempers his own rescue fantasies and need for a "cure," allowing his patient to create his own time frame for recovery. In this way he carefully avoids the role of all-powerful parent, which only promotes further regression.

Working with people in schizophrenic ASCs challenges a healer's creativity and invites boldness and unorthodoxy. An effective therapist delights in ambiguity, recognizing his own limitations in knowing whether sanity or the emotional oblivion of madness is the most desirable mode of existence for each particular individual. Yet he remains decisive in a crisis, using his own strong ego as a container for the fragmented ego of his patient when that is necessary. He is firm in dangerous situations, showing that he is an ally against his patient's primal impulses of hate and rage. He avoids gratuitously encouraging patients to "get their anger out," knowing that repressed rage is seldom a problem for people caught up in second-chakra regressions. Finally, he views his patients as capable of teaching him a great deal about himself, human consciousness, and ordinarily obscure areas of the Ground.

The goals of psychotherapy with people centered in second-chakra consciousness are quite different from those of people at higher levels. Rather than uncovering repressed emotions, which cannot be contained by the weakly bounded self, the artful healer shores up defenses against strong feeling. Every child must master these same defenses during adolescence if he is to advance from the second to the third chakra. This is not to say that feelings should be denied. As they emerge naturally, feelings should be empathically acknowledged and labeled, which teaches the patient to gain control over how they are expressed.

One important new finding about the schizophrenic ASC comes from family-interaction studies. These show that schizophrenics who live with families with high emotional expressivity are more likely to relapse than schizophrenics who live with less emotional intensity. In one study, families of schizophrenics were taught to reduce emotionally laden criticism and face-to-face contact. The relapse rate in those families was only 14 percent, compared with 78 percent for control patients. This is probably because heated emotions stir up dopamine activity in the limbic system, which imbalances its relations with higher brain areas. As we create a system of New Asylums, establishing a quietly warm and supportive emotional tone must be an ongoing concern.

This does not mean that a family's real feelings should be disguised, only that they should be expressed in a gentle and straightforward way. The Jungian psychiatrist John Weir Perry emphasized the need for emotional authenticity in our responses to the schizophrenic ASC.

> One of the chief factors in the genesis of the schizophrenic experience is that such individuals have been raised in families or in conditions . . . where there has been little

acknowledgment of emotional realities. The milieu is usually a subculture in which emotional truth is suppressed—in which there is such an ingrained habit of judging the right and wrong ways about things that the eyes are blinded to actual ways of feeling. If there is a constitutional factor along with this environmental one, it is that these are sensitive individuals who cannot afford to live this way, and who instead need to live in recognition of the truth of their emotional realities. I see the whole stormy process as one of coming to this realization, and to a self-image and a design of life that give full place to it.

Although most transpersonal healers gravitate toward consciousness-expanding techniques that bring already-healthy individuals into greater contact with the Ground, such methods are *contraindicated* for schizophrenics. Spiritual growth for regressed people means ego building, the same as for a child naturally passing through the second chakra. And just as it is crucial for healthy childhood development, empathy is also the key to reparenting. Flowing from the open heart of the healer, empathy is the mortar from which an enduring self-in-the-world is built, or rebuilt.

An unusual first-person article in the *American Journal of Psychiatry* illustrates the value of empathic psychotherapy in schizophrenia. The author, identified only as "a recovering patient," poignantly described how her therapist's willingness to risk caring for her as a valuable individual gradually enabled her to reveal her inner self to another person for the first time:

> I had drawn so far inside myself and so far away from the world, I had to be shown not only that the world was safe, but also that I belonged in it, that I was in fact a person . . . I often felt at odds with my therapist until I could see that he was a real person, and he related to me and I to him not only as patient and therapist, but as human beings. Eventually I began to feel that I, too, was a person, not just an outsider looking in on the world . . . My therapist once told me that he looks at me and treats what he sees—I cannot think of any other thing that has instilled my confidence more than that statement.

This courageous patient further described the rewards that are inherent in helping people in psychotic ASCs.

It seems that only through psychotherapy can the world of unreality truly be dispelled. There are those bad days, but I must admit that there are other days when I am glad that they did not give up on me, and that there is someone standing beside me guiding me to the knowledge of another existence . . . Medication or superficial support alone is not a substitute for the feeling that one is understood by another human being. For me, the greatest gift came the day I realized that my therapist really had stood by me for years and that he would continue to stand by me and to help me achieve what *I* wanted to achieve. With that realization my viability as a person began to grow. I do not profess to be cured—I still feel the pain, fear, and frustration of my illness. I know I have a long road ahead of me, but I can honestly say that I am no longer without hope.

We have every reason to believe recovering schizophrenics who say they are not only alone in their ASC, but also terribly *lonely*, although their fear of intimacy is even greater than the pain of loneliness. From the above description of the healing effect of psychotherapy, we can recognize its power to reduce that crippling fear and release the embryonic desire to establish ties with another human being.

Intellectual Healing

On the intellectual level, ideal therapy for schizophrenics helps them to integrate third-chakra consciousness by teaching them to relate appropriately to others. These are skills that most of us master in high school, but that a persistent schizophrenic ASC relentlessly strips away. Basic social-skill training is best performed in groups. Such simple tasks as practicing eye contact, learning to grant others their personal space, modulating tone of voice, and laughing only when appropriate can greatly affect the quality of a person's life as he tries to reintegrate himself into consensual society. Group meetings in which the only agenda is to read and discuss the morning newspaper can be an ideal forum for helping people in schizophrenic ASCs to regain a fix on consensual matters.

Group therapy is also an ideal medium for teaching recovering schizophrenics to recognize that hallucinated voices usually occur in particular situations—that is, when they expect to hear them. There is a *listening attitude*—an interval between the expectation of the voices and actually perceiving them. It is a subtle point, but most schizophrenics can learn to recognize their internal preparations to make contact with the voices, and then direct their attention elsewhere. Practical techniques such as this are far more effective than churlish attempts to interpret these voices—whatever their mysterious origin—as representing the patient's repressed wishes or fantasies.

A similar tactic can be taken with delusions. There is always a grain of truth in any delusion, and some represent a first step toward insight. The artful healer exploits the correspondence between delusion and consensual reality. First he validates the points of agreement, then painstakingly shows how these have been overextended and misapplied. While the patient may not immediately accept this version of reality, he no longer feels hopelessly out of touch with the consensual world, and also sees that the therapist genuinely wants to understand his feelings rather than merely pretending to do so.

For schizophrenics regressed to first- and lower-second-chakra levels, behavior modification can help restore conditions in which spiritual growth resumes. Transpersonal psychologists have been known to groan aloud when behavior modification is mentioned. It is true that these techniques can be insulting to people whose selves have reached the third chakra or above, and who value their emerging powers of will. Nevertheless, these methods are appropriate for people regressed to lower-chakra consciousness, as long as they are part of a strategy that recognizes the integrity of personal consciousness.

The goal of behavior therapy must not be mindless conformity to prevailing social mores, but to help ingrain adaptive behavior patterns as *options* available to the patient. Creating environments that systematically reward good work habits, personal hygiene, and other healthy social responses can greatly improve the quality of life for people in schizophrenic ASCs. For example, a regressed patient may seek attention by screaming, cursing, banging his head, begging for cigarettes, or urinating on the floor. If the hospital staff ignores him when he does these things, but provides attention and cigarettes when he behaves appropriately, it is likely that after a while he will enjoy an environment in which others respond to him more kindly.

Emotional Healing

Because the schizophrenic ASC lays bare the psyche's underpinnings, mythological images may surface during therapy as delusions or hallucinations. These represent the archetypes inherent in the particular chakra where the regressed self is centered, and they offer the healer a unique opportunity to track his patient to the level where conflict is preventing growth. These dreamlike symbols are unlike the images that characterize higher-chakra openings, which typically contain themes of liberation, reunion, or high mission. In contrast, typical first- and second-chakra archetypes are of seeking protection from malign and monstrous forces; turning into an animal to escape a threat; becoming large, small, or invisible; being lost, hungry, or abandoned; fleeing from hunters; or sexually merging with a powerful fantasy object.

Some therapists have written of telepathic or other paranormal abilities that emerge from the schizophrenic ASC during psycho-therapy. Such phenomena can accompany any ASC that weakens ego boundaries and opens self to Ground. In schizophrenia, as in childhood, paranormal abilities usually appear randomly and lack coherence or control, but they can be quite striking in some people, and contribute to the pre/trans confusion about schizophrenia. Because schizophrenics mingle these inner perceptions with their own projected fears or desires, experienced therapists find that many more patients claim these powers than can objectively demonstrate them. Nonetheless, their content can inform a healer about specific disturbances within his patient's psyche.

Social Healing

On the community level, a system of New Asylums would go far in correcting both the soul-deadening conditions of the old state hospitals and the debacle of deinstitutionalization that made matters even worse. We might foresee a system of rural, agriculturally based therapeutic communities for regressed individuals, with sheltered workshops in small towns and urban centers for less regressed people. The goal of the agricultural communities would be to "graduate" a significant percent-age of residents to community centers, where ego building is continued. The goal of these centers would be to help residents live independently through dignified work and social-skills training, recognizing that a number of these people will stabilize at a level at which a partially pro-tective environment must be maintained.

A fragile schizophrenic who requires medication to maintain a ten-uous hold on consensual reality would certainly be ill suited to guide others through the maze of their own ASC. Yet people in an advanced stage of recovery from psychoses could be of unique service to others. The sensitivity of people in psychotic ASCs was demonstrated in one experiment that showed that mental patients are *twice* as likely as nor-mal controls to help a suffering stranger. A system of New Asylums could number among its staff people whose psychotic experience afforded them empathy for others astray in remote mental planes. Although such tactics are successful in the treatment of addictions, ex-psychotics are systematically excluded from any involvement in mental-health programs.

Spiritual Healing

Modern Western societies can well afford to treat the 1 percent of their population who are schizophrenic with more compassion than they do now. It dehumanizes us to passively observe people wasting their lives in forced indolence in hopelessly outmoded custodial warehouses or on the streets. As humanity collectively prepares to embrace the compassionate consciousness of the fourth chakra, we would do well to open our hearts to these gentle, light-winged souls whose only fault is to hover too close to the same flame of life that warms us all.

For many of us a compassionate response may be no more than buying some street person a toothbrush or a belt to hold his pants up. For others it may be a wholehearted attempt to rebuild the system from within. When Charles Dickens visited Saint Luke's Hospital for the insane during Christmas of 1852 he sensitively perceived the rewards forthcoming to any who devote themselves to the humble nobility of caring for the severely mentally ill.

> To lighten the affliction of insanity by all human means is not to restore the greatest of the Divine gifts; and those who devote themselves to the task do not pretend that it is. They find their sustainment and reward in the substitution of humanity for brutality, kindness for maltreatment, peace for raging fury; in the acquisition of love instead of hatred, and the knowledge that, from such treatment improvement and hope of final restoration will come, if such hope be possible. It may be little to have abolished from the mad-house all that is abolished, and to have substituted all that is substituted. Nevertheless, reader, if you can do a little in any good direction—do it. It will be much some day.

TRANSPERSONAL THERAPIES FOR THE BORDERLINE PATIENT

Experienced psychotherapists tend to rank borderline patients as their most difficult. People with this "in between" form of madness have not developed a coherent self that can stand unsupported.

Individuals with the borderline syndrome form their self-boundaries from those of others—*selfobjects* with whom they seek to merge identities. Although borderlines spend most of their time in touch with consensual reality, their boundaries fragment when their selfobjects prove to be unreliable props. At those moments, they are liable to transient psychotic ASCs.

If a healer accepts a call to work with these challenging patients, he should recognize that they are trying to cope with third-chakra tasks without having first accomplished essential first- and second-chakra passages. They feel a constant backward tug to complete these unfulfilled agendas, so their lives are a constant struggle against the same kind of regression to primitive modes of consciousness to which schizophrenics helplessly succumb.

Yet psychotic regressions of the borderline syndrome are usually not malignant. They may therefore be thought of as lower-chakra spiritual emergencies—efforts to heal old wounds impeding the self's transition to a higher chakra. Yet these are quite different from spiritual emergencies that complicate transitions into higher chakras, and so require different strategies. The obsessions that impede growth are derived from *pre*-ego stages, so the individual lacks the ego strength to control these elemental impulses and rages that threaten the very existence of selfhood.

Therefore, the aim of therapy is not to expose infantile yearnings, but to consolidate a stable sense of selfhood that can operate independently within the often heartless interpersonal milieu of third-chakra societies. The third chakra is also called the "power" chakra, so the healer should assist his borderline patients in achieving spiritual growth through worldly *empowerment*. The early-life failings that haunt the borderline run deep to the core of the personality, and the task of fortifying a fundamentally weak self-structure is long and demanding.

Physical Healing

On the physical level, there is no reason to believe that the borderline syndrome has a genetic component that is anywhere near as irrevocable as in schizophrenia. This is probably why antipsychotic medicines are seldom helpful for borderlines, and can be antitherapeutic if psychotherapy is in progress. Yet they are not contraindicated, as they are in most higher-level spiritual emergencies. There is a dearth of skilled therapists willing to commit themselves to the arduous therapy necessary to heal these trying patients, who usually cannot afford expensive long-term treatment. Psychiatrists often administer neuroleptic drugs to borderlines from simple lack of other available responses. This is far from ideal, but it is understandable in light of the extreme psychic suffering these people experience during moments of ego fragmentation.

Borderlines are frequently afflicted by a particularly dismal kind of depression called *hysteroid dysphoria*. Usually arising following a lost selfobject relationship, this unfortunate state produces a terrifying feeling of falling apart, or losing oneself, accompanied by an implacable sense of inner tension and restlessness that demands immediate relief.

Because living in such anguish seems not worth the trouble, the borderline often seeks release through a dramatic suicide gesture. This is quickly followed by a cry for help, usually a desperate phone call to the therapist. The suicide gesture is studiously sublethal—a series of superficial scratches on the wrist with a dull knife, a small overdose of over-the-counter pills. But by drawing the alarmed attention of mental-health professionals, it seldom fails as an antidote to intolerable loneliness.

Physical release may be the only way to cope with the intense grief and rage that emerge during psychotherapy with borderlines as they realize that they will *never* receive from their parents the nurturing that produces a whole and secure self. The fury of emptiness and loss that follows is beyond release by shedding a sedate tear or two during conventional verbal psychotherapy. It can be discharged only by nonverbal physical techniques, such as those from Gestalt or bioenergetic therapy that stimulate a person to sob or scream from deep in his body while vigorously hitting or kicking a pillow, which can help release impediments to selfhood left over from early life. An artful healer alternates these methods with verbal psychotherapy as the need arises.

Emotional Healing

On the emotional level, intensive long-term psychotherapy is the ideal treatment for borderline disorders. As in other arrests of development, the goal is to restore the individual to a condition in which spiritual growth can resume. The key to this restoration of selfhood is empathy—a heartfelt way of observing, listening, and communicating that is the primary healing force in psychotherapy. The fourth-chakra art of empathy enables a healer to "live into" complex feelings from the vantage of the patient's unique experience rather than from the perspective of an aloof observer or a particular theoretical school.

A healer who commits himself to intensive psychotherapy with a borderline patient must in a very real way *reparent* that individual, sometimes starting at early life stages. This is a demanding task that requires special characteristics from those rare therapists who hear the call. A need to rescue and a personal identification with primal neediness—either of which would be detrimental in therapy with other maladies—are helpful personal characteristics for healers who work with border-lines, provided they are aware of these traits.

Borderline patients can be bottomless vessels of neediness, capable of draining dry a therapist's emotional reserves, yet themselves never full or satisfied. The therapist must sit through phases during which he is idolized as an omnipotent savior, followed by upwellings of primal rage in which he is utterly devalued. His patient may feel entitled to special treatment, while simultaneously believing that the world has no place in it for him. Dramatic suicide attempts follow trivial empathic failures, and the healer lives with the idea that his patient may ultimately succeed in suicide. For these reasons, many therapists feel that they can work with only one or two borderline patients at a time.

Effective psychotherapy requires the therapist to be available at odd hours to respond to innumerable crises in the borderline's world, just as a good mother is available to soothe the hurt feelings of her child. Acting at times as a "prosthesis" for his patient's weakly formed self, the therapist takes pains to *mirror* his patient's talents and accomplishments with unforced admiration, while at the same time allowing his patient to idealize him as a source of strength and protection. Throughout all this, the therapist salves his patient with empathy, gently resisting temptations to offer intellectual interpretations or directly gratify primal needs, no matter how hurtfully presented. Instead, he helps the borderline to *mourn* the fact that his parents were unable or unwilling to love him enough. If all goes well, the patient gradually incorporates the therapist into his own self, transforming the therapist's mirroring admiration into self-esteem, and his placid strength into self-soothing skills.

No healer can offer perfect empathy at all times, however, and failures are inevitable. Whenever a borderline patient shows signs of regression for no apparent reason, the healer needs to review his own recent responses to ferret out an empathic failure. Borderlines experience these as outrages perpetrated upon a fragile self that seeks an affirming selfobject the way a hungry infant seeks nurturing milk. When this is withheld, there is a grave threat to the self.

These unavoidable shortfalls do not have to be harmful. If the healer takes steps to repair the damage and restore himself as a reliable selfobject, a borderline patient builds *stronger* internal self-structures. An artful healer knows he has been unempathic when he observes his patients begin to fragment, and knows he is back on track as they again regain cohesiveness. Through this reparenting process of empathic failure and repair, fragmentation and rebuilding, the patient gradually completes the task of ego-formation left unfinished from early childhood.

The following case illustrates the results of empathic failure and subsequent repair in a borderline patient who was once under my care.

Merrie was a twenty-three-year-old woman who functioned well in her professional life as a legal assistant, but poorly in her personal relationships. It was easy for her to attract a variety of men, but they would typically end the relationship after a few weeks, telling her that she was too clinging and possessive, that they needed more "space," and that her moodiness and explosive overreactions kept them from knowing where they stood. As each relationship ended, Merrie would become depressed and suicidal.

After several psychotherapy sessions, Merrie grew increasingly hostile and evasive, rather than more comfortable in my presence as I had hoped. When I asked if anything was bothering her, she began reciting a litany of my faults, including the way I dressed and how my office was decorated. She complained that I asked too many questions during our first session and didn't care about her, concluding that I was undoubtedly the worst psychiatrist in the checkered history of the profession.

My response was unfortunately defensive. I told her that I was sorry she felt that way, but she was free to change therapists, and I would be glad to make a referral to a colleague with whom she might feel more comfortable. She then abruptly bolted for the door, snatching my prescription pad as she passed my desk, angrily shouting that she would forge a prescription and kill herself. After an extremely ugly confrontation at the clinic door, I retrieved the pad, elicited a promise that she would not attempt suicide, and gave her an appointment for early the next morning.

Later that evening, I discussed the case with a respected colleague who immediately recognized my failure. "Merrie probably has a crush on you and wants to be close, but feels threatened by these feelings," she told me. "Her outburst was her way of warding off intimacy, which has always been painful for her. Don't apologize, though. All you have to do is acknowledge her pain, and she'll feel better."

When Merrie arrived the next morning, I was dismayed to find her disheveled and regressed, rocking a teddy bear in her arms and talking to it as if it were a baby. In a matter-of-fact tone of voice, she informed me with unfeigned sincerity that the doll was indeed her baby, and that I was the father. She said that I should have let her kill herself so that I could gain custody of this orphan child, which she knew I secretly wanted.

I resisted the temptation to hospitalize Merrie at that instant, in favor of asserting my awareness that it was painful for her to be alone and feeling uncared for, and that I understood how she could be furious at me for being so smug and "professional." I also pointed out that my retrieving the prescription pad was a gesture of concern that she not harm herself, and that I would continue to take steps to protect her when she felt that way. Merrie began sobbing deeply, which I did not interrupt, and within an hour, her psychosis vanished before my eyes. Our sessions continued for two more years, with occasional thunderstorms whenever I failed to accurately reflect her feelings, but there were no more psychotic episodes. I had learned my lesson, and took pains to search for my own unempathic blind spots whenever she seemed to lose internal cohesiveness. A few months after her brief psychotic ASC, Merrie professed to have no memory whatsoever of what transpired that morning. I lost contact with her when she married a lawyer in her firm and moved to another state.

Intellectual Healing

On the intellectual level, a seasoned healer negotiates a therapeutic contract with his borderline patients early in therapy. There are no limits to the borderline's primal needs, and there are likewise no limits to his fantasies about the therapist's ability to fulfill those needs. Yet just as a child feels most comfortable when his parents set firm limits on his behavior, even though he may test these repeatedly, the borderline thrives on his therapist's sturdy ego to temporarily supplement his own boundless condition. The healing relationship progresses more smoothly if details of fees, length of sessions, conditions for emergency phone calls, and prohibitions on social contact between patient and therapist are set in advance and firmly maintained.

Intellectual interpretations about what makes the patient "tick," no matter how clever or technically correct, are spectacularly unhelpful to borderline patients, who perceive them as attacks on their fragile selfhood. The artful healer keeps these to himself, accepting the challenge of translating them into gently empathic reflections, with which he "feeds" his patient's hungry emptiness. This requires the healer to rein in his own ego—a fourth-chakra capability—before he accepts the task of working with this difficult group of patients.

Spiritual Healing

On the spiritual level, a sensitive healer shields his borderline patients from tactics that weaken the ego or its defenses. Prolonged meditation, charismatic religious meetings, cultish rituals, and psychedelic drugs are anathema to the borderline's tenuous selfhood, which must be consolidated before it can be transcended. In contrast, borderlines usually respond favorably to the structured ritual, ethical rules, memorized prayer, and affirmative group membership of organized religion, so long as guilt and punishment are deemphasized, and metaphysical ambiguity is minimal. Many modern psychotherapists find such religions more or less distasteful, feeling that they have transcended their need for concretized religious symbols. Yet the artful healer recognizes that traditional religious frameworks can be quite helpful during the ego-building phase of spiritual development.

A spiritual hazard for borderlines is engulfment in cults, which have magnetic appeal to people with frail egos. One has scant need for an ego while in a cult. The charismatic cult leader supplies all the formulas for living one could wish for. Often paranoid and grandiose, the leader courts idealization, even deification, which he draws from people who need powerful selfobjects to fortify their vulnerable selves. The leader maintains power by affecting a degree of aloofness and inaccessibility, hiding behind self-inflating rhetoric that obscures his own human foibles. A cult may be a temporary prop for a faltering ego, but no true healing comes from it, for there is no real empathy, which can emerge only from a symmetrical and nonmanipulative relationship.

Social Healing

On the social level, the artful healer encourages his borderline patients to seek a sense of belongingness through clubs and service groups that stress healthy affiliation, especially through initiation ritual. Just as role learning through group membership smooths the transit from the second to the third chakra during early adolescence, so can it afford external support to a shaky self. The selfobject needs of borderline people are so profound that an individual therapist can seldom provide enough healing energy, so he encourages them to seek all the help they can get from a variety of sources.

Although an old therapeutic adage says, "Borderlines are forever," an empathic healer working under near-ideal conditions can look forward to the day when his patient assembles a self capable of standing alone and resuming spiritual growth. This is necessarily a long-term process—it takes several years, by most accounts—and the termination stage must be handled with uncommon sensitivity, as it is sure to reopen old wounds. Temporary regressions to the separation-individual stage are common during this phase as the patient gradually relinquishes the therapist as a gratifying selfobject, abandons impossible loves, and forms attachments outside of therapy. The reader is referred to several excellent sources from authors in the Western psychological traditions for guidance in this most delicate form of psychotherapy.

CHAPTER 17

Artful Healing II: Spiritual Emergencies & Mania

◆

Here begins the new life.
DANTE

Physician, heal thyself.
LUKE 4:23

IN MEDICAL SCHOOL, I was taught by learned scientists about how modern medicines and surgical techniques heal disease in the body and mind. Later in my psychiatric training, I learned how a caring relationship heals a wounded self through sincere empathy, good listening, sensitive interpretation, and personal respect. These were valuable lessons, which served me well.

But nowhere in all those years of training did my teachers mention the most important ingredient in any healing process: *the state of mind of the healer.* If a physician prescribed penicillin, it did not matter if he or she was hung over, constipated, or unhappy at work; the penicillin accomplished its task unaided. Even in psychoanalysis, the therapist is safely ensconced at the end of a couch, where he or she may be quietly depressed, furious at a spouse, in despair about finances, or even sound asleep. No matter; the cure will be forthcoming after a series of timely interpretations. The psychiatrist is not a real person to the patient anyway, only a fantasy figure constructed from the patient's projected needs.

Insights from modern consciousness research have the power to change that view. A cornerstone of transpersonal psychology and the perennial philosophy—and a recurrent theme of this book—is that sentient beings share a common Ground of being within which energy and information constantly resonate from mind to mind, usually beneath the threshold of ordinary awareness. We are more vulnerable to each other than most of us dare to admit. With this awareness or without it, patient and healer sit together in the midst of a field of consciousness in which both actively participate, sometimes "vibrating" in harmony, sometimes in discord.

This subliminal rapport between therapist and patient governs every aspect of the healing situation. As R. D. Laing pointed out, it is not merely what the patient says, but also *how the therapist listens,* that determines how close they get or how far apart they remain. Healing requires more than an exchange of chemicals from pharmacy to brain, more than the transmission of wisdom from tongue to ear. These are important aspects of healing, but even more essential is an exchange of *spirit* from healer to patient and back again. Once activated, this resonance acquires a self-sustaining momentum, operating beyond the momentary awareness of the participants, as if it had ends of its own. The great healing traditions agree that this exchange of energy is mediated through the heart, through the fourth chakra, through the medium of universal love.

A modern healer commands immensely powerful tools, from medicines that alter the delicate metabolic pathways of the brain to refined psychotherapeutic techniques that plumb the depths of the soul. Wielded by clumsy or uncaring hands, these can destroy as easily as heal. The technical proficiency requisite to artful healing comes from dedicated scientific study. But equally important is the healer's commitment to his own spiritual growth, to clearing the debris of ego attachment. To be effective, the healer must relinquish personal defensive armoring against the pain of life, any indulgence in activities that lower consciousness, and the arrogance that prevents him from learning from patients.

This is not to say that a healer must have all these attributes to be effective, only that he must value them as personal goals. In this regard, he would do well to emulate his predecessors, the shamanic medicine men of earlier times. Author Michael Harner described the willingness of the shaman to join his patient in a mutual search for healing power.

> Through his heroic journey and efforts, the shaman helps his patients transcend their normal, ordinary definition of reality, including the definition of themselves as ill. The shaman shows his patients that they are not emotionally and spiritually alone in their struggles against illness and

death. The shaman shares his special powers and convinces his patients, on a deep level of consciousness, that another human is willing to offer up his own *self* to help them. The shaman's self-sacrifice calls forth a commensurate emotional commitment from his patients, a sense of obligation to struggle alongside the shaman to save one's self. Caring and curing go hand in hand.

By the time a prospective healer of the psyche completes medical school or a graduate program in psychology or social work, he is likely to have mastered most of the tasks of the first three chakras. Yet the rigors of professional training can *retard* his ongoing spiritual growth by forcing him into rigid patterns of linear logic, demanding unbending conformity to orthodoxy, rejecting deviations from consensus reality, and numbing his natural compassion for the sake of objectivity. In the West, spiritual considerations are systematically excluded from scientific training and actively discouraged afterward. To remedy this gap in his education, the first task of a would-be healer upon completing formal training is to set out on a disciplined spiritual path.

Spiritual growth is no more than expanding personal consciousness upward from the present stage of development toward the next-higher level. For most of us, this means mastering the ego-based strivings of the third chakra, then clearing away impediments against opening the heart. Orthodox psychotherapy can be quite effective in resolving stubborn blockages left over from painful childhood experiences and freeing the self for natural growth. Most of the better training programs for mental-health professionals wisely insist on individual psychotherapy before graduation.

There will come a day, however, when orthodox psychotherapy that is focused on personal biography is no longer sufficient to fuel self-realization. Indeed, a healer cannot be fully effective until he personally experiences the universal love of the Ground. This implies that he has transcended his ego's need for excessive wealth and personal prestige as ends in themselves, and so has freed the best of his energies to be in the service of others. In other words, it is essential for any healer of mind or body to be actively integrating fourth-chakra consciousness, a task that for most people requires specific spiritual practice.

If a healer is unable to make contact with a psychotic person, this is simply a reflection of his inability to move freely into other systems of reality. Once a healer is free from attachment to a specific plane of consciousness, he will encounter no state of mind beyond his understanding. That is not to say that he should get stuck where his patients are stuck. Intuitive knowing requires the most careful checking against self-deception. This means that he must become expert at the ruthless art of honest introspection.

So prepared, the artful healer knows he cannot force change. Instead, he seeks to understand, accept, nurture, and finally allow natural and inevitable change to acquire its own impetus. Every living organism has a built-in drive toward health, toward adaptation to its surroundings. But fear and anxiety—fear of fear—undermine that drive. The revolutionary task of the artful healer is to teach his psychotic patients to navigate with courage in their internal environment as he has learned to do. Then he can lead a patient not back to automatic conformity with social expectations, but to an appreciation of social norms when it is *convenient* to play the game. Healer and patient play the consensual game no longer as a life-or-death struggle, but freely, even joyfully.

In this chapter we examine how an artful healer working in a transpersonal mode ideally responds to acute psychoses and openings into higher chakra levels, including mania and spiritual emergencies. This often necessitates his breaking the mold of conventional thinking, taking risks that incur the disfavor of his colleagues, and entering situations in which he may doubt his own hold on consensual reality. Becoming intimately involved with people in psychotic ASCs is an arduous process that requires the best of any healer who undertakes this often thankless and frustrating work.

PREPARING FOR HEALING

For all sentient beings, quality of life is identical to quality of consciousness, the condition of the soul. Those who understand this equation, usually through some form of daily introspection or meditation, learn to direct the healing power of the Spiritual Ground *through* themselves for the sake of reducing suffering. Compassion infuses and informs every genuine act of healing, from lifting a scalpel to writing a prescription to sharing the unbearable pain of a psychotic ASC.

Of the two types of meditation described in chapter 15, receptive meditation (contemplation) is especially suited to the healer's art. By intently observing the ever-changing forms of consciousness ebbing and flowing within his awareness, an artful healer learns *mindfulness,* and with it insight into his inner nature that allows him to bring to others this same realization. The particular religious form of the healer's meditation—even thoughtful agnosticism—matters little, for it is the conditioning of the compassionate heart, which inevitably follows from conscientious meditation, that empowers his healing touch.

I am not saying that it is impossible to be an effective healer without practicing meditation, only that meditation can make any healer more artful. The mindfulness gained from regular meditation enables the healer to live with fullness and presence in each moment. By attending carefully to the flow of consciousness without immediately reacting to it, the healer receives each experience free from judgment or aversion. He freshly perceives his patient's immediate reality, without analysis, comparison, or interpretation, and so gains a clear understanding of that person's world. No matter how wrenching a session with a suffering patient may be, or how much pain the healer absorbs, a moment of mindfulness restores calm and balance and allows him to respond in a caring and heartfelt way.

All psychotic ASCs—schizophrenia, mania, MPD, borderline regressions, and spiritual emergencies—have in common that they disrupt the dynamic relationship between individual consciousness and the Spiritual Ground. Therefore, it is only through the medium of consciousness that healing takes place. So a healer's first task is to observe the state of consciousness of his patient by using his own empathic awareness as his primary tool. He strives to know his patient through what Heinz Kohut called *vicarious introspection*—a form of mindfulness in which he creates within himself an internal image of his patient's moment-to-moment experience.

In this way, the healer practices, *impeccability*—in the sense that Yaqui *brujo* Don Juan taught Carlos Castaneda—conducting his art with personal centeredness, clarity of purpose, and sharply focused will.

This is no easy task. It requires personal familiarity with altered states of consciousness along with skill in shifting to and from the ordinary state. To empathize with a psychotic individual involves training of a very different sort from the aloof objectivity taught in professional schools. This suggests that most healers adept at working with psychotics will have themselves at some time undergone a spiritual emergence or emergency. This may have occurred spontaneously, through spiritual practice, or perhaps during a phase of their lives where they employed psychedelic medicines to explore their own psyches. Once a healer personally experiences the effects of altering the self's relationship with the Ground, he gains a feeling for others caught up in a similar process.

ASSESSING AN ACUTE PSYCHOTIC ASC

With the exception of people in the early stages of mania, most individuals who enter a psychotic ASC for the first time are frightened and confused about their shift in consciousness, and many seek professional help. At that point, there is no way of knowing if the ASC will take a malignant or benign turn. The way a healer responds is crucial in determining how patients view themselves, their ASC, and future helpers. If their caretakers are kind and empathic and their treatment is tailored to the specific characteristics of their ASC, there is an excellent chance that regression can be arrested and spiritual growth resumed. This is true no matter what the source of the shift in consciousness or the level of regression.

Like the antipsychiatrists of the 1960s, some transpersonal therapists reject the very idea of diagnosis, believing that it restricts their ability to relate to a patient as a whole person. They instead prefer a "wellness" orientation that may lead them to misapply "consciousness raising" techniques to everyone who walks through the consulting-room door. This is little different from those orthodox psychiatrists who believe that all psychotic ASCs can be quickly treated with the same class of medicines. Because spiritual growth cannot be hastened by short-circuiting the ego, the potential for harm in the name of treatment can be as great on the transpersonal side as it is on the orthodox side.

An artful healer is alert to nuance as he tries to distinguish malignant from benign regressions. Although he regards his intuition as equal to objective signs and symptoms as he makes a diagnosis, he also collects the following information about any acute ASC:

- the person's current level of regression
- the duration of the regressive process
- whether the ASC began insidiously or abruptly
- the level at which the patient operated before regressing
- what, if any, events precipitated the change
- what meaning the individual assigns to those events
- what previous experience the person has had with ASCs, psychotic or otherwise
- how the person feels about his shift in consciousness—frightened, enlightened, confused, fascinated, and so forth
- how the person defends himself against the inflowing energies of the Ground—paranoia, denial, grandiosity, religiosity, occult beliefs, simple bewilderment, denial that anything is wrong
- how firmly attached the person is to his delusions (for instance, can he say, "I know this sounds crazy, but . . . ")
- the presence or absence of hallucinations, their character, and what beliefs the person has formed around them
- the presence or absence of paranormal manifestations—telepathy, precognitions—and how much control he exerts over them

- the presence or absence of Kundalini phenomena, and the locations of any physical blockages to this energy
- the response of the person's spouse, friends, and family to the ASC

After the healer gains an appreciation of the state of consciousness of his patient, he gathers information about his patient's personal history. This usually requires interviewing the family and includes the following information:

- the highest developmental level the person has ever attained
- his habitual modes of defending himself
- the nature and quality of his relationships with others
- the stability of the person's ego during past stressful life events
- the occurrence of similar psychotic ASCs in any blood relative, and the outcome of these
- recent or past involvement in spiritual practice or religion
- recent or past use of psychedelic medicines or other drugs
- circumstances of the person's conception, his mother's experience of pregnancy, difficulties during labor, and the child's adaptation during infancy
- the person's position in the family, how family members express love and disapproval, and their expectations of him throughout life.

TREATING AN ACUTE PSYCHOTIC ASC

Getting to know someone this well takes time and effort. It also requires rethinking the idea that all acute psychotic ASCs are medical emergencies. This misguided notion has led to the practice of rapid neuroleptization—injecting large doses of antipsychotic medicines hourly until all evidence of the ASC has been stamped out. There is no evidence that this leads to a better long-term outcome, and there is at least some reason to believe that it makes matters worse. Not only does it impede attending to the nuances of the ASC, but it sends a clear message to the patient that his experience is of no value, no matter how reparative it may be on a psychological level.

Ideally, during the early stages of a psychotic ASC antipsychotic medications are appropriate under only three circumstances: (1) when there is obvious danger of suicide or violence to others in the environment (in which case the judicious use of antipsyhotic medicines is preferable to physical restraints); (2) when a person defends himself

399

through paranoia (unchecked paranoid delusions can lead to suicide or assaultiveness, and so require direct intervention; in this case, measured doses of neuroleptics can reduce fearful vigilance and guardedness to the point where the person is receptive to psychological methods); (3) when a patient who has had previous psychotic ASCs is in extreme distress, feels unable to cope, and requests relief from the disturbing mental effects.

For the many cases that do not meet these three criteria, it is better to treat acute psychotic ASCs not as medical emergencies but as *spiritual* emergencies, until proven otherwise. This tactic is labor-intensive, but it is likely to save valuable labor and hospital space in the long run. The best way to handle an acute psychotic crisis is to provide a quiet retreat away from the stressors that precipitated it. For instance, if the healer determines that the patient's family is a source of ongoing stress, he limits the patient's contacts with them and substitutes continuous attention by people trained to provide empathy, support, and soothing. They should keep records of what the patient talks about, and what feelings come to the surface during the acute phase of his psychosis.

If the patient becomes uncomfortably agitated or restless, he is probably overstimulated. A quiet, secluded environment may be all that is necessary to quell anxious arousal. There is reason to believe that quiet rooms of certain colors, especially pink, have sedating effects on hyperaroused people. While in seclusion, a person may find that memories or feelings arise that he wishes to share. A staff member should always be available for this purpose. For a person in a psychotic ASC, being left alone in a secluded room with no one available to attend to his physical or emotional needs can turn into a terrifying nightmare.

The legacy of the psychedelic-infused rock concerts of the late 1960s provides us with much useful information about dealing with panic reactions that arise during psychotic ASCs. People experiencing bad LSD trips—a special form of spiritual emergency—were steered by their sympathetic peers into "freak-out stations" that offered asylum for people whose chemical indiscretions created untoward openings to the Ground. Although neuroleptic medicines—antidotes for LSD trips as well as schizophrenic ones—were readily available, the young counterculture physicians found that they achieved better results by providing a dimly lit environment, speaking in a soft voice, and encouraging a passive "flowing with" the experience rather than forcible resistance. When neuroleptics were given, they effectively slammed the door on the bad trip, but they also left the recipient fearful of similar experiences, prone to unpleasant flashbacks, and depressed for days.

A long-abandoned but harmlessly soothing technique for quieting agitated people in acute psychotic ASCs is to wrap them in cool wet-sheet packs. This tactic was used to good effect until about thirty years ago, when such labor-intensive methods were replaced by quick injections of tranquilizing medicine. Thought by some to be a coercive form of "bughouse torture," the procedure is actually quite pleasant and reassuring and is well known to health-spa habitués, who happily pay for its relaxing effects.

Following an explanation of the procedure, the agitated patient is wrapped in cool wet sheets so that he is comfortable but immobilized, like a swaddled infant. Once wrapped, the patient initially feels cold, but warming is rapid due to circulatory changes. This is usually followed by a welcome respite from an escalating cycle of arousal and anxiety. A staff member sits with the patient, who is encouraged to express whatever is on his mind. The procedure lasts for up to two hours, but may be stopped sooner at the patient's request. I once volunteered to experience this technique, which I found to be both deeply relaxing and evocative of vivid memories from childhood. This method could be combined with repetitive rocking movements and soothing music, which could further reduce the need for more intrusive restraints.

Because it is a greater error to medicate a spiritual emergency out of existence than to temporarily delay treating a malignantly regressive ASC in a safe setting, the least intrusive responses should be tried first. After a medicine-free observation period that may last from several hours to several days, the artful healer is in a position to determine if he is confronted with an authentic spiritual emergency or a severe psychotic regression that requires physically oriented treatment.

The likely outcome of a drug-free observation period conducted by an empathic staff in a soothing environment will be that about one-fourth of those in their first acute psychotic ASC will spontaneously return to the ordinary state of consciousness within a few days without chemical intervention. This is contrary to the common wisdom that all acute psychotic ASCs turn chronic unless promptly squelched with antipsychotic medicines. When a patient spontaneously returns to the consensual state of consciousness, it is an excellent prognostic sign that he is ready to engage in intensive psychotherapy to uncover the underlying conflicts and growth impediments that triggered the regression.

Of the remaining three-fourths whose psychotic ASCs persist, there will still be a significant number who meet the criteria for spiritual emergency. These may be expected to gradually recover with further intensive nondrug treatment. The remainder—somewhat more than half of any original sample of acute psychotics—will be caught up in a regression so intractable that they require physical means to arrest the process before less intrusive methods may be attempted.

In any case, the goal of any treatment for acute psychotic ASCs should be *restoration of the patient to a condition in which spiritual growth can resume.* For some this means surrendering the ego; for others, fortifying it. During spiritual emergencies, for instance, restoration means allowing the process to unfold in a protective and supportive environment with techniques designed to integrate the inflowing energies of the Ground and free the psyche for further expansion. In other words, therapy aims at moving the patient from uncontrolled spiritual emergency to controlled spiritual emergence. For people in schizophrenic ASCs, restoration means arresting regression with the artful use of medicines, then engaging the person in treatments designed to promote third-chakra skills, along with supportive therapy to strengthen the ego.

For extreme manic ASC's, restoration means quelling the escalating hyperarousal with lithium, then helping promote a more gradual expansion into higher-chakra consciousness in order to build tolerance for future openings to the Ground. For borderlines prone to psychotic ASCs, restoration means long-term, intensive psychotherapy in which the therapist provides a reliable surrogate ego, which is slowly grafted onto the patient's self. For MPD victims, restoration means intensive, long-term psychotherapy of a specialized sort in which alter personalities enter into a dialogue that gradually dissolves their psychic boundaries and allows a larger self to emerge, inclusive of each of the alters. (Treatment strategies for MPD were presented at some length in chapter 3.)

TRANSPERSONAL THERAPIES FOR MANIC ASCS

Because manic ASCs have some characteristics in common with both spiritual emergencies and regressive psychoses like schizophrenia, their treatment is complex and requires the artful healer to don the cloak of both physician and guru at different stages of the process. Manic ASCs induce states of extreme arousal accompanied by abrupt expansions of the self into higher chakra levels for which there has not been adequate grounding in past experience. This initially leads to euphoria, followed by a "crash and burn" phase in which the mood turns irritable as hallucinations and paranoia overwhelm consensual reality. When this relentless spiral hits bottom, it results in the bleakest depression, during which the self is spiritually paralyzed and suicide feels like a reasonable alternative to taking one's next breath.

A person in an early manic ASC is in a position reminiscent of the audacious coyote in the popular Roadrunner cartoons, who would take three steps off the edge of a cliff but not fall until he looked down and realized he was no longer standing on terra firma. People in manic ASCs are difficult to convince that anything is amiss, even as they unhinge their families and careers for the sake of an overinflated whimsy. To a manic, there are no limits, and regrets are inconceivable, although inevitably forthcoming.

Physical Healing

Although manic ASCs temporarily catapult the psyche to higher states of consciousness, they are far from easy to treat. Healers who regularly deal with the misguided willfulness of manics know that psychological tactics alone, no matter how sophisticated, are inadequate. For most cases of acute mania, there are virtually no reasonable alternatives to using lithium. And abhorrent though it may be to libertarian sensitivities, if ever there is justification for confining people to safe environments against their will, it is when they are certifiably manic. The alternative is often prison or injury to self or others following reckless behavior. If treatment is offered with requisite artfulness, most people with this affliction will be grateful once their reason is restored.

Before taking steps to physically quell the ASC, however, an artful healer sits with his manic patient for a while and listens mindfully. If people in manic ASCs have not yet reached the point where they are disorganized and incoherent, they can be quite creative and occasionally prescient, with an uncanny knack of picking up subtleties that are ordinarily overlooked. Here is an opportunity for a healer to observe an extraordinary ASC in its pristine state, and it may afford him a rare glimpse into the consciousness of the higher chakras, though this is usually extremely distorted. Often the patient will grow calmer by simply releasing verbal energy in the presence of a good listener.

It is important to realize that the depressive phase of the bipolar disorder is just as biologically driven as the manic phase and is accompanied by a deficiency of the same neurotransmitter that is overactive during mania. Depressions that follow manic highs are made doubly grim by the person's realization that he recently contacted a larger self that now seems irretrievably lost. Whereas the manic self is overpermeable to the Spiritual Ground, the depressed self constricts the inflow of this usually generous source of vitality. This contraction feels so inexorable that the person despairs of ever finding his way back to Eden. Being so cut off from the Ground sets up a vicious cycle that spins the depressed person ever downward.

It is during this cycle that antidepressant medications can restore balance to neurotransmitter function. Although some transpersonal healers may think that I am advocating indiscriminate drug treatment to cover up symptoms that demand psychological work, I would counter that the depressions that follow mania are no garden-variety blues.

A person caught up in this bleak ASC cannot sleep or concentrate on the most simple task, is so irritable that others react negatively toward him, and blames himself for everything amiss in his environment. Because suicide is an ever-present danger, a healer should not risk trying to reverse mania by psychotherapy alone.

Physical exercise is important during both manic and depressive phases of the bipolar cycle. During the manic phase it channels excess energy into harmless activity and helps reestablish the disrupted sleep/wake cycle. Although it can be difficult to motivate a severely depressed person to exercise, it is known that aerobic exercise restores balance to the brain's neurotransmitters in much the same way as do antidepressant medicines. The feeling of mastery associated with becoming physically fit also helps restore one's sense of self-esteem.

Emotional Healing

On the emotional level, transpersonal therapy for people with bipolar disorder means helping them deal with the devastating personal consequences of their mood swings. Individuals with this syndrome have no more core-personality hang-ups than anyone else, although the disorder itself can be a source of great distress. There is no reason to believe that the bipolar syndrome is caused by emotional traumas early in life, although they can make the picture worse. Manic-depressives do, however, encounter extraordinary problems with their marriages and careers, and require consistent emotional support, especially throughout the depressed phase.

Intellectual Healing

On the intellectual level, a conscientious healer takes pains to educate his manic-depressive patients about what causes their ASCs and the need to recognize them early. One often overlooked area is in sleep hygiene. People with a predisposition to extreme mood swings should take pains to maintain regular sleep patterns. Missing even one night's sleep, or not compensating for jet lag while traveling, can trigger a manic episode, which then feeds on itself by further disrupting sleep. Time-honored triggers for manic episodes such as bereavement, childbirth, and falling in love all disrupt sleep. It is also important for the manic patient to shun psychostimulants—caffeine, diet pills, cocaine, amphetamines—which can hurl a susceptible person into a manic ASC at far lower doses than would be required for people not genetically predisposed.

Lithium can prevent manic episodes as well as treat them. However, if patient and healer decide to reserve lithium solely for manic phases— a reasonable strategy when mood swings are widely spaced or if there have been only one or two lifetime manic attacks—the patient must learn to recognize the first symptoms of relapse and trust family and friends to warn him of a precipitous change in mood. Because manics are notorious for using denial to defend their mood swings, the artful healer tailors his message to a hyperaroused sensibility.

Spiritual Healing

Although manic-depressive ASCs have a prominent genetic component, treatment should do more than amend chemical imbalances. Mania prematurely exposes the individual to the unfiltered consciousness of the higher chakras, and therefore confronts him with his latent potential for spiritual development. The problem is that he is unprepared to make use of this blinding realization, so ego inflation spins out of control. This is a dangerous condition, but also full of opportunity for spiritual transformation if the person is guided by a healer who is aware of the potentials inherent in any expansive ASC.

Once the ordinary state of consciousness returns, an artful healer helps his patient establish a disciplined pattern of spiritual growth. Unlike severe schizophrenia, a cycle of mania and depression will eventually run its course, and the individual will return to the highest chakra level he has previously integrated in life. For individuals whose life development has taken them no further than the third chakra, the best tactic for restoring spiritual growth is orthodox insight-oriented psychotherapy augmented by bodywork and emotion-releasing tactics.

Because milder forms of the manic ASC can enhance creativity, the patient should be encouraged to develop his native talents. For advanced manic patients, meditation can condition the psyche to tolerate altered states of consciousness. The more mindfulness the individual acquires in his ordinary state, the more he can cope with hyperaroused states. This course of treatment is similar in principle to *homeopathy,* an alternative system of medicine that opposes the orthodox emphasis on treating symptoms of disease. Instead of giving medicines that produce effects *opposite* to the prominent symptoms, a homeopath prescribes small amounts of substances that induce effects *similar* to the disease. The idea is that this stimulates the body's natural defenses. Likewise, if a person prone to mania regularly enters mild and controllable ASC's through meditation, he can learn to maneuver in far more extraordinary mental states.

Social Healing

It is quite difficult to live with someone whose moods fluctuate for reasons that have little to do with events in the environment. Spouses of manics find that their own emotional reactions are ignored in the flurry of attention directed toward their husbands or wives. The artful healer helps all family members to vent their feelings, including children, who have about a 10 to 15 percent chance of having similar mood swings later in life.

HEALING SPIRITUAL EMERGENCIES

In the opening lines of the *Divine Comedy,* Dante captured both the terror and the ultimate salvation of a spiritual emergency.

> Midway upon the journey of our life
> I found that I was in a dusky wood:
> For the right path, whence I had strayed, was lost.
> Ah! How hard a thing it is to tell
> The wildness of that rough and savage place,
> The very thought of which brings back my fear!
> But that the good I found there may be told,
> I will describe the other things I saw.

Once a healer makes a diagnosis of spiritual emergency, he confronts the most benign of all psychotic ASCs. A spiritual emergency is an abrupt, confusing crisis resembling that of birth, accompanied by an altered state of consciousness that can mimic severe forms of psychosis. If facilitated rather than hampered, it naturally leads to a higher plane of awareness. This form of divine madness arises when a person's natural urges to overcome his ego-based alienation are thwarted by impediments to greater relatedness and unity. These hindrances can come from without, such as a destructive relationship, or from within, such as overvalued attachments or fear of intimacy. In either case, the ego resists growth and clings to its calcified self-concept with a death grip that is broken only with explosive force.

Fortunately, only a minority of spiritual emergences cause such crises. Most are gradual and natural unfoldings of higher consciousness, and so require little more treatment than reassurance and guidance toward spiritual practices appropriate for that individual. Spiritual emergencies, however, temporarily render a person unable to function in the world, and if mishandled could result in permanent damage to the personality. In supportive environments, many spiritual emergencies resolve themselves spontaneously as long as they are not prematurely interrupted, and can result in self-healing, renewal, and spiritual growth.

Chapter 12 contains a detailed description of spiritual emergencies, along with characteristics that distinguish them from virulent psychotic regressions. These criteria are not foolproof, however, and a certain percentage of psychotic ASCs that appear to be spiritual emergencies eventually turn out to be malignant. Nonetheless, anyone whose acute psychotic ASC meets the favorable prognostic criteria outlined in chapter 12 should be given a chance to respond to growth-enhancing therapies.

Giving birth to a new reality that fulfills a person's deepest visions can sensitize him emotionally and physically and render him temporarily unfit for ordinary tasks. Therefore, treatment ideally takes place in a quiet, retreatlike setting close to nature, where the individual can be isolated from the stresses of ordinary life for days or weeks. Treatment should be intensive—several hours a day—and intermixed with periods of solitude to promote integration of material that arises. Models for residential treatment of spiritual emergencies emerged from pioneering experiments at the Soteria and Diabasis communities in California, where psychotic people were allowed latitude to freely express their feelings, beliefs, and imagery.

Although Soteria and Diabasis failed to survive, we might speculate that this was not from a lack of effective methods to treat spiritual emergencies, but from a failure to take the pre/trans fallacy into account when selecting those to whom these methods were applied. If these communities had carefully limited their clientele to people in genuine spiritual emergencies, they would probably still be performing an invaluable service to a significant minority of people who experience psychotic ASCs. Fortunately, the idea behind these therapeutic communities has not faded away. New ones are springing up, offering fresh ideas and opportunities to experiment with spiritual healing techniques.

TRANSPERSONAL THERAPIES FOR SPIRITUAL EMERGENCIES

A transpersonal approach to spiritual emergencies is radically different from orthodox therapies, which aim to "readjust" an individual to the limited consciousness of third-chakra societies—or, in Freud's words, to "return him to that state of unhappiness general to all mankind." In contrast, a transpersonal approach holds that unhappiness is not inherent in the human condition, and strives to help the patient to liberate himself from the root cause of unhappiness: alienation from his larger self and from the Spiritual Ground.

Artful healing of spiritual emergencies requires us to change the way we think about ASCs, beginning with the way we train our healers. The process of earning a professional degree reinforces ways of thinking that prevent empathizing with the inner reality of people in psychotic ASCs. This is not to say that psychiatrists, psychologists, and social workers cannot successfully work with spiritual emergencies, only that they have some *unlearning* to do first. We need a community of healers who are familiar enough with influxes of the Spiritual Ground that they are neither afraid nor condemning of them, and can in fact use them as springboards to apprehend the subjective world of their patients.

This requires the healer to become the agent of his patient rather than of society, standing for the authority of nature rather than the authority of the consensus. Therapist and patient should explore together with *equal status,* in an atmosphere of mutual trust. In an ideal sanctuary, rigid staff/patient hierarchies collapse, and each patient is expected to take charge of his life and his destiny. His personal space is respected, and he is not pushed into intimate relatedness before he feels ready. Instead, it is his task to inform the staff when he feels prepared to tentatively reach beyond his solitary ASC.

Ideally, transpersonal therapy for spiritual emergencies in a residential setting emphasizes the same five areas of healing that apply to other disorders: physical, emotional, intellectual, spiritual, and social. Therapy within each area aims to uncover and remove blockages that prevent the natural expansion of consciousness through the higher chakras.

Few therapists are skilled in all five of these areas, so a team approach is essential. However, each new patient should have a primary therapist to provide reliable companionship and deep understanding and to coordinate the team during daily meetings to exchange ideas. Ideally, the therapist himself has experienced a spiritual emergence or emergency in which he came to terms with his own higher potentials and made headway in integrating the healing consciousness of the heart chakra. Because he knows the territory, he can provide empathic witness to the patient's journey and act as attentive midwife to a spiritual rebirth.

Physical Healing

Healing on the physical level takes into account that a spiritual emergency is stressful to the whole organism. The psyche cannot openly receive healing unless the body is in prime condition. Attention to physical needs includes a medical checkup with special focus on neurology, a survey of the state of nutrition, which is often neglected by people undergoing spiritual emergency, and daily aerobic exercise. Questioning the patient about unexplained sensations of pain, pressure, burning, or tingling in the traditional physical locations of the chakras may lend insight into the character of psychological blockages.

Skilled bodywork and deep-tissue massage can liberate repressed emotions that impede spiritual growth, especially preverbal traumas from birth and early life that cannot be expressed in words and are stored as body armor. Physical methods may be the *only* way to bring them to the surface. Techniques like yoga and breathing exercises add an extra dimension to verbal psychotherapy that is overlooked by orthodox therapies that stiffly prohibit touching. We never outgrow our need for reassurance that a living human being is with us during difficult moments of passage. The power of a gentle touch, so essential to an infant, is exactly what many adults need when lost in self-doubt and despair. A hand on the shoulder, a friendly hug, or a back rub is not inappropriate and can have a grounding effect on an agitated psyche. (Sexualized touching is, of course, *always* harmful in a therapeutic setting.)

Antipsychotic medicines tend to retard the natural process of healing inherent in genuine spiritual emergencies, and in all but a few cases are contraindicated. However, there are times when a temporary cooling off of extreme openings to the Ground is desirable, as long as medicines are used with exceptional sensitivity. The vast outflowings of psychic energy liberated by these upheavals must at times be contained and redirected from chaotic forms into more workable manifestations.

There is a middle ground between total withholding of medicines and officiously prescribing textbook dosages with little regard for the subjective reactions of the patient. For instance, I know of a woman at a three-month meditation retreat who started to experience hallucinations and incipient delusions. A sensitive psychiatrist who happened to be at the retreat recommended that she take a half milligram of Haldol a day—a very small dose. This made a world of difference and allowed her to continue her journey.

It is important that the patient maintain the discipline of internalizing the healing process without projecting it onto others. An emergence of paranoid defenses or agitated states that cannot be safely handled within an open environment are indications for a short trial with low-dose antipsychotics. These should be discontinued as soon as the patient is able to continue with less intrusive therapies. The healer must keep in mind that in nonschizophrenics these medicines dull awareness, inhibit abstract thinking, decrease motivation, and lower mood, all of which retard integration and healing. If it is not possible to safely discontinue these medicines and resume disciplined internal work after a few days, the healer should rethink his diagnosis of spiritual emergency.

Emotional Healing

The emotional level deserves the most attention during early stages of a spiritual emergency. Because spiritual emergencies are accompanied by a broad spectrum of moods—profound depression, inner absorption, intense fear, jubilance, and ecstasy, to name a few—the healer should tailor his treatment strategy to the affective state.

Most people in a spiritual crisis respond to opportunities for intense emotional release. The longer the patient has forced his shadow nature underground, the more volcanic will be its liberation. Therefore, these people need a place where: (1) it is permissible to let loose pent-up feelings that may have been accumulating for years; (2) they are free to physically release what has been poisoning them, without fear of harming others; and (3) it is safe to be emotionally out of control, even raucously so. It is not easy for a healer to sit with a person who is actively casting off emotional blockages that have been festering for a lifetime. But an artful healer is secure enough within his own self to accept his patient's intense feelings with compassion and equanimity.

Many spiritual emergencies in Western cultures take place during transitions from the third to the fourth chakra. Therefore, they often free up the kind of nagging guilt feelings we all accumulate during our frenzied passage through the narcissistic third chakra but do not acknowledge until the empathic heart starts to open. Guilt feelings may have been habitually numbed through addictions, which tend to disappear spontaneously once a person applies compassion toward his own human frailties. A psyche unbound from the constraints of a guilt-ridden ego does not—as many fear—turn out to be that of a wild beast rutting about in the squalor of its own naked instincts. Liberation does not mean losing one's ego-oriented rules of social behavior. It simply means seeing through them, choosing to conform or not to conform according to one's own predilections, all the while accepting responsibility for every willed action.

Ideally, a sanctuary for people in spiritual emergency is also a school for creativity. An unfortunate pattern in cultures that reward creativity but not compassion is that a talented person may be well along into integrating fifth-chakra consciousness without having first opened his heart. In such cases where essential growth tasks were skipped, mild emotional regression is essential for the person to catch up. Because the patient may find it difficult to talk about the unfamiliar emotions swirling within his psyche, the healer encourages him to give them voice through creative expression, avoiding intellectualization. Poetry, journal writing, simple musical expression, and freehand drawing are excellent mediums for expressing one's secret fears and longings.

Striking mythological themes often emerge during spiritual emergencies, taking form in dreams, fantasies, or even transient hallucinations and quasi delusions. Motifs of death and rebirth, setting out on a quest, fulfilling a mission, searching for something lost, and breaking free of restraints are typical. These archetypal themes contain important clues about unfulfilled developmental tasks, and they can inform the healer in guiding his patient's inner imagery.

Yet the artful healer recognizes that hastily interpreting symbols from the subconscious, no matter how cleverly done, has a stifling effect on a nascent feeling. Requests for information, ill-timed reassurances, and giving advice can be subtle ways of nonhearing that distract a patient from proceeding inward. A self-aware healer acknowledges that he may be tempted to speak in order to shelter himself from the impact of his patient's raw emotions. Although prolonged silences may indicate resistance to self-exploration, they also signal periods when the patient is conducting his most important inner work. When the healer's intuition tells him that an interpretation is appropriate, he should strive for the grace of simplicity.

Once caught up with old business, the patient will likely find that life proceeds more smoothly. Nevertheless, some regressions may take an ominous turn. Signs of malignant regression during therapy include the individual progressively distancing himself or losing his self-sense for more than a few hours. In the former instance he should be moved to a safe environment and not left alone. In the latter case, a short trial on antipsychotic medicines may be necessary to restore a state in which he again responds to therapy. In contrast, "mini-regressions" that are potentially restorative are marked by the preservation of most of the patient's higher functions, such as his capacity to observe, reflect, and communicate meaningfully what he is experiencing, and by his acceptance of contact and care—in other words, willfully surrendering to the healing process.

The transpersonal psychotherapists Stanislav and Christina Grof have developed a powerful method, called *holotropic integration,* that releases long-buried emotional traumas. The Grofs point out that Western cultures are unique in that they believe psychotherapy works best when it deals with biographical material from a person's childhood that is discussed in the ordinary state of consciousness and followed by an opinion from a particular theoretical school. In contrast, most other cultures insist on altering the consciousness of either healer or patient in order to mobilize traumatic memories from very early life and open the gates to the subsconscious.

Holotropic therapy is a surprisingly simple and effective method for inducing a mild ASC that triggers a cathartic release of long-repressed emotions. The Grofs instruct people attending their groups in the technique of controlled hyperventilation for up to two hours at a time. With a sitter in attendance, each person breathes as rapidly and deeply as he can and is encouraged to freely express in a nonverbal manner whatever enters awareness. The process is helped along by carefully selected, emotionally evocative music played at concert volume.

Although common wisdom holds that hyperventilation induces an unpleasant ASC associated with hysteria and panic, this does not happen under the controlled circumstances of holotropic therapy. I have personally experienced holotropic breathing sessions on four occasions during the Grofs' workshops at Esalen Institute in Big Sur, California. The experience of rapid hyperventilation was at first mildly unsettling as odd physical sensations passed upward through my arms and legs. This stage passed quickly, however, and was replaced by a lucid, inwardly focused ASC in which emotionally tinged images of exceptional clarity passed through my awareness, evoked by themes of the music. I found that I could easily control the intensity of the ASC by accelerating or slowing my breathing, or stop it altogether by breathing normally.

On several occasions during the breathing sessions, I noticed that my body was moving spontaneously as if reliving the birth passage, and these moments were accompanied by rushes of emotions, some associated with memories of "forgotten" events from early life. After each session there was an opportunity to process what came up in a supportive group meeting. The residual aftereffects of the ASC were no more than mild fatigue, followed by a night of vivid dreams. The next day, I had a definite feeling of lightness and release that sprung from the knowledge that I had effectively dealt with several long-neglected matters.

The Grofs acknowledge that their technique is unsuitable for people in chronic psychotic ASCs, or for people with paranoia. Nor do they work in closed settings such as are appropriate for extreme spiritual emergencies. Holotropic therapy is appropriate for people in mild spiritual emergencies and for nonpsychotic people with stubborn emotional barriers to spiritual emergence. Yet this and similar techniques to induce therapeutic ASCs could be creatively modified for patients in deeper spiritual crises.

Intellectual Healing

Many people caught up in sudden openings to the Ground do not understand what is happening to them and are understandably terrified. They may be thrown off balance by emergent paranormal abilities or simply befuddled by an unfamiliar ASC that they misinterpret as irreversible insanity. If a healer encourages his patient to hazard an un-charted journey through a shadowy underworld, he should first inform that patient about regression in the service of transcendence and the prospects for its resolution leading to a more authentic and fulfilling life.

Hallucinated entities or obviously delusional ideas should be vali-dated not as *consensually* real, but as real indications of inner transforma-tion. An artful healer interprets his patient's apparitions as credible and meaningful only in a *personal* way, clearly distinguished from the con-sensual world. Once this difference is established, he helps the patient to categorize his visions, thereby neutralizing the menace of the name-less. But the healer does not pretend authority as to the exact meaning of symbolic imagery. Instead, he facilitates self-discovery through his supportive presence and honest efforts at empathy. By trusting his pa-tient's innate wisdom, he validates the ASC as a natural healing experi-ence rather than a mental disease.

This healing stance is in sharp contrast to orthodox tactics, in which therapists discourage patients from mentioning their delusions or hallucinations, the better to focus on the immediate concerns of everyday living. The idea is that the upwelling imagery is only gibberish anyway, and that the patient should not be enticed to withdraw further into his nonconsensual world. The trouble with this approach is that the patient's *feelings* will not cower behind a socialized mask, and the split between inner and outer realities grows ever wider. A better re-sponse is for the healer to draw within himself for a moment and em-pathically feel what it would be like to hear his patient's voices or believe his delusions, then reflect this new understanding back in a personal context.

In this way, an artful healer provides an intellectual framework to help the patient accept his experience as a difficult but natural process of renewal, and to reassure him that help is available. The healer may also give his patient books or articles on spiritual crises, and conduct groups with people who have undergone similar ASCs. The healer's goal is to link the intellectual understanding of spiritual emergency with the subjective experience of being in a mildly regressive altered state.

Spiritual Healing

Unlike people caught up in malignant regressions, individuals in spiritual emergencies respond favorably to spiritual therapies. Fore-most among these is meditation, ideally practiced daily. Meditation may at first be quite difficult for people experiencing unfamiliar ASCs, but it is essential for sustaining spiritual growth in a controlled way. For patients who have never before meditated, two daily sittings of ten to twenty minutes are usually well tolerated. Although the healer should remain nearby and available, he will benefit from meditating with his patient, paying close attention to anything that enters his own awareness that might have a bearing on the healing process. As the patient's consciousness gains coherence, the length of the meditation sessions can be extended, recognizing that it is certainly possible to meditate too much. The end of each meditation session is an ideal time for verbal psychotherapy.

In some cases, a spiritual emergency can be precipitated by the immoderate practice of meditation, which temporarily disrupts the ego or leads to uncontrolled Kundalini manifestations. In such a case, residence at a therapeutic retreat provides an ideal opportunity to modify and balance the person's practice, and to try out different forms of meditation. Some, like mantra meditation, have more of a grounding effect, increasing one's control over openings to the Ground. Occasionally a temporary cessation from meditation is necessary in extreme spiritual crises.

During the 1950s and 1960s several creative psychotherapists experimented with psychedelic medicines to treat addictions, reduce fear of death in terminally ill hospice patients, and uncover and release emotional blockages that precipitated spiritual emergencies (although that term had not yet been coined). The idea behind these experiments was to use the psychedelic ASC as a lever to lift a person's consciousness into the higher chakras and afford him a glimpse of his higher potentials, in the hope that this would provide impetus for further spiritual progress. The results of these early experiments were encouraging. Grof, for instance, wrote of his experiments in Czechoslovakia:

> In an extensive therapeutic study of LSD psychotherapy conducted at the Psychiatric Research Institute in Prague, I observed a dramatic improvement in several manifestly psychotic patients that transcended by far anything that can be achieved by the traditional suppressive psychopharmacological treatment. The changes in these patients involved not only the disappearance of symptoms but also a deep and significant restructuring of personalities.

Unfortunately, this promising research has now been forbidden by government edict. Psychiatrists are freely allowed to administer drugs to treat pain, anxiety, depression, insomnia, stress, panic attacks, illogical thinking, mania, hyperactivity, and hallucinations. But giving medicines to help people gain knowledge and insight, or engage in spiritual exploration for the sake of personal growth, is prohibited. Although psychedelics have potential for abuse, so, too, do tranquilizers, stimulants, and opiates, which are not prohibited. Prior to Western acculturation, shamanic societies that used psychedelic plants for ritual and healing did not suffer from the problems of drug abuse that plague contemporary society. Used with skill and artfulness under carefully disciplined conditions, psychedelics could be invaluable tools for treating spiritual emergencies and a variety of other impediments to spiritual growth.

Social Healing

As a spiritual emergency subsides and the self resumes its growth into higher realms of consciousness, therapeutic attention shifts to the community. Because there are very few sheltered retreats equipped to treat spiritual emergencies competently, residential treatment should be limited to a few weeks at most to make room for the greatest number of people, and to reduce the chance of regressive dependence on the therapeutic setting. This means that the individual must be referred to community healers skilled in dealing with spiritual emergencies.

Since 1980, the Spiritual Emergence Network (SEN) has collected and disseminated information related to recognition and treatment of altered states of consciousness. The staff has compiled a list of professionals who are willing to work with people in apparent spiritual emergencies. Although SEN does not screen these sources, it has made a significant start in informing the healing professions about this new concept, which remains outside established psychiatric diagnoses.

The major problem in establishing residential treatment programs for spiritual emergencies is neither a lack of dedicated staff nor a shortage of potential patients in need. It is a real fear of being sued. Anyone devising innovative or unorthodox treatment programs is vulnerable to being hauled into court by a legal profession that insists that the healing professions march in lockstep with a stultified "community standard"—little more than a mandate for mediocrity.

This situation is unlikely to change until mainstream psychiatry, psychology, and social work accept the idea that all spontaneous ASCs are not intrinsically pathological. I believe that modern psychiatry is more ready to integrate spiritual concepts than nonpsychiatrists generally acknowledge. But it will take a concerted effort by transpersonally oriented psychiatrists to spread the word from within.

Epilogue

◆

There is a common goal for all of us. In the end, nobody can
attain redemption while his fellows remain still unredeemed.
PAUL BRUNTON

THE OUTLOOK IS bright. As the collective consciousness of humanity stands poised to expand into the compassionate awareness of
the heart chakra, we grow ready to cultivate ever more healing empathy
for the psychotic people who dwell among us, as well as to draw one step
nearer to our ultimate unitive destiny. Once a majority of humanity
reaches the fourth and fifth chakras, people who regress to our present
third-chakra level will seem mad simply for behaving the way most people on this planet do now.

We may expect that in a decade or so the human genetic structure will
be mapped in its entirety, followed by the means to eliminate from future
generations those genes that predispose a person to mania, schizophrenia,
and other inherited conditions deemed "undesirable" by modern society.
With this newfound command of evolution will come an awesome responsibility, for we will also discover ways to produce human beings with
larger, more powerful brains, or specialized neurochemistry that can operate within realities that are now unthinkable. We will devise ever more
powerful medicines to alter brain function in specific ways that radically
expand our relationship with the Spiritual Ground. These advances will
confront humankind with monumental ethical questions that we have not
yet begun to think through.

As humanity collectively expands into the consciousness of the higher
chakras, we will ideally gain the wisdom to use what lies ahead for our
benefit. This requires that consciousness itself become a subject of intensive objective study and personal exploration in both its ordinary
and altered states. One way to begin is to pay respectful attention to the
extraordinary states of consciousness of those thought mad, as well as to

reown the madman within ourselves. Although we share this planet with people who see reality in many different ways, we have been blind to their potential to help us do the same.

The heart of the psychotic person lies within our heart; his or her mind is in our mind. Even to pretend competence in meeting such an individual, we must seek within ourselves the wellsprings of all human thought and action. We must learn through the fastidious exploration of our deepest selves that every thought, every act ever committed, no matter how hideous or exalted, lies within our own capability. Once we *feel* this through and through, and also lovingly accept it about ourselves, we will be ready for the encounter with the source of our own madness and that of those we seek to heal. The mad can be our teachers.

From schizophrenics we can learn to recognize our evolutionary roots in primal consciousness, which are only tenuously transcended by the relatively modern ego. Once we acknowledge our journey upward through the Great Chain of Being, it is easy to overcome the arrogance that leads us to devalue other states of consciousness, life forms, and cultures. If society condemns the schizophrenic for blurring conventional boundaries between inner and outer, the schizophrenic reminds society that this distinction is ultimately arbitrary and not at all the rigid, inflexible absolute that the ego imagines it to be.

People in manic ASCs challenge us to pierce through the confusion generated by their naive excursions into the numinous to glimpse higher potentials in our own consciousness. People prone to mania are among the most creatively iconoclastic in our culture. They summon us to heal the split between exceptional awareness and social adaptation without sacrificing the integrity of the individual. Once we cultivate an empathic eye, the "crazy wisdom" of mania leads us to a new respect for spontaneous ASCs and other unusual experiences.

People with multiple personalities confront us with the vast depth and mystery of human consciousness in its relationship with the Ground. At the same time that MPD victims force us to take a fresh look at comfortable notions of personal selfhood, they also expose the devastating consequences of child abuse, the magnitude of which has emerged into the awareness of Western societies only during the last two decades. It is a tribute to the healing power of empathy that imaginative therapists are now developing techniques to heal this most enigmatic of psychological maladies.

People in spiritual emergencies teach us that spontaneous ASCs are not always harmful, may lead to uncommon growth, and may even be cultivated as a strategy for enriching our lives. The ordinary state of consciousness is hopelessly limited if we wish to generate breakthrough solutions to multilevel environmental and social problems, see beyond the constrictions of ordinary reality, gain inspiration for a work of art, participate deeply in group experience, cultivate a latent telepathic or healing ability, or directly apprehend our divine nature.

Neither science nor philosophy nor introspection alone can offer final solutions to the questions raised in this book regarding madness— or the experience of being alive and miraculously aware on this planet. Yet it is built into the nature of humanity to seek such solutions. In this quest, and in our encounters with those whose inner flame burns too hot, we might regard the seeds of healing reflected in the most fundamental symbol of the ancient East, the yin-yang circle that represents the primal split within the unity underlying all creation.

This symbol neatly encapsulates the complementarity of all worldly dualities: night and day, male and female, reason and intuition, madness and sanity, God and human. The ancients were careful to show that each element contains the seeds of the other: in yin there is also yang, in yang there is yin. No division is ever complete; the profound chaos of madness pulses in the sanest of us, while true sanity dwells lovingly within the maddest. There lies within each of us this healing seed that can weld our fragmented selves into a greater whole in union with our Source.

Notes

◆

INTRODUCTION

xv. To expect religion For a discussion of differences between scientific observation, rational understanding, and spiritual intuition, see K. Wilber, *Eye to Eye* (New York: Anchor Books, 1983). **xviii.** Under adverse conditions R. Walsh and F. Vaughan, "Comparative Models of the Person and Psychotherapy," in *Transpersonal Psychotherapy,* ed. S. Boorstein (Palo Alto, CA: Science and Behavior Books, 1980), p. 12–27. **xxi.** For indeed, nature C. G. Jung, *The Psychogenesis of Mental Disease,* trans. R. F. C. Hull, Bollingen Series XX (Princeton, NJ: Princeton University Press, 1960), p. 271.

CHAPTER ONE

9. Yet this is S. Grof, *Beyond the Brain* (Albany: State University of New York Press, 1985), p. 22. **11.** But ultimately consciousness Ken Wilber cautioned against making "category errors" that confuse physical, mental, and spiritual phenomena. Wilber, *Eye to Eye.* **12.** This process, called The term *original repression* was coined by Michael Washburn, whose foundational ideas were used for this book. Washburn's "Dynamic Ground" is here called the Spiritual Ground. M. Washburn, *The Ego and the Dynamic Ground* (Albany: State University of New York Press, 1987). **15.** The following is Charles Tart's works have been a major source of ideas for this chapter. See C. Tart, *States of Consciousness* (New York: Dutton, 1975); C. Tart, ed., *Altered States of Consciousness* (New York: Anchor Books, 1972); C. Tart, "Some Assumptions of Orthodox Western Psychology," in *Transpersonal Psychologies,* ed. C. Tart (New York: Harper & Row, 1975), p. 81. **17.** Small quantitative increases For a comparable view of ASCs, see R. Fisher, "A Cartography of the Ecstatic and Meditative States," *Science* 174(1971):897–904. **21.** There were lots Wilber, *Eye to Eye,* p. 193. **22.** "Every human being" Albert Hoffman, "The Transmitter-Receiver Concept of Reality," *ReVision* 10: (Spring 1988): 5–11. **22.** So for our Joseph Chilton Pierce discusses how children learn consensual reality in *The Crack in the Cosmic Egg* (New York: Pocket Books, 1971), and *Magical Child* (New York: Dutton, 1977). **24.** Research has demonstrated K. Pribam, "The Neurophysiology of Remembering," in *Progress in Psychobiology: Readings from Scientific American* (San Francisco: Freeman, 1969), pp. 316–17. **26.** European explorers learned Lawrence Blair, *Rhythms of Vision* (New York: Schocken Books, 1975), p. 22. **26.** James Fadiman and J. Fadiman and D. Kewman, eds., *Exploring Madness* (Monterey, CA: Brooks/Cole, 1973), p. 97.

CHAPTER TWO

30. Some who have For an account of a growth-producing psychotic experience, see M. Vonnegut, *The Eden Express* (New York: Bantam Books, 1975), p. 274. **32.** Similar ASCs of The 1979 version of the diagnostic code was revised in 1987, and will likely undergo an even more extensive revision in the early 1990s. See American Psychiatric Association, *Diagnostic and Statistical Manual of Mental Disorders,* 3rd. ed., rev. (Washington, DC: American Psychiatric Association, 1987). **34.** "Sometimes I'd go" Quoted by D. Heveroch, in B. Freedman, "The Subjective Experience of Perceptual and Cognitive Disturbances in Schizophrenia," *Archives of General Psychiatry* 30(1974): 336–40. **36.** "It's just a" Vonnegut, *Eden Express,* p. 137. **38.** A dark example V. Bugliosi, *Helter Skelter* (New York: Bantam Books, 1974), pp. 324–25. **43.** R. D. Laing called this R. D. Laing discussed implosion in *The Divided Self* (Baltimore: Penguin Books, 1960), p. 45. **44.** This cascade of S. Arieti, *The Interpretation of Schizophrenia,* 2nd ed. (New York: Basic Books, 1974), p. 393. **47.** One-third of these R. Chancro, "Overview of Schizophrenia," in *Comprehensive Textbook of Psychiatry III* (Baltimore: Williams & Wilkins, 1980), pp. 1093–1103. **48.** Yet recent evidence C. M. Harding, G. W. Brooks, et al., "The Vermont

Longitudinal Study of Persons With Severe Mental Illness, I." *American Journal of Psychiatry* 144:6(1987). **50.** Ronald Fieve, a physician   Fieve was instrumental in introducing lithium treatment into the United States. See R. R. Fieve, *Moodswing* (New York: Bantam Books, 1975).

CHAPTER THREE

54. The psychoanalyst Heinz Kohut   Heinz Kohut defines *selfobject* in several works. See, for instance, H. Kohut and E. Wolf, "The Disorders of the Self and Their Treatment: An Outline," *International Journal of Psychoanalytic Medicine* 59(1978): 413–25.   **54.** Similar disruptions of   People concerned with diagnostic subtleties disagree on whether the borderline condition is a mild form of schizophrenia or a separate phenomenon. See S. J. Beck, "Schizophrenia Without Psychosis," *Archives of Neurology and Psychiatry*, 81(1959): 85–96.   **55.** Although they can   S. Snyder, "Pseudologica Fantastica in the Borderline Patient," *American Journal of Psychiatry* 143(1986):1287–89.   **55.** The following is   J. G. Gunderson, and M. C. Zanarini, "Current Overview of the Borderline Diagnosis," *Journal of Clinical Psychiatry* 48(August 1987).   **56.** His sexual confusion   One study showed that homosexuality is ten times more common in men and six times more common in women with the borderline syndrome than in the general population. G. S. Lubenko, et al., "Sexual Practices among Patients with Borderline Personality Disorder," *American Journal of Psychiatry* 144(1987):748–52.   **58.** Controls feigning alternate   C. H. Thigpen and H. Cleckley, "A Case of Multiple Personality," *Journal of Abnormal Psychology* 49(1954):135–51; F. W. Putnam, "The Psychophysiological Investigation of Multiple Personality Disorder: A Review," *Psychiatric Clinics of North America* 7(1984):31–39; P. M. Coons, "EEG Studies of Two Multiple Personalities and a Control," *Archives of General Psychiatry* 39(1982):823–25.   **58.** After studying the   Quote from K. Larimore, A. Ludwig, and R. Cain, "Multiple Personality: An Objective Case Study," *British Journal of Psychiatry* 131(1977):35–40.   **58.** Research reveals other   In writing this section, I combined my personal experience with information gathered from the works of several experts in the field, especially Richard Kluft and Bennett Braun. For more information see *Psychiatric Annals* 14(January 1984); R. P. Kluft, "An Update on Multiple Personality Disorder," *Hospital and Community Psychiatry* 38(April 1987); E. L. Bliss, "Multiple Personalities," *Archives of General Psychiatry* 37(1980):1388–97; B. G. Braun, ed., *The Treatment of Multiple Personality Disorder* (Washington, DC: American Psychiatric Press, 1986). For a discussion of the metaphysical and mind/brain implications of MPD, see "Multiple Personality—Mirrors of a New Model of Mind?" *Investigations, A Research Bulletin of the Institute. (Noetic Sciences* 1, no. 3/4(1985): 5.   **59.** There are known   R. Schultz and B. G. Braun, "Creativity and the Imaginary Companion Phenomenon: Prevalence and Phenomenology in MPD" (Paper presented at the Second International Conference on Multiple Personality, Chicago, 1985).   **60.** As a former patient   Quoted in "Multiple Personality," 5.   **60.** "Specifics, like things"   DiMele was quoted in J. Klimo, *Channeling: Investigations on Receiving Information from Paranormal Sources* (Los Angeles; Jeremy P. Tarcher, 1987), p. 238.   **60.** This kind of history   F. W. Putnam, et al., "The Clinical Phenomenology of MPD: Review of 100 Recent Cases," *Journal of Clinical Psychiatry* 47(1986): 285–93.   **60.** Adults with MPD   M. R. Nash, et al., "Adult Hypnotic Susceptibility, Childhood Punishment, and Child Abuse," *International Journal of Clinical and Experimental Hypnosis* 32 (1984):6–11.   **61.** This idea is   For a discussion of the spirit-possession hypothesis of MPD, see M. Kenny, "Multiple Personality and Spirit Possession," *Psychiatry* 44(1981):337–58.   **62.** This new self-membrane   Pamelor Reagor, a California therapist who works with MPD patients, discussed reparenting techniques at a lecture at the Kaiser-Bellflower Psychiatric Clinic in 1987. She submitted her paper, "A Re-parenting Model for Management of Therapeutic Relationships with Multiple Personalities," for publication.   **62.** It has been shown   B. G. Braun, "Neurophysiologic Changes in MPD Due to Integration," *American Journal of Clinical Hypnosis* 26(1983):84–92.   **62.** Although about one-fourth   G. Gabbard, "Out-of-Body States," *Psychiatric Times,* January 1988. 5–6; G. Gabbard, *With the Eyes of the Mind: An Empirical Analysis of Body States* (New York: Praeger, 1984). OBEs have been the subject of symposia at recent annual American Psychiatric Association conventions.   **62.** They generally follow   The *Tibetan Book of the Dead* is a richly symbolic document that lists discrete stages, or *bardos*, that are said to occur between lifetimes. Modern collections of near-death anecdotes correspond to the first four or five of these stages. W. Y. Evans, ed., *The Tibetan Book of the Dead* (London: Oxford University Press, 1960).   **63.** In one study   Raymond Moody, *Life after Life* (New York: Bantam, 1975).   **63.** For more information   See especially K. Ring, *Heading Toward Omega* (New York: Morrow, 1985).   **63.** There are a few   Kenneth Ring, personal communication, Esalen workshop, 1986.   **63.** During an excursion   R. Monroe, *Journeys Out of the Body* (New York: Anchor Books, 1973).   **63.** Many changed from   Gabbard, "Out-of-Body States."   **64.** Tart also monitored   Charles Tart described his experiment in *PSI, Scientific Studies of the Psychic Realm* (New York: E. P. Dutton, 1977), pp. 183–85. Other laboratory research on OBEs is described in J. Mishlove, *Roots of Consciousness* (New York: Random House, 1975), p. 134.   **64.** "Something else"   Randy Mills, personal communication.   **65.** A final and most eerie N. Lukianowicz, "Autoscopic Phenomena" *AMA Archives of Neurology and Psychiatry* 80(1958):199–220.   **67.** Several subjects felt   B. Aaronson, "Hypnosis, Depth Perception, and Psychedelic Experience," in *Altered States of Consciousness,* ed. Tart; B. Aronson, "Hypnotic Alterations of Space and Time: Their Relation to Psychopathology," in *Exploring Madness,* ed. Fadiman and Kewman, pp. 203–16.   **67.** The fact that any   Readers interested in accounts of dramatic alterations of reality induced through hypnosis are directed to the numerous works of Milton Erickson.   **68.** The disorienting effects   W. Heron, "The Pathology of Boredom," *Scientific American,* January 1957.   **69.** Not surprisingly, after   J. Lilly, *The Center of the Cyclone* (New York: Julian Press, 1972).   **69.** But few people   F. Jeffrey, *John Lilly, so far . . .* (Los Angeles: Tarcher, 1987).   **69.** One prison research   J. Silverman, et al., "Some Perceptual Correlates of Institutionalization," *Journal of Nervous and Mental Diseases* 141(1966):651–57.   **70.** While it is beyond   B. S. Busick and M. Gorman, *Ill Not Insane* (Boulder, CO: New Idea Press, 1986).

CHAPTER FOUR

72. "Uh, yes, but I don't"   Ken Kesey's antipsychiatry novel *One Flew over the Cuckoo's Nest* was written in the early 1950s, when prefrontal lobotomies were still performed on mental patients. The movie version of the late 1970s, however, did not make it clear that the last lobotomy for psychiatric reasons in California is said to have been performed in 1953.   **73.** The book he   L. R. Hubbard, *Dianetics* (Los Angeles: Bridge Publications, 1985; original edition published in 1950).   **74.** "The chronic mentally"   J. Talbott, "Deinstitutionalization: Avoiding the Disasters of the Past," *Hospital and Community Psychiatry* 30(1979):621–24.   **74.** However, as one critic   This cynical but realistic view of the hapless Indian's fate is found in a critical report about deinstitutionalization. See E. Torrey and S. Wolfe, *Care of the Seriously Mentally Ill* (Washington, DC: Public Citizen Health Research Group, 1986).   **75.** Can a society   Conservative columnist George F. Will argues for the "good society" as opposed to the libertarian viewpoint in this universal debate. See *Psychiatric Times,* March 1988, 9.   **76.** In 1843, the reformist   Quoted in Torrey and Wolfe, *The Seriously Mentally Ill.*   **78.** The iatrogenic school   Ernest Goffman's critique of mental hospitals was a prime force behind deinstitutionalization. See E. Goffman, *Asylums: Essays on the Social Situation of Mental Patients and Other Inmates* (New York: Anchor Books, 1961). Thomas Scheff's works integrated labeling theory into Goffman's critique. See T. Scheff, "Schizophrenia as Ideology," In *Radical Psychology,* ed. P. Brown (New York: Harper Colophon, 1973), pp. 53–59.   **80.** "Upon being admitted"   D. L. Rosenhan, "On Being Sane in Insane Places," *Science* 179(1973):256.   **81.** A second antipsychiatry school   T. Szasz, *The Myth of Mental Illness* (New York: Harper and Row, 1961); T. Szasz, *Insanity: The Idea and Its Consequences* (New York: Wiley, 1987).   **81.** "The mind can"   Szasz, *Insanity,* p. 147.   **82.** "Now some of"   T. S. Szasz, "Bang Bang, You're Sick: Shooting the Shrink," *The New Republic,* June 16, 1982, 11–15.   **82.** All of them   T. S. Szasz, *Psychiatric Justice* (New York: Macmillan, 1965), pp. 266–69.   **82.** Unlike Szasz, the   Laing articulated his most potent antipsychiatry statement in an intensely subjective book, *The Politics of Experience* (New York: Pantheon Books, 1967). For an update of his views, see interviews in *Omni,* April 1988, and *East-West Journal,* September 1987.   **85.** "Experience has become"   Laing, interview in *Omni,* 62.   **85.** These drugs, he   Ibid.   **85.** Laing's radical counterpoint   Laing, interview in *East-West Journal,* 40.   **86.** "If I could turn"   Laing, *Politics of Experience.*   **86.** There were reports   O. Friedrich, *Going Crazy,* (New York: Avon, 1975), p. 96. Also my personal communication with an ex-resident of Kingsley Hall.   **87.** As with most controversies   E. Fuller Torrey categorizes all psychotic ASCs as biologically determined, and therefore advocates treatment that is primarily drug based. Nonetheless, his book is helpful to families and schizophrenic patients, with the caveat that it does not distinguish between malignant and benign psychoses. E. F. Torrey, *Surviving Schizophrenia,* rev. ed. (New York: Harper & Row, 1988). After a delay of nearly two decades, mainstream psychiatry has specifically countered the arguments of the antipsychiatrists in M. Roth and J. Kroll, *The Reality of Mental Illness* (Cambridge: Cambridge University Press, 1986).   **90.** If good is to come   G. Zilboorg and G. W. Henry, *A History of Medical Psychology* (London: George Allen & Unwin, 1941).   **92.** For instance, the   J. M. Murphy, "Psychiatric Labelling in Cross-cultural Perspective," *Science* 191(1976):1019–28.   **93.** Similarly, the Yoruba   Ibid.   **93.** "Rather than being"   Ibid.   **94.** Similarly, a World Health   Ibid.

CHAPTER FIVE

Several summaries of recent findings in normal and psychotic brain function were influential in the preparation of this and the following two chapters. For the layperson, the first choice is works that do not hold that psychosis is only aberrant brain function. See J. Hooper and D. Teresi, *The Three-Pound Universe* (New York: Dell, 1986); M. S. Gazzaniga, *Mind Matters* (Boston: Houghton Mifflin, 1988). Also informative for the layperson, but unfortunately reductionistic are N. C. Andreasen, *The Broken Brain* (New York: Perennial Library, 1984); and Busic and Gorman, *Ill, Not Insane*. An excellent review for those trained in the neurosciences is N. C. Andreasen, *Can Schizophrenia Be Localized in the Brain?* (Washington, DC: American Psychiatric Press, 1986). Albert E. Scheflen took a holistic systems-theory approach in *Levels of Schizophrenia* (New York: Brunner/Mazel, 1981). **101.** Given its complexity When a strand of DNA is copied, three separate enzyme systems "proofread" the new DNA strand and correct any mismatches. See M. Radman and R. Wagner, "The High Fidelity of DNA Duplication," *Scientific American*, August 1988, 40–47. **101.** Only when researchers Research on the genetics of schizophrenia has occupied a prominent position in the psychiatric literature since Franz Kallman's landmark work, *The Genetics of Schizophrenia* (New York: Augustin), was published in 1938. Another work utilizing the *folkeregister* is D. Rosenthal and S. Kety, eds., *The Transmission of Schizophrenia* (New York: Pergamon Press, 1968). Also I. Gottesman and J. Shields, "A Critical Review of Recent Adoption, Twin, and Family Studies of Schizophrenia: Behavioral Genetics Perspectives," *Schizophrenia Bulletin*, 1976, 360–401. **102.** One report noted L. Heston, "Psychiatric Disorders in Foster-home-reared Children of Schizophrenic Mothers," *British Journal of Psychiatry* 112(1966):819–25. **103.** Although the genetic Gary Bravo, M.D., personal communication. **103.** Another puzzling question E. Fuller Torry argues that schizophrenia may have come into existence only in the last two hundred years. See Torry, *Surviving Schizophrenia*, pp. 337–52. Other theorists dispute this point. For statistical evidence of an increase in bipolar disorder, see E. Gershon, et al., "Birth-Cohort Changes in Manic and Depressive Disorders in Relatives of Bipolar and Schizoaffective Patients," *Archives of General Psychiatry* 44(April 1987):314–19. **103.** One possibility is M. Bleuler, "A Twenty-three-year Longitudinal Study of 208 Schizophrenics and Impression in Regard to the Nature of Schizophrenia," in *Transmission of Schizophrenia*, ed. Rosenthal and Kety. **103.** Only the more J. Silverman, et al., "Familial Schizophrenia and Treatment Response," *American Journal of Psychiatry* 144(1987):1271–76. **103.** The outcome of A recent trend in psychiatry is to attribute many so-called personality traits, once thought to be psychologically determined, to genetic influence. These include taste in food and music, choice of spouse, craving for alcohol or other drugs, and specific artistic talents. A rebuttal of this line of thinking is found in R. C. Lewontin, S. Rose, and L. Kamin, *Not in Our Genes* (New York: Pantheon, 1984). **103.** Geneticists now suspect J. Egeland, et al., "Bipolar Affective Disorders Linked to DNA Markers on Chromosome 11," *Nature* 325:(1987); 783. M. Baron, et al., "Genetic Linkage between X-chromosome Markers and Bipolar Affective Illness," *Nature* 326(1987):289. **104.** There is reason R. DePaulo, paper presented at the American Psychiatric Association meeting, 1987. Summarized in *Clinical Psychiatry News* 15(6):7. **104.** For the sake P. McLean, "On the Evolution of Three Mentalities," in *New Dimensions in Psychiatry: A World View*, vol. 2, ed. S. Arieti and G. Chrzanowki, (New York: Wiley, 1977). **108.** The progressive upward T. P. Millar, "Schizophrenia, an Etiological Speculation," *Perspectives in Biology and Medicine* 30(1987):597–607. **110.** Similarly, people whose R. W. Sperry, "Split-Brain Approach to Learning," in *The Neurosciences*, ed. G. C. Guarton, et al. (New York: Rockefeller University Press, 1967); R. Ornstein, *The Psychology of Consciousness* (San Francisco: Freeman, 1972). **111.** Despite this intriguing Robust evidence now exists that alterations in limbic-system functioning may underlie many psychotic ASCs. This evidence has come from four directions: (1) implantation of stimulating electrodes directly into the brains of animals; (2) CAT, PET, EEG, and NMR procedures performed on living human beings; (3) studies of the subjective experience of patients with epileptic seizures known to originate within limbic areas; and (4) electrical and chemical stimulation of the brains of awake human beings undergoing surgery. **112.** Other temporal areas The neurosurgeon Wilder Penfield mapped the discrete functional areas of the cortex and underlying structures by correlating his patients' subjective experience with brain areas he stimulated with electricity during surgery. Penfield's work led him to conclude that the brain retains a complete and permanent record of the stream of consciousness throughout life. In his shocking final work, he concluded that the brain mechanisms cannot fully explain the mind, that consciousness is a second fundamental element of existence, and that it derives its energy from sources other than the biological processes of the body. See W. Penfield, *The Mystery of the Mind* (Princeton: Princeton University Press, 1975). **113.** In schizophrenia there is For more on this pleasure center and its role in schizophrenia, see

R. Heath, "Brain Function and Behavior," *Journal of Nervous and Mental Disease* 160(1975):159–75. **114.** As of this writing ̇Both computerized axial tomography (CAT scans) and magnetic resonance imaging have consistently revealed enlarged cerebral ventricles in chronic schizophrenics. See, for instance, N. Andreasen, et al., "Magnetic Resonance Imaging of the Brain in Schizophrenia," *Archives of General Psychiatry* 47(1990):35–44. **115.** But recent research E. Courchesne, et al., "Hypoplastic Cerebellar Vermal Lobules VI and VII in Autism" *New England Journal of Medicine* 318(1988): 1349–54; R. J. Heath, et al., "Cerebellar Patients: An Update," *Biological Psychiatry* 16(1981): 953–962

CHAPTER SIX

121. The development of S. Snyder, *Madness and the Brain* (New York: McGraw-Hill, 1974). **122.** This objection was J. Griffith, "Dextroamphetamine Evaluation of Psychomimetic Properties in Man," *Archives of General Psychiatry* 26(1972):97–100; C. Schulz, "The Amphetamine Challenge Test in Patients with Borderline Disorder," *American Journal of Psychiatry* 145(1988):809–14. **120.** Other researchers then There are exceptions to this that further confound the picture and demonstrate the enormous complexity and interrelatedness of brain processes. See D. Janowsky et al., "Provocation of Schizophrenic Symptoms by Intravenous Methylphenidate," *Archives of General Psychiatry* 28(1973):185. **123.** Medicated patients complained O. W. Sacks, et al., "Effect of Levodopa in Parkinsonian Patients with Dementia," *Neurology* 22(1972): 516–19. **123.** These extra receptors P. Seeman, et al., "Bimodal Distribution of Dopamine Receptor Densities in Brains of Schizophrenics," *Science* 225(1984):728–31. **123.** But recently, Daniel D. Weinberger, "Implications of Normal Brain Development for the Pathogenesis of Schizophrenia," *Archives of General Psychiatry* 44(1987): 660–69. Weinberger's theory generated several letters both challenging and expanding upon the idea in the November 1988 issue of *Archives of General Psychiatry*, 1051–55. **124.** When researchers selectively C. J. Pycock, et al., "Effect of Lesion of Cortical Dopamine Terminals on Subcortical Dopamine in Rats," *Nature* 286(1980):74–77. **124.** Recent studies show that the P. Yakoviev, et al., "The Myelogenetic Cycles of Regional Maturation of the Brain," in *Regional Development of the Brain in Early Life*, ed. A. Minkowski (Boston: Blackwell Scientific Publications, 1964), pp. 3–70. **126.** Anything that interferes Researchers on this subject often succumb to the temptation of reductionism. See A. J. Mandell, "Toward a Psychobiology of Transcendence: God in the Brain," in *The Psychobiology of Consciousness*, ed. J. M. Davidson (New York: Plenum, 1980), pp. 379–464. **126.** In other words Ernest Hartmann, a widely published neuroscientist, described his theory and self-experiment in R. Chancro, ed., *Annual Review of the Schizophrenic Syndrome, 1976–7* (New York: Brunner/Mazel, 1978), pp. 77–104. **127.** "I experienced states" Ibid., pp. 96–97. **130.** Musicians grow more Several experiments demonstrate that experience continuously alters both brain chemistry and anatomy throughout life. See "The Brain of a Salesman: You Are What You Do," *The Omni Whole Mind Newsletter*, June 1988, 1; W. T. Greenough, "Structural Correlates of Information Storage in the Mammalian Brain: A Review and Hypothesis," *Trends in NeuroSciences* 7(1984):229–33. **131.** Vicious cycles then S. Arieti, "The Possibility of Psychosomatic Involvement of the Central Nervous System in Schizophrenia," *Journal of Nervous and Mental Diseases* 123(1956):324–33; N. Q. Brill, "Schizophrenia: A Psychosomatic Disorder?" *Psychosomatics*, 19(1978): 665–70.

CHAPTER SEVEN

135. Modern antipsychotic medicines For a history of mental illness throughout the centuries, see Otto Friedrich, *Going Crazy*. **137.** Neuroleptics also adversely For a technical review of the effects of dopamine-inhibiting drugs on widespread areas of the brain and body, see S. H. Snyder, "Neuroleptic Drugs and Neurotransmitter Receptors," in *Research in the Schizophrenic Disorders: The Stanley R. Dean Award Lectures*, vol. 2, ed. R. Chancro and S. R. Dean (New York: Spectrum, 1985), pp. 193–211. **138.** Most are experiencing Psychiatrists often wonder aloud why so many persons in self-admitted unpleasant ASCs refuse to take medicines that promise relief. Akathisia accounts for as many as 35 percent of this group. See T. Van Putten, et al., "Response to Antipsychotic Medication: The Doctor's and the Consumer's View," *American Journal of Psychiatry* 141(1984):16–19; T. Van Putten, "Behavioral Toxicity of Antipsychotic Drugs," *Journal of Clinical Psychiatry* 48 (September 1987):13–19. **140.** For certain patients M. Rappaport, et al., "Are There Schizophrenics for Whom Drugs May Be Unnecessary or Contraindicated?" *International Pharmacopsychiatry* 13(1978):100–111. **140.** Even for chronically T. Van Putten and S. Marder,

"Low-Dose Treatment Strategies," *Journal of Clinical Psychiatry* 47 (May 1986): 12–16.   **141.** When this was tried   C. P. Chien, "Drugs and Rehabilitation in Schizophrenia," In *Drugs in Combination with Other Therapies*, ed. M. Greenblatt (New York: Grune & Stratton, 1975).   **141.** Reducing delusions and   This question was raised in an article that points out that a doctor's definition of "doing better" does not always accord with the patient's appraisal of how life is going. See R. Diamond, "Drugs and the Quality of Life: The Patient's Point of View," *Journal of Clinical Psychiatry* 46(May 1985): 29–35.   **142.** More recently, psychiatrists   Lithium is more likely to benefit people with schizophreniclike ASCs in which affect is preserved and the core personality is not too regressed. See F. P. Zemlan et al., "Impact of Lithium Therapy on Core Psychotic Symptoms of Schizophrenia," *British Journal of Psychiatry* 144(1984):64–69.   **143.** Antidepressants afford relief   D. J. Kupfer, "Possible Role of Antidepressants in Precipitating Mania and Hypomania in Recurrent Depression," *American Journal of Psychiatry* 147 (1988):804–8.   **143.** In a way yet   M. Zetin, et al., "Effects of Psychoactive Drugs on Circadian Rhythms," *Psychiatric Annals* 17(1987):682–88.   **145.** One of the first   J. L. W. Thudichum, *A Treatise on the Chemical Constitution of the Brain* (London: Baliere, Tindall and Cox, 1884).   **147.** For more information   A. Hoffer and H. Osmond, *How to Live with Schizophrenia* (Secaucus, NJ: Citadel Press, 1974). Also see Linus Pauling and Albert Szent-Gyorgyi's work on vitamin C in I. Stone, *The Healing Factor: Vitamin C against Disease* (New York: Grosset & Dunlap, 1972).   **150.** But in the first   L. Fischman, "Dreams, Hallucinogenic Drug States, and Schizophrenia: A Psychological and Biological Comparison," *Schizophrenia Bulletin* 9, no. 1 (1983):73–94.   **151.** He'd become a   The practice of administering powerful psychoactive drugs to unprepared subjects is a form of torture equivilent to Nazi medical experiments during the holocaust. See J. Marks *The Search for the Manchurian Candidate* (New York: Best Books, 1979).   **151.** Every major hallucinogenic   One of several studies demonstrating this effect is A. E. Wolback, et al., "Comparison of Psilocin with Psilocybin, Mescaline and LSD-25," *Psychopharmacologia* 3(1962):219–23.   **152.** These hint at   Stanislav Grof described his treatment of an acutely psychotic woman by multiple LSD-enhanced psychotherapeutic sessions in S. Grof, "Theoretical and Empirical Basis of Transpersonal Psychotherapy," in *Transpersonal Psychotherapy*, ed. S. Boorstein, (Palo Alto: Science and Behavior Books, 1980), p. 365. Also see S. Grof, *Realms of the Human Unconscious: Observations from LSD Research* (New York: Viking Press, 1975).

CHAPTER EIGHT

156. The original object   For a clear explanation of holography, see P. Pietsch, *Shufflebrain: The Quest for the Hologramic Mind* (Boston: Houghton-Mifflin, 1981).   **156.** It was this characteristic   K. Pribam, *Languages of the Brain* (New York: Prentice-Hall, 1971).   **156.** As he struggled   K. Lashly, *Brain Mechanisms and Intelligence* (Chicago: University of Chicago Press, 1929).   **157.** The arbitrary outline   In his most poetic work, Ken Wilber confronts the reader with the illusion of separateness within a unitary universe. K. Wilber, *No Boundary* (New York: Shambhala, 1981).   **157.** This blending of   The results of this convergence of minds were reported in *Brain/Mind Bulletin*, 4 July 1977, 1–3.   **158.** In the same way   M. Ferguson, "Karl Pribam's Changing Reality," in *The Holographic Pardigm and Other Paradoxes*, ed. K. Wilber (Boston: New Science Library, 1982), p. 25.   **159.** The technically inclined   Terrance and Dennis McKenna presented their theory of the mind/brain interface, which emerged from their research with esoteric chemical hallucinogens in *The Invisible Landscape* (New York: The Seabury Press, 1975); for a taped account of their personal experiences with natural hallucinogens as they trekked about the Amazon basin, see their self-published "talking-book" *True Hallucinations*, available from Lux Natura, Box 1196, Berkeley, CA 94704. Frank Barr, M.D., published his mind/brain theory in the technical article "Melanin: The Organizing Molecule," *Medical Hypothesis* 11(1983):1–140; a self-published companion article, "Melanin and the Mind/Brain Problem," is available through the Institute for the Study of Consciousness, 2924 Benvenue Ave., Berkeley, CA 94705; for a nontechnical summary, see *Brain/Mind Bulletin* 8, no. 12/13 (1983).   **161.** Physics—even quantum   While agreeing that holographic analogies are probably valid as a way of understanding the brain at the quantum level, Wilber argues that it is an invalid conceptual leap to assert that consciousness itself is like *any* physical structure, no matter how subtle. See K. Wilber, "Reflections on the New-Age Paradigm," in *The Holographic Paradigm*, ed. Wilber, pp. 249–94.   **161.** The fit between   See, for instance, Fritjof Capra, *The Tao of Physics* (Berkeley: Shambhala, 1975); Gary Zukav, *The Dancing Wu Li Masters* (New York: William Morrow & Co, 1979); Lawrence LeShan, *The Medium, the Mystic and the Physicist* (New York: Ballantine Books, 1966).   **162.** When Jung learned   Jung was among the first Western theorists to learn of the chakra system and incorporate it into his practice. C. G. Jung, "Psychological Commentary on Kundalini Yoga, Lecture IV," *Spring:*

An Annual of Archetypal Psychology and Jungian Thought 21(1976):17. Jung was quoted in S. Ajaya, *Psychotherapy East and West* (Honesdale, PA: Himalayan International Institute, 1983), p. 244.   **162.** A comprehensive description   Several books deal with the seven chakras: Mary Scott, *Kundalini in the Physical World* (London: Routledge & Kegan Paul, 1983); H. Guenther, *Kundalini Yoga for the West* (Spokane: Timeless Books, 1978); J. Small, *Transformers* (Marina del Rey, CA: DeVorss, 1982); B. Gunther, *Energy Ecstasy and Your Seven Vital Chakras* (North Hollywood, CA: Newcastle Publishing, 1983); A. Judith, *Wheels of Life* (St. Paul, MN: Llewellyn, 1987).   **164.** These are unforgettable   Sudden seventh-chakra infusions may be associated with near-death experiences or occasionally follow large doses of psychedelic medicines. Such confrontations with the naked power of the Ground are often beneficial to people who have at least partly opened to fourth-chakra consciousness, but may be disruptive to people mired at lower levels.   **166.** And at any stage Although Wilber's levels of development do not exactly correspond to the chakras, his work has been especially inspirational to the ideas presented here. For an explanation of "dying" to each level, see his book *Eye to Eye*, p. 234. Wilber originally detailed his model of consciousness in *The Atman Project* (Wheaton, IL: Quest Books, 1980). His description of the historical evolution of consciousness is in *Up from Eden* (Boston: New Science Library, 1986).   **167.** These transformative crises   Ken Wilber summarizes his hierarchical theory of spiritual growth in "Odyssey: A Personal Inquiry into Humanistic and Transpersonal Psychology," *The Journal of Humanistic Psychology* 22(Winter 1982):57–90.   **168.** In Wilber's words   K. Wilber, "The Pre/Trans Fallacy," *Re-Vision* 3(1980):58. Wilber also discusses the pre/trans fallacy in several other works, including *Eye to Eye*, pp. 201–46.

CHAPTER NINE

175. But the fact   Arthur Janov, originator of "primal scream" therapy, recognized that intrauterine and birth trauma play an important part in psychopathology later in life. Although his conclusions often seem overdrawn, his core insights represent a significant contribution. See A. Janov, *Imprints* (New York: Coward-McCann, 1983).   **176.** Stanislav Grof has   Stanislav Grof applies the principles of perinatal trauma to a broad spectrum of psychological maladies. See Grof, *Beyond the Brain*.   **176.** Moreover, one research   Several studies correlating birth trauma with suicide and other psychological maladies were summarized in an article in Omni magazine by Sherry Baker (November 1988, p. 26).   **177.** While we await   Some studies demonstrate a link between obstetrical complications and schizophrenia. Orthodox psychiatry interprets these as meaning that the newborn's brain was physically damaged during its transit. While this may be the case, we might also consider how the psyche is affected by birth complications, and how this in turn may affect brain development. See T. F. McNeil and L. Kaij, "Obstetric Factors in the Development of Schizophrenia," in *The Nature of Schizophrenia*, ed. L. Wynne, R. Cromwell, and S. Matthysse (New York: Wiley & Sons, 1978), pp. 401–29.   **177.** This is called   For a graphic description of the effects of current obstetrical practice on the experience of the neonate, see Pearce's thoughtful *Magical Child*.   **178.** The mind translates   Researchers have identified a specific intracellular protein that increases in repetitively stimulated brain areas and is capable of directing the formation of new synapses on neuronal cell membranes. See C. Aoki, and P. Siekevits, "Plasticity in Brain Development," *Scientific American*, December 1988, 56.   **179.** Although invisible to   W. Condon, and L. Sander, "Neonate Movement Is Synchronized with Adult Speech: Interactional Participation and Language Acquisition," *Science* 11(1974):99–101; W. Condon, and W. Ogston, "A Segmentation of Behavior," *Journal of Psychiatric Research*, 5(1967): 221–35.   **183.** "I wanted to"   M. Hayward, and J. Taylor, "A Schizophrenic Patient Describes the Action of Intensive Psychotherapy," in *Exploring Madness*, ed. Fadiman and Kewman, p. 30.   **184.** Because much parental   Torrey, *Surviving Schizophrenia*.   **187.** One recent study   M. Singer, L. Wynne, and M. Toohey, "Communication Disorders and the Families of Schizophrenics," in *The Nature of Schizophrenia*, ed. Wynne et al.   **188.** Confusion, vertigo and   Modified from T. Scheff, "Schizophrenia as Ideology," *Schizophrenia Bulletin* 2 (Fall 1970):15–19.   **189.** Their conclusion: communication   Over the past several decades, Lyman Wynne and Margaret Singer have studied pathological family interaction. See L. Wynne and M. Singer, "Schizophrenics, Families, and Communication Disorders," in *Research in the Schizophrenic Disorders: The Stanley R. Dean Award Lectures*, vol. 1, ed. R. Chancro and S. Dean (New York: Spectrum, 1985), pp. 231–49.   **189.** Whatever segment of   T. Lidz, "Family Studies and a Theory of Schizophrenia," in *Schizophrenic Disorders*, vol. 1, ed. Chancro and Dean, p. 213.   **189.** Indeed, sometimes after   T. Lidz, *The Origin and Treatment of Schizophrenic Disorders* (New York: Basic Books, 1973), p. 8.   **189.** "The listener is"   Wynne and Singer, "Schizophrenics, Families and Communication Disorders," p. 233.   **190.** One final theory   For an overview of the connection between high-EE environments and relapse rates of schizophrenics, see C. Vaughn, and J. Leff, "The Influence of Family and Social Factors on the Course of Psychiatric Illness," *British Journal of Psychiatry* 129(1976):215–37. **191.** As E. Fuller Torry Torry, *Surviving Schizophrenia*, p. 164. **192.** In this regard Silvano Arieti, "From Schizophrenia to Creativity," *American Journal of Psychotherapy* 33, no. 4(1979): 140–52.

CHAPTER TEN

199. The essence of *Calvin and Hobbes* is syndicated in daily newspapers from coast to coast. Many of the best episodes are collected in a volume with an introduction by Pat Oliphant. See Bill Watterson, *Something under the Bed Is Drooling* (Kansas City: Andrews and McMeel, 1988). **206.** Ken Wilber refers Wilber, *The Atman Project;* Wilber, *Up from Eden.* **203.** Transpersonal philosopher Michael Michael Washburn poetically discusses the interplay between the consciousness of the Ground and a developing pysche in *The Ego and The Dynamic Ground* (Albany: State University of New York Press, 1988). **208.** One day he Acts 9:3–4, 6:14, 9:9. **208.** "Upon this, Mohammed" R. Bucke, *Cosmic Consciousness* (New York: Dutton, 1901), p. 126. **210.** Some patients can L. N. Gould, "Verbal Hallucinations and Activity of Vocal Musculature: An Electromyographic Study," *American Journal of Psychiatry* 105(1948):367–72. **210.** Some patients can P. Bick and M. Kinsbourn, "Auditory Hallucinations and Subvocal Speech in Schizophrenic Patients," *American Journal of Psychiatry* 144(1987):222–25. **210.** *Command hallucinations*—a J. Yesavage, "Inpatient Violence and the Schizophrenic Patient," *Acta Psychiatric Scand.* 67(1983):353–57. **210.** *Command hallucinations*—a D. Hellerstein, et al., "The Clinical Significance of Command Hallucinations," *American Journal of Psychiatry* 144(1987):219–21. **211.** "It was commanded." *New York Times* News Service report, August 12, 1977. **211.** An exception is W. Van Dusen, *The Presence of Spirits in Madness* (New York: Swedenborg Foundation, 1983); W. Van Dusen, *The Natural Depth in Man* (New York: Swedenborg Foundation, 1972), pp. 136–53. **212.** Rarer, higher-order The perception of inner voices by people who demonstrate no conspicuous psychopathology is discussed in M. Heery. "Inner Voice Experiences: An Exploratory Study of Thirty Cases," *The Journal of Transpersonal Psychology* 21, no. 1(1989):73–82. **213.** But he was Jung never wrote of actually conversing with his psychotic patients' voices, but it is probable that he did so. See C. G. Jung, *The Psychogenesis of Mental Disease* (Princeton, NJ: Princeton University Press, 1960), p. 248. **215.** Therapists who work J. Ehrenwald, *The ESP Experience* (New York: Basic Books, 1978), pp. 207–17. **216.** For instance, Princeton J. Jaynes, *The Origin of Consciousness in the Breakdown of the Bicameral Mind* (Boston: Houghton Mifflin, 1976). **217.** In his classic Silvano Arieti, *Interpretation of Schizophrenia* (New York: Basic Books, 1974), p. 268. **217.** L. J. West took L. J. West, "A General Theory of Hallucinations and Dreams," in *Hallucinations: Behavior, Experience, and Theory*, ed. R. K. Siegel and L. J. West (New York: John Wiley & Sons, 1975). **212.** Even the pioneer Tart, *States of Consciousness*, p. 101. **218.** This line of W. Dement, *Some Must Sleep While Some Must Watch. . .* (New York: Norton, 1978). **218.** These include the During the past century, the British Society for Psychical Research (SPR) has lent an air of credibility to the study of death apparitions and allied phenomena. The SPR has published a 1,300-page document, *Phantasms of the Living*, in which 702 separate cases were analyzed. **220.** Exorcisms allegedly rid Three recent books describe variations of these techniques: Murry Hope, *Practical Techniques of Psychic Self-Defense* (New York: St. Martin's Press, 1986); O. Phillips, and M. Denning, *Psychic Self-Defense and Well-Being* (St. Paul, MN: Llewellyn, 1986); E. Fiore, *The Unquiet Dead* (New York: Dolphin, 1987). **221.** In the western For information on theosophy contact the Krotona Institute of Theosophy, in Ojai, California. **221.** Yet they use T. Clifford, *Tibetan Buddhist Medicine and Psychiatry* (York Beach, ME: Weiser, 1981). **221.** When I read Ibid., pp. 147–70. **222.** A contemporary version Klimo's *Channeling* is the definitive book on this phenomenon. **223.** He also sustained Swedenborg's present-day followers maintain study centers in California and New York. For information contact The Swedenborg Foundation, 129 East 23rd Street, New York, NY 10010. **224.** "When spirits begin" Emanuel Swedenborg, quoted in Klimo, *Channeling*, p. 94. **225.** The technique is Susy Smith, *Voices of the Dead?* (New York: Signet, 1977; New York: Taplinger, 1971). **225.** Independent investigators who Ibid., p. 3. **225.** One researcher reported W. Welch, *Talks with the Dead* (New York: Pinnacle Books, 1975). **226.** No one in Carlos Castaneda has published nine Don Juan chronicles since the 1960s. Ideally they should be read in sequence. Information on the assemblage point is in *The Fire Within* (New York: Simon & Schuster, 1984), pp. 283–84. **228.** "In each individual" Carl Jung expressed this opinion in a letter to a friend. See his *Collected Letters*, vol. 1, 1906–1950 (Princeton, NJ: Bollingen, 1977), p. 114.

CHAPTER ELEVEN

233. His transit through For a discussion of how the ego creates the illusion of polarities as it turns away from its spiritual origins, see Ajaya, *Psychotherapy East and West.* **233.** It consists of C. Jung, "The Concept of the Collective Unconscious," in *The Portable Jung,* ed. J. Campbell (New York: Viking Press, 1971). **236.** Such confusion of Psychoanalyst Silvano Arieti rediscovered the logical formulations of an obscure German psychiatrist, Eilhard von Domaraus, and elaborated these ideas into a comprehensive theory of regression in schizophrenia. See Arieti, *Interpretation of Schizophrenia,* pp. 229–35. **238.** The esteemed Swiss Jean Piaget's observations on childhood reasoning did not include the chakra system, but his stages of cognitive development roughly approximate the transitions of logic during the first three chakras as described in ancient yoga texts. See J. Piaget, *The Origins of Intelligence in Children* (New York: International Universities Press, 1952). **240.** When asked if Arieti, *Interpretation of Schizophrenia.* **246.** This is what A. Toynbee, *A Study of History* (New York: Oxford University Press, 1934). **246.** Michael Washburn aptly Washburn distinguishes the psychoanalytical concept of regression in the service of the ego from regression in the service of transcendence in *The Ego and the Dynamic Ground* **248.** Several studies have W. T. Carpenter, et al., "The Treatment of Acute Schizophrenia without Drugs: An Investigation of Some Current Assumptions," *American Journal of Psychiatry* 134(1977):14; M. A. Young and H. Y. Meltzer, "The Relationship of Demographic, Clinical, and Outcome Variables to Neuroleptic Treatment Requirements," *Schizophrenia Bulletin* 6(1980):88. **249.** Images of a In chapter 7 of *The Ego and the Dynamic Ground,* Washburn characterizes archetypal images that emerge during regression in the service of transcendence. **250.** The premier mythologist Joseph Campbell made this statement during a six-part series of televised interviews with Bill Moyers broadcast on PBS during Fall 1988. **252.** "A hero ventures" Joseph Campbell first described the hero's journey in *The Hero with a Thousand Faces* (New York: Pantheon Books, 1949), p. 30. In a later work he connected this with schizophrenia. See J. Campbell *Myths to Live By* (New York: Bantam Books, 1972), ch. 10. **252.** Its theme is John Weir Perry, M.D., is a Jungian analyst who has written extensively of the mythological themes that emerge during psychotic experience. See J. W. Perry, *The Far Side of Madness* (Englewood Cliffs, NJ: Prentice-Hall, 1974). **252.** In either instance David Lukoff presented a case history of a psychotic episode with transpersonal implications in "The Myths in Mental Illness," *The Journal of Transpersonal Psychology* 18, no. 2(1985):123–53. **256.** Transpersonal philosophers such as Wilber, *Up from Eden.*

CHAPTER TWELVE

259. It is said S. S. Radha, *Kundalini Yoga for the West* (Spokane: Timeless Books, 1978). **261.** It embraces all Buddhist meditation teacher Jack Kornfield discusses compassion in his book on Vipassana meditation, coauthored with Joseph Goldstein, *Seeking the Heart of Wisdom* (Boston: Shambhala, 1987), p. 160. **262.** As we saw Washburn coined the term *original repression* in *The Ego and The Dynamic Ground.* **263.** His belief in Roberto Assagioli, founder of "psychosynthesis," discussed spiritual emergencies in "Self-Realization and Psychological Disturbances," *ReVision,* 8, no. 2(1986):21–32. **264.** But if his The terms *spiritual emergence* and *spiritual emergency* were coined by Christina and Stanislav Grof. See S. Grof and C. Grof, *Spiritual Emergency: When Personal Transformation Becomes a Crisis* (Los Angeles: Jeremy P. Tarcher, 1989). **266.** The ASC is E. Bragdon, *A Sourcebook for Helping People in Spiritual Emergency* (Menlo Park, CA: Institute of Transpersonal Psychology, 1987). Much of the information in the following sections of this chapter has been gleaned from this lucid work. **262.** In such cases In addition to *Spiritual Emergency,* Christina and Stanislav Grof describe the various forms of spiritual emergency in "Forms of Spiritual Emergency," *Spiritual Emergency Network Newsletter* 1(3); and "Spiritual Emergency: The Understanding and Treatment of Transpersonal Crises," *ReVision* 8, no. 2(1986):7–20 (This entire issue of *ReVision* examines the border lands between psychosis and spiritual experience.) **266.** Other characteristics that Transpersonal psychologist David Lukoff published a thoughtful paper outlining criteria for a proposed official diagnostic category of "mystical experiences with psychotic features." See D. Lukoff, "The Diagnosis of Mystical Experiences with Psychotic Features," *The Journal of Transpersonal Psychology* 17, no. 2(1985):155–80. **269.** This favorable outcome Lukoff described and interpreted two similar case histories involving flying-saucer sightings in "Diagnosis of Mystical Experiences." **271.** The San Francisco Lee Sanella, M.D., gives a detailed description of the phenomenon, along with a collection of case histories, in *The Kundalini Experience* (Lower Lake, CA: Integral Publishing, 1987). **272.** "The spectacle was" G. Krishna, *Kundalini: The Evolutionary Energy in Man* (Berkeley: Shambhala, 1971), p. 49. **274.** "This led me" Sanella's original self-published account is titled *Kundalini—*

Psychosis or Transcendence?　**276.** That which Roberto　Assagioli, "Self-Realizations," 21–32. **276.** "And when the"　Ibid., 26.　**277.** "I did not"　Lukoff, "Diagnosis of Mystical Experiences," 177.　**277.** "In short, nothing"　Naomi Steinfeld, now a writer, editor, and publications expert, described her spiritual emergency in "Surviving the Chaos of Something Extraordinary," *Shaman's Drum,* Spring 1986, 22–27.　**277.** Michael Washburn termed　Washburn, *The Ego.*　**279.** Ken Wilber calls　Ken Wilber discusses the concept of the centaur in several of his works. See especially *The Spectrum of Consciousness* (Wheaton, IL: Theosophical Publishing House, 1977), pp. 245–65.

CHAPTER THIRTEEN

283. With eyes closed　A. E. Caldwell, "La Malinconia: Final Movement of Beethoven's Quartet op. 18, no. 6: A Musical Account of Manic Depressive States," *Journal of the American Medical Woman's Association* 27(1972):241–48.　**285.** The self could　Wilber dealt with the hierarchal stages of development in *The Atman Project,* p. 89. He has revised and updated his view in his several subsequent works.　**286.** The tree becomes　E. Fromm, "The Creative Attitude," in *Creativity and Its Cultivation* (New York: Harper & Row, 1959), cited in J. Briggs, *The Fire in the Crucible* (New York: A Thomas Dunn Book/St. Martin's Press, 1988), p. 57.　**287.** He no longer　Wilber calls this capacity "vision/logic." See *Eye to Eye,* p. 274.　**288.** All things are　J. Small, *Transformers: The Therapists of the Future* (Marina del Rey, CA: DeVorss, 1982), p. 106.　**291.** "The words seem　A. Lowell, "The Process of Making Poetry," in *The Creative Process,* ed. B. Ghiselin (New York: Mentor Books, 1952), p. 110.　**291.** Yet she was　Example cited in Briggs, *Fire in the Crucible,* pp. 237–45.　**291.** When he tried　Example cited in O. Friedrich, *Going Crazy* p. 54. The effect of Schumann's mental illness on his work is also analyzed in R. Porter, *A Social History of Madness* (New York: Weidenfeld & Nicolson, 1987) and in W. Frosch, "Moods, Madness, and Music. I. Major Affective Disease and Musical Creativity," *Comprehensive Psychiatry* 28(1987):315–22.　**291.** When his wife　Blake's sources of inspiration are discussed in C. Panati, *Supersenses* (New York: Anchor Books, 1976), p. 164. Also see Porter, *Social History of Madness,* p. 64.　**292.** By the later　Washburn discusses the process of reowning the creative aspects of the Ground in *The Ego and the Dynamic Ground.*　**292.** Rilke, for instance　Ranier Maria Rilke made this statement in the introduction to his book of mystically inspired poetry, *Duino Elegies and the Sonnets to Orpheus,* trans. A. Poulin (Boston: Houghton Mifflin, 1977), p. viii.　**292.** In this same vein　Amy Lowell, "The Process of Making Poetry," in *The Creative Process,* ed. Ghiselin, p. 10.　**292.** I just sort of　A. Scaduto, *Bob Dylan* (New York: Signet, 1971), p. 141.　**293.** Toward the end　C. Zervos, "Conversation with Picasso," in *The Creative Process,* ed. Ghiselin, p. 57.　**294.** Our most creative　Another helpful book in differentiating creativity from regressive ASCs is S. Arieti, *Creativity: The Magic Synthesis* (New York: Basic Books, 1976).　**294.** Because both presocial　Wilbur, *The Atman Project,* p. 56.　**295.** "When I examine"　Einstein's creativity was discussed in two books. See A. Storr, *The Dynamics of Creation* (New York: Atheneum, 1972), ch. 6; B. Scharfstein, *Mystical Experiences* (Baltimore: Penguin Books, 1973), ch. 6.　**296.** After a walk　Zervos, "Conversation with Picasso," p. 57.　**296.** "It must be"　Lowell, "The Process of Making Poetry," p. 111.　**296.** "If I didn't　Scaduto, *Bob Dylan,* p. 160.　**300.** While the evocative　Briggs elaborates on this point in chapter 12 of *Fire in the Crucible.*　**300.** It was quite　On page 77 of *The Ego,* Washburn discusses how "paleosymbols" from primitive consciousness sometimes infuse the creative process.　**302.** This holds true　R. Fieve, *Moodswing* chapter 3.　**302.** "It shoots out"　Porter, *Social History of Madness,* p. 60.　**305.** "Blinded by reason"　Ibid., p. 73.　**305.** Researchers found a　E. D. Shaw, J. J. Mann, et al., "Effects of Lithium Carbonate on Associative Productivity and Idiosyncrasy in Bipolar Outpatients," *American Journal of Psychiatry* 143(1986):1166. In *Moodswing,* Fieve takes a contrary view that creative output becomes more consistent when a person prone to manic episodes is on lithium (p. 53).　**306.** Most writers reported　Nancy Andreasen published several updates of her study since its inception fifteen years ago. The latest, "Creativity and Mental Illness: Prevalence Rates in Writers and Their First-Degree Relatives," appears in *American Journal of Psychiatry* 144(1987):1288–92.　**309.** "In itself it"　C. G. Jung, "Psychology and Literature," in *The Creative Process,* ed. Ghiselin, pp. 216–17.　**309.** This suggests that　Andreasen, "Creativity and Mental Illness," 1290.　**309.** Other studies confirm　L. Heston, "Psychiatric Disorders in Foster-Home-Reared Children of Schizophrenic Mothers," *British Journal of Psychiatry* 112(1966):819–25.

CHAPTER FOURTEEN

311. From the modern　This point of view was expounded by the behaviorist B. F. Skinner in his utopian novel *Walden II* (New York: MacMillan, 1976).　**312.** Huxley described the　A. Huxley, "The Perennial Philosophy," in *The Highest State of Consciousness*, ed. J. White (New York: Anchor Books, 1972), p. 58. **314.** The Indian culture S. Ayala, *East and West: A Unifying Paradigm* (Honesdale, PA: Himalayan International Institute, 1983), p. 148. **315.** More than individual Ibid. p. 88. **318.** This creates the L. LeShan, "On the Non-Acceptance of the Paranormal," *International Journal of Parapsychology*, Summer 1966, p. 1349–54. **318.** Not to believe A. Koestler, *The Roots of Coincidence* (New York: Vintage Books, 1972). **319.** Because it is Besides LeShan's "On the Non-Accpetance" and Koestler's *Roots of Coincidence*, the following works are general sources of information about psychic phenomena: L. Vasiliev, *Experiments in Distant Influence* (New York: Dutton, 1963); J. B. Rhine, "On Parapsychology and the Nature of Man," in *Dimensions of Mind*, ed. S. Hook (New York: Collier Books, 1960); S. Ostrander, and L. Schroeder, *Psychic Discoveries Behind the Iron Curtain* (New York: Bantam Books, 1970); C. Panati, *Supersenses* (New York: Anchor Books, 1976); R. Targ and K. Harary, *The Mind Race* (New York: Villard Books, 1984); J. Ehrenwald, *The ESP Experience* (New York: Basic Books, 1978); C. Tart, *PSI: Scientific Studies of the Psychic Realm* (New York: Dutton, 1977); S. Phillips, *Extrasensory Perception of Quarks* (Wheaton, IL: Philosophical Publishing House, 1980); M. Ferguson, *The Brain Revolution* (New York: Bantam Books, 1973); D. S. Rogo, *Exploring Psychic Phenomena: Beyond Mind and Matter* (Wheaton, IL: Quest Books, 1976). **319.** Researchers found that Ostrander and Schroeder, *Psychic Discoveries*, p. 32. **320.** The recording showed Ferguson, *The Brain Revolution*, p. 346. **320.** This voodoolike R. White, "The Influence of Persons Other Than the Experimenter on the Subject's Scores in Psi Experiments," *Journal of American Social Psychology Research* 70(1976):133–66; R. White, "The Limits of Experimenter Influence on Psi Test Results: Can Any Be Set?" *Journal of American Social Psychology Research* 70(1976):333–70. **320.** Scientists have been Theories of how information could be transmitted across "dimensions of being" are described in chapter 8 of Klimo's *Channeling*. **321.** Interest in this The most recent article on the subject was written by Bruce Greyson, M.D.; it contains a review of previous studies, as well as the negative results of his own research: "Telepathy in Mental Illness: Deluge of Delusion?" *Journal of Nervous and Mental Disease* 165(1977):184–200. **321.** Telepathy to him Ehrenwald described in *The ESP Experience* numerous incidents of telepathy during his long years of practice. He felt they were especially apt to occur with paranoids. **323.** Pathological hallucinations occur I. Stevenson, "Do We Need a New Word to Supplement *Hallucination*?" in *The American Journal of Psychiatry* 140(1983):1609–11. **325.** The goal of A. Hastings, "A Counseling Approach to Parapsychological Experience," *The Journal of Transpersonal Psychology* 15(1983):143–67; this article also appeared in *ReVision* 8, no. 2(1986):61–73. **326.** A world gone LeShan, *The Medium*, p. xii. **326.** As it is true H. Schmidt, *Journal of Parapsychology* 34(1970):3–4. **327.** For instance if For a detailed discussion of experiments with psychokinesis, see C. Tart, "The Physical Universe, the Spiritual Universe and the Paranormal," in *Transpersonal Psychologies*, ed. Tart. **329.** They were more W. Tenhaeff, "Summary of the Results of the Psychodiagnostic Investigation of Forty Paragnots," *Proceedings of the Parapsychological Institute of the State University of Utrecht* 2(1962). **329.** Other studies reveal G. Schmeidler, "The Psychic Personality," *Psychic*, April 1974. **330.** Channeling is the Klimo, *Channeling*, p. 2. **331.** Despite this impressive Tart's Dictum appears in Hastings, "Parapsychological Experience." **331.** You! This passage was channeled by J. Z. Knight and cited in Klimo, *Channeling*, p. 43. **332.** It is merely *A Course in Miracles* is published with no author specified, but is said to be channeled by the psychologist Helen Cohn Schucman. See *A Course in Miracles*, vol. 1, *Text* (Tiburon, CA: Foundation for Inner Peace, 1975), p. 358. **330.** "One has to" William James left us with this thought in 1909 in "Report on Mrs. Piper's Hodgson Control," *Proceedings of the English Society for Psychical Research* 23:1, p. 121. **330.** "In each individual" Jung, *Letters*, vol. 1, cited in Klimo, *Channeling*, p. 217. **335.** In other words E. Hartmann, "Dreams and Other Hallucinations: An Approach to the Underlying Mechanism," in *Hallucinations, Behavior, Experience, and Theory*, ed. R. K. Siegel and L. J. West (New York: John Wiley & Sons, 1975), ch. 3. **335.** Thirteen hours of Peter Tripp's ordeal was described in M. Ferguson, *The Brain Revolution* (New York: Bantam Books, 1973), p. 152. **336.** The connection between For more details of research on dreams and their connection with the normal and psychotic brain, see William Dement's *Some Must Sleep While Some Must Watch* (New York: Norton, 1978). **337.** One of the S. LaBerge, *Lucid Dreaming: The Power of Being Awake and Aware in Your Dreams* (Los Angeles: Jeremy P. Tarcher, 1985). **337.** As Don Juan Despite Carlos Castaneda's occasional stretching the limits of poetic license, his works capture the flavor of an opening to the sixth chakra through the ancient shamanic vocation. This lesson appears in the third book of the series, *Journey to Ixtlan* (New York: Simon & Schuster, 1972), pp. 126–27. **338.** Whereas, in contrast Campbell, *Myths to Live By*, p. 214. **339.** He becomes a My information on shamanism was gathered from J. Silverman, "Shamans and Acute Schizophrenia, *American Anthropologist* 69(1967):21–31; T. McKenna and

D. McKenna, *The Invisible Landscape* (New York: Seabury Press, 1975), pp. 8–25; A. Krober, "Psychosis or Social Sanction," in *Exploring Madness*, ed. Fadiman and Kewman, pp. 77–86; M. Harner, *The Way of the Shaman* (New York: Bantam Books, 1980). **340.** This maintained equilibrium   LeShan, "On the Non-Acceptance."

CHAPTER FIFTEEN

341. It has been   The higher seven chakras are, in some esoteric systems, followed by seven more, recollecting the seven levels of heaven in Dante's *Divine Comedy*. Some systems hold that the Muladhara chakra, the first chakra of human beings, is the seventh and highest chakra of lower animals. For more information, the reader is referred to the ancient Vedic texts, especially The Upanishads.   **345.** The story could   The Ten Bulls are illustrated in D. T. Suzuki. Another version is found in P. Reps, *Zen Flesh, Zen Bones* (Garden City, NY: Anchor Books).   **345.** "Or as if "   Saint Teresa wrote this in *Interior Castle*, a mystical treatise written in 1577. Quoted by Kenneth Wapnick in "Mysticism and Schizophrenia," in *The Highest State of Consciousness*, ed. J. White (New York: Anchor Books, 1973), p. 162.   **345.** Every experience in   Da Free John, *The Knee of Listening* (Clearlake, CA: Dawn Horse Press, 1978), quoted in Sanella, *The Kundalini Experience*, p. 126.   **346.** The individual attains   S. Dean, *Psychiatry and Mysticism* (Chicago: Nelson-Hall, 1975), p. 11.   **346.** The Sanskrit term   Ajaya, *Psychotherapy East and West*, p. 177ff.   **347.** Freud, for instance   S. Freud, *Civilization and Its Discontents* (New York: WW Norton, 1930/1961).   **347.** Similarly, the eminent   F. Alexander, "Buddhist Training as an Artificial Catatonia," *Psychoanalytic Review* 18(1931):1245.   **347.** More recently, the   For a review of theories linking mystical experience to temporal-lobe function, see D. Stacy, "Transcending Science," *Omni*, December 1988, 55.   **348.** Some argue, against   One statement of this idea is in E. Podvoll, "Psychosis and the Mystic Path," *The Psychoanalytic Review* 66(1979):571–90.   **348.** It is therefore   A. Deikman, "Deautomatization and the Mystic Experience," in *Altered States of Consciousness*, ed. Tart, 1972, p. 43.   **349.** The essence of   For a debate on the distinctions between regression and mysticism, see two articles of differing viewpoints in *The Highest States of Consciousness*, ed. In the first, Raymond Prince and Charles Savage argue that mysticism is essentially regression to an infantile state (pp. 114–34). The second, by Claire Myers Owens, offers a counterpoint (pp. 135–52). An article by Kenneth Wapnick in the same collection offers further thoughts on the subject (pp. 153–75).   **350.** This is what   A. Weil, *The Natural Mind* (Boston: Houghton Mifflin, 1973), pp. 177–79.   **350.** "What I am"   Campbell, *Myths to Live By*, pp. 215–16, 226.   **352.** "I must recognize"   The author of this quote, Daniel Paul Schreber, a jurist in the Kingdom of Saxony during the nineteenth century, was thought to be schizophrenic by some historians, but by today's more refined diagnostic standards he clearly demonstrated symptoms of the manic ASC. See his biographical account: *Memoirs of My Nervous Illness* (London: R. Dawson, 1955).   **353.** Efforts to popularize   H. Bensen, *The Relaxation Response* (New York: William Morrow, 1975). For a comprehensive bibliography on physical and psychological effects of medication, see M. Murphy, and S. Donovan, "A Bibliography of Meditation Theory and Research: 1931–1983," *The Journal of Transpersonal Psychology* 15(1983):181–228.   **353.** Buddhist "insight" meditation   I have found that the most helpful guide for a beginning meditator is L. LeShan, *How to Meditate* (New York: Bantam Books, 1974). Also, J. Goldstein and J. Kornfield, *Seeking the Heart of Wisdom* (Boston: Shambhala, 1987).   **354.** "Or better, we"   Thomas, Merton "What Is Contemplation?" *Catholic Agitator*, June 1988, 3.   **354.** When the moon   R. Ornstein, *The Psychology of Consciousness* (San Francisco: Freeman, 1972).   **350.** These moments are   For a transpersonal interpretation of the effects of mediation on the psyche, see chapter 4 of Wilber, *Eye to Eye;* and chapter 6 of Washburn, *The Ego*.   **355.** It is the   Wilber, *Eye to Eye*, p. 116.   **356.** Perhaps Carl Jung   C. Jung, "Psychological Commentary on *The Tibetan Book of The Dead*," in *Collected Works*, vol. 11, 2nd ed. (Princeton, NJ: Princeton University Press, 1969).   **357.** For these people   R. Walsh, and L. Roche, "Precipitation of Acute Psychotic Episodes by Intensive Meditation in Individuals with a History of Schizophrenia," *American Journal of Psychiatry* 136(1979):1085–85; A. P. French, et al., Transcendental Meditation, Altered Reality Testing, and Behavioral Change: A Case Report," *Journal of Nervous and Mental Disease* 161(1975):55–58.   **357.** Or, as the   J. Engler, "Therapeutic Aims in Psychotherapy and Meditation: Developmental Stages in the Representation of Self," in *Transformations of Consciousness*, ed. J. Engler, K. Wilber, and D. Brown (Boston: New Science Library, 1981).   **359.** But until that   Wilber, *The Atman Project*, p. 78.   **359.** Schizophrenics pass beyond   N. O. Brown, *Love's Body* (New York: Vintage Books, 1966), pp. 159–60.   **361.** As pychiatrist M. Scott   M. S. Peck, *The Road Less Traveled* (New York: Touchstone, 1978), p. 97.

CHAPTER SIXTEEN

374. He also created   K. Isumi, "LSD and Architectural Design," in *Psychedelics*, ed. B. Aaronson, and H. Osmond (New York: Anchor Books, 1970), pp. 381–97.   374. Many schizophrenics improve   J. Silverman, "Perceptual and Neurophysiological Analogues of Experience in Schizophrenia and LSD Reactions," in *Exploring Madness*, ed. Fadiman and Kewman, pp. 151–73.   376. To many patients   R. Diamond, "Drugs and the Quality of Life: The Patient's Point of View," *Journal of Clinical Psychiatry* 46 (May 1985):29–35.   376. Recent studies indicate   J. M. Kane, A. Rifkin, et al., "Low-dose Neuroleptic Treatment of Outpatient Schizophrenics: I. Preliminary Results for Relapse Rates," *Archives of General Psychiatry* 27(1972):893–96.   377. Where this has   C. P. Chien, "Drugs and Rehabilitation in Schizophrenia," in *Drugs in Combination with Other Therapies*, ed. M. Greenblatt (New York: Grune & Stratton, 1975).   377. Contrary to the   W. Fenton, and T. McGlashan, "Sustained Remission in Drug-Free Schizophrenic Patients," *American Journal of Psychiatry*, October 1987, 1306–9.   377. Given our current   We may expect laboratory tests to be helpful in making this discrimination in the near future. For a review of recent progress, see Busic and Gorman, *Ill, Not Insane*.   377. People who have   J. Lieberman and J. Kane eds., *Predictors of Relapse in Schizophrenia* (Washington, DC: American Psychiatric Press, 1986).   377. Dance therapies are   V. Goertzel, et al., "Body-Ego Technique: An Approach to the Schizophrenic Patient," *The Journal of Nervous and Mental Disease* 141(1965):53–60.   377. For more advanced   H. Higdon, "Can Running Cure Mental Illness?" and "Can Running Put Mental Patients on Their Feet?" *Runner's World*, January and February 1978; F. Leer, "Running as an Adjunct to Psychotherapy," *Social Work*, January 1980, 20–25.   379. Finally, he views   T. McGlashan, "Intensive Individual Psychotherapy of Schizophrenia," *Archives of General Psychiatry* 40(1983):909–20.   379. The relapse rate   J. Leff, et al., "A Controlled Trial of Social Intervention in the Families of Schizophrenic Patients: Two Year Follow-up," *British Journal of Psychiatry* 146(1985):594–600.   380. "I see the whole"   Perry, *Far Side of Madness*, p. 120.   381. "I know I"   "'Can We Talk?': The Schizophrenic Patient in Psychotherapy," *American Journal of Psychiatry* 143(1986):68–70.   381. Such simple tasks   R. Liberman, "Social Skills Training for Schizophrenic Individuals at Risk for Relapse," *American Journal of Psychiatry* 143(1986):523–26.   381. There is a   S. Arieti, "Hallucinations, Delusions, and Ideas of Reference Treated with Psychotherapy," *American Journal of Psychotherapy* 16(1962):52–60; I. Faloon and Ralph Talbot, "Persistent Auditory Hallucinations: Coping Mechanisms and Implications for Management," *Psychological Medicine* 11(1981):329–39.   377. While the patient   Arieti, "Hallucinations."   383. Some therapists have   Ehrenwald, *The ESP Experience*.   383. The sensitivity of   "When in Trouble, Call a Psychotic," *Brain/Mind Bulletin*, May 16, 1977, 2.   386. It can be   S. Gilman, *Seeing the Insane* (New York, John Wiley & Sons and Brunner/Mazel), 1982, p. 150.   386. The fourth chakra   H. Kohut, "Introspection Empathy and Psychoanalysis, *Journal of the American Psychoanalytic Association* 7(1959):459–83; Kohut and Wolf, "The Disorders of the Self." 413–25.   387. If all goes   H. Kohut, *The Restoration of the Self* (New York: International Universities Press, 1977).   391. The reader is   A review of the borderline syndrome and therapeutic approaches is in W. Goldstein, *An Introduction to the Borderline Conditions* (Northwall, NJ: Aronson, 1985). Also L. Boyer and P. Giovacchini, *Psychoanalytic Treatment of Characterological and Schizophrenic Disorders* (New York: Aronson, 1967).

CHAPTER SEVENTEEN

394. As R. D. Laing   R. D. Laing, *The Voice of Experience* (New York: Pantheon Books, 1982).   395. Caring and curing   Harner, *Way of the Shaman*, p. xiv.   396. By intently observing   Goldstein and Kornfield, *Seeking the Heart of Wisdom*.   397. He strives to   Heinz Kohut discussed the central place of empathy in the psychotherapeutic healing process in his two major works, *The Analysis of the Self* and *The Restoration of the Self* (Madison, CT: International Universities Press, 1971 and 1977).   397. In this way   Carlos Castaneda expands on the concept of the impeccible warrior throughout his series of books, starting with *The Teachings of Don Juan: A Yaqui Way of Knowledge* (New York: Simon & Schuster, 1966). Also see D. Williams, *Border Crossings: A Psychological Perspective on Carlos Castaneda's Path of Knowledge* (Toronto: Inner City Books, 1981), pp. 63–67.   401. The procedure lasts   D. R. Ross, et al., "The Psychiatric Uses of Cold Wet Sheet Packs," *The American Journal of Psychiatry* 145(1988):242–48.   404. Time-honored triggers   R. Wehr and D. Sack, "Sleep Disruption: A Treatment for Depression and a Cause of Mania," *Psychiatric Annals* 178(1987):654–59.   407. Models for residential   For a description of the Soteria project, see L. Mosher, and A. Menn, "Soteria: An Alternative to Hospitalization for Schizophrenics," in *New Direction for Mental Health Services*, 1, (San Francisco: Jossey-Bass, 1979),

pp. 73–84. Diabasis, another residential treatment facility, is described in J. W. Perry, "Spiritual Emergence and Renewal," *ReVision*, Winter/Spring 1986, 33–38. **407.** New ones are One of these communities, Tamanawas, is described in J. Dallett, *When the Spirits Come Back* (Toronto: Inner City Books, 1988). **407.** In contrast, a R. Walsh, and F. Vaughan, "Comparative Models of the Person and Psychotherapy," in *Transpersonal Psychotherapy*, ed. Boorstin, pp. 12–27. **409.** This made a Gary Bravo, M.D., personal communication. **410.** It simply means Alan Watts made a similar point in *Psychotherapy East and West* (New York: Ballantine Books, 1961), pp. 25–32, 193. **411.** In contrast, most Stanislav Grof, at the annual conference of the International Association for Transpersonal Psychology, October 1988. **412.** Yet this and S. Grof, *The Adventure of Self-Discovery* (Albany: State University of New York Press, 1987). **413.** The healer may S. Grof, and C. Grof, *Spiritual Emergency*. **414.** Occasionally a temporary Ken Wilber describes specific treatments for a variety of higher spiritual derailments in chapter five of *Transformations of Consciousness*, coauthored by Jack Engler and Daniel P. Brown (Boston: New Science Library, 1986), pp. 127–156. **414.** The changes in S. Grof, *Beyond the Brain*, p. 302. **415.** Used with skill G. Bravo and C. Grob, relate psychedelics in shamanic cultures to possible use in modern psychiatry. See "Shamans, Sacraments, and Psychiatrists," *The Journal of Psychoactive Drugs* 21(1989):123–28. For an account of employing psychedelics therapeutically, see S. Grof, *LSD and Psychotherapy* (Claremont, CA: Hunter House, 1980). **415.** Although SEN does not The Spiritual Emergence Network (SEN), 250 Oak Grove Avenue., Menlo Park, CA 94025; tel. (415)327-2776. For more information about spiritual emergencies, see Bragdon, *Helping People in Spiritual Emergency* (available through SEN). **415.** This situation is For criteria for a proposed official diagnostic category of "mystical experiences with psychotic features," see D. Lukoff, "The Diagnosis of Mystical Experiences with Psychotic Features," *The Journal of Transpersonal Psychology* 17(1985):155–80.

Index

◈

HEALING THE SPLIT
Integrating Spirit Into Our Understanding of the Mentally Ill
REVISED EDITION

With a Foreword by Ken Wilber and a Preface by Michael Washburn

JOHN E. NELSON, M.D.

"An enormously impressive, profound, and important book."–Ken Wilber

"An overwhelmingly valuable book."–Robert M. Pirsig, author of *Zen and the Art of Motorcycle Maintenance*

The links between madness, creative genius, and spiritual experiences have tantalized philosophers and scientists for centuries. In *Healing the Split*, John Nelson brings the lofty ideas of transpersonal psychology down to earth so they can be applied in a practical way to explain the bizarre effects of insanity on the human mind. Drawing on a vast knowledge of Eastern philosophy and mainstream neuropsychiatry, he heals the split between orthodox and alternative views with a comprehensive approach that goes beyond both. Starting where R. D. Laing and Thomas Szasz left off, Nelson revises and expands their radical views in light of modern brain science. He then turns to ancient tantric yoga for a synthesis that weaves brain, psyche, and spirit into a compelling new conception of mental illness.

For professionals who seek to meet the needs of their patients more creatively, this book offers a unique synthesis. For people in emotional crisis, it clarifies the distinctions among intractable psychosis, temporary breakdowns in the service of healing (spiritual emergencies), and psychic breakthroughs (spiritual emergence). And for anyone interested in the seemingly inexplicable workings of the human mind gone mad, this fascinating exploration of psychotic states of consciousness will be exciting reading.

"John Nelson has written an important and compelling book. He provides us with a thorough, well-referenced review of contemporary theories of psychotic illness, including a broad sweep of how conventional psychiatry views the psychoses."–*The Association for Humanistic Psychology Newsletter*

"Nelson's level of expertise with both the Western medical model and the Hindu chakra system is quite exceptional and perhaps unique among transpersonal theorists. *Healing the Split* would make an ideal textbook for a transpersonal psychology course."–*The Journal of Transpersonal Psychology*

John E. Nelson, M.D., is a practicing psychiatrist certified by the American Board of Psychiatry and Neurology. He has worked with psychiatric patients since 1969 and has been a long time student of transpersonal psychology and Eastern philosophy.

A volume in the SUNY series in the Philosophy of Psychology
Michael Washburn, editor

State University of New York Press
ISBN 0-7914-1985-1

ISBN 0-7914-1986-X

9 780791 419861